# Readings in Games and Information

**Blackwell Readings for Contemporary Economics**

This series presents collections of writings by some of the world's foremost economists on core issues in the discipline. Each volume dovetails with a variety of existing economics courses at the advanced undergraduate, graduate, and MBA levels. The readings, gleaned from a wide variety of classic and contemporary sources, are placed in context by a comprehensive introduction from the editor. In addition, a thorough index facilitates research.

# Readings in Games and Information

Edited by

**Eric Rasmusen**
*Indiana University, Bloomington*

 BLACKWELL
*Publishers*

First published 2001

2 4 6 8 10 9 7 5 3 1

Blackwell Publishers Inc.
350 Main Street
Malden, Massachusetts 02148
USA

Blackwell Publishers Ltd
108 Cowley Road
Oxford OX4 1JF
UK

*Library of Congress Cataloging-in-Publication Data*

Readings in games and information / edited by Eric Rasmusen.
    p. cm.—(Blackwell readings for contemporary economics)
    Includes bibliographical references and index.
    ISBN 0–631–21556–5 (alk. paper)—ISBN 0–631–21557–3 (pb. : alk. paper)
    1. Game theory.   I. Rasmusen, Eric.   II. Series.

    QA269 .R42 2001
    519.3—dc21                                        00–042937

*British Library Cataloguing in Publication Data*

A CIP catalogue record for this book is available from the British Library.

Typeset in 10/11.5 pt Ehrhardt
by Kolam Information Services, Pvt. Ltd Pondicherry, India


This book is printed on acid-free paper.

# Contents

# Preface

Good tools are half the battle; any repairman will tell you that. The home handyman has a garage full of tools, gadgets, and specialized gewgaws for two reasons. One is that they're beautiful in construction, fascinating in design, and thrilling to use. The other is that they're cost-effective. In America, capital is cheap and labor is expensive. Any tool that saves a skilled worker two hours of labor, or an unskilled worker ten hours over its lifetime is worth buying. And if you are a self-employed professional, no matter how poorly paid, you will also want to buy top quality.

Top quality does not mean top complexity. This year I bought the Sears Craftsman 6-Inch Pocket Socket adjustable box-end wrench shown in figure 1. This tool should be a model for us all. It is adjustable, replacing an assortment of fixed wrenches and removing the need to figure out which is which. Adjusting it is not only possible, but easy, and the handle coating makes it a pleasure to heft. It is simple in construction, and of good materials – which means it will be durable. Sears offers a lifetime guarantee, and means it. The wrench is even offset slightly, a nice touch for avoiding scraped knuckles, and has a hole in the handle for hanging from a nail.

Yet the Pocket Socket was not invented until 1989. Why not? As far as I can tell, its materials (except perhaps for the handle coating) and construction were feasible in 1789. The need has been there for quite some time. There was even profit to be made – Mr. Richard Cones, working for Midwest Tool and Cutlery, was able to acquire US patent 4,967,613 and make a deal with Sears to distribute it.[1] Why did this invention come only after almost five million others? I don't know.

Students and scholars should meditate on the pocket socket. It shows that there are still simple discoveries to be made long after the best minds in the business have acquired fancy theoretical university training and been agonizing over useless frontier projects. (This is not to say, however, that Mr. Cones did not have fancy training, or did not need it to come up with his simple idea!) A corollary is that when superior new tools are discovered, that does not necessarily make life harder, and students should be especially

---

[1] Go to the U.S. patent office site at www.uspto.gov/patft/index.html and search by patent number. Sears's description of the Pocket Socket can be found by searching for that name at www.sears.com.

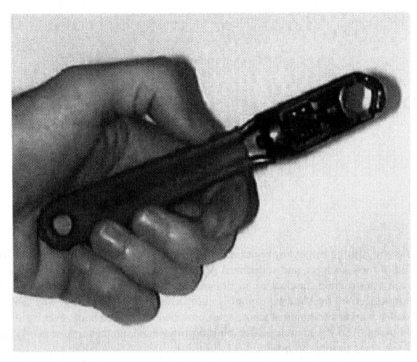

**Figure 1**   The Pocket Socket

happy about them. The pocket socket allowed me to discard several other tools, and I can abandon my vain quest to learn how to tell at a glance whether a nut size is $\frac{1}{4}$ inch or 11 mm. Game theory is much the same. The new way of thinking has made life easier, not harder.

The tools of game theory will save you a good deal of effort if you know which tools you need and if you have acquired them and stored them close at hand. That is why a Ph.D. advisor can, after ten minutes of casual discussion, find a flaw in a student dissertation that it would take the student twenty hours of scrawled algebra to uncover.

This book does not contain the magical tools of the ideas of game theory. (Those are in my other book, *Games and Information*.) It does, however, contain more humble tools that should be in your kit. Essentially, it is a stripped-down, cleaned-up version of the readings packet I use in my game theory course at Indiana University. I doubt anyone will march through and read all of these articles. Rather, you will put your hand into the toolbox and select an item that you need now or think you will need in the future, or just think looks fun to heft and to twiddle.

Books are the tools of the scholar's trade, and he should lay in a good stock of them, even if he hasn't much money. (Remember Erasmus: "When I get a little money I buy books; and if any is left I buy food and clothes.") In particular, anybody who liked *Games and Information* should buy this book. Like that book, it is deliberately eccentric, and you will find things here that you will not find elsewhere. I reckon the "Notes on Writing" alone are worth the price of admission. I expect the readers to be a diverse crowd, ranging from political science professors in Macao to economics undergraduates in Boston.

I've included only readings that are interesting and useful to read, leaving out some undoubted classics that I would not recommend for current reading. Thus, I have omitted the following very important articles, to which a historian of thought would have to devote much careful reading:

- Harsanyi, John (1967) "Games with Incomplete Information Played by 'Bayesian' Players, I: The Basic Model" *Management Science*. November 1967. 14: 159–82.
- Kreps, David and Robert Wilson (1982) "Sequential Equilibria" *Econometrica* 50: 863–94.
- Spence, A. Michael (1973) "Job Market Signalling" *Quarterly Journal of Economics* 87: 355–74.
- von Neumann, John (1928) "Zur Theorie der Gesellschaftspiele" *Mathematische Annalen* 100: 295–320. Translated by Sonya Bargmann as "On the Theory of Games of Strategy" in *Contributions to the Theory of Games*, Vol. IV, D. Luce and A. Tucker (eds.), Princeton: Princeton University Press, 1959, 13–42.

There exist other collections of articles on game theory which have a mixture of classic and readable articles, two categories which do, of course, overlap. They include:

- Baumol, William and Stephen Goldfeld (1968) *Precursors in Mathematical Economics: An Anthology*. London: London School of Economics and Political Science.
- Diamond, Peter and Michael Rothschild, eds. (1978) *Uncertainty in Economics: Readings and Exercises*. New York: Academic Press.
- Harold W. Kuhn, ed. (1997) *Classics in Game Theory*. Princeton, N.J.: Princeton University Press.

What I've included is a combination of readings that would be recommended by every teacher of game theory and readings that probably none of them but me know. I've inclined towards articles not published in easily available book or journals, such as Ariel Rubinstein's 1979 article, "An Optimal Conviction Expectation Regime for Offenses that May Have Been Committed by Accident," which appeared in *Applied Game Theory*. And I've included newspaper articles and cartoons, not for relief from hard thinking but rather for the opposite reason. The hardest part of game theory to learn is which tool applies to which situation, and the way to learn that is by practice.

Quite a lot of the material is about how to do research. An example is the old but good item by Harry Roberts and Roman Weil, "The University of Chicago. Starting Research Early." There is also some history that I think good for inspiration and direction in how to think about research, such as the chapter by Sylvia Nasar, "School of Genius." If you aren't at a department like 1948 Princeton mathematics, try creating one. It's not just the brains, which you can't replicate – the style matters just as much.

The Net, of course, is reducing the advantage that scholars at top departments in crossroads such as Chicago and Princeton have over the rest of the profession. As an example, let me use this very book. It has a web page up at Php.indiana.edu/~erasmuse/ GI/gireader.htm at which I may post items of interest to readers. Just as important, though, I invite you to use the Games and Information Bulletin Board that I have set up at Pacioli.bus.indiana.edu/erasmuse/GI/bbs.htm. If you have any comments on the readings in this collection, or any new articles, clippings, or cartoons you think might be of interest, please let me know there or at my email address, Erasmuse@Indiana.edu.

# Acknowledgments

Adams, Scott (nd): "Dilbert, I Want You to Manage Wally's Project While He's on Vacation in Aruba," Dilbert. © United Media, courtesy of Knight Features, London.

Adams, Scott (nd): "Look Ted! We Get Paid the Same as You but All We're Doing is Standing Around and Flicking our Fingers," Dilbert. © United Media, courtesy of Knight Features, London.

Adams, Scott (1997): "Ratbert the Consultant." © United Feature Syndicate, Inc., courtesy of Knight Features, London.

Agins, Teri (1985): "Bonded Worker is No Guarantee of a Perfect Job," *Wall Street Journal*, September 30.

Akerlof, George A. (1970): "The Market for 'Lemons': Quality Uncertainty and the Market Mechanism," *Quarterly Journal of Economics* 84(3) August, 488–500. © by the President and Fellows of Harvard College.

Anderson, Carl (nd): "Henry and the Candy Shop," © Allsorts Media Limited.

Axelrod, Robert and William D. Hamilton (1981): "The Evolution of Cooperation," *Science* 211 (March). © 1981 American Association for the Advancement of Science.

Ayres, Ian and Jeremy Bulow (1997/8): "The Donation Booth," *The Boston Review*, December–January, 26–7.

Bagehot, Walter (pseudonym for Jack Treynor) (1971): "The Only Game in Town," *Financial Analysts Journal* 27 (March–April). © 1971 Financial Analysts Journal. Reproduced and republished with permission from the Association for Investment Management and Research. All Rights Reserved.

Bagwell, Kyle and Michael H. Riordan (1991): "High and Declining Prices Signal Product Quality," *The American Economic Review* 81(1) March, 224–39. © 1991 American Economic Association. Reprinted with their permission and that of the authors.

Bailey, Jeff (1993): "To Ensure High Prices, Some Haulers Have Been Known to Break the Rules," *Wall Street Journal*, November 8.

Barro, Robert J. and Alan Stockman (1986): "This Tax Amnesty Will Work Only Once," *Wall Street Journal*, August 7.

Blackmon, Douglas A., Martha Brannigan, Glenn Burkins, and Laura Jereski (1997): "UPS Faces More Than $1 Billion a Year in New Labor Expenses: Pact Calls for

Substantial Pay Increases, Full-time Jobs and a Union Pension Plan," *Wall Street Journal*, August 20.

Buss, Dale D. (1983): "Unions Say Auto Firms Use Interplant Rivalry to Raise Work Quotas," *Wall Street Journal*, November 8.

Cox, Meg (1988): "At Many Auctions, Illegal Bidding Thrives as a Longtime Practice Among Dealers," *Wall Street Journal*, February 19.

Davis, John W. (1940): "The Argument of an Appeal," *American Bar Association Journal* 26 (December), 895–909. Reprinted with permission.

Davis, Philip, J. Reuben Hersh, and Elena Marchisotto (1981): "The Creation of New Mathematics: An Application of the Lakatos Heuristic," *The Mathematical Experience*. New York: Springer-Verlag Inc.

Edgeworth, Francis (1922): "The Mathematical Economics of Professor Amoroso," *Economic Journal* 30 (September), 400–7.

Farrell, Joseph (1983): "Monopoly Slack and Competitive Rigor: A Simple Model," MIT mimeo, February. Reprinted by courtesy of the author.

Farrell, Joseph (1987): "Cheap Talk, Coordination, and Entry," *Rand Journal of Economics* 18(1) Spring, 34–9.

Fisher, Ed (1954): "Say, I Think I See Where We Went Off…" © 1954 The New Yorker Collection, Ed Fisher from cartoonbank.com. All Rights Reserved.

Fudenberg, Drew and Jean Tirole (1984): "The Fat-Cat Effect, the Puppy-Dog Ploy, and the Lean and Hungry Look," *American Economic Review, Papers and Proceedings* 74 (May), 361–6.

Gasparino, Charles and Josh P. Hamilton (1998): "Cash Flow: 'Pay to Play' is Banned, but Muni-Bond Firms Keep the Game Going," *Wall Street Journal*, May 13.

Gonik, Jacob (1978): "Tie Salesmen's Bonuses to Their Forecasts," *Harvard Business Review* 56 (May–June). © 1978 the Presidents and Fellows of Harvard College. All Rights Reserved. Reprinted by permission of Harvard Business Review.

Guiles, Melinda Grenier (1985): "Car-Buying Services Can Save Money, Especially for Those who Hate Haggling," *Wall Street Journal*, April 23.

Harris, Sidney (nd): "That's it? That's Peer Review?" © 2000 by Sidney Harris.

Harris, Sidney (nd): "Whatever Happened to *Elegant* Solutions?" © 2000 by Sidney Harris.

Hemp, Paul (1985): "Dutch Accountants Take on a Formidable Task: Ferreting Out 'Cheaters' in the Ranks of OPEC," *Wall Street Journal*, February 26.

Hoff, Sidney (1951): "Of Course, That's Only an Estimate…" © 1951 The New Yorker Collection, Sidney Hoff from cartoonbank.com. All Rights Reserved.

Hoff, Sidney (1955): "Yes, but the Trouble is he *Always* Wears that Mysterious Smile," © 1955 The New Yorker Collection, Sidney Hoff from cartoonbank.com. All Rights Reserved.

Hotelling, Harold (1929): "Stability in Competition," *Economic Journal* 39 (March), 41–57.

King, Ralph T. Jr. (1998): "Drugs: Novel Heart-Drug Deal Protects Sales, Spurs Suit," *Wall Street Journal*, August 21.

Kreps, David M., Paul Milgrom, John Roberts, and Robert Wilson (1982): "Rational Cooperation in the Finitely Repeated Prisoners' Dilemma," *Journal of Economic Theory* 27, 245–52. © 1982 Academic Press. Reprinted by permission of the publisher.

Lachman, Judith (1984): "Knowing and Showing Economics and Law," *Yale Law Journal* 93 (July), 1598–1604. (A review of Polinsky, A. Mitchell (1983): *An Introduction to Law and Economics*.)

Larson, Gary (nd): "Frank's Neurosurgery," The Far Side by Gary Larson. © 1982 Far Works, Inc. Used with Permission. All Rights Reserved.

Larson, Gary (nd): "Einstein Discovers that Time is Actually Money," The Far Side by Gary Larson. © 1985 Far Works, Inc. Used with permission. All Rights Reserved.

Livy (circa 29 BC): "The Horatii and the Curiatii," *The Roman History by Titus Livius with the Entire Supplement of John Freinsheim* (1744): 1(1), excerpts from chapters 23, 24, and 25. (Punctuation modernized.)

McAfee, R. Preston and John McMillan (1996): "Analyzing the Airwaves Auction," *Journal of Economic Perspectives* 10(1) Winter, 159–75.

McDonald, John and John W. Tukey (1949): "Colonel Blotto: A Problem of Military Strategy," *Fortune*, June, 102. © 1949 Time Inc. Reprinted by permission.

Martin, Henry (1979): "All Those in Favor say 'Aye'." ©1979 The New Yorker Collection, Henry Martin from cartoonbank.com. All Rights Reserved.

Mathews, Anna Wilde (1997): "Shipping Price-Fixing Pacts Hurt Consumers, Critics Say," *Wall Street Journal*, October 7.

Nasar, Sylvia (1948): "School of Genius," *A Beautiful Mind: A Biography of John Forbes Nash, Jr.* Reprinted with permission of Simon and Schuster © 1998 by Sylvia Nasar.

Nash, John F. Jr (1950): "Equilibrium Points in N-Person Games," *Proceedings of the National Academy of Sciences* 36 (January), 48–9.

Nash, John F. Jr (1950): "The Bargaining Problem," *Econometrica* 18 (April), 155–62. Reprinted by permission of The Econometric Society, Evanston, Illinois.

Nash, John F. Jr (1951): "Non-Cooperative Games," *Annals of Mathematics* 54(2) September, 286–95.

Nomani, Asra Q. (1990): "Fare Warning: How Airlines Trade Price Plans," *Wall Street Journal*, October 9.

Pasztor, Andy (1985): "Busting a Trust: Electrical Contractors Reel Under Charges That They Rigged Bids," *Wall Street Journal*, November 29.

Pileggi, Nicholas (1985): "Wise Guy: Life in a Mafia Family," © 1985 Pileggi Literary Properties Inc. Reprinted by permission of Pocket Books, a division of Simon & Schuster.

Rasmusen, Eric (1998); "Examples of Plea Bargains," excerpted from "Mezzanatto and the Economics of Self Incrimination," *Cardozo Law Review* 19 (May), 1541–84.

Rasmusen, Eric (2000): "Aphorisms on Writing, Speaking and Listening," unpublished notes, February.

Roberts, Harry V. and Roman L. Weil (1970): "Starting Research Early," unpublished notes, University of Chicago Business School, August 14. Reprinted by courtesy of the authors.

Rogers, Rob (1999): "The Next Item up for Bid is the Presidency of the United States..." © 1999 United Feature Syndicate, Inc., courtesy of Knight Features, London.

Rogers, Rob (1999): "Isn't it Great that We Don't Get Any More Pesky Calls during Dinner Asking us to Switch Long-Distance Companies?" © 1999 United Feature Syndicate, Inc., courtesy of Knight Features, London.

Rothkopf, Michael H. (1980): "TREES – A Decision-Maker's Lament," *Operations Research* 28(1) January–February, 3.

Rubinstein, Ariel (1979): "An Optimal Conviction Policy for Offenses that May Have Been Committed by Accident," in *Applied Game Theory: Proceedings of a Conference at the Institute for Advanced Studies, Vienna, June 13–16, 1978*, edited by S. J. Brams, A. Schotter, and G. Schwödiauer, 406–13. © Physica-Verlag, Wurzburg, Germany.

Rubinstein, Ariel (1982): "Perfect Equilibrium in a Bargaining Model," *Econometrica* 50 (January), 97–109. Reprinted by permission of The Econometric Society, Evanston, Illinois.

Schelling, Thomas C. (1960): *The Strategy of Conflict*, Harvard University Press, Cambridge, Mass. and London, England, 119–50.

Seeger, Elizabeth (1967): "Shooting the Bird's Eye," in *The Five Sons of King Pandu: The Story of The Mahabhárata*, 18–19. New York: William R. Scott.

Shaked, Avner (1982): "Existence and Computation of Mixed Strategy Nash Equilibrium for 3-Firms Location Problem," *Journal of Industrial Economics* 31 (September–December), 93–6. Reprinted by permission of Blackwell Publishers.

Shubik, Martin (1954): "Does the Fittest Necessarily Survive?" in *Readings in Game Theory and Political Behavior*, Martin Shubik (ed.), New York: Doubleday, 43–6.

Shubik, Martin (1971): "The Dollar Auction Game: A Paradox in Noncooperative Behavior and Escalation," *Journal of Conflict Resolution* 15 (March), 109–11. Reprinted by permission of Sage Publications, Inc., Thousand Oaks.

Stigler, George (1977): "The Conference Handbook," *Journal of Political Economy* 85(2), 441–3. Reprinted by permission of The University of Chicago Press.

Straffin, Philip D. Jr (1980): "The Prisoner's Dilemma," *UMAP Journal* 1, 101–3.

Tucker, Albert W. (1950): "A Two-Person Dilemma." Unpublished notes, May.

Unger, Jim (1988): "Very Guilty." © United Media, courtesy of Knight Features, London

Varian, Hal R. (1999): "How to Build an Economic Model in Your Spare Time," *Passion and Craft: Economists at Work*, Michael Szenberg (ed.), Ann Arbor: University of Michigan Press.

Zermelo, Ernst (1913): "On An Application of Set Theory to the Theory of the Game of Chess," *Proceedings, Fifth International Congress of Mathematicians* 2. Translated by Ulrich Schwalbe and Paul Walker in "Zermelo and the Early History of Game Theory," forthcoming, *Games and Economic Behavior*.

Ziegler, Bart (1996): "Are Advertisers Ready to Pay Their Viewers?" *Wall Street Journal*, November 14. © 1997 Dow Jones and Company, Inc. All Rights Reserved.

## PART ONE

# The Rules of the Game

# Introduction

Two major themes of Part One of this book, of my book *Games and Information*, and of the entire field of game theory are the Prisoner's Dilemma and Nash equilibrium.

The Straffin and Tucker readings present the story of how the Prisoner's Dilemma came to be. When I was working on the first edition of *Games and Information* in 1988, I wanted to be careful in my citations, but I found it hard to track down the origin of the Prisoner's Dilemma. I asked Lloyd Shapley, who was nearby at UCLA, and he told me to write to Albert Tucker, still alive and living in Princeton. Tucker referred me to this article. See also the oral history project, "The Princeton Mathematics Community in the 30's" http://www34.homepage.villanova.edu/robert.jantzen/princeton_math/pmob.htm, and Chapter 6 of Willam Poundstone, *Prisoner's Dilemma: John von Neumann, Game Theory, and the Puzzle of the Bomb*, New York: Doubleday (1992).

The story told in the Straffin article raises a profound question for the philosophy of science. Who discovered the Prisoner's Dilemma – Dresher and Flood, who came up with the payoff matrix, or Albert Tucker, who came up with the story? Should the contribution of any of the three be enough for tenure, if that were all the person had ever done? In any case, which is more important, the matrix or the story?

The Prisoner's Dilemma is a game whose equilibrium can be found by either the idea of dominance or consistency of best responses. The second of these is the idea of Nash equilibrium. I tell my students that understanding Nash equilibrium is the most important thing to learn in a course on game theory. It is easy to memorize the definition, and to think that you understand the idea, but invariably I have questions on the midterm that rely on it and most students get the questions wrong without even realizing why. All I can do is tell you that, and tell you that once you really know game theory you will realize why Nash's idea deserved a Nobel Prize. The two articles reprinted here are the publications that earned him the prize.

Sylvia Nasar has written an excellent book on John Nash – on his early successes, his insanity, and his subsequent life up to winning the Nobel Prize. I have included a chapter from it that is not about Nash directly, but about the Princeton economics department which trained him. Princeton had one of the best mathematics department in the world in 1948. This is a good model for how a department should work. Note that the good qualities here described are not due to money or fame, but to attitude. The worst college in the world could do the same. But attitude is often the hardest thing to acquire, and a scholarly attitude seems to be strongly correlated with scholarly talent. Why? *A priori*, I see no reason why a department of morons could not have good coffee hours during which they fanatically discuss mathematics or economics, even if what they discuss is long division or the idea of a supply curve. They would enjoy themselves and increase their knowledge just as much as Nash and his colleagues, even if no new discoveries would be made for the wider world.

The two articles from the *Wall Street Journal* on garbage collection and municipal bond underwriting both are about Prisoner's Dilemma games. How? I will leave it to you. These are good stories on which to base the exercise of taking a verbal story and converting it to a formal game theory model by describing Players, Actions, Payoffs, and Information. They are also good for practice in finding Nash equilibria.

Finally, just to motivate you for the rest of the book, the Dilbert cartoon shows the easiest way to make money from game theory. But it raises good questions, too. Why do people hire consultants? How do they know which people to hire as consultants? Later chapters on information asymmetry will help you to understand.

# ONE

# The Prisoner's Dilemma

PHILIP D. STRAFFIN, JR.

Source: *UMAP Journal* 1, 1980, pp. 101–3.

Albert W. Tucker's note [see selection 2 of this book] which is published here for the first time, was the first written description of what has come to be known as the "prisoner's dilemma." The example in that note, with its accompanying story, has played a major role in social thought in the last thirty years. It is an example of a simple idea, originating in mathematical analysis, which can be said to have changed the way we think about our social world.

In 1944, John von Neumann and Oskar Morgenstern published the *Theory of Games and Economic Behavior* and founded the theory of games as a branch of mathematics. Von Neumann's celebrated minimax theorem stated that every finite two-person zero-sum game has an equilibrium outcome in mixed strategies. By 1950, John Nash, then a Ph.D. student under Tucker, had generalized this result to prove that finite two-person non-zero-sum games also have equilibria. However, it was clear that the equilibria of non-zero-sum games could have a number of strange and undesirable properties. The payoff matrix in the note was one of a number of examples devised by Melvin Dresher and Merrill Flood at the RAND Corporation to exhibit some of these strange properties. Tucker recalls that he first saw the matrix in Dresher's office on a visit to RAND in 1950. Somewhat later, Tucker was asked by the psychology department at Stanford to give a talk on game theory. He thought that this example would be an interesting illustration of the difficulty of analyzing non-zero-sum games, but that it should be presented with a "story" to accompany it. The famous story of the note is the result.

As the prisoner's dilemma was popularized among social scientists by Howard Raiffa, Duncan Luce, and Anatol Rapoport in the 1950s and early 1960s, it became apparent that Dresher and Flood's simple game was a useful model for a large number of social situations. Must an invisible hand govern economics in such a way that individually rational behavior always leads to a socially optimal outcome? Not always, and the prisoner's dilemma illustrates why not. For two nations engaged in an arms race, the payoffs for the strategies "continue to arm" and "disarm" may look like those of the prisoner's dilemma, and arms races persist. A prisoner's dilemma game with a larger number of players lies at the heart of Garrett Hardin's influential 1968 essay, "The Tragedy of the

Commons," which shows how environmental pollution and over-exploitation of resources can be dominant strategies that lead to disastrous social outcomes.

The prisoner's dilemma game became a useful experimental tool for psychologists interested in attributes that govern human behavior in social situations. Experimental literature on prisoner's dilemma grew steadily throughout the 1960s: Rapoport estimates that 200 experiments related to it were reported between 1965 and 1971. The game has been at least as fruitful for theoreticians. Any modern discussion of the meaning of rationality in social behavior must come to terms with the prisoner's dilemma.

What kinds of mathematical ideas can be most productive to social science? A simple idea may be best. Mathematical thinking, for instance concentrating on properties of equilibria in non-zero-sum games, can pare away inessentials and reveal a core common to many social situations. It can provide a simple model embodying that core, perhaps even a model around which experimental work can be done. It helps if the model comes with a clever story and an attractive title. The prisoner's dilemma was born in mathematical analysis, and proved so useful that it has become part of the jargon of the social sciences.

## Acknowledgments

We are grateful to Professor Tucker for his permission to publish "A Two-Person Dilemma," to William Lucas for keeping a mimeograph copy of the note in circulation, and Tucker and Merrill Flood for their accounts of the events of 1950.

# TWO

# A Two-Person Dilemma

## ALBERT TUCKER

*Source*: Unpublished notes, Stanford, May 1950.

Two men, charged with a joint violation of law, are held separately by the police. Each is told that

1 if one confesses and the other does not, the former will be given a reward of one unit and the latter will be fined two units,
2 if both confess, each will be fined one unit.

At the same time each has good reason to believe that

3 if neither confesses, both will go clear.

This situation gives rise to a simple symmetric two-person game (*not* zero-sum) with the following table of payoffs, in which each ordered pair represents the payoffs to I and II, in that order:

|   |   | II confess | not confess |
|---|---|---|---|
| I | confess | $(-1, -1)$ | $(1, -2)$ |
|   | not confess | $(-2, 1)$ | $(0, 0)$ |

Clearly, for each man the pure strategy "confess" dominates the pure strategy "not confess." Hence, there is a unique *equilibrium point** given by the two pure strategies "confess." In contrast with this *non-cooperative* solution one sees that both men would profit if they could form a *coalition* binding each other to "not confess."

The game becomes zero-sum three-person by introducing the State as a third player. The State exercises no choice (that is, has a single pure strategy) but receives payoffs as follows:

* See J. Nash, *Proc. Nat. Acad. Sci.* 36 (1950) 48–49.

|   | | II | |
|---|---|:---:|:---:|
|   |   | confess | not confess |
| I | confess | 2 | 1 |
|   | not confess | 1 | 0 |

# THREE

# Equilibrium Points in N-Person Games*

JOHN F. NASH, JR.

Source: *Proceedings of the National Academy of Sciences* 36 (January), 1950, pp. 48–9.

One may define a concept of an $n$-person game in which each player has a finite set of pure strategies and in which a definite set of payments to the $n$ players corresponds to each $n$-tuple of pure strategies, one strategy being taken for each player. For mixed strategies, which are probability distributions over the pure strategies, the pay-off functions are the expectations of the players, thus becoming polylinear forms in the probabilities with which the various players play their various pure strategies.

Any $n$-tuple of strategies, one for each player, may be regarded as a point in the product space obtained by multiplying the $n$ strategy spaces of the players. One such $n$-tuple counters another if the strategy of each player in the countering $n$-tuple yields the highest obtainable expectation for its player against the $n - 1$ strategies of the other players in the countered $n$-tuple. A self-countering $n$-tuple is called an equilibrium point.

The correspondence of each $n$-tuple with its set of countering $n$-tuples gives a one-to-many mapping of the product space into itself. From the definition of countering we see that the set of countering points of a point is convex. By using the continuity of the pay-off functions we see that the graph of the mapping is closed. The closedness is equivalent to saying: if $P_1, P_2, \ldots$ and $Q_1, Q_2, \ldots, Q_n, \ldots$ are sequences of points in the product space where $Q_n \to Q, P_n \to P$ and $Q_n$ counters $P_n$ then $Q$ counters $P$.

Since the graph is closed and since the image of each point under the mapping is convex, we infer from Kakutani's theorem[1] that the mapping has a fixed point (i.e., point contained in its image). Hence there is an equilibrium point.

In the two-person zero-sum case the "main theorem"[2] and the existence of an equilibrium point are equivalent. In this case any two equilibrium points lead to the same expectations for the players, but this need not occur in general.

## Acknowledgments

The author is indebted to Dr. David Gale for suggesting the use of Kakutani's theorem to simplify the proof and to the A.E.C. for financial support.

---

* Communicated by S. Lefschetz, November, 1949.
[1] Kakutani, S., *Duke Math. J.*, 8, 457–459 (1941).
[2] Von Neumann, J., and Morgenstern, O., *The Theory of Games and Economic Behaviour*, Chap. 3, Princeton University Press, Princeton, 1947.

FOUR

# Non-Cooperative Games

JOHN F. NASH, JR.

*Source*: *Annals of Mathematics* 54(2) September, 1951, pp. 286–95.

## Introduction

Von Neumann and Morgenstern have developed a very fruitful theory of two-person zero-sum games in their book *Theory of Games and Economic Behavior*. This book also contains a theory of *n*-person games of a type which we would call cooperative. This theory is based on an analysis of the interrelationships of the various coalitions which can be formed by the players of the game.

Our theory, in contradistinction, is based on the *absence* of coalitions in that it is assumed that each participant acts independently, without collaboration or communication with any of the others.

The notion of an *equilibrium point* is the basic ingredient in our theory. This notion yields a generalization of the concept of the solution of a two-person zero-sum game. It turns out that the set of equilibrium points of a two-person zero-sum game is simply the set of all pairs of opposing "good strategies."

In the immediately following sections we shall define equilibrium points and prove that a finite non-cooperative game always has at least one equilibrium point. We shall also introduce the notions of solvability and strong solvability of a non-cooperative game and prove a theorem on the geometrical structure of the set of equilibrium points of a solvable game.

As an example of the application of our theory we include a solution of a simplified three person poker game.

## Formal Definitions and Terminology

In this section we define the basic concepts of this paper and set up standard terminology and notation. Important definitions will be preceded by a subtitle indicating the concept defined. The non-cooperative idea will be implicit, rather than explicit, below.

## Finite game

For us an *n-person game* will be a set of *n players*, or *positions*, each with an associated finite set of *pure strategies*; and corresponding to each player, *i*, a *payoff function*, $p_i$, which maps the set of all *n*-tuples of pure strategies into the real numbers. When we use the term *n-tuple* we shall always mean a set of *n* items, with each item associated with a different player.

## Mixed strategy, $s_i$

A *mixed strategy* of player *i* will be a collection of non-negative numbers which have unit sum and are in one to one correspondence with his pure strategies.

We write $s_i = \sum_\alpha c_{i\alpha} \pi_{i\alpha}$ with $c_{i\alpha} \geqq 0$ and $\sum_\alpha c_{i\alpha} = 1$ to represent such a mixed strategy, where the $\pi_{i\alpha}$'s are the pure strategies of player *i*. We regard the $s_i$'s as points in a simplex whose vertices are the $\pi_{i\alpha}$'s. This simplex may be regarded as a convex subset of a real vector space, giving us a natural process of linear combination for the mixed strategies.

We shall use the suffixes *i, j, k* for players and $\alpha$, $\beta$, $\gamma$ to indicate various pure strategies of a player. The symbols $s_i$, $t_i$, and $r_i$, etc. will indicate mixed strategies; $\pi_{i\alpha}$ will indicate the $i^{\text{th}}$ player's $\alpha^{\text{th}}$ pure strategy, etc.

## Payoff function, $p_i$

The payoff function, $p_i$, used in the definition of a finite game above, has a unique extension to the *n*-tuples of mixed strategies which is linear in the mixed strategy of each player [*n*-linear]. This extension we shall also denote by $p_i$, writing $p_i(s_1, s_2, \ldots, s_n)$.

We shall write $\mathfrak{s}$ or $\mathfrak{t}$ to denote an *n*-tuple of mixed strategies and if $\mathfrak{s} = (s_1, s_2, \ldots, s_n)$ then $p_i(\mathfrak{s})$ shall mean $p_i(s_1, s_2, \ldots, s_n)$. Such an *n*-tuple, $\mathfrak{s}$, will also be regarded as a point in a vector space, the product space of the vector spaces containing the mixed strategies. And the set of all such *n*-tuples forms, of course, a convex polytope, the product of the simplices representing the mixed strategies.

For convenience we introduce the substitution notation $(\mathfrak{s}; t_i)$ to stand for $(s_1, s_2, \ldots, s_{i-1}, t_i, s_{i+1}, \ldots, s_n)$ where $\mathfrak{s} = (s_1, s_2, \ldots, s_n)$. The effect of successive substitutions $((\mathfrak{s}; t_i); r_j)$ we indicate by $(\mathfrak{s}; t_i; r_j)$, etc.

## Equilibrium point

An *n*-tuple $\mathfrak{s}$ is an *equilibrium point* if and only if for every *i*

$$p_i(\mathfrak{s}) = \max_{\text{all } r_i\text{'s}} \; [p_i(\mathfrak{s};r_i)] \tag{1}$$

Thus an equilibrium point is an *n*-tuple $\mathfrak{s}$ such that each player's mixed strategy maximizes his payoff if the strategies of the others are held fixed. Thus each player's strategy is optimal against those of the others. We shall occasionally abbreviate equilibrium point by eq. pt.

We say that a mixed strategy $s_i$ *uses* a pure strategy $\pi_{i\alpha}$ if $s_i = \sum_\beta c_{i\beta}\pi_{i\beta}$ and $c_{i\alpha} > 0$. If $\mathfrak{s} = (s_1, s_2, \cdots, s_n)$ and $s_i$ uses $\pi_{i\alpha}$ we also say that $\mathfrak{s}$ uses $\pi_{i\alpha}$.

From the linearity of $p_i(s_1, \cdots, s_n)$ in $s_i$,

$$\max_{\text{all } r_i\text{'s}} [p_i(\mathfrak{s}; r_i)] = \max_\alpha [p_i(\mathfrak{s}; \pi_{i\alpha})] \tag{2}$$

We define $p_{i\alpha}(\mathfrak{s}) = p_i(\mathfrak{s}; \pi_{i\alpha})$. Then we obtain the following trivial necessary and sufficient condition for $\mathfrak{s}$ to be an equilibrium point:

$$p_i(\mathfrak{s}) = \max_\alpha p_{i\alpha}(\mathfrak{s}) \tag{3}$$

If $\mathfrak{s} = (s_1, s_2, \cdots, s_n)$ and $s_i = \sum_\alpha c_{i\alpha}\pi_{i\alpha}$ then $p_i(\mathfrak{s}) = \sum_\alpha c_{i\alpha}p_{i\alpha}(\mathfrak{s})$, consequently for (3) to hold we must have $c_{i\alpha} = 0$ whenever $p_{i\alpha}(\mathfrak{s}) < \max_\beta p_{i\beta}(\mathfrak{s})$, which is to say that $\mathfrak{s}$ does not use $\pi_{i\alpha}$ unless it is an optimal pure strategy for player $i$. So we write

$$\text{if } \pi_{i\alpha} \text{ is used in } \mathfrak{s} \text{ then } p_{i\alpha}(\mathfrak{s}) = \max_\beta p_{i\beta}(\mathfrak{s}) \tag{4}$$

as another necessary and sufficient condition for an equilibrium point.

Since a criterion (3) for an eq. pt. can be expressed by the equating of $n$ pairs of continuous functions on the space of $n$-tuples $\mathfrak{s}$ the eq. pts. obviously form a closed subset of this space. Actually, this subset is formed from a number of pieces of algebraic varieties, cut out by other algebraic varieties.

## Existence of Equilibrium Points

A proof of this existence theorem based on Kakutani's generalized fixed point theorem was published in the Proceedings of the National Academy of Sciences of the U.S.A., 36, pp. 48–9. The proof given here is a considerable improvement over that earlier version and is based directly on the Brouwer theorem. We proceed by constructing a continuous transformation $T$ of the space of $n$-tuples such that the fixed points of $T$ are the equilibrium points of the game.

THEOREM 1.   *Every finite game has an equilibrium point.*

PROOF   Let $\mathfrak{s}$ be an $n$-tuple of mixed strategies, $p_i(\mathfrak{s})$ the corresponding pay-off to player $i$, and $p_{i\alpha}(\mathfrak{s})$ the pay-off to player $i$ if he changes to his $\alpha^{\text{th}}$ pure strategy $\pi_{i\alpha}$ and the others continue to use their respective mixed strategies from $\mathfrak{s}$. We now define a set of continuous functions of $\mathfrak{s}$ by

$$\varphi_{i\alpha}(\mathfrak{s}) = \max(0, p_{i\alpha}(\mathfrak{s}) - p_i(\mathfrak{s}))$$

and for each component $s_i$ of $\mathfrak{s}$ we define a modification $s_i'$ by

$$s_i' = \frac{s_i + \sum_\alpha \varphi_{i\alpha}(\mathfrak{s})\pi_{i\alpha}}{1 + \sum_\alpha \varphi_{i\alpha}(\mathfrak{s})},$$

calling $\mathfrak{s}'$ the $n$-tuple $(s_1', s_2', s_3' \cdots s_n')$.

We must now show that the fixed points of the mapping $T: \mathfrak{s} \to \mathfrak{s}'$ are the equilibrium points.

First consider any $n$-tuple $\mathfrak{s}$. In $\mathfrak{s}$ the $i^{\text{th}}$ player's mixed strategy $s_i$ will use certain of his pure strategies. Some one of these strategies, say $\pi_{i\alpha}$, must be "least profitable" so that $p_{i\alpha}(\mathfrak{s}) \leqq p_i(\mathfrak{s})$. This will make $\varphi_{i\alpha}(\mathfrak{s}) = 0$.

Now if this $n$-tuple $\mathfrak{s}$ happens to be fixed under $T$ the proportion of $\pi_{i\alpha}$ used in $s_i$ must not be decreased by $T$. Hence, for all $\beta$'s, $\varphi_{i\beta}(\mathfrak{s})$ must be zero to prevent the denominator of the expression defining $s_i'$ from exceeding 1.

Thus, if $\mathfrak{s}$ is fixed under $T$, for any $i$ and $\beta$ $\varphi_{i\beta}(\mathfrak{s}) = 0$. This means no player can improve his pay-off by moving to a pure strategy $\pi_{i\beta}$. But this is just a criterion for an eq. pt. [see Nash (1950)].

Conversely, if $\mathfrak{s}$ is an eq. pt. it is immediate that all $\varphi$'s vanish, making $\mathfrak{s}$ a fixed point under $T$.

Since the space of $n$-tuples is a cell the Brouwer fixed point theorem requires that $T$ must have at least one fixed point $\mathfrak{s}$, which must be an equilibrium point.

## Symmetries of Games

An *automorphism*, or *symmetry*, of a game will be a permutation of its pure strategies which satisfies certain conditions, given below.

If two strategies belong to a single player they must go into two strategies belonging to a single player. Thus if $\phi$ is the permutation of the pure strategies it induces a permutation $\psi$ of the players.

Each $n$-tuple of pure strategies is therefore permuted into another $n$-tuple of pure strategies. We may call $\chi$ the induced permutation of these $n$-tuples. Let $\xi$ denote an $n$-tuple of pure strategies and $p_i(\xi)$ the payoff to player $i$ when the $n$-tuple $\xi$ is employed. We require that

$$\text{if } j = i^\psi \quad \text{then} \quad p_j(\xi^\chi) = p_i(\xi)$$

which completes the definition of a symmetry.

The permutation $\phi$ has a unique linear extension to the mixed strategies. If

$$s_i = \sum_\alpha c_{i\alpha}\, \pi_{i\alpha}$$

we define

$$(s_i)^\phi = \sum_\alpha c_{i\alpha}\, (\pi_{i\alpha})^\phi$$

The extension of $\phi$ to the mixed strategies clearly generates an extension of $\chi$ to the $n$-tuples of mixed strategies. We shall also denote this by $\chi$.

We define a *symmetric $n$-tuple* $\mathfrak{s}$ of a game by $\mathfrak{s}^\chi = \mathfrak{s}$ for all $\chi$'s

**THEOREM 2.** *Any finite game has a symmetric equilibrium point.*

**PROOF** First we note that $s_{i0} = \sum_\alpha \pi_{i\alpha} / \sum_\alpha 1$ has the property $(s_{i0})^\phi = s_{j0}$ where $j = i^\psi$, so that the $n$-tuple $\mathfrak{s}_0 = (s_{10}, s_{20}, \cdots, s_{n0})$ is fixed under any $\chi$; hence any game has at least one symmetric $n$-tuple.

If $\mathfrak{s} = (s_1, \cdots, s_n)$ and $\mathfrak{t} = (t_1, \cdots, t_n)$ are symmetric then

$$\frac{\mathfrak{s} + \mathfrak{t}}{2} = \left( \frac{s_1 + t_1}{2}, \frac{s_2 + t_2}{2}, \cdots, \frac{s_n + t_n}{2} \right)$$

is also symmetric because $\mathfrak{s}^\chi = \mathfrak{s} \leftrightarrow s_j = (s_i)^\phi$, where $j = i^\psi$, hence

$$\frac{s_j + t_j}{2} = \frac{(s_i)^\phi + (t_i)^\phi}{2} = \left( \frac{s_i + t_i}{2} \right)^\phi$$

hence

$$\left( \frac{\mathfrak{s} + \mathfrak{t}}{2} \right)^\chi = \frac{\mathfrak{s} + \mathfrak{t}}{2}$$

This shows that the set of symmetric $n$-tuples is a convex subset of the space of $n$-tuples since it is obviously closed.

Now observe that the mapping $T : \mathfrak{s} \to \mathfrak{s}'$ used in the proof of the existence theorem was intrinsically defined. Therefore, if $\mathfrak{s}_2 = T \mathfrak{s}_1$ and $\chi$ is derived from an automorphism of the game we will have $\mathfrak{s}_2^\chi = T \mathfrak{s}_1^\chi$. If $\mathfrak{s}_1$ is symmetric $\mathfrak{s}_1^\chi = \mathfrak{s}_1$ and therefore $\mathfrak{s}_2^\chi = T \mathfrak{s}_1 = \mathfrak{s}_2$. Consequently this mapping maps the set of symmetric $n$-tuples into itself.

Since this set is a cell there must be a symmetric fixed point $\mathfrak{s}$ which must be a symmetric equilibrium point.

## Solutions

We define here solutions, strong solutions, and sub-solutions. A non-cooperative game does not always have a solution, but when it does the solution is unique. Strong solutions are solutions with special properties. Sub-solutions always exist and have many of the properties of solutions, but lack uniqueness.

$S_1$ will denote a set of mixed strategies of player $i$ and $\mathfrak{S}$ a set of $n$-tuples of mixed strategies.

Solvability:

A game is *solvable* if its set, $\mathfrak{S}$, of equilibrium points satisfies the condition

$$(\mathfrak{t}; r_i) \in \mathfrak{S} \text{ and } \mathfrak{s} \in \mathfrak{S} \to (\mathfrak{s}; r_i) \in \mathfrak{S} \text{ for all } i\text{'s} \tag{5}$$

This is called the *interchangeability* condition. The *solution* of a solvable game is its set, $\mathfrak{S}$, of equilibrium points.

Strong Solvability:

A game is *strongly solvable* if it has a solution, $\mathfrak{S}$, such that for all $i$'s

$$\mathfrak{s} \in \mathfrak{S} \text{ and } p_i(\mathfrak{s}; r_i) = p_i(\mathfrak{s}) \rightarrow (\mathfrak{s}; r_i) \in \mathfrak{S}$$

and then $\mathfrak{S}$ is called a *strong solution*.

## *Equilibrium strategies*

In a solvable game let $S_i$ be the set of all mixed strategies $s_i$ such that for some t the $n$-tuple $(\mathbf{t}; s_i)$ is an equilibrium point. [$s_i$ is the $i^{\text{th}}$ component of some equilibrium point.] We call $S_i$ the set of *equilibrium strategies* of player $i$.

## *Sub-solutions*

If $\mathfrak{S}$ is a subset of the set of equilibrium points of a game and satisfies condition (1); and if $\mathfrak{S}$ is maximal relative to this property then we call $\mathfrak{S}$ a *sub-solution*.

For any sub-solution $\mathfrak{S}$ we define the $i^{\text{th}}$ *factor set*, $S_i$, as the set of all $s_i$'s such that $\mathfrak{S}$ contains $(\mathbf{t}; s_i)$ for some t.

Note that a sub-solution, when unique, is a solution; and its factor sets are the sets of equilibrium strategies.

THEOREM 3. *A sub-solution, $\mathfrak{S}$, is the set of all n-tuples $(s_1, s_2, \cdots, s_n)$ such that each $s_i \in S_i$ where $S_i$ is the $i^{\text{th}}$ factor set of $\mathfrak{S}$. Geometrically, $\mathfrak{S}$ is the product of its factor sets.*

PROOF Consider such an $n$-tuple $(s_1, s_2, \cdots, s_n)$. By definition $\exists \, \mathbf{t}_1, \mathbf{t}_2, \cdots, \mathbf{t}_n$ such that for each $i$ $(\mathbf{t}_i; s_i) \in \mathfrak{S}$. Using the condition (5) $n - 1$ times we obtain successively $(\mathbf{t}_1; s_1) \in \mathfrak{S}, (\mathbf{t}_1; s_1; s_2) \in \mathfrak{S}, \cdots, (\mathbf{t}_1; s_1; s_2; \cdots; s_n) \in \mathfrak{S}$ and the last is simply $(s_1, s_2, \cdots, s_n) \in \mathfrak{S}$, which we needed to show.

THEOREM 4. *The factor sets $S_1, S_2, \cdots, S_n$ of a sub-solution are closed and convex as subsets of the mixed strategy spaces.*

PROOF It suffices to show two things:

(a) if $s_i$ and $s_i' \in S_i$ then $s_i^* = (s_i + s_i')/2 \in S_i$; (b) if $s_i^{\#}$ is a limit point of $S_i$ then $s_i^{\#} \in S_i$.

Let $\mathbf{t} \in \mathfrak{S}$. Then we have $p_j(\mathbf{t}; s_i) \geqq p_j(\mathbf{t}; s_i; r_j)$ and $p_j(\mathbf{t}; s_i') \geqq p_j(\mathbf{t}; s_i'; r_j)$ for any $r_j$, by using the criterion of (1) for an eq. pt. Adding these inequalities, using the linearity of $p_j(s_1, \cdots, s_n)$ in $s_i$, and dividing by 2, we get $p_j(\mathbf{t}; s_i^*) \geqq p_j(\mathbf{t}; s_i^*; r_j)$ since $s_i^* = (s_i + s_i')/2$. From this we know that $(\mathbf{t}; s_i)$ is an eq. pt. for any $\mathbf{t} \in \mathfrak{S}$. If the set of all such eq. pts. $(\mathbf{t}; s_i^*)$ is added to $\mathfrak{S}$ the augmented set clearly satisfies condition (5), and since $\mathfrak{S}$ was to be maximal it follows that $s_i^* \in S_i$.

To attack (b) note that the $n$-tuple $(\mathbf{t}; s_i^{\#})$, where $\mathbf{t} \in \mathfrak{S}$, will be a limit point of the set of $n$-tuples of the form $(\mathbf{t}; s_i)$ where $s_i \in S_i$, since $s_i$ is a limit point of $S_i$. But this set is a set of eq. pts. and hence any point in its closure is an eq. pt., since the set of all eq. pts. is closed. Therefore $(\mathbf{t}; s_i^{\#})$ is an eq. pt. and hence $s_i^{\#} \in S_i$ from the same argument as for $s_i^*$.

Values:

Let $\mathfrak{S}$ be the set of equilibrium points of a game. We define

$$v_i^+ = \max_{\mathfrak{s} \in \mathfrak{S}} \; [p_i(\mathfrak{s})], \quad v_i^- = \min_{\mathfrak{s} \in \mathfrak{S}} \; [p_i(\mathfrak{s})].$$

If $v_i^+ = v_i^-$ we write $v_i = v_i^+ = v_i^- \cdot v_i^+$ is the *upper value* to player $i$ of the game; $v_i^-$ the *lower value*; and $v_i$ the *value*, if it exists.

Values will obviously have to exist if there is but one equilibrium point.

One can define *associated values* for a sub-solution by restricting $\mathfrak{S}$ to the eq. pts. in the sub-solution and then using the same defining equations as above.

A two-person zero-sum game is always solvable in the sense defined above. The sets of equilibrium strategies $S_1$ and $S_2$ are simply the sets of "good" strategies. Such a game is not generally strongly solvable; strong solutions exist only when there is a "saddle point" in *pure* strategies.

## Simple Examples

These are intended to illustrate the concepts defined in the paper and display special phenomena which occur in these games.

The first player has the roman letter strategies and the payoff to the left, etc.

| Ex. 1 | 5 | $a\alpha$ | −3 | Solution $\left(\frac{9}{16}a + \frac{7}{16}b, \frac{7}{17}\alpha + \frac{10}{17}\beta\right)$ |
|---|---|---|---|---|
| | −4 | $a\beta$ | 4 | |
| | −5 | $b\alpha$ | 5 | $v_1 = \frac{-5}{17}, v_2 = +\frac{1}{2}$ |
| | 3 | $b\beta$ | −4 | |
| Ex. 2 | 1 | $a\alpha$ | 1 | Strong Solution $(b, \beta)$ |
| | −10 | $a\beta$ | 10 | |
| | 10 | $b\alpha$ | −10 | $v_1 = v_2 = −1$ |
| | −1 | $b\beta$ | −1 | |
| Ex. 3 | 1 | $a\alpha$ | 1 | Unsolvable; equilibrium points $(a, \alpha), (b, \beta),$ |
| | −10 | $a\beta$ | −10 | and $\left(\frac{a}{2} + \frac{b}{2}, \frac{\alpha}{2} + \frac{\beta}{2}\right)$. The strategies in the last |
| | −10 | $b\alpha$ | −10 | case have maxi-min and mini-max properties. |
| | 1 | $b\beta$ | 1 | |
| Ex. 4 | 1 | $a\alpha$ | 1 | Strong Solution: all pairs of mixed strategies. |
| | 0 | $a\beta$ | 1 | |
| | 1 | $b\alpha$ | 0 | $v_1^+ = v_2^+ = 1, v_1^- = v_2^- = 0.$ |
| | 0 | $b\beta$ | 0 | |
| Ex. 5 | 1 | $a\alpha$ | 2 | Unsolvable; eq. pts. $(a, \alpha), (b, \beta)$ and |
| | −1 | $a\beta$ | −4 | $\left(\frac{1}{4}a + \frac{3}{4}b, \frac{3}{8}\alpha + \frac{5}{8}\beta\right)$. However, empirical tests |
| | −4 | $b\alpha$ | −1 | show a tendency toward $(a, \alpha)$. |
| | 2 | $b\beta$ | 1 | |
| Ex. 6 | 1 | $a\alpha$ | 1 | Eq. pts.: $(a, \alpha)$ and $(b, \beta)$, with $(b, \beta)$ an |
| | 0 | $a\beta$ | 0 | example of instability. |
| | 0 | $b\alpha$ | 0 | |
| | 0 | $b\beta$ | 0 | |

## Geometrical Form of Solutions

In the two-person zero-sum case it has been shown that the set of "good" strategies of a player is a convex polyhedral subset of his strategy space. We shall obtain the same result for a player's set of equilibrium strategies in any solvable game.

THEOREM 5. *The sets* $S_1, S_2, \cdots, S_n$ *of equilibrium strategies in a solvable game are polyhedral convex subsets of the respective mixed strategy spaces.*

PROOF   An $n$-tuple $\mathfrak{s}$ will be an equilibrium point if and only if for every $i$

$$p_i(\mathfrak{s}) = \max_{\alpha} \ p_{i\alpha}(\mathfrak{s}) \tag{6}$$

which is condition (3). An equivalent condition is for every $i$ and $\alpha$

$$p_i(\mathfrak{s}) - p_{i\alpha}(\mathfrak{s}) \geqq 0 \tag{7}$$

Let us now consider the form of the set $S_j$ of equilibrium strategies, $s_j$, of player $j$. Let $\mathfrak{t}$ be any equilibrium point, then $(\mathfrak{t}; s_j)$ will be an equilibrium point if and only if $s_j \in S_j$, from Theorem 2. We now apply conditions (2) to $(\mathfrak{t}; s_j)$, obtaining

$$s_j \in S_j \longleftrightarrow \text{for all } i, \alpha \quad p_i(\mathfrak{t}; s_j) - p_{i\alpha}(\mathfrak{t}; s_j) \geqq 0 \tag{8}$$

Since $p_i$ is $n$-linear and $\mathfrak{t}$ is constant these are a set of linear inequalities of the form $F_{i\alpha}(s_j) \geqq 0$. Each such inequality is either satisfied for all $s_j$ or for those lying on and to one side of some hyperplane passing through the strategy simplex. Therefore, the complete set [which is finite] of conditions will all be satisfied simultaneously on some convex polyhedral subset of player $j$'s strategy simplex. [Intersection of half-spaces.]

As a corollary we may conclude that $S_j$ is the convex closure of a finite set of mixed strategies [vertices].

## Dominance and Contradiction Methods

We say that $s_i'$ dominates $s_i$ if $p_i(\mathfrak{t}; s_i') > p_i(\mathfrak{t}; s_i)$ for every $\mathfrak{t}$.

This amounts to saying that $s_i'$ gives player $i$ a higher payoff than $s_i$ no matter what the strategies of the other players are. To see whether a strategy $s_i'$ dominates $s_i$ it suffices to consider only pure strategies for the other players because of the $n$-linearity of $p_i$.

It is obvious from the definitions that *no equilibrium point can involve a dominated strategy* $s_i$.

The domination of one mixed strategy by another will always entail other dominations. For suppose $s_i'$ dominates $s_i$ and $t_i$ uses all of the pure strategies which have a higher coefficient in $s_i$ than in $s_i'$. Then for a small enough $\rho$

$$t_i' = t_i + \rho(s_i' - s_i)$$

is a mixed strategy; and $t_i$ dominates $t_i'$ by linearity.

One can prove a few properties of the set of undominated strategies. It is simply connected and is formed by the union of some collection of faces of the strategy simplex.

The information obtained by discovering dominances for one player may be of relevance to the others, insofar as the elimination of classes of mixed strategies as possible components of an equilibrium point is concerned. For the $t$'s whose components are all undominated are all that need be considered and thus eliminating some of the strategies of one player may make possible the elimination of a new class of strategies for another player.

Another procedure which may be used in locating equilibrium points is the contradiction-type analysis. Here one assumes that an equilibrium point exists having component strategies lying within certain regions of the strategy spaces and proceeds to deduce further conditions which must be satisfied if the hypothesis is true. This sort of reasoning may be carried through several stages to eventually obtain a contradiction indicating that there is no equilibrium point satisfying the initial hypothesis.

## A Three-Man Poker Game

As an example of the application of our theory to a more or less realistic case we include the simplified poker game given below. The rules are as follows:

(a)  The deck is large, with equally many *high* and *low* cards, and a hand consists of one card.
(b)  Two chips are used to ante, open, or call.
(c)  The players play in rotation and the game ends after all have passed or after one player has opened and the others have had a chance to call.
(d)  If no one bets the antes are retrieved.
(e)  Otherwise the pot is divided equally among the highest hands which have bet.

We find it more satisfactory to treat the game in terms of quantities we call "behavior parameters" than in the normal form of *Theory of Games and Economic Behavior*. In the normal form representation two mixed strategies of a player may be equivalent in the sense that each makes the individual choose each available course of action in each particular situation requiring action on his part with the same frequency. That is, they represent the same behavior pattern on the part of the individual.

Behavior parameters give the probabilities of taking each of the various possible actions in each of the various possible situations which may arise. Thus they describe behavior patterns.

In terms of behavior parameters the strategies of the players may be represented as follows, assuming that since there is no point in passing with a *high* card at one's last opportunity to bet that this will not be done. The greek letters are the probabilities of the various acts.

|  | First Moves | Second Moves |
|---|---|---|
| I | $\alpha$ Open on *high*<br>$\beta$ Open on *low* | $\kappa$ Call III on *low*<br>$\lambda$ Call II on *low*<br>$\mu$ Call II and III on *low* |
| II | $\gamma$ Call I on *low*<br>$\delta$ Open on *high*<br>$\varepsilon$ Open on *low* | $v$ Call III on *low*<br>$\xi$ Call III and I on *low* |
| III | $\zeta$ Call I and II on *low*<br>$\eta$ Open on *low*<br>$\theta$ Call I on *low*<br>$\iota$ Call II on *low* | Player III never gets a second move |

We locate all possible equilibrium points by first showing that most of the greek parameters must vanish. By dominance mainly with a little contradiction-type analysis $\beta$ is eliminated and with it go $\gamma, \zeta$, and $\theta$ by dominance. Then contradictions eliminate $\mu, \xi, \iota, \lambda, \kappa$, and $v$ in that order. This leaves us with $\alpha, \delta, \varepsilon$, and $\eta$. Contradiction analysis shows that none of these can be zero or one and thus we obtain a system of simultaneous algebraic equations. The equations happen to have but one solution with the variables in the range (0, 1). We get

$$\alpha = \frac{21 - \sqrt{321}}{10}, \ \eta = \frac{5\alpha + 1}{4}, \ \delta = \frac{5 - 2\alpha}{5 + \alpha}, \ \varepsilon = \frac{4\alpha - 1}{\alpha + 5}.$$

These yield $\alpha = .308$, $\eta = .635$, $\delta = .826$, and $\varepsilon = .044$. Since there is only one equilibrium point the game has values; these are

$$v_1 = -.147 = -\frac{(1 + 17\alpha)}{8(5 + \alpha)}, \quad v_2 = -.096 = -\frac{1 - 2\alpha}{4},$$

and

$$v_3 = .243 = \frac{79}{40}\left(\frac{1 - \alpha}{5 + \alpha}\right).$$

A more complete investigation of this poker game is published in Annals of Mathematics Study No. 24, *Contributions to the Theory of Games*. There the solution is studied as the ratio of ante to bet varies, and the potentialities of coalitions are investigated.

## Applications

The study of *n*-person games for which the accepted ethics of fair play imply non-cooperative playing is, of course, an obvious direction in which to apply this theory.

And poker is the most obvious target. The analysis of a more realistic poker game than our very simple model should be quite an interesting affair.

The complexity of the mathematical work needed for a complete investigation increases rather rapidly, however, with increasing complexity of the game; so that analysis of a game much more complex than the example given here might only be feasible using approximate computational methods.

A less obvious type of application is to the study of cooperative games. By a cooperative game we mean a situation involving a set of players, pure strategies, and payoffs as usual; but with the assumption that the players can and will collaborate as they do in the von Neumann and Morgenstern theory. This means the players may communicate and form coalitions which will be enforced by an umpire. It is unnecessarily restrictive, however, to assume any transferability or even comparability of the payoffs [which should be in utility units] to different players. Any desired transferability can be put into the game itself instead of assuming it possible in the extra-game collaboration.

The writer has developed a "dynamical" approach to the study of cooperative games based upon reduction to non-cooperative form. One proceeds by constructing a model of the pre-play negotiation so that the steps of negotiation become moves in a larger non-cooperative game [which will have an infinity of pure strategies] describing the total situation.

This larger game is then treated in terms of the theory of this paper [extended to infinite games] and if values are obtained they are taken as the values of the cooperative game. Thus the problem of analyzing a cooperative game becomes the problem of obtaining a suitable, and convincing, non-cooperative model for the negotiation.

The writer has, by such a treatment, obtained values for all finite two person cooperative games, and some special $n$-person games.

## Acknowledgments

Drs. Tucker, Gale, and Kuhn gave valuable criticism and suggestions for improving the exposition of the material in this paper. David Gale suggested the investigation of symmetric games. The solution of the Poker model was a joint project undertaken by Lloyd S. Shapley and author. Finally, the author was sustained financially by the Atomic Energy Commission in the period 1949-50 during which this work was done.

*Bibliography*

H. W. KUHN, *Extensive Games*, Proc. Nat. Acad. Sci. U.S.A., 36 (1950) 570–576.

JOHN NASH, *Two Person Cooperative Games*, to appear in Econometrica.

J. F. NASH, Jr., *Equilibrium Points in N-Person Games*, Proceedings of the National Academy of Sciences of the U. S. A. 36 (1950) 48–49.

J. F. NASH and L. S. SHAPLEY, A Simple Three-Person Poker Game, in H. Kuhn and A. Tucker (eds), *Contributions to the Theory of Games*, Vol. 1, Annals of Mathematics Study No. 24, Princeton University Press, 1950, pp. 105–16.

VON NEUMANN, MORGENSTERN, Theory of Games and Economic Behavior, Princeton University Press, 1944.

# FIVE

# To Ensure High Prices, Some Haulers Have Been Known to Break the Rules

JEFF BAILEY

*Source*: *Wall Street Journal*, November 8, 1993.

To enforce the high prices of the cartel system, protect their positions of influence and enrich themselves, mob members and their associates have engaged in murder, environmental crimes, bribery of public officials and truck sabotage. Based on allegations in indictments, affidavits and other fillings in federal court in Manhattan and Brooklyn, here are some of the key players:

James Failla has controlled much of New York hauling while working at the Manhattan haulers group, Associations of Trade Waste Removers of Greater New York, and via his control until recently of Teamsters Local 813, which represents workers in the hauling business.

Known as "Jimmy Brown," he was at Sparks Steak House in Manhattan on Dec. 16, 1985, waiting to have dinner with Paul Castellano, boss of the Gambino crime family. Mr. Castellano was gunned down as he arrived, by order of John Gotti, who took over the family but allegedly kept Mr. Failla, now 74 years old, as a family captain.

Mr. Failla was indicted last April on charges that he and Mr. Gotti arranged the 1989 murder of Thomas Spinelli, a mobster who was about to testify before a federal grand jury, and on racketeering charges involving his control of hauling activities. He pleaded not guilty; trial is in April.

Martin McLaughlin, a lobbyist for the haulers' umbrella group, Council of Trade Waste Associations Inc., says Mr. Failla's role with the Manhattan group is diminished and perhaps over. "He's very sick and hasn't been around for three or four months. Maybe he won't be back."

Salvatore Avellino provided perhaps the most extensive look at mob control of hauling by doing business while driving around Long Island in his Jaguar, in which the government had placed listening devices. A captain in the Lucchese family, another of the five organized-crime families in New York, Mr. Avellino owned a hauling company and oversaw the industry through the Private Sanitation Industry Association of Nassau/ Suffolk Inc.

He collected so much cash from haulers in return for policing the cartel that he complained to an associate in 1983: "I can't even...carry that." According to federal prosecutors, half the money went to his Lucchese boss – Antonio "Tony Ducks" Corallo, at the time – and half to Mr. Failla because Local 813 operated on Long Island, too.

On tape, Mr. Avellino discussed the finer points of punishing a hauler who doesn't abide by the cartel's rules. "We... put, ah, nuts and bolts into the engines." Mr. Corallo told him to be more subtle: "You put [metal] shavings in the oil."

Mr. Avellino also discussed legal maneuvers to conceal the ownership of his hauling company. The talk became too much for Lucchese underboss Salvatore Santoro, who declared: "F – legitimate businesses. They're a pain in the f – a –."

Robert Kubecka was a Long Island hauler who wouldn't cooperate with the cartel's price fixing, competing for customers instead. It was Mr. Avellino's job to bring him into line, but law-enforcement scrutiny was tying his hands. He felt he was letting the haulers down. "I know in my heart I'm not servicing these people," he told Mr. Santoro. "Gotta go there and take the f – money... you know what an embarrassment that is."

The government brought a civil racketeering case against Mr. Avellino and others in June 1989, and Mr. Kubecka was expected to testify. That August, Mr. Kubecka and his brother-in-law, Donald Barstow, were shot to death. Mr. Avellino, who allegedly approached another Mafia member as early as late 1988 to arrange the killing, was indicted last April on murder charges. He pleaded not guilty. A federal judge barred him from the trash industry last December. He was denied bail in the murder case. Trial is set for February.

Louis J. and Robert A. Mongelli, haulers north of the city and associates of Genovese family members, heard about the bug in Mr. Avellino's car. Robert insisted on talking in a noisy garage to avoid being taped. "That's how they got all those guys... bugs right in the dashboard..."

By the time Robert said that, in October 1988, the government had bug-wearing informants in the Mongelli brothers' midst. The Mongellis sought to divvy up hauling territories, Louis noting in one instance that "then they can all raise their price 30 percent across the board."

They laundered millions of dollars to avoid taxes. They pleaded guilty to that as well as to racketeering and tax evasion. They abandoned a dump that became a $14 million cleanup site, "leaving Robert's mother-in-law as the sole stockholder, director and officer," according to prosecutors' sentencing memorandum. And they offered hundreds of thousands of dollars – plus "free use of Louis's condominium in Palm Beach, Fla., a 92-foot yacht, and a 'broad,'" – in bribes to a state official for help with dump permits.

Anthony Vulpis and Angelo Paccione, big haulers in Brooklyn and Queens, both had mob ties, according to documents filed in federal court in Manhattan. In 1988, they got permits to run a "clean fill" on Staten Island but turned it into a full-scale dump – taking trash, medical waste and asbestos. The cleanup bill would hit $15 million.

They also ran a medical-waste business that advertised aggressively: "Is Your Medical Waste Being Washed Up On A Beach? You Could Be Prosecuted! Let Us Handle Your Waste Problems." But their permits were bogus and the operation slipshod. A truck full of medical waste, including blood vials and human organs, sat on the street leaking for two weeks.

## SIX

# Cash Flow: 'Pay to Play' is Banned, But Muni-Bond Firms Keep the Game Going

CHARLES GASPARINO AND JOSH P. HAMILTON

*Source*: *Wall Street Journal*, May 13, 1998.

The biggest municipal-bond deal in history gets under way today, as underwriters price the first of $7 billion in bonds issued for a partial state takeover of Long Island Lighting Co. Whatever the policy merits of the state takeover, there is no question it is a good deal for the underwriters. They stand to collect about $40 million in fees. The contenders for this lucrative business were put "through a competitive process," then selected on the basis of their skill and experience, says the state agency that is handling the deal. That seems a reasonable contention; the winning underwriters are, after all, highly experienced firms. Still, they are more than that. The firms that walked away with the biggest chunks of the issue also all have extensive links to political figures in a position to influence the selection of underwriters. And all have made substantial political contributions that found their way to powerful New York politicians, despite the supposed demise of the ethically questionable political/muni-bond nexus known as "pay to play."

In attacking that system four years ago, the Securities and Exchange Commission put in place a rule barring from muni-bond underwriting any firm that gives to state or local officials in position to influence underwriter selection. It also sharply limits giving by firms' employees. Rule G-37, as it is called, was promulgated by an industry self-regulatory group called the Muncipal Securities Rulemaking Board. But judging by the mammoth Lilco underwriting, the game didn't end, it just got more complicated. Muni-bond underwriters are barred from direct giving to a great many state and local campaigns now. But they have their ways. Bond firms and employees of the firms ship money off to a variety of legal destinations: state-party "housekeeping accounts," bond-act committees, federal political-action committees and national party kitties that ostensibly finance federal candidacies. At the same time, the underwriting firms burnish their welcome by hiring politically connected law firms, lobbyists and consultants, who sometimes proceed to make campaign contributions of their own to muni-bond decision makers.

Rule G-37 isn't violated. But officials influencing decisions about bond offerings often can easily find out the source of money wending its way to their coffers. None of this proves that the money and connections are buying influence. But then, even in its heyday, "pay to play" never did produce a smoking gun. What it produced was a suspicious pattern – lots of money flowing from bond firms to local politicians, and then lots of muni-bond business flowing from government offices to bond firms. That pattern is still abundantly in evidence.

In New York, the office handling the huge offering in the Lilco case is a state agency called the Long Island Power Authority, or LIPA. In February, its board selected four senior managers of the offering: Bear Stearns Cos., Lehman Brothers Inc., the Salomon Smith Barney unit of Travelers Group and Morgan Stanley, Dean Witter & Co. Bear Stearns won the coveted role of lead underwriter of the first $3 billion of bonds, the ones to be priced today. Later this month, $1.5 billion more of bonds will be priced, and then the rest in coming months. The board that selected the underwriters has 15 members (there is one vacancy). New York Gov. George Pataki names nine of the members, including the chairman. Three more are named by a close Pataki ally, the Republican leader of the state senate, with the other three picked by the Democratic leader of the state assembly. This makes Gov. Pataki someone the bond firms want to be sure they are on good terms with. And by virtue of that fact, it makes a central player of Gov. Pataki's political patron, Sen. Alfonse D'Amato. Not that Sen. D'Amato needs any reflected glory. Before becoming a senator, Mr. D'Amato was a leading municipal politician on Long Island; the powerful senator has ties to several members of the LIPA board, to say nothing of the influence he wields through such federal roles as chairman of the Senate Banking Committee and a member of the Senate Finance Committee.

Messrs. Pataki and D'Amato are close. A former chief fund-raiser for Sen. D'Amato had the same role in Mr. Pataki's successful 1994 campaign for governor, then became the governor's economic-development czar. They have a joint fund-raising committee called New York Salute, 1998, whose affiliated committees include one called Friends of Pataki, according to a document filed with the Federal Election Commission. They occasionally hold joint fund-raising events. State and federal campaign-contribution records show that all four of the firms chosen to lead the Lilco underwriting have contributed to various political committees and funds that exist to get Messrs. Pataki and D'Amato re-elected or to further causes they are promoting. Both are up for re-election this year.

Bear Stearns is one of Sen. D'Amato's very biggest boosters on Wall Street. In 1996, Bear Stearns and its chief executive, James Cayne, chipped in a total of $50,000 to promote a state environmental-bond act, ads for which prominently and favorably featured Sen. D'Amato as an environmentally concerned senator. In 1997, Bear Stearns officials exceeded their counterparts at other firms in total contributions to the senator, giving $42,750. That isn't all. Bear Stearns employs lobbyists, law firms and muni-bond execut-ives with extensive political and business relationships with the D'Amato – Pataki political partnership. Bear Stearns manages a blind trust of Sen. D'Amato's personal investments. And the firm employs Sen. D'Amato's son, Daniel, as a stockbroker.

Does all this mean anything? The firm says no. Although it won't comment on its handling of the senator's finances or employment of his son, Bear Stearns says in a statement that "every meeting, every decision, every selection by LIPA has been part of an open process. . . ." It adds: "Based on merit, expertise and past performance, Bear Stearns will successfully bring our portion of the bond issue to market." Sen. D'Amato, asked about the notion that bond firms feel they have to hire consultants who are close to him or the governor, says in a statement: "That's absolute nonsense. . . . There are a multitude of people and companies involved at every level. . . . I've been the senator from New York for almost 20 years, and it would be ridiculous for me not to know the kinds of people who may be involved in this endeavor." As for Bear Stearns, Sen. D'Amato says his "blind trust was placed there for precisely its reputation for integrity. My son is a stockbroker and has nothing even remotely to do with Long Island Lighting Co." Gov. Pataki declines to comment, apart from a statement read by his spokeswoman, Zenia Mucha: "We live in a democracy. People have a right to participate in the political process. It's their right to choose to participate and their right to choose not to participate."

A pattern similar to Bear Stearns's is evident at Salomon Smith Barney, one of the second-place winners in the underwriting competition. It, too, has cultivated political ties to decision makers. Salomon Smith Barney's main munibond investment banker in New York state is Bartley Livolsi. He is a Pataki appointee to New York's Temporary State Commission on Lobbying, where he is vice chairman. The firm says Mr. Livolsi doesn't wish to comment about his role. Salomon Smith Barney also uses as a muni-bond consultant John Klein, a former political leader of Long Island's Suffolk County. Late last year, the Republican-controlled Suffolk County Legislature voted to put the proposed Lilco takeover before voters, in a move that might have scuttled the entire project. But the effort was a nonstarter, thanks to a lawsuit filed by an influential community group called the Association for a Better Long Island. The association's general counsel: Mr. Klein. Association for a Better Long Island is influential in another way: One of its board members, Vince Polimeni, heads LIPA's finance committee. This was the committee that recommended to the full board the final group of underwriters. Mr. Klein, whose law firm receives $180,000 a year from Salomon Smith Barney for muni-related services, says he had no role in helping the firm secure a chunk of the LIPA bond deal. Salomon Smith Barney likewise says Mr. Klein played no role in its LIPA underwriting efforts. Mr. Polimeni, a Pataki appointee to the LIPA board, didn't return calls. A LIPA spokesman says any suggestion that industry connections influence Mr. Polimeni's decision is "absurd."

The utility at the heart of this, Lilco, has charged some of the highest rates in the U.S. for years, partly because of one ill-fated project: its construction – and subsequent abandonment, under public pressure – of a $5.5 billion nuclear-power plant known as Shoreham. The costly blunder saddled the Hicksville, N.Y., company's more than a million customers with huge utility bills. During the 1994 gubernatorial campaign, then-Gov. Mario Cuomo proposed easing the burden by having the state take over Lilco. Mr. Pataki initially questioned the idea, but after defeating Mr. Cuomo, he began to promote it. With Wall Street's help, state officials began drawing up plans for a takeover of about $4 billion in Shoreham-related debt as well as Lilco's transmission and distribution lines. The transaction was designed to slash Lilco customers' bills by 20 percent, largely by refinancing the debt with tax-exempt municipal bonds. Lilco would continue to exist as a publicly held power-generation company free of the Shoreham debt.

In 1995, LIPA officials began interviewing firms for the short-term post of financial adviser. Though white-shoe firms Morgan Stanley and Goldman, Sachs Co. seemed the favorites, Bear Stearns won the job. LIPA officials say the others were outhustled and underbid by Bear Stearns. Its CEO, Mr. Cayne, campaigned personally for the role, at one point showing up for a meeting with LIPA despite a 103-degree fever. Bear Stearns's two-year gig as financial adviser brought it about $2 million, and the firm eventually will collect $2 million to $4 million more, contingent on future utility-rate reductions.

In September 1995, Bear Stearns hired Dennis Francis Gill as a trading-floor clerk. He is a son of James Gill, who at the time was chairman of LIPA, the agency that would select the giant bond deal's underwriters. James Gill also is a prominent D'Amato-Pataki supporter and a partner at the well-connected law firm of Robinson, Silverman, Pearce, Aronsohn & Berman in New York City. Dennis Gill joined Bear Stearns the same month LIPA chose Bear Stearns as financial adviser, according to records at the National Association of Securities Dealers and minutes of LIPA's Sept. 22 meeting. The minutes say his father abstained from voting on Bear Stearns's selection, explaining that several "investment-banking firms, including Bear Stearns, were clients of his" law firm and that "his son worked for Bear Stearns in an area of the firm unrelated to the consulting services to be provided to LIPA." Dennis Gill has left Bear Stearns and couldn't be located.

By this time, Bear Stearns and its Wall Street rivals were vying for a piece of what would be the biggest muni-bond issue in U.S. history. PaineWebber Group Inc. hired, as an investment banker in its muni-bond department, a man named Frank Mahoney. He is a former Pataki administration official, and he also is the brother of a Pataki D'Amato political adviser, Kieran Mahoney. Lehman Brothers, meanwhile had hired investment banker Ronald Stack. Mr. Stack had served on one of Mr. Pataki's postelection transition committees. Morgan Stanley also hired a politically connected investment banker, Paula Dagen. PaineWebber declined to comment and didn't make Mr. Mahoney available. Morgan Stanely and Lehman said the hirings of Mr. Stack and Ms. Dagen were merit-based, and both firms said the bankers didn't wish to comment.

Bear Stearns outgunned them all. In 1996 it hired as a managing director in its muni-bond department Paul Atanasio, one of the most prominent rainmakers in the muni-bond business. Mr. Atanasio has made contributions to Mr. Pataki's campaign dating back to 1992, campaign records show. He served on Gov. Pataki's panel on privatization. He also advises the chairman of New York state's Conservative Party, Michael Long, who is a key player in Gov. Pataki's administration and one of Sen. D'Amato's biggest supporters.

In 1996, Bear Stearns made some of the largest corporate donations to the National Republican Senatorial Committee, at a time when Sen. D'Amato was its chairman. Bear Stearns gave $150,000 to the committee's building fund. Bear Stearns hadn't given to the committee in the two years before the Senate banking chairman took it over. After he left, the firm cut its giving to the committee in half.

While Sen. D'Amato headed the national-party senatorial committee, he oversaw its distribution of nearly $2 million to the New York gubernatorial re-election campaign of Mr. Pataki, even though the election remained more than a year away. Sen. D'Amato also had the committee pass along more than $500,000 to the New York State Republican Party and thousands of dollars to New York candidates, including over $100,000 to Gov. Pataki's apparent choice for running mate this fall, Judge Mary O. Donohue. The GOP senatorial committee says muni-bond funds' contributions don't trickle down to the state level. Bear Stearns also retained Nixon Hargrave Devans & Doyle, a New York law and lobbying firm. In 1997, Nixon Hargrave gave $8,000 to an account at the New York State Republican Committee, called the "reporting" account. Nixon Hargrave employs as senior counsel John V. Scaduto. He is a major Pataki fund-raiser, a childhood friend of Sen. D'Amato and a former treasurer of Long Island's Nassau County. Mr. Scaduto didn't return calls. Mr. Atanasio had no comment.

Throughout 1997, Wall Street executives met with state officials to push for an underwriting position. Some traveled to Washington to discuss the issue with Sen. D'Amato's chief of staff, Michael Kinsella. Through a spokeswoman, Mr. Kinsella says he had "no contact with anyone at LIPA with regard to this matter."

In April 1997, Gov. Pataki held a fund-raiser at Manhattan's South Street Seaport and invited a number of Wall Street executives, including some who were competing for a piece of the LIPA deal. The invitations included a morsel of advice to muni-bond executives barred by Rule G-37 from giving to him directly: Make any gifts payable to the state Republican Party's housekeeping account. In the weeks after receiving the invitations, Wall Street muni-bond houses and executives gave thousands of dollars to this account, records show. One of the biggest gifts came from Travelers, the parent of Salomon Smith Barney. A Travelers spokesman says that through several subsidiaries, it contributed $100,000 to the state GOP's housekeeping account. Travelers says that "no money was given in Smith Barney's name because of the sensitivity to pay-to-play issues."

Gov. Pataki's spokeswoman says his campaign committee "abides by the letter of the law," and all contributions "are fully disclosed and fully documented." Nonetheless, at the time, his solicitation came to the attention of the Municipal Securities Rulemaking Board. The board was gradually realizing that Wall Street had figured out ways around Rule G-37. It had identified common tactics, including contributing to public officials' favorite charities and sponsoring quasipolitical conferences attended by governors and other state officials. Rule G-37 includes a clause barring firms from making indirect contributions when they can't contribute directly, but proving such violations is difficult. Essentially, regulators have to prove that munibond executives intended to funnel their donations to state and local officials, a task that is nearly impossible.

The Pataki fund-raiser helped trigger a broad review by the Municipal Securities Rulemaking Board, but ultimately it concluded its hands were tied: Any rule aimed at stopping indirect transfers of money from muni-bond firms to politicians "wouldn't have passed constitutional muster," says its executive director, Christopher Taylor. The board, however, is currently considering a new rule under which consultants hired to assist on specific bond deals would have to disclose any contributions they themselves make to politicians involved in municipal finance. Mr. Taylor says there is no way to close every loophole in the contribution restrictions. "Politicians have an insatiable appetite for money," he says, adding: "It's a shakedown." But one participant in the bond market suggests that it is naive to be surprised by firms' efforts to build ties to the influential. "People don't do arm's-length relationships with everything they do," says Michael Shamosh, a fixed-income strategist at Tucker Anthony Inc. in New York City. "It's not possible to do business without influence. Influence is always there and available, and it's used in government and business. You can't legislate away relationships."

SEVEN

# School of Genius

SYLVIA NASAR

*Source*: *A Beautiful Mind: A Biography of John Forbes Nash, Jr.*
Reprinted with permission of Simon and Schuster. © 1998 by Sylvia Nasar.

> *Conversation enriches the understanding, but solitude is the school of genius.*
> EDWARD GIBBON

On Nash's second afternoon in Princeton, Solomon Lefschetz rounded up the first-year graduate students in the West Common Room.[1] He was there to tell them the facts of life, he said, in his heavy French accent, fixing them with his fierce gaze. And for an hour Lefschetz glared, shouted, and pounded the table with his gloved, wooden hands, delivering something between a biblical sermon and a drill sergeant's diatribe.

They were the best, the very best. Each of them had been carefully handpicked, like a diamond from a heap of coal. But this was Princeton, where real mathematicians did real mathematics. Compared to these men, the newcomers were babies, ignorant, pathetic babies, and Princeton was going to make them grow up, damn it!

Entrepreneurial and energetic, Lefschetz was the supercharged human locomotive that had pulled the Princeton department out of genteel mediocrity right to the top.[2] He recruited mathematicians with only one criterion in mind: research. His high-handed and idiosyncratic editorial policies made the *Annals of Mathematics*, Princeton's once-tired monthly, into the most revered mathematical journal in the world.[3] He was sometimes accused of caving in to anti-Semitism for refusing to admit many Jewish students (his rationale being that nobody would hire them when they completed their degrees),[4] but no one denies that he had brilliant snap judgment. He exhorted, bossed, and

[1] Solomon Leader, professor of mathematics, Rutgers University, interview, 6.9.95.

[2] The portrait of Solomon Lefschetz is based on interviews with Harold W. Kulm, J L 97; William Baumol, 1.95; Donald Spencer, 11.18.95; Eugenio Calabi, 3.2.96; Martin Davis, 2.20.96; Melvin *Haqueci* 2.6.96; Solomon Leader, 6.9.95; and other contemporaries of Nash's at Princeton. Also consulted were several memoirs, including Solomon Lefschetz, "Reminiscences of a Mathematical Immigrant in the United States," *American Mathematical Monthly*, vol. 77 (1970); A. W. Tucker, *Solomon Lefschetz: A Reminiscence*; Sir William Hodge, *Solomon Lefschetz, 1884–1972*; Phillip Griffiths, Donald Spencer, and George Whitehead, *Solomon Lefschetz: Biographical Memoirs* (Washington, D.C.: National Academy of Sciences, 1992); Gian Carlo Rota, *Indiscrete Thoughts*, op. cit.

[3] Lefschetz's obituary in *The New York Times* (October 7, 1972) credits him for "developing [the *Annals of Mathematics*] into one of the world's foremost mathemalical journals."

[4] "It should be noted that although Lefschetz was Jewish, he was not above engaging in a mild form of anti-semitism. He told Henry Wallman that he was the last Jewish graduate student that would he admitted to Princeton because Jews could not get a job anyway and so why bother," Ralph Phillips, "Reminiscences of the 1930s," *The Mathematical Intelligencer*, vol. 16, no. 3 (1994). Lefschetz's attitude toward Jewish students was well known. Phillips's impressions were confirmed by Leader, interview, 6.9.95; Kuhn, interview. 11.97; Daith interview, 2.20.96; and Hausner, interview, 2.6.96.

bullied, but with the aim of making the department great and turning his students into real mathematicians, tough like himself.

When he came to Princeton in the 1920s, he often said, he was "an invisible man."[5] He was one of the first Jews on the faculty, loud, rude, and badly dressed to boot. People pretended not to see him in the hallways and gave him wide berth at faculty parties. But Lefschetz had overcome far more formidable obstacles in his life than a bunch of prissy Wasp snobs. He had been born in Moscow and been educated in France.[6] In love with mathematics, but effectively barred from an academic career in France because he was not a citizen, he studied engineering and emigrated to the United States. At age twenty-three, a terrible accident altered the course of his life. Lefschetz was working for Westinghouse in Pittsburgh when a transformer explosion burned off his hands. His recovery took years, during which he suffered from deep depression, but the accident ultimately became the impetus to pursue his true love, mathematics.[7] He enrolled in a Ph.D. program at Clark University, the university famous for Freud's 1912 lectures on psychoanalysis, soon fell in love with and married another mathematics student, and spent nearly a decade in obscure teaching posts in Nebraska and Kansas. After days of backbreaking teaching, he wrote a series of brilliant, original, and highly influential papers that eventually resulted in a "call" from Princeton. "My years in the west with total hermetic isolation played in my development the role of 'a job in a lighthouse' which Einstein would have every young scientist assume so that he may develop his own ideas in his own way."[8]

Lefschetz valued independent thinking and originality above everything. He was, in fact, contemptuous of elegant or rigorous proofs of what he considered obvious points. He once dismissed a clever new proof of one of his theorems by saying, "Don't come to me with your pretty proofs. We don't bother with that baby stuff around here."[9] Legend had it that he never wrote a correct proof or stated an incorrect theorem.[10] His first comprehensive treatise on topology, a highly influential book in which he coined the term "algebraic topology," "hardly contains one completely correct proof. It was rumored that it had been written during one of Lefschetz' sabbaticals . . . when his students did not have the opportunity to revise it."[11]

He knew most areas of mathematics, but his lectures were usually incoherent. Gian-Carlo Rota, one of his students, describes the start of one lecture on geometry: "Well a Riemann surface is a certain kind of Hausdorff space. You know what a Hausdorff space is, don't you? It's also compact, ok. I guess it is also a manifold. Surely you know what a manifold is. Now let me tell you one non-trivial theorem, the Riemann-Roch theorem."[12]

On this particular afternoon in mid-September 1948, with the new graduate students, Lefschetz was just warming up. "It's important to dress well. Get rid of that thing," he

[5] Baumol, interview, 1.95.

[6] See, for example, Gian-Carlo Rota, "Fine Hall in Its Golden Age," op. cit. DOD personnel security application. 3.10.56. Princeton University Archives.

[7] Solomon Lefschetz, "A Self Portrait," typewritten, 1.54, Princeton University Archives.

[8] Ibid., p. iii.

[9] Donald Spencer, interviews, 11.28.95; 11.29.95; 11.30.95.

[10] Rota, op. cit.

[11] Ibid.

[12] Ibid.

said, pointing to a pen holder. "You look like a workman, not a mathematician," he told one student.[13] "Let a Princeton barber cut your hair," he said to another.[14] They could go to class or not go to class. He didn't give a damn. Grades meant nothing. They were only recorded to please the "goddamn deans." Only the "generals" counted.[15]

There was only one requirement: come to tea.[16] They were absolutely required to come to tea every afternoon. Where else would they meet the finest mathematics faculty in the world? Oh, and if they felt like it, they were free to visit that "embalming parlor," as he liked to call the Institute of Advanced Study, to see if they could catch a glimpse of Einstein, Gödel, or von Neumann.[17] "Remember," he kept repeating, "we're not here to baby you." To Nash, Lefschetz's opening spiel must have sounded as rousing as a Sousa march.

Lefschetz's, hence Princeton's, philosophy of graduate mathematics education had its roots in the great German and French research universities.[18] The main idea was to plunge students, as quickly as possible, into their own research, and to produce an acceptable dissertation quickly. The fact that Princeton's small faculty was, to a man, actively engaged in research itself, was by and large on speaking terms, and was available to supervise students' research, made this a practical approach.[19] Lefschetz wasn't aiming for perfectly polished diamonds and indeed regarded too much polish in a mathematician's youth as antithetical to later creativity. The goal was not erudition, much as erudition might be admired, but turning out men who could make original and important discoveries.

Princeton subjected its students to a maximum of pressure but a wonderful minimum of bureaucracy. Lefschetz was not exaggerating when he said that the department had no course requirements. The department offered courses, true, but enrollment was a fiction, as were grades. Some professors put down all *A*s, others all *C*s, on their grade reports, but both were completely arbitrary.[20] You didn't have to show up a single time to earn them and students' transcripts were, more often than not, works of fiction "to satisfy the Philistines." There were no course examinations. In the language examinations, given by members of the mathematics department, a student was asked to translate a passage of French or German mathematical text. But they were a joke.[21] If you could make neither heads nor tails of the passage – unlikely, since the passages typically contained many mathematical symbols and precious few words – you could get a passing grade merely by promising to learn the passage later. The only test that counted was the general examination, a qualifying examination on five topics, three determined by the department, two by the candidate, at the end of the first, or at latest, second year. However, even the generals were sometimes tailored to the strengths and weaknesses of a student.[22] If, for example, it

---

[13] Leader, interview, 6.9.95.
[14] Danis, interview, 2.6.96.
[15] Hausner, interview, 2.6.96.
[16] Leader, interview, 6.9.95.
[17] Spencer, interviews.
[18] Virginia Chaplin, "Princeton and Mathematics," op. cit.; Davis, interview, 2.20.96; Hartley Jogers, interview, 1.26.96.
[19] Ibid.
[20] Hausner, interview.
[21] Ibid.
[22] Ibid.

was known that a student really knew one article well, but only one, the examiners, if they were so moved, might restrict themselves to that paper. The only other hurdle, before beginning the all-important thesis, was to find a senior member of the faculty to sponsor it.

If the faculty, which got to know every student well, decided that so-and-so wasn't going to make it, Lefschetz wasn't shy about not renewing the student's support or simply telling him to leave. You were either succeeding or on your way out. As a result, Princeton students who made it past the generals wound up with doctorates after just two or three years at a time when Harvard students were taking six, seven, or eight years.[23] Harvard, where Nash had yearned to go for the prestige and magic of its name, was at that time a nightmare of bureaucratic red tape, fiefdoms, and faculty with relatively little time to devote to students. Nash could not possibly have realized it fully that first day, but he was lucky to have chosen Princeton over Harvard.

That genius will emerge regardless of circumstance is a widely held belief. The biographer of the great Indian mathematician Ramanujan, for example, claims that the five years that the young Ramanujan spent in complete isolation from other mathematicians, having failed out of school and unable to get as much as a tutoring position, were the key to his stunning discoveries.[24] But when writing Ramanujan's obituary, G. H. Hardy, the Oxford mathematician who knew him best, called that view, held earlier by himself, "ridiculous sentimentalism." After Ramanujan's death at thirty-three, Hardy wrote that the "the tragedy of Ramanujan was not that he died young, but that, during his five unfortunate years, his genius was misdirected, side-tracked, and to a certain extent distorted."[25]

As was to become increasingly obvious over the months that followed, Princeton's approach to its graduate students, with its combination of complete freedom and relentless pressure to produce, could not have been better suited to someone of Nash's temperament and style as a mathematician, nor more happily designed to elicit the first real proofs of his genius. Nash's great luck, if you want to call it luck, was that he came onto the mathematical scene at a time and to a place tailor-made for his particular needs. He came away with his independence, ambition, and originality intact, having been allowed to acquire a truly first-class training that was to serve him brilliantly.

Like nearly all the other graduate students at Princeton, Nash lived in the Graduate College. The College was a gorgeous, faux-English edifice of dark gray stone surrounding an interior courtyard that sat on a crest overlooking a golf course and lake. It was located about a mile from Fine Hall on the far side of Alexander Road, about halfway between Fine and the Institute for Advanced Study. Especially in winter, when it was dark by the time the afternoon seminar ended, it was a good long walk, and once you were there, you didn't feel like going out again. Its location was the outcome of a fight between Woodrow Wilson and Dean Andrew West.[26] Wilson had wanted the graduate students to mix and

[23] Joseph Kohn, interview, 7.25.96.

[24] Robert Kanigel, *The Man Who Knew Infinity* (New York: Pocket Books, 1991); G. H. Hardy, "The Indian Mathematician Ramanujan," lecture delivered at the Harvard Tercentenary Conference of Arts and Sciences. August 31, 1936, reprinted in *A Century of Mathematics* (Washington, D.C.: Mathematical Asociation of America, 1994), p. 110.

[25] Hardy, op. cit.

[26] J. Dasies, op. cit.: Gerard Washmitzer, professor of mathematics, Princeton University, interview, 9.25.96.

mingle with the undergraduates. West wanted to re-create the atmosphere of one of the Oxbridge colleges, far removed from the rowdy, snobbish undergraduate eating clubs on Prospect Street.

In 1948, there were about six hundred graduate students, their ranks swelled by the numbers of returning veterans whose undergraduate or graduate careers had been interrupted by the war.[27] The College, a bit shabbier than before the war and in need of sprucing up, was full, overflowing really, and a good many less lucky first-year students had been turned away and were being forced to lodge in rented rooms in the village. Almost everyone else had to share rooms. Nash, who lived in Pine Tower, was lucky to get a private room, one of the perks of his fellowship.[28] About fifteen or twenty of the mathematics students, second- and third-year as well as first-year students, and a couple of instructors lived in the college at the time.

Life was masculine, monastic, and scholarly, exactly as Dean West had envisioned.[29] The graduate students ate breakfast, lunch, and dinner together at the cost of fourteen dollars a week. Breakfast and lunch were served in the "breakfast" room, hurried meals that were taken on the run. But dinner, served in Proctor Hall, a refectory very much in the English style, was a more leisurely affair. There were tall windows, long wooden tables, and formal portraits of eminent Princetonians on the walls; the evening prayer was led by Sir Hugh Taylor, the college's dean, or his second in command, the college's master. Grace was said. There were no candles and no wine, but the food was excellent. Gowns were no longer required as before the war (they were briefly reinstated in the early 1950s, but soon disappeared for good), but jackets and ties were required.

The atmosphere at dinner was a combination of male debating society, locker room, and seminary. Though historians, English scholars, physicists, and economists all lived cheek by jowl with the mathematicians, the mathematicians segregated themselves as strictly as if they were living under some legal system of apartheid, always occupying a table by themselves.[30] The older, more sophisticated students, namely Harold Kuhn, Leon Henkin, and David Gale, met for sherry in Kuhn's rooms before dinner. Conversation at dinner, sometimes but not always mathematical, was more expansive than at teatime. The talk, one former student recalls, frequently revolved around "politics, music, and girls." Political debate resembled discussions about sports, with more calculation of odds and betting than ideology. In that early fall, the Truman-Dewey race provided a great deal of entertainment. Being a more diverse group, the graduate students were more evenly split between the candidates than the Princeton undergraduates; 98 percent of the undergraduates at Princeton, it turned out, were Dewey supporters. One graduate student even wore a Wallace button for Henry Wallace, the candidate supported by the American Labor party, a Communist front organization.[31]

[27] Graduate Catalog, Princeton University, various years; Report to the President, Princeton University, various years.

[28] Letter from John Nash Forbes, Jr., to Solomon Lefschetz referring to request for private room, 4.46; Calabi, interview.

[29] Interviews with Kulun, 11.97; Washnitzer, 9.25.96; Felix Browder, 11.2.96; Calabi, 3.12.96; John Toler, professor of mathematics, Princeton University, 9.30.97; John Isbell, professor of mathematics, State University of New York at Buffalo, 8.97; Leader, 6.9.95; Davis, 2.6.96.

[30] Kuhn, interview.

[31] Davis, interview.

Girls, or rather the absence of girls, the difficulty of meeting girls, the real or imagined exploits of certain older and more worldly students, were also hot subjects.[32] Very few of the students dated. Women were not allowed in the main dining hall, and, of course, there were no female students. "We are all homosexuals here" was a famous remark made by a resident to fluster the dean's wife.[33] Isolation made the real prospects of meeting a girl remote. A few venturesome souls, organized by a young instructor named John Tukey, went to Thursday night folk dances at the local high school.[34] But most were too shy and self-conscious to do even that. Sir Hugh, a stuffed shirt roundly disliked by the mathematicians, did his best to discourage what little socializing there was. One student was called into the dean's office because a pair of women's panties had been found in his room; it turned out his sister had been visiting and he, to preserve appearances, had moved out for the night. At one point, a seemingly unnecessary rule was handed down that residents of the Graduate College were not allowed to entertain a woman past midnight. The very few students who actually had girlfriends interpreted the rule literally to mean that a woman could be in the room, but couldn't be entertained. Harold Kuhn spent his honeymoon there.[35] The only time and place that women were allowed to join the larger group was Saturday lunch in the Breakfast Room.

In short, social life was rather enveloping – it would be hard to become really lonely – and at the same time limited to other men, in Nash's case specifically to other mathematicians. The parties held in student rooms were thus mostly all-male affairs. Such evenings, as often as not, were devoted to mathematical parties organized by one of the graduate students at Lefschetz's request to entertain some visitor but actually to get his students much-needed job contacts.[36]

The quality, diversity, and sheer volume of mathematics talked about in Princeton every day, by professors, Institute professors, and a steady stream of visitors from all over the world, not to mention the students themselves, were unlike anything Nash had ever imagined, much less experienced. A revolution was taking place in mathematics and Princeton was the center of the action. Topology. Logic. Game theory. There were not only lectures, colloquia, seminars, classes, and weekly meetings at the institute that Einstein and von Neumann occasionally attended, but there were breakfasts, lunches, dinners, and after-dinner parties at the Graduate College, where most of the mathematicians lived, as well as the daily afternoon teas in the common room. Martin Shubik, a young economist studying at Princeton at that time, later wrote that the mathematics department was "electric with ideas and the sheer joy of the hunt. If a stray ten-year-old with bare feet, no tie, torn blue jeans, and an interesting theorem had walked into Fine Hall at tea times, someone would have listened."[37]

[32] Interviews with Washnitzer and Kuhn.
[33] Washnitzer, interview.
[34] Tukey, interview.
[35] Kuhn, interview.
[36] Calabi, interview.
[37] Martin Shubik, "Game Theory at Princeton: A Personal Reminiscence," Cowles Foundation Preliminary Paper 901019, undated.

Tea was the high point of every day.[38] It was held in Fine Hall between three and four between the last class and the four-thirty seminar that went until five-thirty or six. On Wednesdays it was held in the west common room, or the professor's room as it was also called, and was a far more formal affair, where the self-effacing Mrs. Lefschetz and the other wives of the senior faculty, wearing long gowns and white gloves, poured the tea and passed the cookies. Heavy silver teapots and dainty English bone china were brought out.

On other days, tea was held in the east common room, also known as the students' room, a much-lived-in, funky place full of overstuffed leather armchairs and low tables. The janitor would bring in the tea and cookies a few minutes before three o'clock and the mathematicians, tired from a day of working alone or lecturing or attending seminars, would start drifting in, one by one or in groups. The faculty almost always came, as did most of the graduate students and a sprinkling of more precocious undergraduates. It was very much a family gathering, small and intimate. It is hard to think where a student could get to know as many other mathematicians as well as at Princeton teatime.

The talk was by no means purely formal. Mathematical gossip abounded – who was working on what, who had a nibble from what department, who had run into trouble on his generals. Melvin Hausner, a former Princeton graduate student, later recalled, "You went there to discuss math. To do your own version of gossiping. To meet faculty. To meet friends. We discussed math problems. We shared our readings of recent math papers."[39]

The professors felt it their duty to come, not only to get to know the students but to chat with one another. The great logician Alonzo Church, who looked "like a cross between a panda and an owl," never spoke unless spoken to, and rarely then, would head straight for the cookies, placing one between the fingers of his splayed hand, and munch away.[40] The charismatic algebraist Emil Artin, son of a German opera singer, would fling his gaunt, elegant body into one of the leather armchairs, light a Camel, and opine on Wittgenstein and the like to his disciples, huddled, more or less literally, at his feet.[41] The topologist Ralph Fox, a Go master, almost always made a beeline for a game board, motioning some student to join him.[42] Another topologist, Norman Steenrod, a good-looking, friendly midwesterner who had just created a sensation with his discovery of fiber bundles, usually stopped in for a game of chess.[43] Albert Tucker, Lefschetz's righthand man, was the straitlaced son of a Canadian Methodist minister and Nash's eventual thesis adviser. Tucker always surveyed the room before he came in and would make fussy little adjustments – such as straightening the curtain weights if the drapes happened to be awry, or issuing a word-to-the-wise to a student who was taking too many cookies.[44] More often than not, a few visitors, often from the Institute for Advanced Study, would turn up as well.

---

[38] Interviews with Hausner; Davis; Kuhn; Spencer; Leader; Rogers; Calabi; and John McGarthy, professor of computer science, Stanford University, 2.4.96.

[39] Flausner, interview, 2.6.96.

[40] Interviews with Davis, Leader, Spencer; Rota. op. cil.

[41] Roda, op. cit.

[42] Isbell, interview.

[43] Tukey, interview.

[44] David Yarmush, interview, 2.6.96.

The students who gathered at teatime were as remarkable, in a way, as the faculty. Poor Jews, new immigrants, wealthy foreigners, sons of the working classes, veterans in their twenties, and teenagers, the students were a diverse as well as brilliant group, among them John Tate, Serge Lang, Gerard Washnitzer, Harold Kuhn, David Gale, Leon Henkin, and Eugenio Calabi.[45] The teas were heaven for the shy, friendless, and socially awkward, a category in which many of these young men belonged. John Milnor, the most brilliant freshman in the history of the Princeton mathematics department, described it this way: "Everything was new to me. I was awkward socially, shy and isolated. Everything was wonderful. This was a whole new world. Here was a whole community in which I felt very much at home."[46]

The atmosphere was, however, as competitive as it was friendly.[47] Insults and one-upmanship were always major ingredients in teatime banter. The common room was where the young bucks warily sized each other up, bluffed and postured, and locked horns. No culture was more hierarchical than mathematical culture in its precise ranking of individual merit and prestige, yet it was a ranking always in a state of suspense and flux, in which new challenges and scuffles erupted almost daily. Back in their undergraduate colleges, most of these young men had gotten used to being the brightest and best, but now they were bumping up against the brightest and best from other schools. One of the graduate students who entered with Nash admitted, "Competitiveness, it was sort of like breathing. We thrived on it. We were nasty. This guy, he's dumb, we'd say. Therefore he no longer existed."[48]

There were cliques, mostly based on fields. *The* clique at the top of the hierarchy was the topology clique, which clustered around Lefschetz, Fox, and Steenrod. Then came analysis, grouped around Lefschetz's archrival in the department, a civilized and erudite lover of music and art named Bochner. Then came algebra, which consisted of Emil Artin and a handful of anointed followers. Logic, for some reason, was not highly regarded, despite Church's towering reputation among early pioneers of computer theory. The game theory clique around Tucker was considered quite déclassé, an anomaly in this ivory tower of pure mathematics. Each clique had its own thoughts about the importance of its subject and its own way of putting the others down.

Nash had never in his life encountered anything like this exotic little mathematical hothouse. It would soon provide him with the emotional and intellectual context he so much needed to express himself.

---

[45] Princeton Alumni Directory 1997.

[46] John W. Milnor, professor of mathematics and director, Institute for Mathematical Sciences, State University of New York at Stony Brook, interviews, 10.28.94 and 7.95.

[47] Interviews with Kuhn, Hausner, John McCarthy.

[48] Interviews with Hausner and Davis.

# EIGHT

# Ratbert the Consultant

SCOTT ADAMS

*Source*: © 1997 United Feature Syndicate, Inc., courtesy of Knight Features, London.

# PART TWO
# Information

# Introduction

The Ayres and Bulow article that opens Part Two illustrates one of its basic points: information matters. They suggest that the key to campaign finance reform is not to change who is allowed to make contributions (the players) or how big a contribution can be (the actions) or who politicians can work for after they leave office (the payoffs), but just to change the information, leaving everything else the same. If the politician doesn't know you gave him the contribution, he won't do you any special favors. For a longer version of their idea, see Ian Ayres and Jeremy Bulow, "The Donation Booth: Mandating Donor Anonymity to Disrupt the Market for Political Influence," *Stanford Law Review* 50: 837–91 (February 1998).

Ayres and Bulow's idea is similar to the "Australian ballot." This is the secret written ballot, introduced into the United States in the nineteenth century. The main argument was not that the ballot's secrecy would prevent harassment of the voter. What was it? And why was the Australian ballot adopted, but we see no signs of any country adopting the Ayres and Bulow idea? Think about players, actions, and payoffs – *cui bono*, or, as Rush Limbaugh likes to say, *follow the money*.

I include the story of the Horatii because it is the source for a good homework problem. This shows how a story can be converted to a model. How would you model this? Is everybody behaving rationally? It is possible to set a model up with everybody behaving rationally, albeit with imperfect information, or with the Curiatii being dimwitted and irrational. It is also quite possible to set it up with the Curiatii being dimwitted but nonetheless rational. For my own model, see this book's website, at http://php.indiana.edu/~erasmuse/GI/gireader.htm

The Rothkopf poem is a bit of humor from decision theory. As you can perhaps tell already, I think humor is an important part of learning game theory. Even in subjects less full of twists and paradoxes than game theory, humor is useful. John Littlewood said, "A good mathematical joke is better, and better mathematics, than a dozen mediocre papers" (John Littlewood, *A Mathematician's Miscellany*, London: Methuen [1953]). So rather than include another paper, I'll tell a joke:

> One day a mathematician decided that he was sick of math. He walked down to the fire department and announced he wanted to be a fireman. The fire chief said, "You look

dependable. I'd be glad to hire you, but first I have to give you a little test." He took the mathematician to an alley behind the firehouse where there was a dumpster, a spigot, a can of gasoline, and a hose. The chief said, "Suppose you were walking in the alley to smoke a cigarette and you saw the dumpster on fire. What would you do?"

The mathematician said, "Well, I'd hook up the hose to the spigot, turn the water on, and put out the fire."

The chief said, "That's great...perfect! The test isn't over, though, because we get some strange characters wanting to be firemen. What would you do if you were walking down the alley to smoke a cigarette and you saw the dumpster and gasoline, but the dumpster wasn't on fire?"

The mathematician puzzled over the question, looking for the trick. Finally, he said, "First, I'd light the dumpster on fire with the gasoline and my cigarette...."

The chief whistled. "I knew it! When PhDs show up wanting to be firemen, there's something wrong with them. So why would you light the dumpster on fire?"

The mathematician replied, "Well, I couldn't figure out what the trick was in the question, but I knew there must be one. So I decided just to reduce the problem to one I'd already solved. I'm sorry it isn't a more elegant proof – does that mean I don't get the job? (Adapted from a joke at David Shay, "Mathematicians," www.geocities.com/Cape-Canaveral/4661/, July 25, 1999.)

The cartoon at the end of Part Two is more humor. It points to the importance of common knowledge. Would the managers behave the same way if they all knew what everybody's opinion was? What if everybody but the CEO knew everybody's opinions? How would you model this?

# NINE

# The Donation Booth

IAN AYRES AND JEREMY BULOW

*Source*: *The Boston Review*, December–January 1997/8, pp. 26–7.

"I think it's disingenuous for anybody in public life to say that it doesn't help you to be considered for [a trade mission] if you help the person who happens to win an election . . . And it is a good thing to do. That's the way the political system works."

**President Clinton**

Thus sayeth the President. With this mindset, it's not surprising that Clinton was obsessed with learning the identity of his campaign contributors. But contrary to the President's views, giving donors preferential treatment is not "a good thing to do." And it's not the way the political system has to work.

If we could stop candidates from learning the identity of contributors, big donors would not be able to buy perks or policy. Mandating anonymous donations would make it harder for candidates to sell access or influence, because they would never know that the donor had paid the price. Imagine a world with anonymous donations: No more selling nights in the Lincoln bedroom. No more ambassadorships or trade missions for successful fundraisers.

There is no good reason why politicians need to know the identity of their donors, or why donors need to reveal their identities. People can signal the intensity of their preferences by marching on Washington – barefoot if need be. An individual's power to influence government should not turn on personal wealth. Small donors are already effectively anonymous, because $100 doesn't buy very much face time with the president. Mandating anonymity is likely to level the playing field of influence by making small contributions count for relatively more.

The privacy of the voting booth is a core feature of our democracy. This privacy makes it much more difficult for candidates to buy votes, because at the end of the day they can never be sure who voted for them. We should replicate the privacy of the voting booth by creating a "donation booth" – a screen that forces donors to funnel campaign contributions through blind trusts.

Several states have already experimented with prohibiting judicial candidates from learning who donates to their election or reelection campaigns. The logic of course is

We have secret ballots to avoid corruption. Why not keep campaign contributions secret too?

that judges don't need to know the identity of their donors: judicial decisions should be based on the merits of each case, not on contributors' money. But it is difficult to explain why this logic does not apply to the other two branches of government as well. Our experience with judicial elections shows that donor anonymity can be enforced and can deter contributors who would otherwise seek to influence judicial decision making.

## PAC Bundling and Soft Money

Mandating anonymous donations could also help mitigate two of the biggest influence abuses: PAC bundling and soft money. Even though political action committees (PACs) are not supposed to give more than $5,000 to an individual federal candidate, PACs can bundle together individual $1,000 contributions and pass them on *en masse*. PAC bundles are often 10 to 20 times greater than the statutory limit.

Our proposal would radically reduce the amount of bundling because candidates would not know the identity of the PAC that had procured the bundle of individual donations. Currently, the PACs make sure that the candidates understand who is responsible for the bundle. Under our proposal, PACs could still solicit contributions for candidates, but they could not buy access from the victors.

Channeling donations through blind trusts could also mitigate the "soft money" loophole that allowed Clinton and Dole to spend $250 million more than what was intended by existing campaign finance regulation. Soft-money contributions to political parties can be used for television commercials that openly disparage the other party's candidate as long as the commercials refrain from using magic words such as "vote for candidate X." Reformers have attempted to stop "soft money" by expanding what counts as a campaign ad or allocating part of soft-money expenditures to candidates' campaign limits.

But "no disclosure" is better than "full disclosure." If we simply kept President Clinton in the dark about the identity of his soft-money contributors, he would have a much harder time extracting six-figure gifts from James Riady and company. Instead of trying to discern whether soft money is being used to promote a particular candidate, the donation booth would reduce the incentive for donors to write large soft-money checks in the first place.

## How Would It Work?

The proposal might operate through a privatized system of blind trusts – operated by established trust companies with substantial, preexisting assets (of say, more than $100 million). All candidates, political parties and political action committees would establish blind trust accounts at qualified institutions. The core regulation would require that all donations to candidates, political parties, and PACs be made by mail to the blind trusts. Campaigns would no longer be allowed to accept money in cash or check. Large donors would have the option of having the trust disclose that they had given at least $200, but under no circumstance would the trust identify a donor as having contributed more than $200. The blind trusts would then report to the candidates on a weekly or a biweekly basis the total amount that had been donated, but not detail any individual donations exceeding $200. Representatives of the blind trust could not be employed in positions influencing access or policy – and as a prophylactic should be required not to privately communicate with candidates or campaign workers.

Candidates could still ask individuals for support, but could not close the deal. This by itself might free politicians from the current fund-raising marathon of constantly seeking contributions. A candidate like Dole could still have fundraisers and limit invitations to rich, registered Republicans. But under our regime of mandated anonymity, the dinner could not be priced above cost. Instead, campaign workers could do no more than distribute postage-free envelopes addressed to the blind trust – so that attendees could later mail in a contribution.

The trust's books would be publicly audited only some number of years after the candidate left office. This *ex post* auditing would allow donors to be sure that their donations had in fact gone to their candidate and to allow the public to assess whether donations were – notwithstanding the trust – purchasing access or influence.

What's to stop a donor from telling a candidate on the sly about a large "soft money" contribution? Probably nothing. But talk is cheap. Anyone can claim to have voted for Clinton, but the voting booth makes it impossible to prove that you voted for him. Most generally, non-donors should be able to easily mimic any signals of real donors. For example, we recommend a 10-day cooling-off period in which contributors could cancel their contribution. A cooling-off period would give non-donors as well as donors the ability to acquire canceled checks from the trust. And allowing donors to privately cancel their donations would also reduce the "mailbox" problem of donors trying to mail their contribution in the presence of a campaign worker.

Of course, candidates would still know a lot. Ross Perot would know how much he gave to himself. Clinton would know how many New Hampshire cocktail parties a particular supporter threw on his behalf. Donating your time to fundraising might still get you an ambassadorship. But the effect would be muted, because – as with PAC bundling – the candidate wouldn't be able to see how much money a particular person raised.

Mandating anonymous donations would undoubtedly lead some donors to directly purchase television ads supporting a candidate. Our constitution does not permit limiting individuals' ability to speak directly. Direct speech, uncoordinated with candidate campaigns, would therefore allow rich individuals to continue to signal their willingness to spend money on behalf of particular candidates. But "direct speech" end runs would not completely undermine the effectiveness of mandated anonymity. Current law limits the ability of corporations and labor unions to engage in direct speech. Moreover, independent "direct speech" ads are not as valuable to candidates (and therefore wouldn't purchase as much influence) because candidates cannot control their content. And few individuals have sufficient resources to purchase effective broadcast campaigns.

Undoubtedly candidates would find ways to identify some donors. But when you make something more costly, you are likely to produce less of it. In the end, we predict that mandating donor anonymity would substantially reduce the number of six-figure donations. This drop itself would be evidence that many donors are not donating merely to help their candidate win, but are also hoping to purchase access and/or influence.

## Is It Politically Feasible?

Cynics will argue that any reform worth doing has no chance of passing. And more than likely the incumbent chairs of powerful congressional committees would want to oppose our proposal – because a large proportion of their "access" money would dry up. But opponents would have difficulty explaining why they need to know the identity of their donors. An expanding group of CEOs is pledging not to give soft money to either political party. These and other donors should support our proposal, because mandated anonymity removes the political pressure to give.

At a minimum, we should change the law to give individual candidates the option of using blind trusts to finance their campaigns. The first question candidates should be asked when they announce their candidacy is whether they will commit to donor anonymity. Unlike many of the other reforms that have been proposed, mandated anonymity is constitutional. Just as there is no constitutional right to be able to prove that you voted for Clinton, there is no constitutional right to be able to prove that you gave Clinton money. In either instance, you will be able to say that you did – you just won't be able to prove it.

A growing number of politicians are embracing full and immediate disclosure as the only effective means to discourage politicians from selling access or influence. But the opposite strategy of keeping the candidate as well as the public in the dark has a long pedigree. Maimonides long ago extolled the benefits of anonymous charity. We should remind ourselves why we choose to make voting a solitary act. The "donation booth" might not be a panacea, but it would keep faith with the simple and widely held belief that the amount of your political donation should not determine your access to government.

# TEN

# The Horatii and the Curiatii

LIVY

*Source*: *The Roman History by Titus Livius with the Entire Supplement of John Freinsheim*, Volume 1; London: James Bettenham, 1744. Excerpts from Book 1, Chapters 23, 24, and 25. (Punctuation modernized)

As both armies stood in *battalia*, the chiefs, with a few nobles, advanced into the middle between them. At this conference, the Alban dictator expressed himself thus:

"Methinks I have heard our king Cluilius alledge, as causes of the present war, injuries done us by the Romans and goods not restored according to treaties when they were demanded; neither do I doubt, O Tullus, but you will urge the same things; yet were we to speak truth instead of using specious arguments, the true motive which prompts two nearly allied and neighboring nations to take up arms is an ambition of sovereignty, whether justly or unjustly I say not; let the first aggressor answer for that."

"The Albans have chosen me general for carrying it on. I would only have you, Tullus, consider how closely we both, but you more particularly, are hemmed in by the powerful state of Hetruria. But as you are nearer to it, you must be more sensible of the common danger. Its strength by land is considerable, and very mighty by sea. Be assured, that as soon as you shall give the signal for battle, our two armies will be an agreeable fight to them, who will fall both on the conquerors and the conquered, wearied and spent with fighting against each other."

"Therefore, in the name of the Gods, seeing we are not contented with certain liberty but will run the risk of either sovereignty or slavery, let us agree on some expedient whereby it may be determined which shall reign over the other without great mischief to or shedding much blood of either nation."

Tullus, though naturally inclined to war and elated with the hope of victory, was not averse to the proposal. After deliberation on both sides, a method to decide the contest was agreed to, and fortune pointed out the proper persons.

24. It happened that there were in each of the two armies three brothers born at one birth, of equal age and strength. It is very certain that they were called Horatii and Curiatii; nor is there any action among the ancients either more celebrated or better known; yet however distinctly the other circumstances of this story are related, a doubt remains concerning their names: to which nation the Horatii and to which the Curiatii belonged. Authors are divided about it, yet I find the greater number agree that the Horatii were on the Roman side. My inclination leads me to follow them.

The kings dealt with the three brothers to decide the fate of their country in combat, assuring them that the sovereignty over both nations should be theirs whose side should get the victory. They readily consented, and the time and place were appointed. But before they engaged, a treaty between the Romans and the Albans was agreed to upon this condition: "That that nation whose champions should come off conquerors in the combat should peaceably reign over the other."

Different treaties are made on different terms, but they are all concluded in the same general method. This is the most ancient treaty recorded in history, which was ratified in the following form: a *Fecialis* asked king Tullus thus, "Do you command me, O king, to conclude a treaty with the *pater patratus* of the Alban people?" After the king gave him orders, he said, "I demand of thee, O king, vervain." To which the king replied, "Bring some that is pure." The *Fecialis* brought some pure grass from the altar, and again asked the king, "Do you, O king, appoint me the royal ambassador of the Romans? Do you assign me equipage and a retinue?" The king answered, "What can be done without detriment to my right or to that of the Roman people, I do." The Fecialis was M. Valerius, who appointed Sp. Fusius *pater patratus*, touching his head and hair with vervain.

The office of *pater patratus* is to administer the oath, that is, to ratify the treaty, which he repeats in a long form of words too tedious to be recited. After setting forth the conditions, he says, "O Jupiter, hear, O *pater patratus* of the Alban people, and ye Alban people hear. The Romans will not first break those articles which have been, from first to last read out of waxed tables without deceit and this day fully understood. If they by publick authority or fraud shall first violate them, do thou, O Jupiter, in that day so strike the Romans as I this instant strike this hog, and let thy stroke be proportionably heavier as thou art more mighty and powerful." Having done this, he struck the hog dead with a flint stone. The Albans took the oaths and ratified the treaty in form by their dictator and priests.

25. The treaty being concluded, the twin brothers, as had been agreed, took their arms. Each side encouraged their own champions by putting them in mind, "that the Gods of their country, their country and parents, all their fellow-citizens, both at home and in the army, under the greatest anxiety had their whole dependence on their weapons and hands." They, naturally bold and animated by these exhortations of their countrymen, advanced into the middle between the two armies, which stood before their several camps rather out of danger for the present than free from solicitude, for empire was at stake and depended on the bravery and fate of so few. Therefore, being distracted between hope and fear, their attention was at that instant entirely fixed upon the disagreeable scene.

The signal was given, and the champions, three of a side, animated with the courage of great armies, engaged with all the fury of mighty hosts. It was not their own particular danger, but public sovereignty or slavery, that presented themselves to each of their minds; and the thoughts that they were to decide the future fate of their country. But when at the first encounter the spectators heard the clashing of their arms and saw the glittering of their burnished swords, they were seized with great horror, and as neither side had greater ground of hope than the other, it was with difficulty they could either speak or breathe. But on their coming to grapple hand to hand, when not only the motions of their bodies and the brandishings of their dangerous weapons and arms but the very wounds and blood were seen, the three Albans were wounded and two of the Romans fell and expired the one above the other. At whose fall, while the Alban army shouted for joy, the Roman legions, though they had lost all hopes of victory, were yet under great concern for their surviving champion, whom the three Curiatii surrounded.

As good luck would have it, he was not wounded, and though not able to fight all the three at once, was yet an overmatch for them singly. Therefore, in order to separate them, he retreated, being convinced that they would pursue him at such distances as their bodies, differently galled with wounds, would permit them.

He had already run a good way from the place they had fought in when, looking back, he perceived them following him at a great distance from one another. Observing one not far from him, he turned short on him with great fury. And while the Alban army called out to the Curiatii to assist their brother, the victorious Horatius, having killed the first, was running to encounter the second. Then the Romans, with such shouts as are commonly made on success after despairing of victory, encouraged their champion, who made all possible haste to finish the combat. And before the third, who was not far off, could come up, he dispatched the second.

And now there remained but one champion on each side to decide the quarrel, but their strength and hopes were very unequal. A body free from wounds and a double victory encouraged Horatius boldly to encounter his antagonist, while he, dragging after him a body weakened with loss of blood, fatigued with running, and dispirited with the sight of his two brothers slain before his eyes, presented himself an easy prey to his victorious enemy.

It could not be called a fight. The Roman, in triumph, said, "I have sacrificed two persons to the *manes* of my brothers; the third I will sacrifice to the decision of this war, and that the people of Rome may obtain the sovereignty over the people of Alba." And as he tottered under the weight of his arms, Horatius struck him on the throat, and stript him as he lay dead.

The Romans, triumphing on account of the victory, received Horatius with hearty gratulations, and their joy was the greater because they had almost despaired of success. Then they set about burying their dead, but with very different hearts, for the one side was become sovereigns and the other subjects of a foreign state.

# ELEVEN

# TREES – A Decision-Maker's Lament

MICHAEL H. ROTHKOPF

Source: *Operations Research* 28(1) January–February, 1980, p. 3.

[W]ith apologies to Joyce Kilmer and to competent, conscientious decision analysts everywhere

**Michael H. Rothkopf**

I think that I shall never see
A decision complex as that tree—

A tree with roots in ancient days
(At least as old as Reverend Bayes);

A tree with trunk all gnarled and twisted
With axioms by Savage listed;

A tree with branches sprouting branches
And nodes declaring what the chance is;

A tree with flowers in its tresses
(Each flower made of blooming guesses);

A tree with utiles at its tips
(Values gleaned from puzzled lips);

A tree with stems so deeply nested
Intuition's completely bested;

A tree with branches in a tangle
Impenetrable from any angle;

A tree that tried to tell us "should"
Although its essence was but "would";

A tree that did decision hold back
'Til calculation had it rolled back.

Decisions are reached by fools like me,
But it took a consultant to make that tree.

TWELVE

# Knowing and Showing Economics and Law

JUDITH LACHMAN

*Source*: *Yale Law Journal* 93 (July), 1984, pp. 1598–1604. (A review of *An Introduction to Law and Economics*, A. Mitchell Polinsky (1983)).

## A Word From A Sponsor: Abstractions and Their Assumptions

Fortunately for us – and despite Professor Polinsky's humble caveats to the contrary* – his book comes equipped with everything. In particular, it comes equipped with an early chapter about the role of assumptions, and about the uses of abstraction in the process of economic inquiry. There Polinsky points out that "[e]conomists make assumptions for the obvious reason that the world, viewed economically, is too complicated to understand without some abstraction." He therefore suggests isolating one or two issues at a time "by making simplifying assumptions that eliminate the others," and later expanding the inquiry by adding various complications to the framework. In other words, the challenge of economic thinking is the proper use of abstraction; in determining how properly to use abstraction, one needs to take into account concerns about tractability, the realism of assumptions, the particular questions to be pursued, and the relationship of the assumptions to the goals of the inquiry. To use Polinsky's phrasing, "[t]he art of economics is picking assumptions that without inevitably causing those features to be unimportant ones."

Because the process of economic abstraction is, by assumption, unfamiliar to the book's readers, I approach it by analogy to a more familiar concept, specifically, to abstraction in the form of maps. A map is an abstraction of the world, and its use requires a theory by which one can link the abstraction with the world.[67] Before this linkage is established, however, one needs to know the questions the map should answer. Humbug. A map is a map is a map, you say? Then, by all means, help yourself to a soundscape map of Boston: "A composite view of the variety of city sounds [as] perceived along a sequence of

* [Lachman's footnotes 1-66, which are to page numbers of Polinsky, have been omitted.]

[67] See, e.g., A. Robinson, R. Sale & J. Morrison, *Elements of Cartography* 50–75 (4th ed. 1978) (theory and systems of transformation for map projections); id. at 149–80 (theories of cartographic generalization); Board, Maps as Models, in *Models in Geography* 671 (R. Chorley & P. Haggett, eds. 1967); Lam, Spatial Interpolation Methods: A Review, 10 *Am. Cartography* 129 (1983).

streets... [in which s]ymbols represent qualities of sounds..., for example, soft, intense, roaring, muffled, sharp, echoing, expansive."[68] Or if that's not quite what you had in mind, how about an Eskimo Coastline Relief Carving (yes, you read that correctly), convenient for carrying on and around your ship?[69] Or a color-coded map showing "The Percent of [the U.S] Population Unchurched...1971"?[70] And so on.

Somehow, these maps offer little help in getting from Madison to Chicago. Instead I want a road map, and a certain kind at that: I need to be given the details of the street plan for the cities at each end, but *not* such details for everywhere in between. I need to know about the roads, and seasonal temperature and precipitation indicators would be nice. What about cloud movements, wind direction and color-keyed info on vegetation? National and local parks, population centers, and Howard Johnson restaurants? The map darkens progressively with colors and symbols, and darkens still some more until ...until I notice that even as I gave free rein to my desire to know more, I consigned myself to a map from which I could only know less.

This is the paradox of abstraction to which Polinsky succinctly referred.[71] The skillful use of abstraction requires one to forego including some considerations that would indeed add information, so that the resulting abstraction will, in the end, tell us more. In other words, even as one chooses *which* details or assumptions to include, she necessarily chooses an overall level of complexity appropriate to the task.[72] This choice then constitutes a fund, a budget of complexity, from which any particular penny, once spent cannot be spent again.

Now, within this budget, as in any other, there are allocative choices to be made. If I spend most of the available complexity showing parks and schools, there will not be much left for depicting the alternative street routes that can take me to my destination. So among the details of which the world is so rich, one must discern those details most important for the purpose at hand,[73] and in the austerity that is the elegance of abstraction, select only the highest in priority from among these.[74] The best abstraction, or even the better one, cannot be determined without reference to the abstraction's purpose. In order to judge the better map from the worse, a critic must know these goals – must even, for purposes of judging, accept them – and carry on the criticism from there.

[68] M. Southworth & S. Southworth, *Maps* 190 (1982).

[69] L. Bagrow & R. Skelton, *Meister der Kartographie* (1973), reprinted in M. Southworth & S. Southworth, *supra* note 68, at 51. For examples of map abstractions of a different sort, see M. Kidron & R. Segal, *The State of the World Atlas*, map no. 29 (1981) (entitled "Bullets and Blackboards," map depicts ratios of soldiers to teachers, by county, in 1974); G. Bula, Gospel Temperance Railroad Map (1908), reprinted in *An Atlas of Fantasy* 33–35 (J. Post ed. 1973) (Railroad of Life can go past Mount Terror into State of Darkness or take more northerly route toward Celestial City).

[70] Glenmary Research Center, Percent of Population Unchurched, By Counties of the United States: 1971 (1974).

[71] See *supra* p. 1599; pp. 3–4.

[72] See, e.g., A. Robinson, R. Sale & J. Morrison, *supra* note 67, at 201–16 (theories of representation by point symbols in cartography); cf. M. Blaug, *The Methodology of Economics, or How Economists Explain* 254–55 (1980) (simplifying assumptions made in conjunction with development of growth theory result in this having "extremely limited practical implications").

[73] See Klevorick, *supra*, note 5, at 244–45 (more formal models can "give insights about more complicated settings in which the results of the more 'stripped down' models are relevant"); cf. Kelman, *Misunderstanding Social Life: A Critique of the Core Premises of "Law and Economics,"* 33 J. *Legal Educ.* 274, 274–75 (in its attempt to organize reaity, legal economics appears also relentless in its attempt to "filter the complexity of both social life and individual identity").

[74] This choice is not irreversible, but a rerun of the selection requires reconstructing the framework.

But then, to where? To the investigation of two sets of things: the choice about the allocation of complexity, and the technical integrity with which the abstracting process is carried out. The former I will turn to in a moment; the latter I discuss briefly here. Good mapmaking means certain things, and two mapmakers pursuing the same objectives with the same information can nevertheless produce maps of differing quality. Similarly, a single task in economic abstracting can be done better or more poorly as a function of the economist's efforts, imagination, and skill. The integrity of the abstraction is, I think, in part a matter of casting the problem in such a way that the research can bring to bear the intellectual metaphors of the field.

Differing senses of "like" are what distinguish one discipline from another, one form of answer from another.[75] To my amazement in the first few days of law school, I learned that water can be like cows. When is water like cows? Answer: When it's escaping from land.[76] A lawyer might be equally surprised to find that hay-bailing wire can be like San Francisco housing. When is this so? When both are in short supply due to price controls.[77] Within a discipline, the sense of like goes yet deeper: Does the demand for potatoes fall when prices rise, as demand does for many other products, or could its relationship to price be otherwise?[78] Do jobs for minority group members rise in a simple stairstep fashion as neighborhoods come to be more integrated?[79] Or do these jobs rise in number with some integration, taper off with more, and still after that decline?[80] Clearly, there are important judgments to be made about the way that those within a discipline go about constructing their abstractions, even once the goals of the inquiry have been set. Assuming, however, that the technical-integrity expectations have been met, satisfaction or dissatisfaction with an abstraction most likely links in some way to its original assumptions.

It is here that reasonable people must often agree to disagree. For the assumptions acceptable to one abstractor or another can on occasion be as varied as the persons from

---

[75] See Hansmann, *The Current State of the Law-and-Economics Scholarship*, 33 *J. Legal Educ.* 217, 221 n.12 (1983) (characterizing lawyerly thinking as entailing treating "like" things alike); Kornhauser; *A Guide to the Perplexed Claims of Efficiency in the Law*, 8 Hofstra L. Rev. 591, 637–38 (1980) (discussing sense of analogy in economics and in law); Priest, *Social Science Theory and Legal Education: The Law School as University*, 33 *J. Legal Educ.* 437, 439 (1983) (economics brings to the law different presuppositions and organizing thoughts). These systems of analogy and classification distinguish one system of thought from another. Cf. M. Foucault, *The Order of Things* XV (1966, trans. 1970) (quoting and discussing set of categories from a "'certain Chinese encyclopaedia' in which it is written that 'animals' are divided into: (a) belonging to the Emperor, (b) embalmed, (c) tame, (d) sucking pigs, (e) sirens, (f) fabulous, (g) stray dogs, (h) included in the present classification, (i) frenzied, (j) innumerable, (k) drawn with a very fine camelhair brush, (l) et cetera, (m) having just broken the water pitcher, (n) that from a long way off look like flies").

[76] See Rylands v. Fletcher, [1866] 1 *L.R.* Ex. 265, aff'd, [1868] 3 *L.R.-E.* & I. App. 330.

[77] See J. Hirshleifer, *Price Theory and Applications* 40–41, 321–29 (2d ed. 1980) (discussing market effects of imposing price controls, and example of San Francisco housing). See generally *Guidelines: Informal Controls and the Market Place* (G. Schultz & R. Aliber eds. 1966) (collection of essays on consequences of various forms of price controls); Cheung, *A Theory of Price Control*, 17 *J.L. & Econ.* 52 (1974) (price controls analyzed as limitations on contracting).

[78] See J. Henderson & R. Quandt, *supra* note 29, at 34 (although demand usually declines as price rises, the reverse relationship is possible; goods for which this occurs are called Giffin goods); Dwyer & Lindsay, *Robert Giffin and the Irish Potato*, 74 *Am. Econ. Rev.* 188, 191 (1984) (Giffin goods are more likely to be found in poor communities that import most of their food).

[79] See Kain, *Housing Segregation, Negro Employment, and Metropolitan Decentralization*, 82 *Q.J. Econ.* 175 (1968).

[80] See Offner & Saks, *A Note on John Kain's Housing Segregation, Negro Employment, and Metropolitan Decentralization*, 85 *Q.J. Econ.* 147 (1971).

whom they derive. Not always, of course: There are times when the findings of one episode of research become the assumptions of yet another, so that the wheel need not be continually reinvented. And at other times the assumptions based at first on intuition can quickly be verified by a test.

But there are also times (most of the time, in my experience) when at least one of the assumptions entailed in the abstraction relates to the expertise of another discipline,[81] or to the ordinary knowledge that human beings have,[82] or possibly to both. When this is the case, evaluation of the goodness of an abstraction becomes itself complex. For the choice about one assumption, intertwined as it is with other such choices made within the budget of complexity, may become of necessity a choice about the package of assumptions all together. Nevertheless, if one focuses first on these extra-disciplinary assumptions, progress in framing a judgment can yet be made.

Here we consider, by assumption, assumptions about which the discipline's "expert" offers no special expertise. The economist, for example, is no more expert than other lay persons when the necessary assumptions must include a specification of attitudes toward childbirth or a direction from which the sun is believed to rise.[83] When it comes to assumptions such as these, the economist constructing an abstraction relies upon the expertise of others, or upon ordinary experience. It is therefore possible that a similarly situated economist, with identical skills and technical expertise, would nevertheless obtain results at odds with those of the first, and not because of lack of technical integrity in the work: Assumptions intimately affect outcomes, of course, and for some sets of contrasting outcomes, assumptions will be the only source of difference.

What then should be the relationships between ordinary knowledge and professional expertise, and between the world of the abstraction and the world it seeks to reflect? How, then, should lawyers relate to the expertise economists bring to bear?

---

[81] See, e.g., Akerlof & Dickens, *supra* note 7 (economic analysis of workplace safety, with assumptions about cognitive dissonance made in light of previous psychology research); cf. Tushnet, *Legal Scholarship: Its Causes and Cure*, 90 *Yale L.J.* 1205, 1212 (1981) (problem of some economic analysis of law is the use of unsupported abstraction).

[82] See C. Lindblom & D. Cohen, *Usable Knowledge* 8, 12 (1979) (defining ordinary knowledge as "knowledge that does not owe its origin, testing, degree of verification, truth status, or currency to distinctive [professional social inquiry] techniques but rather to common sense, casual empiricism, or thoughtful speculation and analysis"); cf. Tushnet, *supra* note 81, at 1214 ("[I]n traditional policy analysis, common sense is used both to select a goal and to determine how to achieve it.").

Lindblom and Cohen point out:
The most basic knowledge we use in social problem solving is ordinary.
Everyone has ordinary knowledge – has it, uses it, offers it. It is not, however, a homogeneous commodity. Some ordinary knowledge, most people would say, is more reliable, more probably true, than other. People differ from each other in the kind and quality of ordinary knowledge they possess. C. Lindblom & D. Cohen, *supra*, at 15 (footnote omitted). The line between ordinary knowledge and scientific knowledge is not a hard and fast one, and indeed may depend upon the state of the knowledge. For example, the most important way in which ordinary knowledge grows is by turning into scientific knowledge. K. Popper, *The Logic of Scientific Discovery* 18–19 (1959). Cf. C. Lindblom & D. Cohen, *supra*, at 13 n.2 (some ordinary knowledge was once scientific knowledge).

[83] See C. Lindblom & D. Cohen, *supra* note 81 (professional social inquiry may have "no distinct advantages in stock or use of ordinary knowledge helpful to public policy and many other forms of social problem solving"); D. North & R. Miller, *The Economics of Public Issues* 8 (2nd ed. 1973) (economist is not qualified "to answer the pivotal question of whether life begins at conception, at 24 weeks, or at birth, [n]or ... whether or not abortion should be legally permitted or proscribed," but can analyze the economic aspects of the issues).

## A Word From Another Sponsor: Ordinary Knowledge and the Process of Abstraction

An economist thinks in terms of models and theories. But so does the rest of the world. To grab hold of the thought style of economics must mean, then, that one think not only in terms of models and theories, but also in terms of such models and theories as economists employ. This sense of "economicsiness" provides the commonality for binding these thought patterns one to another, while distinguishing them from the thought patterns of other kinds of inquiries and of ordinary experience. Yet, apart from this peculiar economic flavor, the economist's mode of abstraction is not all that different from the mapmaker's or from the thinking entailed in ordinary experience.

I said above that everyone thinks in terms of models and theories, a statement of dubious truthfulness. Unless, that is, one adopts a generously energetic definition of the verb "thinks" – which I now do. Every day we go about life on the basis of very powerful yet unarticulated theories, about the world and how we relate to it. We believe in replication, for example, in that we expect that if we do the same thing today as we did yesterday – eating breakfast, catching a bus – things will turn out the same as they did before. We believe that if we go to sleep in one location we will wake up the next day in the same spot, that flipping certain switches makes a room lighter rather than colder, that drinking water stifles thirst, and so on. None of these propositions need be true day after day. But they usually are, and indeed the regularity is so striking that we can forget the essential role of theory – here, a theory that the future will be like the past – in even the most simple of daily tasks.

Sometimes this overarching theory, that the future will be like the past, is incorrect. I expect the bridge to be where it has always been because it's always been there, and then one day it is located below its usual spot, having collapsed into the Mianus River. Or, having functioned on the theory that my memory replicates reality, I fail to find the bridge because I am myself in a different spot. And so it goes: We live by theories, by assumptions of regularity, despite the fact that they fail us. We do this because abstractions about the world are necessary to function in it; we must see things in patterns if we are to deal with much information at all. And these abstractions, although they fail us, are better than no abstractions at all. Like the infinite regress of attempting to define all words by using other words, we cannot comprehend everything all at once, without understanding some things first. And those first understandings, inarticulable except in terms of themselves, become the first two-by-fours in the framework within which we build our thoughts. Then, when our theories fail us, we can use that experience to revise the plan of the structure, so that in the future our theories will fail us less.

All of this is what we human beings, not just economists, do every day, and our learning from it constitutes "ordinary knowledge."[84] It is the wellspring from which we draw and to which we replenish knowledge as we go about the continual processes of explanation and prediction, re-explanation and, at times, simply wondering about the world in which

---

[84] C. Lindblom & D. Cohen, *supra* note 82, at 12; n.78; cf. B. Ackerman, *Private Property and the Constitution* 10–20 (1977) (distinguishing "ordinary observer" and "scientific policymaker" based on "the existence of a divergent understanding of the nature of legal language").

we live. This "ordinary knowledge," viewed as both a process of thinking and a reservoir of its results, figures importantly in the development of "scientific theories" such as those of economics.[85] The reservoir services the daily experiences that form the main estate of ordinary knowledge, and also serves as a perception of reality against which scientific theories may be tested.

---

[85] K. Popper, *supra* note 82, at 22 (scientific knowledge is result of growth of common sense knowledge, and "[i]ts very problems are enlargements of the problems of common-sense knowledge"); cf. id. at 47 (social scientists can draw on introspection as a source of knowledge about behavior, and because of this, have an inherent advantage over those studying natural phenomena).

THIRTEEN

# "All Those in Favor Say 'Aye'"

HENRY MARTIN

*Source*: © The New Yorker Collection 1987 Henry Martin from cartoon bank.com. All Rights Reserved. First published in the *New Yorker*, April 23, 1979.

"All Those in Favor Say 'Aye,'"
"Aye"  "Aye"  "Aye"  "Aye"

# Introduction

An entire class of games is called "Colonel Blotto games." The *Fortune* article that begins Part Three shows one way of illustrating the payoffs from mixed strategies. You might find it instructive to try to set up the game other ways instead. Also, can you think of how to adapt this game to conflict between firms?

Auditing is not the same as using a mixed strategy. Why not? What problems might arise from the method the OPEC members use to try to discover if any of them are cheating on their agreement to limit oil output? Can you think of any alternatives?

OPEC is a cartel made up of oil-producing countries, which is why it is exempt from the anti-trust laws of the US and other countries. Many countries, including the US, also exempt certain industries, especially sales of labor by labor unions. The article on ocean shipping cartels shows that even when cartels are legal, the price does not necessarily go to the monopoly price. Much depends on the particular industry.

I include Stigler's conference handbook for the reader's general education in how to do economic research. Though it dates from 1977, most of the questions in it are still just as standard. Game theory adds a few more:

1 Is your equilibrium subgame perfect?
2 Did you take into account deviations using mixed strategies?
3 Why didn't you use out-of-equilibrium belief refinement [insert questioner's favorite refinement here] to eliminate unreasonable equilibria?
4 Why did you use out-of-equilibrium belief refinement [insert speaker's refinement here], which eliminates reasonable equilibria?
5 What happens with incomplete information?
6 Your model is too simple.
7 Your model is too complicated.
8 Is there even one market in the history of the world that fits the assumptions of your model?

The "Very Guilty" cartoon is about the discomfort of having a discrete instead of a continuous strategy set. In common law countries such as England and the United States, the jury decides whether a criminal defendant is innocent or guilty, but the judge decides what the penalty will be, taking the jury's decision as given. Whether the jury is completely sure that the defendant is guilty and was able to decide in five minutes or whether the jury barely decided that he was guilty and took five days, the judge is supposed to impose the same penalty. Does this actually happen, though? What are the payoffs for the judge and jury? Will the judge really ignore the likelihood of guilt and concentrate on the heinousness of the crime, the past record of the criminal, and other such things that are supposed to determine the punishment? Will the jury really ignore the heinousness of the crime and concentrate on the likelihood of guilt? How else might a court be organized? Which way is best?

# FOURTEEN

# Colonel Blotto: A Problem of Military Strategy

JOHN MCDONALD AND JOHN W. TUKEY

*Source*: *Fortune*, June 1949, p. 102. © 1949 Time Inc. Reprinted by permission.

Colonel Blotto's problem is a classical dilemma in strategy. The solution is supplied by a direct application of the theory of two-person zero-sum games. A diagrammatic solution has been given here which enables the reader to get some idea of the type of computation faced with and the result obtained in a simple example of a game. This type of problem may be made considerably more complicated and has led to the development of many game applications to the examination of strategic military decisions, as well as work on weapons evaluation.

The "Colonel Blotto" game is a military deployment problem, found in Caliban's *Weekend Problems Book*. The version shown here illustrates in elementary, graphic form the basic idea of von Neumann's theory of games. With patience it is not too difficult for the layman to follow.

The problem is given to Colonel Blotto by his general as a test of competence. Blotto has four units of armed force with which to oppose an enemy of three units. Between the opposing forces is a mountain with four passes; in each pass is a fort. War is declared in the evening. The issue will be decided in the morning. Decisions are based on who outnumbers the other at each pass. One point is scored for each fort taken, and one point for each unit taken. In the original form of this game the opponent's units turn up where they do in the night as a matter of luck. Blotto thus deployed his forces against a known probability that his opponent's forces would be grouped as follows: one unit in each of three passes, two in one and one in another, or all three in one pass.

In Princeton during World War II, two mathematicians, Charles P. Winsor and John W. Tukey, working on practical military problems, spent odd moments bringing Colonel Blotto's problem closer to reality. They allowed the units of Blotto's opponent to communicate and employ counter-strategies. The illustration above, shown here by courtesy of Professor Tukey, indicates the solution. Here is the way it goes:

Blotto has available four forms of "pure" strategy (pure as distinguished from mixed): he may deploy his four units singly, one to a pass; or three and one; or two and two; or all four in one pass. To simplify the problem for the purposes of this illustration, a special rule is introduced forbidding Blotto to send all four units into one pass. This leaves him three possible pure strategies. His opponent likewise has three possible pure strategies.

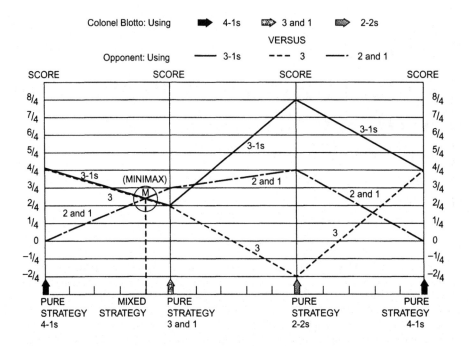

Beginning at the left-hand side of the graph, Blotto's pure strategy "4-1's" (one in each pass) is tried against his opponent's pure strategy "2 and 1." They would meet in the mountain passes like this: 1 1 1 1

2 1

In the first pass Blotto will lose one fort and one unit for a loss of two points; the second, one against one, is a standoff; in the third Blotto will gain a fort for one point and in the fourth another fort for a second point. The result will be the same no matter which passes his opponent enters with this strategy (if there were a difference as there is when other deployments are used, all scoring positions would simply be averaged to get the score for that strategy). In this instance the score is two for Blotto and two for his opponent: or zero. No gain for either. This is indicated on the graph where pure-strategy "4-1's" meets pure-strategy "2 and 1."

The same simple arithmetic will show that when Blotto deploys his forces in the same way (singly) against his opponent's deployment of three ones (singly) or three together, the average result will be one point for Blotto (shown as four-fourths, since Blotto's vertical line is measured for convenience in fourths).

The second vertical line represents Blotto's pure strategy "3 and 1." Arithmetic will show that Blotto gains an average of one-half a point (two-fourths) in contact with his opponent's deployments of "3-1's" and "3"; and he will gain an average of three-fourths of a point in contact with his opponent's "2 and 1."

The third vertical line continues Blotto's score with pure-strategy two two's against his opponent's three deployments. The fourth vertical line is a repetition of the first. Of the three pure strategies available to Blotto, then, he will do best with "3 and 1," with a possible high score of three-fourths or a low of two-fourths or one-half. But can he do better?

The alternative, on von Neumann's principle, is to give up pure strategy for a mixed strategy. (The "mixture" could be made by rolling a five-sided die with one side marked "3 and 1" and the others marked "4-1's.") When lines are drawn between the average scoring points for each contact of strategies, all three lines intersect at the point "M." If then he mixes strategies to achieve this point, Blotto can win an average of more than two-fourths, no matter what strategy his opponent chooses. This is fact is also the best that he can do, assuming his opponent uses his best strategy. This is "minimax" — Blotto's highest minimum and lowest maximum.

An example of a similar problem in economics is the distribution (deployment) of spare parts. Thus, as Professor Tukey observes, "games of strategy . . . may have considerable practical value in diverse fields."

FIFTEEN

# Dutch Accountants Take on a Formidable Task: Ferreting out "Cheaters" in the Ranks of OPEC

PAUL HEMP

*Source*: *Wall Street Journal*, February 26, 1985.

Brussels, Belgium – A big Dutch accounting firm has taken on what may be "Mission Impossible" in the auditing field. KMG Klynveld Kraayenhoff Co. has been hired by the Organization of Petroleum Exporting Countries to monitor OPEC member states' oil prices and production figures. KMG got the job because the 13 OPEC members don't trust one another. They suspect that member nations have been cheating on OPEC policies designed to keep prices high. The suspicion, of course, is justified; falling petroleum spot-market prices reflect the defections from official price levels. However, KMG, a member of the world-wide accounting group Klyveld Main Goerdeler, faces a major obstacle: Its job is to ferret out cheating, but it has to rely on OPEC states, including the cheaters, for information on prices, production and so on.

For OPEC, hiring an auditor is seen as an important move. The cartel is trying desperately to hold firm on price levels and maintain unity while pressures against it mount. Some suspect that the cartel's future could be affected by the audit's success. "If this doesn't work, there will be no OPEC," a member of the Iraqi delegation gloomily speculates. Others don't see it that seriously, but the difficulty of keeping OPEC members honest mirrors the strains in the group.

For KMG, the contract potentially is worth more than $1 million. But some find the audit firm's position so difficult as to be downright comical. "KMG has a virtually impossible task, one that lots of firms of auditors wouldn't relish; it will depend wholly on the good will of the member states," says John Thompson, an oil analyst at Fielding, Newsom-Smith Co., London stockbrokers. Mr. Thompson drops his voice: "It's a joke." KMG Chairman J. A. Steenmeijer concedes that his firm has its work cut out for it, but he rejects the comedy scenarios. "We wouldn't have taken the job if we didn't think we could be helpful," he says. He could get an assist; falling oil prices alone might help bring panicky OPEC members into line on production quotas and other matters (on the other hand, that might increase the cartel's disarray).

OPEC has been through a similar exercise before. In 1983, OPEC's market monitoring committee hired the U.S. consulting firm Arthur D. Little to track members' output and prices. Sheik Ahmed Zaki Yamani, the Saudi oil minister, who had been feuding with the committee's chairman, United Arab Emirates Oil Minister Manei Saeed al-Otaiba, upbraided Little for allegedly failing to provide accurate information – even though the firm hadn't been given access to key OPEC statistics. The Arthur Little contract was terminated last December. Sheik Yamani then arranged for the hiring of KMG.

KMG ideally needs to keep an exact, daily, barrel-by-barrel tally of more than a third of the noncommunist world's oil; make sure that none of those barrels is sold below a floor price that is being broken daily; report to an organization whose members bitterly accuse one another of cheating; and do all of those tasks in remote corners of the globe where secretive oil producers may be hostile to the firm's endeavors. A small group of KMG experts is working overtime designing the auditing project. Partners soon will be making get-acquainted visits to wary officials in the OPEC nations. KMG will report to OPEC's ministerial executive council, headed by Sheik Yamani. Mr. Steenmeijer concedes, "If there's no cooperation, it will be very difficult." But, he says, if any nation fails to cooperate, "We'll bring it up with the ministry council." Even with full OPEC cooperation, the logistical problems could be staggering. OPEC oil is shipped from more than 50 ports. And stationing dockside observers at each port mightn't be effective; industry analysts note that crude oil could be diverted before reaching shipping terminals, or be trucked over land to other destinations.

However, industry and OPEC sources say KMG won't attempt to construct an independent profile of the group's production and price figures. Instead, the sources say, the firm will agree, or disagree, with OPEC members' estimates of their own operations. That tactic has two virtues. It allows the audit firm to start the undertaking quickly, without waiting for permission to station its inspectors in each OPEC nation, a process that could take months. Also, it could give Sheik Yamani greater leeway in disciplining wayward member nations by waving at them KMG's "disapproval" of their figures.

Industry sources point to a growing problem: The prices and volume figures on refined crude products increasingly being exported by OPEC members such as Saudi Arabia, Algeria and Libya aren't included yet in the monitoring system. An oil specialist at the Middle East office of one major international accounting firm says, "The farther upstream you move, the more accurate your estimate will be." But a voyage upstream may lead to an oil field that also is a battlefield in the Iran–Iraq war. "I don't think many neutral experts would like to go to those fields," the specialist comments.

However, Mr. Steenmeijer says, "Our biggest challenge is to get the right information about prices." One way to do that is to focus on the most likely violators. "An auditor of a company doesn't look at every single invoice," notes Carol Ferguson, an oil analyst at Wood, Mackenzie Co. in Edinburgh, Scotland. "You identify where the problems are – in this case, the countries most likely to cheat – and concentrate on those."

KMG has almost 2,000 employees and nearly 50 offices world-wide. Some observers think its nationality played a part in its selection. "Politically the Netherlands doesn't take stands too clearly" on controversial petroleum issues, a KMG official notes. But the firm also has a lot of experience in the industry; the Royal Dutch/Shell Group is among its clients.

SIXTEEN

# Shipping Price-Fixing Pacts Hurt Consumers, Critics Say

ANNA WILDE MATHEWS

*Source*: *Wall Street Journal*, October 7, 1997.

Rutherford, N.J. – Every two weeks, in an unobtrusive office building here, about 20 shipping-line managers gather for their usual meeting. They sit around a long conference table, exchange small talk over bagels and coffee and then begin discussing what they will charge to move cargo across the Atlantic Ocean.

All very routine, except for one detail: They don't work for the same company. Each represents a different shipping line, supposedly competing for business. Under US antitrust law, most people doing this would end up in court.

But shipping isn't like other businesses. Many of the world's big shipping lines, from Sea-Land Service Inc. of the US to A.P. Moller/Maersk Line of Denmark, are members of a little-noticed cartel that for many decades has set rates on tens of billions of dollars of cargo.

## Impact Enormous

Most US consumer goods exported or imported by sea are affected to some degree. The cartel – really a series of cartels, one for each major shipping route – can tell importers and exporters when shipping contracts start and when they end. They can favor one port over another, enough to swing badly needed trade away from an entire city. And because the shipping industry has an antitrust exemption from Congress, all of this is legal.

"This is one of the last legalized price-setting arrangements in existence," says Robert Litan, a former Justice Department antitrust official. Airlines and banks couldn't do this, he says, "but if you're an ocean shipping line, there's nothing to stop you from price fixing."

You could call them the OPEC of shipping, though not quite as powerful because they can't keep members from building too many ships. To get more business, some of the shipping cartels' own members undercut cartel rates or make special deals with big customers. They also face the emergence of new competitors, which are keeping rates down in some markets.

Nonetheless, the industry is playing a bigger role now in the US economy as American companies plunge more deeply into world trade. Exports over the seas have jumped 26 percent in the past two years and 50 percent since the start of the decade.

For consumers, the impact is hard to measure. Transportation costs make up 5 percent to 10 percent of the price of most goods, and increases in shipping rates are usually passed on to consumers. A limited 1993 survey by the Agriculture Department, examining $5 billion of US farm exports, concluded that the cartels were raising ocean shipping rates as much as 18 percent. A different report, by the Federal Trade Commission in 1995, found that when shipping lines broke free of cartel rates, contract prices were about 19 percent lower.

## Viewed as Base Prices

"The cartels' whole makeup is anticonsumer," says John Taylor, a transportation professor at Wayne State University in Detroit. "They're designed to keep prices up."

Some moves are afoot to change all this. The US Senate is considering a bill that, for the first time in a decade, would weaken the cartels, by reducing their power to police their members. The bill, sponsored by Sen. Kay Bailey Hutchinson of Texas, has the support of some other high-ranking Republicans, including Majority Leader Trent Lott. Even some major cartel members, including Sea-Land and Maersk, support it, under pressure from customers seeking world-wide contracts.

But even supporters think that only a watered-down bill could pass the Senate; a similar measure passed the House last year and went nowhere. Moreover, the US has only limited jurisdiction over cartel members; most of them are based in Europe, like Maersk, or in Asia, like Orient Overseas (International) Ltd., which is controlled by the family of Hong Kong's top official, Tung Chee Hwa. Even if the US banned cartel-like behavior, foreign shipping lines probably could still meet abroad to set rates. The biggest US player, Sea-Land, is a unit of CSX Corp., which is far better known as a railroading giant.

## Cartels Unapologetic

The companies' executives are unapologetic about the cartels, which they say help limit the pressure toward both mergers and bankruptcies. They contend that a wave of acquisitions would leave even less competition, with just a few world-wide companies dominating ocean trade. Some note America's uneven experience with deregulation in other transportation industries, such as airlines and railroads, where quick consolidation reduced prices but hurt on-time performance and other aspects of service in many markets.

In many ways, some shipping executives say, cartels are pro-consumer. "Unfettered competition is not in the public interest," says Conrad Everhard, chairman of Cho Yang (America) Inc., a Rutherford, N.J., subsidiary of a South Korean cartel member. "You would get a chaotic rate war."

But many US companies say they would welcome a little unfettered competition. Blue Diamond Growers, one of the nation's biggest agricultural exporters, says that in the early 1990s its shipping rates to Europe jumped almost 50 percent in 18 months – when a cartel decided prices were too low. The cooperative recently was able to switch to noncartel lines, but for years, the only carrier near the co-op's Sacramento, Calif., base was too busy carrying lumber. A Blue Diamond attempt to send thousands of boxes of almonds overland, by railroad to the port of Montreal, ended disastrously when the train ran late and the nuts missed the boat. Transportation Manager Jilian Morley says negotiation is out of the question; the cartel officials sometimes don't even return her phone calls. In a letter, the cartel, now called the Trans-Atlantic Conference Agreement, told the co-op to "let nature take its course" and pay the rates. Cartel officials didn't return repeated phone calls about the letter and other matters.

In Scarborough, Maine, David Hefler says cartel rates have discouraged free trade, at least in eggs, the main product he exports. When the cartel that dominates US routes to the Mideast raises prices, he can't afford to ship there for months at a time. "An egg is an egg is an egg," he says. "A difference of three cents a dozen can put us out of the ballgame."

## The Service Issue

For many companies, especially large ones, bad service can be an even more of an issue. Although Polaroid Corp. is only 20 miles from the port of Boston, the company trucks its film and chemical exports more than 300 miles to Montreal, where a noncartel line's rates are 20 percent lower and service is more consistent, says Rodney Schonland, manager of trade and regulations. In addition, Polaroid would have to pay an extra tax in the US.

Even General Motors Corp. has to take orders from the big Atlantic cartel, which tells it to sign its annual shipping contract every December, eight months before the auto-model cycle begins. Cartel lines "dictate to us," says Cynthia Bridgeman, GM's director of international transportation.

Cartel members say they aren't nearly as powerful as critics contend. Many lines suffer from a glut of ships and are engaged in a commercial war of sorts. Some members say that if they didn't break cartel agreements and cut rates for big customers, they would lose too much business to noncartel lines. Hanjin Shipping Co., a major South Korean line with a small trans-Atlantic operation, has gone even further, withdrawing from a 16-line Atlantic cartel so it could set its own rates.

Moreover, the cartels are facing a rising breed of aggressive lines that are cherry-picking shippers with lower rates. Sometimes, the customers can play the new competitors off against conference lines, cartel officials say. Because of such tactics, shipping rates on the Pacific have slipped in recent years; from 1992 to 1997, for example, they fell 7 percent to the US from Asia.

There aren't "fearsome cartels wringing monopoly rates out of anyone," says Christopher Koch, Sea-Land's senior vice president and general counsel. "Conferences have shown they're ineffective."

## The Subsidy Problem

And cartel members have another argument: Many ship lines, even in the US, get various -subsidies. That can make for irrational, politically influenced pricing. "The general public is better off today with the system we have than with any other system," says Olav Rakkenes, chairman of the main Atlantic cartel. "You have to have some reliability and stability."

The cartels try to present an innocuous front. They never use the word "cartel," for instance. The Trans-Atlantic Conference Agreement not only avoids calling itself a cartel, but it has its small office suite in the same building in Rutherford as the local chamber of commerce. Harold Holden, the shipping group's genial top administrator, goes by the nickname "Lucky" and says he worked his first sea passage by chipping rust off a freighter.

Now, he oversees an organization that sets rates on about 70 percent of the cargo shipped between the US and Northern Europe – about $60 billion of products each year, from apples to suits to beer. Members enforce strict secrecy about their meetings, barring reporters and nonmember companies. But the meetings are hardly dramatic; the participants, usually midlevel managers, confer on the tiniest of minutiae. One 65-item agenda included prices for moving bad shrimp from the US to Europe. " 'Somewhat tedious' is how I would describe it," one participant says.

But the results can be anything but tedious for US ports. As the main conduit for international trade, the nation's ports are a major source of jobs and business revenues in big coastal cities. Port authorities are in the uneasy position of dealing with cartels that, in a single stroke, could abruptly change a port's future.

That's about what happened in Philadelphia in 1991. Members of an Atlantic cartel decided to cut off service to the city, ignoring a port that had handled $8 billion a year in cargo, in favor of larger ports, such as New York. Frantic officials in Philadelphia set out to win smaller, noncartel lines. That softened the blow, but even now many companies in the area have to put their freight through New York. To Mafco Worldwide Corp., Philadelphia "is a dead port," says Lynn Talotta, traffic manager for the licorice-flavoring maker. She can see Philadelphia's piers from her office but loads her European shipments on trucks to New York.

## "Victory" in New Orleans

In New Orleans, port officials went on the offensive in 1995 against the cartel that dominated trade lanes from Latin America. In a complaint filed with the Federal Maritime Commission, the port argued, in effect, that the cartel was pricing New Orleans out of the market by favoring Florida ports with lower rates. The port cited frozen broccoli, which cost 83 percent more to ship from Guatemala to New Orleans than to Florida, and unfinished clothing, which cost 132 percent more to ship to Honduras from New Orleans than from Florida. Cartel members contended that the price discrepancies didn't apply to all products and that their rates were fair. But they didn't wait to find out whether the government agreed; they dissolved the New Orleans arrangement, and companies there declared it an enormous victory.

But if it was – some Louisiana shippers now believe they lost some business forever – it was rare. For eight decades, shipping cartels have been protected by Congress under the Shipping Act of 1916, passed at the behest of American shipping customers, who thought cartels would guarantee reliable service. The law was revised significantly only twice, in 1961 and 1984, but both times the industry's antitrust immunity was left intact.

The most recent major review was done in 1991 by a congressional commission. It heard more than 100 witnesses, produced a 250-page report – and offered no conclusions or recommendations. One commission member who represented shipping customers complained, in his official comments, of the cartels' "almost unlimited monopolistic power." Another participant disagreed, praising shipping lines' "agreements that promote efficiency of operation." In an executive summary, the commissioners said they hoped the report would serve as a "valuable policy tool."

# SEVENTEEN

# The Conference Handbook

GEORGE STIGLER

*Source*: *Journal of Political Economy* 85(2), 1977, pp. 441–3. Reprinted by permission of the University of Chicago Press.

There is an ancient joke about the two traveling salesmen in the age of the train. The younger drummer was being initiated into the social life of the traveler by the older. They proceeded to the smoking parlor on the train, where a group of drummers were congregated. One said, "87," and a wave of laughter went through the group. The older drummer explained to the younger that they traveled together so often that they had numbered their jokes. The younger drummer wished to participate in the event and diffidently ventured to say, "36." He was greeted by cool silence. The older drummer took him aside and explained that they had already heard that joke. (In another version, the younger drummer was told that he had told the joke badly.)

This parable has often recurred to me as I attend conferences of economists. Economists travel together a great deal, and there is no reason why the discussions which follow the presentation of papers should not utilize a handbook of commentary. The following is a preliminary list of numbered comments, which itself will cover a large share of the comments elicited in most conferences. If the proposal meets approval, the list can be extended, and a second list of the standard replies to these comments can be provided.

## Introductory Remarks

A   The paper is a splendid review of the literature, but unfortunately it does not break new ground.

B   The paper admirably solves the problem which it sets for itself; unfortunately, this was the wrong problem.

C   What a pity that the vast erudition and industry of the author were misdirected.

D   I am an amateur in this field so my remarks must be diffident and tentative. However, even a novice must find much to quarrel with in this piece.

E   I can be very sympathetic with the author; until 2 years ago I was thinking along similar lines.

F   It is good to have a nonspecialist looking at our problem. There is always a chance of a fresh viewpoint, although usually, as in this case, the advantages of the division of labor are reaffirmed.

G   This paper contains much that is new and much that is good.

H   Although the paper was promised 3 weeks ago, I received it as I entered this room.

## Comments

1   Adam Smith said that.

2   Unfortunately, there is an identification problem which is not dealt with adequately in the paper.

3   The residuals are clearly nonnormal and the specification of the model is incorrect.

4   Theorizing is not fruitful at this stage: we need a series of case studies.

5   Case studies are a clue, but no real progress can be made until a model of the process is constructed.

6   The second-best consideration would of course vitiate the argument.

7   That is an index number problem (obs., except in Cambridge).

8   Have you tried two-stage least squares?

9   The conclusions change if you introduce uncertainty.

10   You didn't use probit analysis?

11   I proved the main results in a paper published years ago.

12   The analysis is marred by a failure to distinguish transitory and permanent components.

13   The market cannot, of course, deal satisfactorily with that externality.

14   But what if transaction costs are not zero?

15   That follows from the Coase theorem.

16   Of course, if you allow for the investment in human capital, the entire picture changes.

17   Of course the demand function is quite inelastic.

18   Of course the supply function is highly inelastic.

19   The author uses a sledgehammer to crack a peanut.

20   What empirical finding would contradict your theory?

21   The central argument is not only a tautology, it is false.

22   What happens when you extend the analysis to the later (or earlier) period?

23   The motivation of the agents in this theory is so narrowly egotistic that it cannot possibly explain the behavior of real people.

24   The flabby economic actor in this impressionistic model should be replaced by the utility-maximizing individual.

25   Did you have any trouble in inverting the singular matrix?

26   It was unfortunate that the wrong choice was made between $M_1$ and $M_2$.

27   That is alright in theory, but it doesn't work out in practice (use sparingly).

28   The speaker apparently believes that there is still one free lunch.

29   The problem cannot be dealt with by partial equilibrium methods: it requires a general equilibrium formulation.

30   The paper is rigidly confined by the paradigm of neoclassical economics, so large parts of urgent reality are outside its comprehension.

31   The conclusion rests on the assumption of fixed tastes, but of course tastes have surely changed.

32   The trouble with the present situation is that the property rights have not been fully assigned.

# EIGHTEEN

# "Very Guilty"

JIM UNGER

*Source*: © 1988 United Media, courtesy of Knight Features, London.

# PART FOUR
# Dynamic Games with Symmetric Information

# Introduction

Existence of equilibrium is not a big concern in game theory once mixed strategies are admitted, since an equilibrium exists except in pathological cases. Economists, however, frequently need to try to prove such things as existence of an equilibrium in pure strategies, non-existence of asymmetric equilibria, or uniqueness of the equilibrium. Zermelo's paper proves an existence theorem about the best strategy for the game of chess. Schwalbe and Walker provide us with the first English translation of Zermelo's German article. Since most game theorists could not read the original article, there has been much confusion over what Zermelo proved. Did he prove that there is a winning strategy for White? That either White can win, or Black can win, or both can force a draw? That the winning strategy, if it exists, involves less than a certain number of moves? That in a finite game of perfect information, backwards induction shows that each player has a best strategy? Try to figure out what Zermelo's theorem actually says, and then see Ulrich Schwalbe and Paul Walker, "Zermelo and the Early History of Game Theory," forthcoming, *Games and Economic Behavior*. Sometimes it is easier to re-prove something than to figure out someone else's proof. Think how you would go about proving whichever of these things Zermelo did not prove.

The game of chess continues to be popular despite Zermelo's Theorem because knowing that an optimal strategy exists or even knowing of its features does not tell you what it is. Hilbert's Hair Theorem illustrates this too. David Hilbert would say to his mathematics class in Gottingen, "Among the people now in this lecture hall, there is one who has the least number of hairs on his head." (He always got a laugh, because characterization was not actually so difficult in that special case, Hilbert himself being bald.) Howard Eves, *Mathematical Circles Squared*, p. 128, Boston: Prindle, Weber Schmidt (1972).

Thomas Schelling's 1960 book ought to be read by every person as a requirement for obtaining a bachelor's degree from college. Although nontechnical, it conveys a large number of strategic ideas through clear writing and striking examples. It took twenty years before the profession caught up with the book's two big themes of precommitment and information transfer. This excerpt is just an appetizer. See also his *Arms and Influence*,

New Haven: Yale University Press (1966), and *Micromotives and Macrobehavior*, New York: W. W. Norton (1978).

Martin Shubik's note on duelling is one of those papers better known than read, since it appeared in a book long out of print. Think how it could be applied to primary elections, political intrigue, and international diplomacy.

The *Mahabharata* is, with the *Ramayana*, one of the two great classic epics of India. You must imagine me as Drona and yourself as Arjuna, and think about the difficulty of bringing a situation down to its essentials when you choose the players, actions, payoffs, and information in a game. Think also of the mathematician Euler, who said, after going blind in one eye after extraordinary effort put into a particular proof, "Now I will have less distraction." Howard Eves, *In Mathematical Circles*, p. 48 of Volume II, Boston: Prindle, Weber and Schmidt (1969). The cartoon for this chapter, however, "That's it? That's peer review?" will remind us to be humble. Sometimes the arrow misses anyway.

## NINETEEN

# On An Application of Set Theory to the Theory of the Game of Chess

Ernst Zermelo

*Source*: *Proceedings, Fifth International Congress of Mathematicians* 2, 1913, pp. 501–4. Translated by Ulrich Schwalbe and Paul Walker "Zermelo and the Early History of Game Theory," forthcoming, *Games and Economic Behavior*.

The following considerations are independent of the special rules of the game of chess and are valid in principle just as well for all similar games of reason, in which two opponents play against each other; for the sake of determinateness they shall be exemplified by chess as the best known of all games of this kind. Also they do not deal with any method of practical play, but only with the answer to the question: can the value of an arbitrary position, which could possibly occur during the play of a game as well as the best possible move for one of the playing parties be determined or at least defined in a mathematically-objective manner, without having to make reference to more subjective-psychological notions such as the "perfect player" and similar ideas? That this is possible at least in singular special cases is shown by the so called "chess problems", i.e. examples of positions in which it can be proved that the player whose turn it is to move can enforce checkmate in a prescribed number of moves. However, it seems to me worth considering whether such an evaluation of a position is at least theoretically conceivable and does make any sense at all in other cases as well, where the exact execution of the analysis finds a practically insurmountable obstacle in the enormous complication of possible continuations, and only this validation would give the secure basis for the practical theory of the "endgames" and the "openings" as we find them in textbooks on chess. The method used in the following for the solution of the problem is taken from the "theory of sets" and the "logical calculus" and shows the fertility of these mathematical disciplines in a case, where almost exclusively *finite* totalities are concerned.

Since the number of squares and of the moving pieces is finite, so also is the set $P$ of possible positions $p_0, p_1, p_2, \ldots, p_t$, where positions always have to be considered as different, depending on whether white or black has to move, whether one of the parties already has castled, a given pawn has been "promoted" etc.

Now let $q$ be one of these positions, then starting from $q$, "endgames" $\mathbf{q} = (q, q_1, q_2, \ldots)$ are possible, that is sequences of positions, which begin with $q$ and follow each other in accordance with the rules of the game, so that each position $q_\lambda$ emerges from the previous one $q_{\lambda-1}$ by an admissible move of either white or black in an alternating way. Such a possible endgame $\mathbf{q}$ can find its natural end either in a "check-mate" or in a "stalemate" position but could also – at least theoretically – go on forever in which case the game would without doubt has to be called a draw or "remis". The totality $Q$ of all these "endgames" $\mathbf{q}$ associated with $q$ is always a well defined, finite or infinite subset of the set $P^a$, which comprises all possible countable sequences formed by elements $p$ of $P$.[1]

Among these $\mathbf{q}$ endgames some can lead to a win for white in $r$ or less "moves" (i.e. simple changes of position $p_{\lambda-1} \to p_\lambda$, but not double moves) however this also depends in general on the play of the opponent. What properties does a position $q$ have to have so that white, independently of how black plays, can *enforce* a win in at most $r$ moves? I claim, the necessary and sufficient condition for that is the existence of a non-vanishing subset $U_r(q)$ of the set $Q$ with the following properties:

1 All elements $\mathbf{q}$ of $U_r(q)$ end in at most $r$ moves with a win for white, such that no sequence contains more than $r + 1$ elements and $U_r(q)$ is definitely finite.

2 If $\mathbf{q} = (q, q_1, q_2, \ldots)$ is an arbitrary element of $U_r(q)$, $q_\lambda$ an arbitrary element of this sequence which corresponds to a move carried out by black, i.e. always one of even or odd order, depending on whether at $q$ it is white's or black's turn to move, and finally $q'_\lambda$ a possible variant, such that black could have moved from $q_{\lambda-1}$ to $q'_\lambda$ as well as to $q_\lambda$, then $U_r(q)$ contains in addition at least an element of the form $\mathbf{q}'_\lambda = (q, q_1, \ldots, q_{\lambda-1}, q'_\lambda, \ldots)$, which shares with $\mathbf{q}$ the first $\lambda$ elements. Indeed in this and only in this case white can start with an arbitrary element $q$ of $U_r(q)$ and in every case, where black plays $q'_\lambda$ instead of $q_\lambda$ white can carry on playing with a corresponding $\mathbf{q}'_\lambda$, i.e. win under all contingencies in at most $r$ moves.

Of course there can be several such subsets $U_r(q)$, but the sum of any two always has the same properties and also the union $\bar{U}_r(q)$ of all such $U_r(q)$, which is uniquely determined by $q$ and $r$ and definitely has to be different from $0$,[2] i.e. has to contain at least one element if such $U_r(q)$ exist at all.

Thus, $\bar{U}_r(q) \neq 0$ is the necessary and sufficient condition such that white can enforce a win in at most $r$ moves. If $r < r'$ then $\bar{U}_r(q)$ is always a subset of $\bar{U}_{r'}(q)$ since every set $U_r(q)$ definitely satisfies the conditions imposed on $U_{r'}(q)$, i.e. has to be contained in $\bar{U}_{r'}(q)$, and to the smallest $r = \rho$, for which $\bar{U}_r(q) \neq 0$ corresponds the common compon-ent $U^*(q) = \bar{U}_\rho(q)$ of all such $\bar{U}_r(q)$; this contains all continuations such that white must win in the shortest time. Now all these minimum values $\rho = \rho_q$ have on their part a maximum $\tau \leq t$ which is independent of $q$, where $t + 1$ denotes the number of possible positions, thus $U(q) = \bar{U}_\tau(q) \neq 0$ is the necessary and sufficient condition that in position $q$ some $\bar{U}_r(q)$ does not vanish and white is "in a winning position" at all. Namely if in a position $q$ the win can be enforced at all, then it can be enforced in at most $t$ moves as we want to show. Indeed every endgame $\mathbf{q} = (q, q_1, q_2, \ldots, q_n)$ with $n > t$ would have to

---

[1]  In modern terminology, $P^a$ would be called the game tree and $Q$ a subgame.
[2]  To denote an empty set, Zermelo uses the symbol 0 instead of $\emptyset$.

contain at least one position $q_\alpha = q_\beta$ a second time and white could have played at the first appearance of it in the same way as at the second and thus could have won earlier than by move $n$, i.e. $\rho \leq t$.

If on the other hand $U(q) = 0$, so that white can only achieve a draw, if the opponent plays correctly, but white can also be "in a losing position" and will try in this case to postpone a checkmate as long as possible. If he should hold out until the $s$th move there must exist a subset $V_s(q)$ with the following properties:

1    There is no endgame contained in $V_s(q)$ where white loses before the $s$th move.
2    If $\mathbf{q}$ is an arbitrary element of $V_s(q)$ and if in $\mathbf{q}$ the element $q_\lambda$ can be replaced with $q'_\lambda$ by black using an allowed move, then $V_s(q)$ contains at least one element of the form

$$\mathbf{q}'_\lambda = (q, q_1, \ldots, q_{\lambda-1}, q'_\lambda, \ldots)$$

that coincides with $\mathbf{q}$ up to the $\lambda$th member and then continues with $q'_\lambda$.

Also these sets $V_s(q)$ are all subsets of their union $\bar{V}_s(q)$ which is uniquely determined by $q$ and $s$ and which has the same property as $V_s(q)$ itself, and for $s > s'$ now $\bar{V}_s(q)$ becomes a subset of $\bar{V}_{s'}(q)$. The numbers $s$ for which $\bar{V}_s(q)$ differs from 0 are either infinite or $\leq \sigma \leq \tau \leq t$, since the opponent, if he can win at all, must be able to enforce a win in at most $\tau$ moves.[3] Thus if and only if $V(q) = \bar{V}_{\tau+1}(q) \neq 0$ white can obtain a draw and in the other case, by virtue of $V^*(q) = \bar{V}_\sigma(q)$ he can postpone the loss for at least $\sigma \leq \tau$ moves. Since every $U_r(q)$ certainly satisfies the conditions imposed on $V_s(q)$, each $\bar{U}_r(q)$ is a subset of each set $\bar{V}_s(q)$, and $U(q)$ is a subset of $V(q)$. The result of our examination is thus the following:

To each of the positions $q$ that are possible during play, there correspond two well-defined subsets $U(q)$ and $V(q)$ of the totality of the endgames beginning with $q$ where the second contains the first. If $U(q)$ is different from 0, then white can enforce a win, independently of how black might play and can do so in at most $\rho$ moves by virtue of a certain subset $U^*(q)$ of $U(q)$, but not for certain in fewer moves. If $U(q) = 0$ but $V(q) \neq 0$, then white can at least enforce a draw by virtue of the endgames contained in $V(q)$. However, if $V(q)$ vanishes also and the opponent plays correctly, white can postpone the loss up until the $\sigma$th move at best by virtue of a well defined subset $V^*(q)$ of continuations. In any case only the games contained in $U^*$ respectively $V^*$ have to be considered as "correct" for white, with any other continuation he would, if in a winning position, forfeit or delay the certain win or otherwise make possible or accelerate the loss of the game given that the opponent plays correctly. Of course an exact analogy exists for black and only those games that satisfy both conditions *simultaneously* could be considered as played "correctly" until the end, in any case they form a well defined subset $W(q)$ of $Q$.

The numbers $t$ and $r$ are independent of the position and only determined by the rules of the game. To each possible position there corresponds a number $\rho = \rho_q$ or $\sigma = \sigma_q$ smaller than $\tau$, depending on whether white or black can enforce a win in $\rho$ respectively $\sigma$

---

[3] Zermelo doesn't define the number $\sigma$; it denotes the smallest number of moves for which white can postpone his loss.

moves but not less. The special theory of the game would have, as far as possible, to determine these numbers or at least include them within certain boundaries, which hitherto has only been possible for special cases such as the "problems" or the real "endgames". The question as to whether the starting position $p_0$ is already a "winning position" for one of the parties is still open. Would it be answered exactly, chess would of course lose the character of a game at all.

# TWENTY

# The Strategy of Conflict

THOMAS C. SCHELLING

Source: *The Strategy of Conflict*. Cambridge, Mass. and London, England: Harvard University Press (1960), pp. 119–50.

## Enforcement, Communication, and Strategic Moves

Whenever we speak of deterrence, atomic blackmail, the balance of terror, or an open-skies arrangement to reduce the fear of surprise attack; when we characterize American troops in Europe as a trip wire or plate-glass window or propose that a threatened enemy be provided a face-saving exit; when we advert to the impotence of a threat that is so enormous that the threatener would obviously shrink from carrying it out or observe that taxi drivers are given a wide berth because they are known to be indifferent to dents and scratches, we are evidently deep in game theory. Yet formal game theory has contributed little to the clarification of these ideas. The author suggests that nonzero-sum game theory may have missed its most promising field by being pitched at too abstract a level of analysis. By abstracting from communication and enforcement systems and by treating perfect symmetry between players as the general case rather than a special one, game theory may have overshot the level at which the most fruitful work could be done and may have defined away some of the essential ingredients of typical nonzero-sum games. Preoccupied with the solution to *the* nonzero-sum game, game theory has not done justice to some typical game situations or game models and to the "moves" that are peculiar to nonzerosum games of strategy.

What "model," for example, epitomizes the controversy over massive retaliation? What conditions are necessary for an efficacious threat? What in game theory corresponds to the proverbial situation "to have a bear by the tail"; how do we identify the payoff matrix, the communication system, and the enforcement system that it embodies? What are the tactics by which pedestrians intimidate automobile drivers, or small countries large ones; and how do we formulate them in game-theoretical terms? What is the information or communication structure, or the complex of incentives, that makes dogs, idiots, small children, fanatics, and martyrs immune to threats?

The precarious strategy of cold war and nuclear stalemate has often been expressed in game-type analogies: two enemies within reach of each other's poison arrows

on opposite sides of a canyon, the poison so slow that either could shoot the other
before he died;[1] a shepherd who has chased a wolf into a corner where it has no choice
but to fight, the shepherd unwilling to turn his back on the beast; a pursuer armed
only with a hand grenade who inadvertently gets too close to his victim and dares not
use his weapon; two neighbors, each controlling dynamite in the other's basement,
trying to find mutual security through some arrangement of electric switches and
detonators.[2] If we can analyze the structures of these games and develop a working
acquaintance with standard models, we may provide insight into real problems by the
use of our theory.

To illustrate, an instructive model is that of twenty men held up for robbery or ransom
by a single man who has a gun and six bullets. They can overwhelm him if they are willing
to lose six of themselves, if they have a means of deciding which six to lose. They can
defeat him without loss if they can visibly commit themselves to a threat to do so, if they
can simultaneously commit themselves to a *promise* to abstain from capital punishment,
once they have caught him. He can deter their threat if he can visibly commit himself to
shoot in disregard of any subsequent threat they might make, or if he can show that he
could not believe their promise. If they cannot deliver their threat – if, say, he understands
only a foreign language – they cannot disarm him verbally. Nor can they make a threat
unless they agree on it themselves; so if he can threaten to shoot any two who talk
together, he can deter agreement. If the twenty cannot find a way to divide the risk,
there may be no one to go first to carry out the threat, hence no way to make the threat
persuasive; and if he can announce a formula for shooting, such as that those who move
first get shot first, he can deter them unless they find a way to move together without a
"first." If fourteen of the twenty can overpower the remaining six and force them to
advance, they can demonstrate that they could overwhelm the man; if so, the threat
succeeds and the gunman surrenders, and even the six "expendables" gain through
their own inability to avoid jeopardy. If the twenty could overwhelm the man but
have no way of letting him escape, a promise of immunity may be necessary; but if
they cannot deny their capacity to identify him and testify against him later, it may be
necessary to let him take a hostage. This, in turn, depends on the ability of nineteen to
enforce their own agreement to protect, by silence, whoever is currently the
hostage...and so on. When we have identified the critical ingredients in several games
of this sort, we may be in a better position to understand the basis of power of an
unpopular despot or of a well-organized dominant minority, or the conditions for
successful mutiny.

This chapter is an attempt to suggest the kinds of typical moves and structural elements
that deserve to be explored within the framework of game theory. They include such
moves as "threat," "promise," "destruction of communication," "delegation of decision,"
and so forth, and such structural elements as the communication and enforcement
provisions.

---

[1] Compare C. W. Sherwin, "Securing Peace Through Military Technology," *Bulletin of the Atomic Scientists*,
12: 159–164 (May 1956).

[2] Compare Herman Kahn and Erwin Mann, "Game Theory," The RAND Corporation, Paper P–1166 (Santa
Monica, 1957), pp. 55 ff. The authors work out a number of problems involving dynamite, detonators, and
deterrence.

## An Illustrative Move

An example of a standard "move" is the commitment, analyzed at some length in Chapter 3. If the institutional environment makes it possible for a potential buyer to make a single "final" offer subject to extreme penalty in the event he should amend the offer – to commit himself – there remains but a single, well-determined decision for the seller: to sell at the price proposed or to forego the sale. The possibility of commitment converts an indeterminate bargaining situation into a two-move game; one player assumes a commitment, and the other makes a final decision. The game has become determinate.[3]

This particular move, analyzed at length in Chapter 3, is mentioned here only as a particularly simple illustration of a typical move. As noted in Chapter 3, the availability and the efficacy of this move depend on the communication structure of the game and the ability of the player to find a way to commit himself, to "enforce" the commitment against himself. Furthermore, we have allowed the move structure of the game to be asymmetrical; the "winner" is the one who can assume the commitment or, if both can, the one who can do it first. (We can consider the special case of a tie, but we have not, by an assumption of symmetry, made ties a foregone conclusion.)

But, although we have made the game "determinate" in the sense that we have no difficulty in identifying the "solution," once we have identified which of the two players can first commit himself, it remains a game of *strategy*. Though the winner is the one who achieves his commitment first, the game is not like a foot race that goes to the fastest. The difference is that the commitment does not automatically win under the rules of the game, either physically or legally. The outcome still depends on the second player, over whom the first player has no direct control. The commitment is a *strategic* move, a move that induces the other player to choose in one's favor. It constrains the other player's choice by affecting his expectations.

The power to commit one's self in this kind of game is equivalent to "first move." And if the institutional arrangements provide no means for incurring an irrevocable commitment in a legal or contractual sense, one may accomplish the same thing by an irreversible maneuver that reduces his own freedom of choice. One escapes an undesired invitation by commitment when he arranges a "prior" engagement; failing that, he can deliberately catch cold. Luce and Raiffa have pointed out that the same tactic can be used by a person against himself when he wants, for example, to go on a diet but does not trust himself. "He announces his intention, or accepts a wager that he will not break his diet, so that later he will *not* be free to change his mind and to optimize his actions according to his tastes at *that* time."[4] The same thing is accomplished by maneuver rather than by

---

[3] In the real estate example of Von Neumann and Morgenstern referred to earlier (p. 116) buyer B (whose top price is 15) might raise the limit on what he can extract from buyer C (whose top price is 25) if he can find some means to bind himself to buy the house for 20 and keep or destroy it (that is, not be free to resell it to C for a loss) unless he gets a specified large fraction of, say, $20 - P$, where $P$ is the ultimate price paid by C. In effect, B changes his own "true" top price, thus raising the limit on what he may extract from C. Of course, D and E may try to do the same; and the first to get properly committed, or the one who can find a means if only one of them can, is the winner. If D, who attaches no personal value to the house, is committed to pay up to 22 for it, he is a bona fide member of the game with a true reservation price of 22; his *bona fides* is even greater than was B's originally, if the commitment is demonstrable while subjective valuations are not.

[4] *Games and Decisions*, p. 75.

commitment when one deliberately embarks on a vacation deep in the wilds without cigarettes.

## Threats

The distinctive character of a threat is that one asserts that he will do, in a contingency, what he would manifestly prefer not to do if the contingency occurred, the contingency being governed by the second party's behavior. Like the ordinary commitment, the threat is a surrender of choice, a renunciation of alternatives, that makes one worse off than he need be in the event the tactic fails; the threat and the commitment are both motivated by the possibility that a rational second player can be constrained by his knowledge that the first player has altered his own incentive structure. Like an ordinary commitment, a threat can constrain the other player only insofar as it carries to the other player at least some appearance of obligation; if I threaten to blow us both to bits unless you close the window, you know that I won't unless I have somehow managed to leave myself no choice in the matter.[5]

The threat differs from the ordinary commitment, however, in that it makes one's course of action *conditional* on what the other player does. While the commitment fixes one's course of action, the threat fixes a course of reaction, of response to the other player. The commitment is a means of gaining *first move* in a game in which first move carries an advantage; the threat is a commitment to a strategy for *second move*.

A threat can therefore be effective only if the game is one in which the first move is up to the other player or one can force the other player to move first. But if one must, in a mechanical sense, move first or simultaneously, he can still force the legal equivalent of "first move" on the other by attaching his threat to a demand that the other promise in advance how he will behave – if the game has communication and enforcement structures that make promises feasible and that the party to be threatened cannot destroy in advance. The holdup man whose rich victim happens to have no money on him at the time can make nothing of his opportunity unless he can extract a hostage while he awaits payment; and even that will not work unless he can himself find a way to assume a convincing commitment to return the hostage in a manner that does not subject himself to identification or capture.

---

[5] In ordinary language, "threat" is often used also for the case in which one merely points out to an adversary, or reminds him, that one would take action painful to the adversary if the latter fails to comply, it being clear that one would have incentive to do so. To "threaten" to call the police on a trespasser is of this sort, the threat to shoot him is not. But it seems better to use a different word for these cases – I suggest "warning" rather than "threat" – because the "threat" either is superfluous, and does not constitute a move, or it conveys true information and relates to situations with an information structure and communication structure worth keeping distinct. In this latter case it is a mutually beneficial move, precluding a jointly undesired outcome by improving the second party's understanding. The main point of analytical similarity, between this "warning" case and that of the "threat," is in the possible difficulty of conveying true information credibly, of conveying *evidence* for the assertion that one would have, ex post, incentive for doing as one warns he will. As a matter of fact, if a threat is of such nature (as it often is) that the act of commitment is not contained in the act of communicating it – if the commitment precedes the conveyance of the threat, with evidence for believing it, to the threatened party – the first act in the process of threatening changes the "true" incentive structure, and the second is, in effect, a "warning."

The fact that *some* kind of commitment, or at least appearance of commitment, must lie behind the threat and be successfully communicated to the threatened party is in contradiction to another notion that often appears in game theory. This is the notion that a threat is desirable, or admissible, or plausible, only if the reaction threatened would cause worse damage to the threatened party than to the party making the threat. This is the view of Luce and Raiffa, who characterize threats by the phrase, "This will hurt you more than it hurts me," explicitly making threats depend on interpersonal utility comparisons. In the event that both players attempt to make plausible threats, they say, the result becomes indeterminate, depending on the "bargaining personalities" of the players; "and to predict what will in fact happen without first having a complete psychological and economic analysis of the players seems foolish indeed."[6]

But the issue is both simpler and more precise than that. Consider the left-hand matrix in Figure 9, where Column is assumed to have "first move." Without threats, Column has an easy "win." He chooses strategy I, forcing Row to choose between payoffs of 1 and 0; Row chooses strategy i, providing Column a payoff of 2. But if we allow Row to make a threat, he declares that he will choose strategy ii unless Column chooses II; that is, he gives Column a choice of ii, I or i, II by committing himself to that conditional choice. *If* Column went ahead and chose I, of course, Row would prefer to choose i; and they both know it. The tactic succeeds only if Column believes that Row *must* choose ii in the event of I.

---

[6] Pp. 110–11, 119–20, 143–4. Morton A. Kaplan, in applying game theory to international relations, also takes the position that "any criterion giving weight to the threat positions of the players involves an interpersonal comparison of utilities." (See his *System and Process in International Politics* [New York, 1957].) Luce and Raiffa may partly be led to their view that only one of the players has a "plausible" threat to make, by confining their brief discussion to 2 × 2 matrices. It is impossible to show, with a 2 × 2 matrix, a game in which both players could be interested in making threats. A threat is essentially a credible declaration of a *conditional* choice for second move. It is profitable only if it yields a better payoff than either first move or second move alone and when one can make the other player move first either actually or by promise. (If second move alone is as good, the threat is unnecessary; and if first move were as good, one needs only an unconditional commitment to his strategy choice, not a commitment to a conditional choice.) But if this preference order holds for one player in a 2 × 2 matrix, it cannot hold for the other player. The actual matrices used by Luce and Raiffa in discussing the point show no "plausible" threat strategy for player No. 2, not because the absolute size of his gains or losses is greater than player I's but for the much simpler reason that player 2 has no use for a threat. He wins if he moves first; he wins if he moves second; and he wins with simultaneous moves, in the games shown. His only interest in a threatlike declaration would be to forestall his partner's threat; and for that purpose he needs only an *unconditional* commitment to his preferred strategy – that is, the legal equivalent of "first move" in advance of his partner's threat. The "threat" tactic of J. F. Nash, which applies to bargaining games that have a continuous range of efficient outcomes – or that can be made to, by agreement on the odds in a drawing of lots – differs from the threat discussed here, in that the threatener does not demand, on pain of mutual damage, a *particular* outcome but only *some* outcome in the efficient range; that is, he shifts the zero point corresponding to "no agreement." The motive for that threat is the expectation of a particular mathematically determinate outcome whose locus is shifted by the shift in the payoffs corresponding to nonagreement. This is the kind of threat assumed by Luce and Raiffa (p. 139) in the "asymmetrical" game. The implicit legal structure of the game apparently honors no irrevocable commitments (otherwise, first commitment would easily win the game for either player). Each player is subject to the legal "disability" that he can always, by the overt act of explicit agreement with his partner on any outcome, evade his own commitment. This being so, the revocable commitments can only shift the zero point – the "status quo" that will rule unless explicit agreement on some outcome is reached. The "asymmetry" that is present in the particular game shown by Luce and Raiffa is thus a feature of the particular legal system that implicitly prevails. In practice it might correspond, say, to the deliberate incurring of social disapproval on failure to reach agreement, with such disapproval constituting cost or punishment (perhaps asymmetrical between participants) in addition to the cost of nonagreement but with the public not concerned with what the agreement provides as long as some agreement is reached.

Figure 9 [Figures 1–8 are in earlier chapters of Schelling's book.]

Either he does believe this, or he does not. If he does not, the "threat" is nothing at all to him; he goes ahead and makes his "best" first move, choosing I. If he does believe that Row must follow a strategy of i, II or ii, I, Column prefers 1 to 0 and chooses II. But this is true of any numbers that we might put in the matrix that reflect the same order of preferences. It is true of the right-hand matrix as well. That one dramatizes the essential character of the threat more than the first one, since the penalty on Row of an irrational choice by Column is greater in this case; but for rational play and full information, Row need not worry. Column's preference is clear; and, once Row has given him the pair to choose from – ii, I versus i, II – there is no doubt what Column will do. If I threaten to blow my brains all over your new suit unless you give me that last slice of toast, you'll give me the toast or not depending on whether you know that I've arranged to have to do so, exactly as if I'd only threatened to throw my scrambled eggs at you.[7]

The issue here is in whether or not we admit that the game has "moves," that is, that it is possible for one player or both players to take actions in the course of the game that irreversibly change the game itself – that in some fashion alter the payoff matrix, the order of choices, or the information structure of the game. If the game by its definition admits no moves of any sort, except mutual agreement and refusal to agree, then it may be true that the "personalities" of the players determine the outcome, in the sense that their expectations in a "moveless" game converge by a process that is wholly psychic. But, if a threat is anything more than an assertion that is intended to appeal to the other player by power of suggestion, we must ask what more it can be. And it must involve some notion of commitment – real or fake – if it is to be anything.

---

[7] Edward Banfield showed me this irresistible quotation about the Bháts and Charáns of the west of India, revered as bards. "In Guzerát they carry large sums in bullion, through tracts where a strong escort would be insufficient to protect it. They are also guarantees of all agreements of chiefs among themselves, and even with the government.

Their power is derived from the sanctity of their character and their desperate resolution. If a man carrying treasure is approached, he announces that he will commit tràga, as it is called: or if an engagement is not complied with, he issues the same threat unless it is fulfilled. If he is not attended to, he proceeds to gash his limbs with a dagger, which, if all other means fail, he will plunge into his heart; or he will first strike off the head of his child; or different guarantees to the agreement will cast lots who is to be first beheaded by his companions. The disgrace of these proceedings, and the fear of having a bard's blood on their head, generally reduce the most obstinate to reason. Their fidelity is exemplary, and they never hesitate to sacrifice their lives to keep up an ascendency on which the importance of their cast depends" (The Hon. Mountstuart Elphinstone, *History of India* [ed. 7; London, 1889], p. 211).

"Commitment" is to be interpreted broadly here. It includes maneuvers that leave one in such a position that the option of nonfulfilment no longer exists (as when one intimidates the other car by driving too fast to stop in time), maneuvers that shift the final decision beyond recall to another party whose incentive structure would provide an ex post motive for fulfilment (as when the authority to punish is deliberately given to sadists, or when one shifts his claims and liabilities to an insurance company), and maneuvers that simply "worsen" one's own payoff in the contingency of nonfulfilment so that even the horror of a mutually damaging fulfilment becomes more attractive (as when one arranges for himself to appear a public coward if he fails to fulfil, or when he puts a plate-glass window in front of his wares or stations women and children on the particular bit of territory that he has threatened somewhat implausibly to defend at great cost). A nice everyday example is given by Erving Goffman, who reminds us that "salesmen, especially street stemmers, know that if they take a line that will be discredited unless the reluctant customer buys, the customer may be trapped by considerateness and buy in order to save the face of the salesman and prevent what would ordinarily result in a scene."[8]

There are, however, some ways in which this notion of commitment to a threat can be usefully loosened. One is to recognize that "firm" commitment amounts to the invocation of some wholly potent penalty, such that one would in all circumstances prefer to carry out what he was committed to. It is a penalty of infinite (or at least of superfluous) size that one voluntarily, irreversibly, and visibly attaches to all patterns of action but the one that he is committed to do. This concept can be loosened by supposing that the penalty is of finite size and not necessarily so large as to be controlling in all cases. In Fig. 10 Column will win if he has first move, unless Row can commit himself to i. (Commitment obtains "first move" for Row.) But, if commitment means the attachment of a finite penalty to the choice of row ii and we show this in the matrix by subtracting from each of Row's payoffs in ii some finite amount representing the penalty, then the commitment will be effective only if the penalty is greater than 2. Otherwise it is clear to Column that Row's response to II will be ii, in spite of the commitment. In this case the commitment is simply a loss that Row would impose on himself, so he avoids it.

|     | I   |     | II  |     |
|-----|-----|-----|-----|-----|
| i   |     | 2   |     | 1   |
|     | 4   |     | 1   |     |
| ii  |     | 2   |     | 3   |
|     | 4   |     | 3   |     |

**Figure 10**

---

[8] Goffman's paper is a brilliant study in the relation of game theory to gamesmanship and a pioneer illustration of the rich game-theoretic content of formalized behavior structures like etiquette, chivalry, diplomatic practice, and – by implication – the law.

Similarly with a threat. In Fig. 11 without threats, the solution is at iii, II whether the rules call for Row to choose first, Column first, or both to choose simultaneously. Either player can win if he can move second and confront the other with a threat.[9] Column would threaten I against iii, Row would threaten i against II. But if the threat is secured by a penalty, the lower limit to any persuasive penalty that Column could invoke would be 4; any smaller penalty leaves him preferring II to I when Row chooses iii. The lower limit to a persuasive penalty on Row's noncompliance would be 3. If, then, the situation is one in which penalties come in a single "size," a size less than 3 goes unused and the outcome is at iii, II; a size greater than 4 is adequate for either player, and the "winner" is the one who can avail himself of the threat first; a size between 3 and 4 is of use only to Row, who wins. In this latter case the player who would be hurt the more by his own unsuccessful threat is the one who cannot threaten – but only through the paradox that he is incapable of calling a sufficiently terrible penalty on his own head.

Note that the "hurt-more" comparison in this case refers not to whether Row or Column would be hurt more by what Row threatens but to whether Row would be hurt more by having to fulfil his own threat than Column would be hurt if, instead, Column had made *his* threat. Actually, in the particular payoff matrix shown, Row's *successful* threat is one that would hurt him *more* in the fulfilment than it would hurt Column, while Column's potential *unsuccessful* threat would hurt him *less* to fulfil than it would hurt Row. Another loosening of the threat concept is to alter our assumption of rationality. Suppose there is some probability Pr for player R, and some probability Pc for player C, that he

|  | I | II | III |
|---|---|---|---|
| **i** | −5 <br> −5 | −1 <br> −2 | −1 <br> −2 |
| **ii** | −3 <br> −4 | 3 <br> 0 | 2 <br> 2 |
| **iii** | −3 <br> −4 | 0 <br> 0 | 0 <br> 3 |

**Figure 11**

[9] If a player, Column, for example, cannot force first move on Row in a mechanical sense, he can do so in a "legal" sense by threatening to choose I unless Row *promises* to chose ii. Full analysis in this case requires attention to the penalties on promises as well as on threats. Since the physical and institutional arrangements for promises (that is, for commitments to the second party) are generally of a quite different nature from those for unilateral commitments (that is, commitments that the second player cannot himself dissolve), available penalties could differ drastically as between threats and promises – just as, in general, they would differ as between the first and second players. The particular payoffs shown in Fig. 11 would require penalties of at least 1 on a promise by Column or by Row. Note that in the case of a promise extracted by a threat, it is an advantage to the threatener to be able to invoke penalty and a disadvantage to the victim to be able to invoke penalty on his own breach of contract, that is, to be able to comply.

will make a mistake or an irrational move, or that he will act in an unanticipated way because the other player is mistaken about the first player's payoffs.[10] This yields us a game in which the possible gains and losses in committing one's self to a threat must take into account the possibility that a fully committed threat will not be heeded. If, then, the potential loss that will ensue from having to carry out the threat is greater for one player than for another, there could be symmetrical circumstances – the P's being equal and the threat penalties equal for the two players – in which one player may find it advantageous to make the threat and the other player not, considering the possibility of "error." (A somewhat similar calculation may be involved if both players have opportunities for threats and there is danger of simultaneous commitment through the failure of one to observe the other's commitment and to stop in time to save both.)

This modification in the threat concept – in the rationality postulate that underlies it – goes somewhat in the direction of the "hurt-more" criterion. On the whole, though, game theory adds more insight into the strategy of bargaining by emphasizing the striking truth that the threat does *not* depend on the threatener's having less to suffer than the threatened party if the threat had to be carried out rather than by exaggerating the possible truth contained in the intuitive first impression. Threats of war, of price war, of damage suit; threats to make a "scene"; most of the threats of organized society to prosecute crimes and misdemeanors; and the concepts of extortion and deterrence generally cannot be understood except by denying the utility-comparison criterion. It is indeed the asymmetries in the threat situation, as between the two players, that make threats a rich subject for study; but the relevant asymmetries include those in the communication system, in the enforcibility of threats and of promises, in the speed of commitment, in the rationality of expected responses, and, finally (in some cases) in the relative-damage criterion.

## Promises

Enforcible promises cannot be taken for granted. Agreements must be in enforcible terms and involve enforcible types of behavior. Enforcement depends on at least two things – some authority somewhere to punish or coerce and an ability to discern whether punishment or coercion is called for. The postwar discussions of disarmament proposals and inspection schemes indicate how difficult it may be, even if both sides should desperately desire to reach an enforcible agreement or find a persuasive means of enforcement. The problem is compounded when neither party trusts the other and each recognizes that neither trusts the other and that neither can therefore anticipate the other's compliance. Many of the technical problems of arms inspection would disappear if there were some earthly means of making enforcible promises or if the nations of the world all rendered unquestioned allegiance to some unearthly authority. But, since noncompliance may be undetectable, promises of compliance could not be enforced even if punishment could be guaranteed. The problem is doubled by the fact that punishment cannot be guaranteed, except such punishment as can unilaterally be meted out by the other party in its act of denouncing the original agreement. Furthermore, some seemingly desirable agreements must be left out for

---

[10] Situations of this sort are explored in Chapters 7 and 9.

being undefinable operationally; agreements not to discriminate against each other will work only if defined in objective terms capable of objective supervision.

Promises are generally thought of as bilateral (contractual) commitments, given against a quid pro quo that is often a promise in return. But there is incentive for a unilateral promise when it provides inducement to the other player to make a choice in the mutual interest. In the left-hand matrix of Fig. 12, if choices are to be simultaneous, only a *pair* of promises can be effective; in the right-hand matrix, Row's promise brings its own reward: Column can safely choose II, yielding superior outcomes for both players. (If, in the left-hand matrix, moves are in turn, the player who chooses *second* must have the power to promise. If the players are themselves to agree on the order of moves and only one of the two can issue promises, they can agree that the other one move first. These promises, in contrast to those for the right-hand matrix, must be conditional on the second player's performance. A unilateral unconditional promise does the trick on the right-hand side but not on the left with moves in turn.) The witness to a crime has a motive for unilateral promise if the criminal would kill to keep him from squealing.[11] A nation known to be on the threshold of an absolutely potent surprise-attack weapon may have reason to foreswear it unilaterally – if there is any possible way to do so – in order to forestall a desperate last-minute attempt by an enemy to strike first while he still has a chance.

The exact definition of a promise – for example, in distinction to a threat – is not obvious. It might seem that a promise is a commitment (conditional or unconditional) that the second party welcomes, one that is mutually advantageous, as in both the games shown in Fig. 12. But Fig. 13 shows a situation in which Row must couple a threat and a promise; he threatens ii against I and promises i in the event of II. The promise insures Column a payoff of 4 rather than zero, once he has made a choice of II, and in that sense it is favorable to him; it does so at a cost of 1 unit to Row. But, if Row could not make the promise, Column would win 5; he would because the threat would be ineffectual without the promise, and the threat would not be incurred. A threat of ii against I by itself is no good; it cannot force Column to choose II, since a choice of II leaves him with an outcome

**Figure 12**

[11] This notion is celebrated in "Wet Saturday," by John Collier, recently reproduced by Alfred Hitchcock on TV. An inadvertent eavesdropper on a murder is ordered at gunpoint to seal his lips by leaving his own fingerprints and other incriminating evidence, so that if the body is found he will be charged with the murder. He should have insisted, however, on fabricating the evidence so as to share the guilt with the actual murderer; as it was, he got badly cheated. (*Short Stories from the "New Yorker"* [London, 1951], pp. 171–178.)

|     | I | II |
|-----|---|----|
| i   | 5 / 2 | 4 / 4 |
| ii  | 1 / 1 | 0 / 5 |

Figure 13

at ii, II, zero instead of I. Row's threat can work only if the promise goes with it; the net effect of the promise is to make the threat work, yielding Column 4 instead of 5, gaining 5 rather than 2 for Row. One cannot force spies, conspirators, or carriers of social diseases to reveal themselves solely by the *threat* of a relentless pursuit that spares no cost; one must also promise immunity to those that come forward.[12]

A better definition, perhaps, would make the promise a commitment that is controlled by the second party, that is, a commitment that the second party can enforce or release as he chooses. But timing is important here. The promise just discussed will work *after* the threat is fully committed; but if the victim of the promise (Column) can renounce the promise in advance, so that Row knows that Column expects zero if he chooses II, the threat itself is deterred. And, if the threat and promise are contrived in such a way as to be "legally" inseparable or if they are accomplished by some irreversible maneuver, the definition becomes obscured. (In fact, the definition breaks down whenever the equivalent of a promise is obtained by some irrevocable act rather than by a "legal" commitment.)

Actually, whenever the alternative choices are more than two, threat and promise are likely to be mixed in any "reaction pattern" that one presents to the other. So it is probably best to consider the threat and the promise to be names for different aspects of the same tactic of selective and conditional self-commitment, which in certain simple instances can be identified in terms of the second party's interest.

### Enforcement schemes

Agreements are unenforcible if no outside authority exists to enforce them or if noncompliance would be inherently undetectable. The problem arises, then, of finding forms of agreement, or terms to agree on, that provide no incentive to cheat or that make noncompliance automatically visible or that incur the penalties on which the possibility of enforcement rests. While the possibility of "trust" between two partners need not be ruled out, it should also not be taken for granted; and even trust itself can usefully be studied in game-theoretic terms. Trust is often achieved simply by the continuity of the relation between parties and the recognition by each that what he might gain by cheating

[12] Somewhat related is the grant of immunity that strips a reticent witness of protective danger of self-incrimination, and so opens him to the ordinary sanction of contempt proceedings.

in a given instance is outweighed by the value of the tradition of trust that makes possible a long sequence of future agreement. By the same token, "trust" may be achieved for a single discontinuous instance, if it can be divided into a succession of increments.

There are, however, particular game situations that lend themselves to enforcible agreement. One is an agreement that depends on some kind of coordination or complementarity. If two people have disagreed on where to meet for dinner; if two criminal accomplices have disagreed on what joint alibi to give; or if members of a business firm or football team have disputed about what prices they will quote or what tactic they will follow, they nevertheless have an overriding interest in the ultimate consistency of their actions. Once agreement is formally reached, it constitutes the only possible focal point for the necessary subsequent tacit collaboration; no one has a unilateral preference now to do anything but what he is expected to do. In the absence of any other means of enforcement, then, parties might be well advised to try to find agreements that enjoy this property of interdependent expectations, even to the extent of importing into their agreement certain elements whose sole purpose is to create severe jeopardy for noncoordination. Tearing the treasure map in half or letting one partner carry the gun and the other the ammunition is a familiar example.

The institution of *hostages* is an ancient technique that deserves to be studied by game theory, as does the practice of drinking wine from the same glass or of holding gang meetings in places so public that neither side could escape if it subjected the other to a massacre. The reported use of only drug addicts as agents or employees in a narcotics ring is a fairly straightforward example of a unilateral hostage.

Perhaps a sufficient interchange of populations between nations that hate each other or an agreement to move the governing agencies of both countries to a single island where they would occupy alternate blocks of the city could be resorted to if both sides became sufficiently desperate to avoid mutual destruction. A principal drawback to the exchange of hostages, on the assumption of rational behavior, is the inherent unknowability of each other's value system adverted to earlier. The king who sends his daughter as a hostage to his enemy's court may be incapable of assuaging his enemy's fears that he really dislikes the girl. We could probably guarantee the Russians against an American surprise attack by having the equivalent of "junior year abroad" at the kindergarten level: if every American five-year-old went to kindergarten in Russia – in American establishments constructed for the purpose, designed solely for "hostage" purposes and not for cultural interchange – and if each year's incoming group arrived before the graduating class left, there would not seem to be the slightest chance that America would ever initiate atomic destruction in Russia. We cannot be quite sure that the Russians would be quite sure of this. Nor can we be quite sure that a reciprocal program would be as much of a deterrent to the Russian government; unfortunately, even if the Russian government were bound by the fear of harming Russian children, it seems nearly impossible for it to persuade us so. Still, in many surprise-attack situations a unilateral promise is better than none; and the idea of hostages may be worth considering, even when symmetrical exchanges do not seem available.[13]

---

[13] The precise definition of hostages is a little difficult. They seem to be as pertinent to threats as to promises: the American divisions that were stationed in Europe principally to demonstrate that America could not avoid becoming engaged in a European conflict can probably be viewed as hostages; if they cannot, their wives and children can, and perhaps their wives and children have been a more persuasive commitment or "trip wire" than the troops themselves. As a general rule, invaders may have to avoid the peak tourist season in countries they covet, to avoid provoking the countries that have yielded inadvertent hostages.

Actually, the hostage idea is logically identical with the notion that a disarmament agreement between the major powers might be more efficacious (and probably more subject to technical control) if it related to *defensive* weapons and structures. To eschew defense is, in effect, to make hostages of your entire population without bothering to put them physically into the other's possession. Thus we can put our children at the mercy of the Russians and receive similar power over Russian children not only by physically trading them, with enormous discomfort and breach of constitutional rights, but also by simply agreeing to leave them so unprotected that the other can do them as much damage where they are as if he had them in his grasp. Thus the "balance of terror" that is so often adverted to is – if, in fact, it exists and is stable – equivalent to a total exchange of all conceivable hostages. (The analogy requires that the balance be stable, i.e., that neither side be able, by surprise attack, to destroy the other's power to strike back, but just able to inflict a surfeit of civilian agony.)[14]

### Denial of enforcement

Enforcement of promises is also relevant to the influence of a third party that wishes to make an efficient outcome more difficult for the other two players. A potent means of banning illegal activities has often been the outlawing of them, so that contracts became unenforcible. Failure to enforce gambling contracts or contracts in restraint of trade or contracts for the delivery of liquor during prohibition has always been part of the process of discouraging the activities themselves. Sometimes, of course, prohibition of this sort delivers enormous power into the hands of anyone who can enforce contracts or make enforcible promises.[15] The denial of copyright liquor labels during prohibition meant that only the bigger gangs could guarantee the quality of their liquor and hence assisted them in developing monopoly control of the business. By the same token, laws to protect brands and labels can perhaps be viewed as devices that facilitate business based on unwritten contracts.

## Relinquishing the Initiative

What makes the threat or ordinary commitment a difficult tactic to employ and an interesting one to study is the problem of finding a means to commitment, the available "penalty" to invoke against one's own nonperformance. There is consequently a related set of tactics that consists of maneuvering one's self into a position in which one no longer has any effective choice over how he shall behave or respond. The purpose of these tactics is to get rid of an embarrassing initiative, making the outcome depend solely on the other party's choice.

This is the kind of tactic that Secretary of State John Foster Dulles was looking for in the following passage:

[14] This concept is developed at length in Chapter 10.

[15] It has been argued that an important function of the racketeer is sometimes to help enforce agreements that are beyond the law. Price-cutting in the Chicago garment trade was punishable by explosion – the fee for the explosion being paid by the price-fixing organization – according to R. L. Duffus, "The Function of the Racketeer," *New Republic* (March 27, 1929), pp. 166–68.

In the future it may thus be feasible to place less reliance upon deterrence of vast retaliatory power.... Thus, in contrast to the 1950 decade, it may be that by the 1960 decade the nations which are around the Sino-Soviet perimeter can possess an effective defense against full-scale conventional attack and thus confront any aggressor with the choice between failing or himself initiating nuclear war against the defending country. Thus the tables may be turned, in the sense that instead of those who are non-aggressive having to rely upon all-out nuclear retaliatory power for their protection, would-be aggressors would be unable to count on a successful conventional aggression, but must themselves weigh the consequence of invoking nuclear war.[16]

The distinction between the type of deterrence he imputes to the 1950's and the type he imputes to the 1960's differs in the matter of who has to make that final decision; and the difference is important because the United States cannot find, or bring itself to trust, a persuasive means of commitment to the threat of massive retaliation against certain types of aggression.

There was a time, shortly after the first atomic bomb was exploded, when there was some journalistic speculation about whether the earth's atmosphere had a limited tolerance to nuclear fission; the idea was bruited about that a mighty chain reaction might destroy the earth's atmosphere when some critical number of bombs had already been exploded. Someone proposed that, if this were true and if we could calculate with accuracy that critical level of tolerance, we might neutralize atomic weapons for all time by a deliberate program of openly and dramatically exploding $n-1$ bombs.

This tactic of shifting responsibility to the other player was nicely accomplished by Lieutenant Colonel (then Major) Stevenson B. Canyon, U.S.A.F., in using his aircraft to protect a Chinese Nationalist surface vessel about to be captured by Communist surface forces in his comic strip. Unwilling and unauthorized to initiate hostilities and knowing that no threat to do so would be credited, he directed his planes to jettison gasoline in a burning ring about the aggressor forces, leaving to them the last clear chance of reversing their engines to avoid the flames. He could neither drop gasoline on the enemy ships nor threaten to; so he dropped the initiative instead.

The same tactic is involved in those dramatic forms of "passive resistance" that might be better called "active nonresistance." According to *The New York Times*, "Striking railway workers sat down on the tracks at more than 300 stations in Japan today, halting 48 passenger and 144 freight trains."[17]

---

[16] J. F. Dulles, "Challenge and Response in U. S. Policy," *Foreign Affairs* (October, 1957). Very similar language is used by Dean Acheson (*Power and Diplomacy* [Cambridge, Mass., 1958], pp. 87–88) in discussing the role of a sizable defense force in Europe: by requiring of the enemy a major attack, rather than a small one, it makes him believe that retaliation would ensue, because "he would be making the decision for us.... A defense in Europe of this magnitude will pass the decision to risk everything from the defense to the offense."

[17] "Rail Strikers Sit in Tracks," *The New York Times* (May 13, 1957), pp. 14L f. The appropriate counter-tactic seems to be the following: The engineer sets the throttle for slow forward speed, conspicuously climbs down from his cab and jumps off the moving train, walks through the station and jumps back on his engine when it catches up with him. The weakness of his position while he is driving the train is that he can stop it more quickly than his adversaries can get off the tracks, particularly if they have arranged to crowd themselves so that they could not vacate the track quickly. They can forestall his countertactic by locking themselves to the tracks and throwing away the key – if they can persuasively inform the engineer of this before he has relinquished his own control of the engine.

A more dramatic instance, also Japanese, was reported in the same paper: "A public debate is being held here this week on whether to send a suicide sit-down fleet to the forbidden waters around Christmas Island, the site of the forthcoming British hydrogen bomb experiment.... The first object of the expedition would be to prevent the British blast."[18]

## Identification

An important characteristic of any game is how much each side knows about the other's value system; but a similar information problem arises with respect to sheer identification. The bank employee who would like to rob the bank if he could only find an outside collaborator and the bank robber who would like to rob the bank if only he could find an inside accomplice may find it difficult to collaborate because they are unable to identify each other, there being severe penalties in the event that either should declare his intentions to someone who proved not to have identical interests. The boy who is afraid to ask a girl for a date because she might rebuff him is in a similar position. Similarly, the kidnaper cannot operate properly if he cannot tell the rich from the poor in advance; and the antisegregation minority in the South may never know whether it is large or small because of the penalties on declaration.

Identification, like communication, is not necessarily reciprocal; and the act of self-identification may sometimes be reversible and sometimes not. One may achieve more identification than he bargained for, once he declares his interest in an object. A nice example occurs in Shakespeare's *Measure for Measure*. Angelo, acting in place of the Duke, has a prisoner whom he proposes to kill. He could torture him, but he has no incentive to. The victim has a sister, who arrives to plead for his life. Angelo, finding the sister attractive, proposes a dishonorable bargain; the sister declines, Angelo then threatens to torture the brother unless the sister submits. At this point the game has been expanded simply by the establishment of identity and of a line of communication. Angelo's only interest in torturing the brother is in what he may gain by making a threat to do so; once there is somebody available to whom the threat can profitably be communicated, the possibility of torture has value for Angelo – not the torture itself, but the threatening of it. The sister has gotten negative value out of her trip; having identified her interest and made herself available to receive the threatening message, she has been forced to suffer what she would not have had to suffer if she had never made her identity known or if she could have disappeared into the crowd before the threat was made.

A nice identification game was uncovered in a New York suburb a few years ago. Certain motorists carried identity cards which identified them to policemen as members in a club; if the motorist with a membership card was arrested, he simply showed the card to the policeman and paid a bribe. The role of these cards was to identify the motorist as a person who, if the bribe was received, would keep quiet. It identified the motorist as a man whose promise was enforcible. But the card identifies the motorist only *after* he has been

[18] "Japan Debating Atomic Suicide," *The New York Times* (March 5, 1957), p. 16.

arrested; if the police could identify card-carrying motorists by looking at them, they could concentrate their arrests on card-carrying drivers, threatening a ticket unless payment were received. The card is contingent identification, at the option of the motorist. A similar situation – pertinent to the discussion of promises as well as to identification – is described by Sutherland: "Most coppers are more or less fair in their dealings with thieves simply because it pays them to be so. They will extend favors even after a pinch which they would not extend to nonprofessionals whom they lock up. They realize that it is safe to do this and that high officials will not be informed, as might be the case if favors were extended to amateurs."[19]

Identification is also relevant to an important economic fact that tends to be ignored in the conventional economics of production and exchange, namely, the enormous potential for destruction that is available and that is relevant because of the extortionate threats that could be supported by it. The ordinary healthy high-school graduate, of slightly below average intelligence, has to work fairly hard to produce more than $3,000 or $4,000 of value per year; but he could destroy a hundred times that much if he set his mind to it, according to the writer's hasty calculations. Given an institutional arrangement in which he could generously abstain from destruction in return for a mere fraction of the value that he might have destroyed, the boy clearly has a calling as an extortionist rather than as a mechanic or clerk. It is fortunate that extortion usually depends on self-identification and overt communication by the extortionist himself.

The importance of self-identification is attested by the significance attached to the doctrine that an accused person should be permitted to know and to confront his accuser. It is also reflected in secret testimony before a Grand Jury, in cases where identifiable witnesses might be intimidated by potential defendants, and in efforts to keep secret the identity of eyewitnesses to a crime until the criminal is apprehended. (The strategy of law and of law enforcement and criminal deterrence is a rich field for the application of game theory.)

## Delegation

Another "move" that is sometimes available is the delegation of part or all of one's interest, or part or all of one's initiative for decision, to some agent who becomes (or perhaps already is) another player in the game. Insurance schemes permit the sharing of interests; the insurance company has a different incentive structure from the insured party and may be better able to make threats or resist them for that reason. Requiring several signatures on a check accomplishes a similar purpose. The use of a professional collecting agency by a business firm for the collection of debts is a means of achieving unilateral rather than bilateral communication with its debtors and of being therefore unavailable to hear pleas or threats from the debtors. Providing ammunition to South Korean troops or giving them access to prisoner-of-war camps so that they can unilaterally release prisoners is a tactical means of relinquishing an embarrassing power of decision – embarrassing because it subjects one to coercive or deterrent threats or leaves one

---

[19] E. H. Sutherland, *The Professional Thief* (Chicago, 1954), p. 126.

the capacity to back out of his own threat, hence the incapacity to make the threat persuasive.

The mutual-defense agreement with the Nationalist government of China is probably to be viewed partly as a means of shifting the decision for response to someone whose resolution would be less doubtful; and more recently the proposal to put nuclear weapons in the hands of European governments has been explicitly argued on grounds that it would enhance deterrence by giving the visible power to retaliate to countries that might in certain contingencies be thought less irresolute than the United States.

The use of thugs and sadists for the collection of extortion or the guarding of prisoners, or the conspicuous delegation of authority to a military commander of known motivation, exemplifies a common means of making credible a response pattern that the original source of decision might have been thought to shrink from or to find profitless, once the threat had failed. (Just as it would be rational for a rational player to destroy his own rationality in certain game situations, either to deter a threat that might be made against him and that would be premised on his rationality or to make credible a threat that he could not otherwise commit himself to, it may also be rational for a player to select irrational partners or agents.)

In the matrix in Fig. 14 – disregarding the numbers in parentheses – if Row has second move, he loses in the lower right-hand corner, Column gaining his own preferred outcome. If a third party without power of decision is scheduled to receive, as a by-product, the payoff in parentheses, Row can win if some means is available for irreversibly surrendering his move to the third player. The payoffs of the latter are such that with second move he wins in the upper left-hand corner, leaving the original Row-player. The payoffs of the latter are such that with second move had to be financed by Row, whose own payoffs were correspondingly reduced, it would still be worth his while to make an irrevocable assignment of portions of his various payoffs to the third player, together with assignment of the decision; with the figures shown, he would still carry away a net value of 3 in the upper left-hand corner, in contrast to 1 in the lower right.)

|  | I | II |
|---|---|---|
| i | (2)<br>3<br>5 | (1)<br>2<br>0 |
| ii | (1)<br>4<br>0 | (0)<br>5<br>1 |

Figure 14

## Mediation

The role of mediator is another element for analysis in game theory. A mediator, whether imposed on the game by its original rules or adopted by the players to facilitate an efficient outcome, is probably best viewed as an element in the communication arrangements or as a third player with a payoff structure of his own who is given an influential role through his control over communication. But a mediator can do more than simply constrain communications – putting limits on the order of offers, counter-offers, and so forth – since he can invent contextual material of his own and make potent suggestions. That is, he can influence the other player's expectations on his own initiative, in a manner that both parties cannot help mutually recognizing. When there is no apparent focal point for agreement, he can create one by his power to make a dramatic suggestion. The bystander who jumps into an intersection and begins to direct traffic at an impromptu traffic jam is conceded the power to discriminate among cars by being able to offer a sufficient increase in efficiency to benefit even the cars most discriminated against; his directions have only the power of suggestion, but coordination requires the common acceptance of some source of suggestion. Similarly, the participants of a square dance may all be thoroughly dissatisfied with the particular dances being called, but as long as the caller has the microphone, nobody can dance anything else. The white line down the center of the road is a mediator, and very likely it can err substantially toward one side or the other before the disadvantaged side finds advantage in denying its authority. The principle is beautifully illustrated by the daylight-saving-time controversy; a majority that wants to do everything an hour earlier just cannot organize to do it unless it gets legislative control of the clock. And when it does, a well-organized minority that opposed the change is usually quite unable to offset the change in clock time by any organized effort to change the nominal hour at which it gets up, eats, and does business.

Mediators can also be a means by which rational players can put aside some of their rational faculties. A mediator can consummate certain communications while blocking off certain facilities for memory. (In this regard he serves a function that can be reproduced by a computing machine.) He can, for example, compare two parties' offers to each other, declaring whether or not the offers are compatible without revealing the actual offers. He is a scanning device that can suppress part of the information put into it. He makes possible certain limited comparisons that are beyond the mental powers of the participants, since no player can persuasively commit himself to forget something.

The problem of persuasively denying one's self the knowledge that one receives by the left hand, while actively seeking it with the right hand, is nicely illustrated by the efforts of parts of governments to obtain accurate data on incomes for the purpose of statistical programs, while another part of the government is seeking the same data in order to impose taxes or to prosecute evasion. Governments have found it important to seek ways of guaranteeing that the statistical agency will deny the information it receives to the taxing agency, in order to receive the information in the first place. An analogous case of relying on an explicit mediator is that of companies that turn trade secrets over to a statistical bureau that is committed to destroy the individual data after computing the sums and averages that it will make public for the benefit of the contributing companies, or of public opinion services that suppress potentially embarrassing individual data on political or sexual practices, publishing only the aggregates. The use of mediators to forestall identification seems to be a common tactic when a buyer of large resources thinks a painting or a right-of-way can be bought cheap if the owner is unaware who it is that is interested.

Mediators may be converted into arbitrators by the irrevocable surrender of authority to him by the players. But arbitration agreements have to be made enforcible by the players' deliberately incurring jeopardy, providing the referee with the power to punish or surrendering to him something complementary to their own value systems. In turn, they must be able to trust him or to extract an enforcible promise from him. But in any case he increases the totality of means for enforcing promises: two people who do not trust each other may find a third person that they both trust, and let him hold the stakes.[20]

## Communication and Its Destruction

Many interesting game tactics and game situations depend on the structure of communication, particularly asymmetries in communication and unilateral options to initiate communication or to destroy it. Threats are no good if they cannot be communicated to the persons for whom they are intended; extortion requires a means of conveying the alternatives to the intended victim. Even the threat, "Stop crying or I'll give you something to cry about," is ineffectual if the child is already crying too loud to hear it. (It sometimes appears that children know this.) A witness cannot be intimidated into giving false testimony if he is in custody that prevents his getting instructions on what to say, even though he might infer the sanction of the threat itself.

When the outcome depends on coordination, the timely destruction of communication may be a winning tactic. When a man and his wife are arguing by telephone over where to meet for dinner, the argument is won by the wife if she simply announces where she is going and hangs up. And the status quo is often preserved by a person who evades discussion of alternatives, even to the extent of simply turning off his hearing aid.

As discussed in the earlier part of this chapter, mob action often depends on communication in a way that makes it possible for the authorities to obstruct mob action by forbidding groups of three or more to congregate. But mobs can themselves intimidate the authorities if they are able to identify them and to communicate with them. Even a tacit threat of subsequent ostracism or violence may be communicated from a riotous mob to the local police, if the police are known to them and are persons who have to reside among them when the occasion is over. In that case the use of outsiders may forestall the mob's intimidating threats against the authorities, partly by reducing the subsequent occasion for carrying out the threat but partly also through the difficulty of tacit communication between mob and police. Federal troops in Little Rock may have enjoyed some immunity

---

[20] I have been told that in countries where no strong tradition of business morality exists, a few partners or directors for a business may deliberately be chosen from another culture where simple honesty and fairness are considered to be common traits or where a reputation for them is considered of much higher value.

to intimidation just by being outside the tacit communication structure of the local populace and being patently less conversant with the local value system than were the local police. State troops were dramatically successful in quelling the Detroit race riot of 1943, when the local police were ineffectual. The use of Moors, Sikhs, and other foreign-language troops against local uprising may owe some of its success to their poor capacity to receive the threats and promises that the enemies or victims might otherwise seek to convey. Even the isolation of officers from enlisted men in military service may tend to make officers less capable of receiving and perceiving threats, hence less capable of being effectively threatened, and thus deterring intimidating threats themselves.

It is important, of course, whether or not the threatener knows that his threat cannot be received; for if he thinks it can, and it cannot, he may make the threat and fail in his objective, being obliged to carry out his threat to the subsequent disadvantage of both himself and the one threatened. So the soldiers in quelling the riot should not only be strangers and not only keep moving sufficiently to avoid "acquaintance" with particular portions of the mob; they should behave with an impassivity to demonstrate that no messages are getting through. They must catch no one's eye; they must not blush at the jeers; they must act as if they cannot tell one rioter from another, even if one has been making himself conspicuous. Figuratively, if not literally, they should wear masks; even the uniform contributes to the suppression of identification and so itself makes reciprocal communication difficult.

## Conveyance of evidence

"Communication" refers to more than the transmission of messages. To communicate a threat, one has to communicate the commitment that goes with it, and similarly with a promise; and to communicate a commitment requires more than communication of words. One has to communicate *evidence* that the commitment exists; this may mean that one can communicate a threat only if he can make the other person see something with his own eyes or if he can find a device to authenticate certain allegations. One can send a signed check by mail, but one cannot demonstrate over the telephone that a check bears an authentic signature; one may show that he has a loaded gun but not prove it by simply saying so. From a game-theory point of view, the Paris *pneumatique* differs from an ordinary telegraph system, and television differs from radio. (One role of a mediator may be to authenticate the statements that the players make to each other; for example, a code system for identification might make it possible for people to transmit funds orally by telephone, the recipient being assured by the bank's code response that it is in fact the bank at the other end of the line assuring him that the payer has been identified by code and that the transaction is complete.) The importance and the difficulty of communicating evidence is exemplified by President Eisenhower's "open-skies" proposal and other suggested devices for dealing with the instability that may be caused by the reciprocal fear of surprise attack. Leo Szilard has even pointed to the paradox that one might wish to confer immunity on foreign spies rather than subject them to prosecution, since they may be the only means by which the enemy can obtain persuasive evidence of the important truth that we are making no preparations for embarking on a surprise attack.[21]

---

[21] L. Szilard, "Disarmament and the Problem of Peace," *Bulletin of the Atomic Scientists*, 2: 297–307 (October, 1955).

It is interesting to observe that political democracy itself depends on a game structure in which the communication of evidence is impossible. What is the secret ballot but a device to rob the voter of his power to sell his vote? It is not alone the secrecy, but the *mandatory* secrecy, that robs him of his power. He not only *may* vote in secret, but he *must* if the system is to work. He must be denied any means of proving which way he voted. And what he is robbed of is not just an asset that he might sell; he is stripped of his power to be intimidated. He is made impotent to meet the demands of blackmail. There may be no limit to violence that he can be threatened with if he is truly free to bargain away his vote, since the threatened violence is not carried out anyway if it is frightening enough to persuade him. But when the voter is powerless to prove that he complied with the threat, both he and those who would threaten him know that any punishment would be unrelated to the way he actually voted. And the threat, being useless, goes idle.

An interesting case of tacit and asymmetrical communication is that of a motorist in a busy intersection who knows that a policeman is directing traffic. If the motorist sees, and evidently sees, the policeman's directions and ignores them, he is insubordinate; and the policeman has both an incentive and an obligation to give the man a ticket. If the motorist avoids looking at the policeman, cannot see the directions, and ignores the directions that he does not see, taking a right of way that he does not deserve, he may be considered only stupid by the policeman, who has little incentive and no obligation to give the man a ticket. Alternatively, if it is evident that the driver knew what the instructions were and disobeyed them, it is to the policeman's advantage not to have seen the driver, otherwise he is obliged, for the reputation of the corps, to abandon his pressing business and hail the driver down to give him a ticket. Children are skilled at avoiding the receipt of a warning glance from a parent, knowing that if they perceive it the parent is obliged to punish noncompliance; adults are equally skilled at not requesting the permission they suspect would be denied, knowing that explicit denial is a sterner sanction, obliging the denying authorities to take cognizance of the transgression.[22]

The efficacy of the communication structure can depend on the kinds of rationality that are imputed to the players. This is illustrated by the game situation known as "having a bear by the tail." The minimum requirement for an efficient outcome is that the bear be able to incur an enforcible promise and that he be able to transmit credible evidence that he is committed, either by a penalty incurred or by a maneuver that destroys his power not to comply (like extracting his own teeth and claws). But if the bear is of limited rationality, having a capacity for making rational and consistent choices among the alternatives that he perceives but lacking the capacity to solve games – that is, lacking the capacity to determine introspectively the choices that a partner would make – the communication

---

[22] What might be called the "legal status" of communication is nicely developed by Goffman: "Tact in regard to face-work often relies for its operation on a tacit agreement to do business through the language of hint – the language of innuendo, ambiguities, well placed pauses, carefully worded jokes, and so on. The rule regarding this unofficial kind of communication is that the sender ought not to act as if he had officially conveyed the message he has hinted at, while the recipients have the right and the obligation to act as if they have not officially received the message contained in the hint. Hinted communication, then, is deniable communication." He refers to the "unratified" participation that can occur in spoken interaction: "A person may overhear others unbeknown to them; he can overhear them when they know this to be the case and when they choose either to act as if he were not overhearing them or to signal to him informally that they know he is overhearing them." He points out that the obligation to respond, for example, to an insulting remark that one has inadvertently overheard may depend on whether the overhearing has acquired "ratification" (pp. 224, 226).

system must make it possible for him to receive a message from his partner. The partner must then formulate the proposition (choice) for the bear and communicate it to him, in order that the bear may then respond by accepting the promise (now that he sees what the "solution" is) and transmitting authoritative evidence back to his own partner.

# TWENTY-ONE

# Does the Fittest Necessarily Survive?

MARTIN SHUBIK

Source: *Readings in Game Theory and Political Behavior*, pp. 43–6, M. Shubik (ed.), New York: Doubleday, 1954.

Below is an application of a simple model from the theory of non-cooperative games to the evaluation of the strength of an individual in a situation involving three countervailing powers. This model emphasizes the difference between the maximization problems of the natural sciences and the "cross-purposes maximization" situations which are found on the political and social scene. A principle of strength through weakness is observed.

Still present in the more naïve folklore of the study of politics is the concept formulated by Spencer of the "survival of the fittest." The origins of this term may be traced to simplified interpretations or misinterpretations of Darwinism in attempts to draw social and political analogies from the work in the biological sciences.

Coexistent with the above much misinterpreted hypothesis has been Thomas Hobbes's frequently quoted description of the state of nature as the ultimate in individualism. "No arts, no letters, no society, and which is worst of all, continual fear and danger of violent death, and the life of men solitary, poor, nasty, brutal and short."

The quotes of atomistic competition are many and many analogies with "the laws of the jungle," "dog-eat-dog," have been made. Behind all of these statements there has been some type of implicit assumption that the strong fare the best. Voltaire observed that: "It is said that God is on the side of the heaviest battalions."

It is evident that if Spencer's statement is to be more than a mere tautology, some operational meaning has to be attached to the word *fittest*. This involves stating the properties of "power" and devising a method whereby we can measure the power in the possession or control of an individual. This is obviously one of the major and most difficult tasks of political science. We will avoid most of this difficulty here by restricting the discussion to a very simple model in which the concept of power is easily defined. Yet even in this almost trivially simple example certain interesting aspects of individualistic maximization against countervailing powers are illustrated.

Given a Hobbesian state of nature, given a definition of individual power, then let us ask what sort of individual is best suited to survive in a state in which every man acts for himself and by himself. In the following two examples, the former appears to support the observation of Voltaire, whereas in the latter the "heaviest battalion" seems to have lost the Deity's favor.

The two-person duel at one time helped to rid society of its excess of aristocrats as well as the occasional man of talent in fields other than dueling. We consider a duel that is fought with revolvers; each man fires one shot; they randomize to decide who shoots first. There is a quite natural manner in which we can define "power" in dueling. We may imagine that the duelists have been rated for their shooting ability. A rating of 0.8, for instance, means that eight out of ten bullets fired by a marksman will hit the target. In this example we will regard the duel as being fought for a prize which will be split among the survivors in proportion to their strength. Suppose that the duelists are rated 0.8 and 0.7, respectively; then, if they both survived the duel, one would get $\frac{8}{15}$ and the other $\frac{7}{15}$ of the prize. (This artifice of introducing a prize is not necessary; however, it will make the computation in the second example considerably easier and will not have any effect on the qualitative results.) Which of the two duelists has the best chance of survival? A simple computation indicated that the one who is the best shot has the best chance to survive. This somewhat unimpressive result is in the spirit of the quotations given at the start of this discussion. The actual chances for survival are given below:

A's chances for survival $1 - (1/2) (.7) (1 - .8) - (1/2) (.7) = .58$

B's chances for survival $1 - (1/2) (.8) (1 - .7) - (1/2) (.8) = .48$

This takes into account the equiprobabilities of each duelist's having to fire either first or last.

We now consider a somewhat more complicated duel involving three individuals. Their ratings are respectively, A, 0.8; B, 0.7; and C, 0.6. They fight a duel by each firing one shot at either of the other two. They randomize to determine the order in which they fire, and they stand equidistant from each other. There are six possible orders of firing: ABC, ACB, BAC, BCA, CAB, CBA, and they are all equiprobable. We will compute through in detail only the first case. Suppose that the order of firing is ABC. This happens to coincide with the order of their relative strengths. As A wishes to maximize his chances of surviving, he is forced to fire at B, hence B's chances of survival are: $1 - (.8) = .2$. If B is alive when it is his turn to shoot, he will fire at C because A having shot no longer represents a threat to him whereas C could still kill him with a high probability. The chances of C's surviving depend upon B's rated accuracy as a marksman and upon B's chances of being alive, hence his chances are: $1 - (.2) (.7) = .86$. If C survives and only A survives, then C will shoot at A. If both A and B are still alive at this stage, C will shoot at A because although neither of them represents a threat to him, he would prefer to see A dead because if alive he would be entitled to more of the prize than B. The chances of A's surviving depend upon C's rated accuracy and upon the chances of C's being alive when it is his turn to fire, hence his survival possibilities are: $1 - (.86) (.6) = .484$. We note that the chances of survival are 0.484 for A, 0.2 for B, and 0.86 for C. The worst shot has by far the highest probability of survival! Upon reflection, the cause of this paradox is easily seen. If all participants act completely individually without any type or form of *esprit de corps*, then the strong will be forced to eliminate the strong in order to maximize their chances to survive. Thus in a noncooperative world in which more than two battalions fought all comers, Voltaire's observation would not hold. The meek would apparently inherit Hobbes's earth. This conclusion does not depend upon the order of firing in the above example. If we work out all other possibilities and then average the results, we obtain the chances of survival for A are 0.260; for B, 0.488; for C, 0.820.

The political analogies to this type of situation are many. In elections very often the competition of two strong candidates gives the third and weaker candidate a chance to win. A weak country's political position may be made stronger by being involved in dealings with two stronger countries which are acting noncooperatively. At various times recently Iran's position could have been described as one involving strength due to weakness when caught between the interests of Great Britain and Russia.

The problem of the three-person duel was originally proposed as a mathematics problem by H. D. Larson.[1] His formulation was somewhat different from the one presented here. Essentially the same is to be found in Kinnaird, *Encyclopedia of Puzzles and Pastimes* (p. 246). Many variants and complications may be introduced in order to make the model more "realistic," however, the basic feature of the noncooperation will not be changed. We note that if the disparity in relative strengths is great enough, then it is possible to find situations in which the strongest player does actually have the best chance for survival. In a noncooperative environment it apparently does not pay to be slightly stronger than the others for this invites action against oneself.

These two duel models are examples of what are called noncooperative games. As such, these simple mathematical models lay stress upon certain essential features of human interaction. They are information patterns, individual powers, and the elements of cooperation or conflict in situations which involve cross-purpose maximizations, i.e., situations in which there is not an absolute identity of interests. In the models above, power was easily defined as shooting ability; motivation was specified as the desire both to survive and to obtain as great a share of the prize as possible; coalitions were ruled out; the information conditions were such that the power of all participants was known beforehand; the information pattern was specified inasmuch as the firing order was determined and it was assumed that each would know when his predecessor had fired. As some of these conditions are changed slightly, the quantitative results will vary. Depending upon the amount and the type of change, the qualitative results may also vary. For instance, a change in the information pattern may be brought about by considering a silent instead of a noisy duel. These types of duels have been studied in military situations using models in which the participants approach each other at given rates and may fire at any time but are unable to hear each other's shots.

We ruled out coalitions because we were primarily interested in examining models that portrayed as much individualism as possible. It is of interest to note that in any situation involving more than two parties, it is impossible to define pure opposition. There is always some element of common interest to some group if the participants are strategically interlinked. In the three-person duel discussed, it would pay the two strong ones to eliminate first the weakest participant before falling out among themselves. It is a matter of empirical research to determine whether or not in certain biological, sociological, and political situations the strong eliminate the weak or themselves first. We have noted that for three or more participants in a strategically interlinked situation there will always be a community of interests between at least two. Even when there are only two individuals involved, it is difficult to define a situation in which there is only pure opposition and hence no opportunity for cooperation. The closest approximation to such a situation can be found in games played for amusement, such as matching pennies, chess, or checkers. In

---

[1] H. D. Larson, "A Dart Game," *American Mathematical Monthly*, December 1948, pp. 640–641.

these games the winnings of one side equal precisely the losings of the other side. A game of this variety is called "zero-sum." In most political situations it is possible for both sides to gain by cooperation and to lose by individual action. A situation of this type is called "non-zero-sum." Many wars are of this nature, both the winner and the loser may be worse off than they would have been had they negotiated rather than fought. The duels could have been set up as cooperative games in which the participants negotiate to decide how to split the prize and use their rated shooting power for threat purposes rather than actually resort to fighting the duel. The present state of game theory is such that no completely satisfactory theory of the solution to cooperative games exists. Nevertheless, the methods used here serve both to clarify some of the basic concepts of individual and group action as well as to indicate results that are by no means intuitively obvious and yet appear to arise even from very simple models of situations involving the presence of more than one decision-making group with power.

TWENTY-TWO

# Shooting the Bird's Eye

ELIZABETH SEEGER

*Source*: *The Five Sons Of King Pandu: The Story of the Mahabhárata*. New York: William R. Scott, 1967, pp. 18–19.

[ . . . ] One day when their education was finished, Drona wished to test them in the use of the bow. He had an artificial bird set on the top of a tree as a target; then he called them all together and said, "Take up your bows and arrows and stand here beside me, with your arrows fixed on the bowstring, aiming at the bird. When I give the order, shoot at the bird's head. I shall give each of you a turn, my children."

He first addressed Yudhistra, since that prince was the eldest. "Behold," he said, "the bird on yonder tree."

"I see it," answered Yudhistra.

But Drona spoke again to the young prince standing bow in hand. "What else do you see, O Yudhistra? Do you see the tree, or me, or your brothers?"

"I see the tree and you, my brothers and the bird," replied the eldest son of Pandu.

And Drona was vexed with him and said, "Stand aside! It is not for you to hit the target."

The master asked the same question of all the sons of Kuru, one after another, and of Bhima and the twins and the other pupils who had come to him from afar. The answer was always the same, "I see the tree and you, my comrades and the bird." They were all reproachfully told by their teacher to stand aside.

Then Drona turned smiling to Arjuna, saying, "You must hit the target; therefore turn your eyes to it with an arrow fixed on the string." Arjuna stood aiming at the bird as the master had commanded, and Drona asked him, "Do you see the bird, the tree, and me?"

"I see only the bird," answered Arjuna, "not the tree or you."

Then Drona, well pleased, said, "If you see the bird, describe it to me."

Arjuna said, "I see only the head of the bird, not its body."

At these words Drona's hair stood on end with delight. "Shoot!" he commanded, and Arjuna instantly let fly his arrow and struck off the bird's head. The master clasped him to his heart, exclaiming, "You will never be vanquished by any foe, and you will win everlasting fame."

TWENTY-THREE

# "That's It? That's Peer Review?"

SIDNEY HARRIS

*Source*: © 2000 by Sidney Harris.

"That's it? That's peer review?"

# Introduction

Repeated games are important in economic transactions where it is hard to write enforceable contracts, but they are even more important in non-economic transactions, since writing contracts is much harder when money does not change hands. Axelrod and Hamilton apply the idea even to non-human transactions – to animals and insects whose evolutionary strategies can be modeled as if they were rationally choosing strategies in a game. Robert Barro is a macroeconomist, but his two best-known articles, on debt in an overlapping-generations model with bequests and on reputation in monetary policy, are both about repeated games. (Robert Barro, "Are Government Bonds Net Wealth?" *Journal of Political Economy* 82:1095–117 [Nov.–Dec. 1974] and Robert Barro and David Gordon, "Rules, Discretion and Reputation in a Model of Monetary Policy," *Journal of Monetary Economics* 12:101–21 [July 1983].) This newspaper piece by Barro and Stockman is about the usefulness of ruining a reputation in the political sphere. But why does past behavior give any indication of future behavior? The last of the three readings on repeated games *per se* is in an economic context, airline pricing, and takes us back to the old problem of oligopoly pricing. It is yet another reminder that there can be no single model of oligopoly, because the institutional features of different markets – the type of product and the marketing channels – matter to pricing behavior.

The notes on dissertation writing by Robert and Weil are part of the unpublished lore that makes doing doctoral work at a top department so valuable. They have kindly given permission for me to make attending Chicago less valuable by publishing their notes here so that the rest of us can enjoy the benefit of their wisdom. The lessons, of course, are valuable for research beyond dissertations too. The cartoon, "Einstein discovers that time is actually money," is relevant to discounting future payoffs. This is a profound idea. Why is the discount rate positive? Is it the price of time? Can you think of strategic situations where a player would rather receive income later rather than earlier?

TWENTY-FOUR

# The Evolution of Cooperation

ROBERT AXELROD AND WILLIAM D. HAMILTON

Source: *Science* 211 (March), 1981, 1390–6. © 1981 American Association for the Advancement of Science.

Cooperation in organisms, whether bacteria or primates, has been a difficulty for evolutionary theory since Darwin. On the assumption that interactions between pairs of individuals occur on a probabilistic basis, a model is developed based on the concept of an evolutionarily stable strategy in the context of the Prisoner's Dilemma game. Deductions from the model, and the results of a computer tournament show how cooperation based on reciprocity can get started in an asocial world, can thrive while interacting with a wide range of other strategies, and can resist invasion once fully established. Potential applications include specific aspects of territoriality, mating, and disease.

The theory of evolution is based on the struggle for life and the survival of the fittest. Yet cooperation is common between members of the same species and even between members of different species. Before about 1960, accounts of the evolutionary process largely dismissed cooperative phenomena as not requiring special attention. This position followed from a misreading of theory that assigned most adaptation to selection at the level of populations or whole species. As a result of such misreading, cooperation was always considered adaptive. Recent reviews of the evolutionary process, however, have shown no sound basis for a pervasive group-benefit view of selection; at the level of a species or a population, the processes of selection are weak. The original individualistic emphasis of Darwin's theory is more valid [1].[1]

To account for the manifest existence of cooperation and related group behavior, such as altruism and restraint in competition, evolutionary theory has recently acquired two kinds of extension. These extensions are, broadly, genetical kinship theory [2] and reciprocation theory [3].[2] Most of the recent activity, both in field work and in further developments of theory, has been on the side of kinship. Formal approaches have varied,

---

[1] For the best recent case for effective selection at group levels and for altruism based on genetic correction of non-kin interactants see D. S. Wilson, *Natural Selection of Populations and Communities* (Benjamin/Cummings, Menlo Park, Calif., 1979).

[2] For additions to the theory of biological cooperation see I. D. Chase [*Am. Nat.* 115, 827 (1980)], R. M. Fagen [*ibid.*, p. 858 (1980)], and S. A. Boorman and P. R. Levitt [*The Genetics of Altruism* (Academic Press, New York, 1980)].

but kinship theory has increasingly taken a gene's-eye view of natural selection [4]. A gene, in effect, looks beyond its mortal bearer to interests of the potentially immortal set of its replicas existing in other related individuals. If interactants are sufficiently closely related, altruism can benefit reproduction of the set, despite losses to the individual altruist. In accord with this theory's predictions, apart from the human species, almost all clear cases of altruism, and most observed cooperation, occur in contexts of high relatedness, usually between immediate family members. The evolution of the suicidal barbed sting of the honeybee worker could be taken as paradigm for this line of theory [5].

Conspicuous examples of cooperation (although almost never of ultimate self-sacrifice) also occur where relatedness is low or absent. Mutualistic symbioses offer striking examples such as these: the fungus and alga that compose a lichen; the ants and ant-acacias, where the trees house and feed the ants which, in turn, protect the trees [6]; and the fig wasps and fig tree, where wasps, which are obligate parasites of fig flowers, serve as the tree's sole means of pollination and seed set [7]. Usually the course of cooperation in such symbioses is smooth, but sometimes the partners show signs of antagonism, either spontaneous or elicited by particular treatments.[3] Although kinship may be involved, as will be discussed later, symbioses mainly illustrate the other recent extension of evolutionary theory, the theory of reciprocation.

Cooperation per se has received comparatively little attention from biologists since the pioneer account of Trivers [3]; but an associated issue, concerning restraint in conflict situations, has been developed theoretically. In this connection, a new concept, that of an evolutionarily stable strategy, has been formally developed [4, 8]. Cooperation in the more normal sense has remained clouded by certain difficulties, particularly those concerning initiation of cooperation from a previously asocial state [9] and its stable maintenance once established. A formal theory of cooperation is increasingly needed. The renewed emphasis on individualism has focused on the frequent ease of cheating in reciprocatory arrangements. This makes the stability of even mutualistic symbioses appear more questionable than under the old view of adaptation for species benefit. At the same time other cases that once appeared firmly in the domain of kinship theory now begin to reveal relatednesses of interactants that are too low for much nepotistic altruism to be expected. This applies both to cooperative breeding in birds [10] and to cooperative acts more generally in primate groups [11]. Here either the appearances of cooperation are deceptive – they are cases of part-kin altruism and part cheating – or a larger part of the behavior is attributable to stable reciprocity. Previous accounts that already invoke reciprocity, however, underemphasize the stringency of its conditions [12].

Our contribution in this area is new in three ways.

1    In a biological context, our model is novel in its probabilistic treatment of the possibility that two individuals may interact again. This allows us to shed new light on certain specific biological processes such as aging and territoriality.

2    Our analysis of the evolution of cooperation considers not just the final stability of a given strategy, but also the initial viability of a strategy in an environment

---

[3] M. Caullery, *Parasitism and Symbiosis* (Sidgwick and Jackson, London, 1952). This gives examples of antagonism in orchid-fungus and lichen symbioses. For the example of wasp-ant symbiosis, see [5].

dominated by noncooperating individuals, as well as the robustness of a strategy in a variegated environment composed of other individuals using a variety of more or less sophisticated strategies. This allows a richer understanding of the full chronology of the evolution of cooperation than has previously been possible.

3   Our applications include behavioral interaction at the microbial level. This leads us to some speculative suggestions of rationales able to account for the existence of both chronic and acute phases in many diseases, and for a certain class of chromosomal nondisjunction, exemplified by Down's syndrome.

## Strategies in the Prisoner's Dilemma

Many of the benefits sought by living things are disproportionally available to cooperating groups. While there are considerable differences in what is meant by the terms "benefits" and "sought," this statement, insofar as it is true, lays down a fundamental basis for all social life. The problem is that while an individual can benefit from mutual cooperation, each one can also do even better by exploiting the cooperative efforts of others. Over a period of time, the same individuals may interact again, allowing for complex patterns of strategic interactions. Game theory in general, and the Prisoner's Dilemma game in particular, allow a formalization of the strategic possibilities inherent in such situations.

The Prisoner's Dilemma game is an elegant embodiment of the problem of achieving mutual cooperation,[4] and therefore provides the basis for our analysis. To keep the analysis tractable, we focus on the two-player version of the game, which describes situations that involve interactions between pairs of individuals. In the Prisoner's Dilemma game, two individuals can each either cooperate or defect. The payoff to a player is in terms of the effect on its fitness (survival and fecundity). No matter what the other does, the selfish choice of defection yields a higher payoff than cooperation. But if both defect, both do worse than if both had cooperated.

Figure 1 shows the payoff matrix of the Prisoner's Dilemma. If the other player cooperates, there is a choice between cooperation which yields $R$ (the reward for mutual cooperation) or defection which yields $T$ (the temptation to defect). By assumption, $T > R$, so that it pays to defect if the other player cooperates. On the other hand, if the other player defects, there is a choice between cooperation which yields $S$ (the sucker's payoff) or defection which yields $P$ (the punishment for mutual defection). By assumption $P > S$, so it pays to defect if the other player defects. Thus, no matter what the other player does, it pays to defect. But, if both defect, both get $P$ rather than the larger value of $R$ that they both could have gotten had both cooperated. Hence the dilemma.[5]

---

[4] A. Rapoport and A. M. Chammah, *Prisoner's Dilemma* (Univ. of Michigan Press, Ann Arbor, 1965). There are many other patterns of interaction which allow gains for cooperation. See for example the model of intraspecific combat in J. Maynard Smith and G. R. Price, in [8].

[5] The condition that $R > (S + T)/2$ is also part of the definition to rule out the possibility that alternating exploitation could be better for both than mutual cooperation.

| Player A | Player B<br>C<br>Cooperation | D<br>Defection |
|---|---|---|
| C<br>Cooperation | R=3<br>Reward for<br>mutual cooperation | S=0<br><br>Sucker's payoff |
| D<br>Defection | T=5<br>Temptation to<br>defect | P=1<br>Punishment for<br>mutual defection |

**Figure 1** The Prisoner's Dilemma game. The payoff to player A is shown with illustrative numerical values. The game is defined by $T > R > P > S$ and $R > (S + T)/2$

With two individuals destined never to meet again, the only strategy that can be called a solution to the game is to defect always despite the seemingly paradoxical outcome that both do worse than they could have had they cooperated.

Apart from being the solution in game theory, defection is also the solution in biological evolution.[6] It is the outcome of inevitable evolutionary trends through mutation and natural selection: if the payoffs are in terms of fitness, and the interactions between pairs of individuals are random and not repeated, then any population with a mixture of heritable strategies evolves to a state where all individuals are defectors. Moreover, no single differing mutant strategy can do better than others when the population is using this strategy. In these respects the strategy of defection is stable.

This concept of stability is essential to the discussion of what follows and it is useful to state it more formally. A strategy is evolutionarily stable if a population of individuals using that strategy cannot be invaded by a rare mutant adopting a different strategy [8]. In the case of the Prisoner's Dilemma played only once, no strategy can invade the strategy of pure defection. This is because no other strategy can do better with the defecting individuals than the $P$ achieved by the defecting players who interact with each other. So in the single-shot Prisoner's Dilemma, to defect always is an evolutionarily stable strategy.

In many biological settings, the same two individuals may meet more than once. If an individual can recognize a previous interactant and remember some aspects of the prior outcomes, then the strategic situation becomes an iterated Prisoner's Dilemma with a much richer set of possibilities. A strategy would take the form of a decision rule which determined the probability of cooperation or defection as a function of the history of the interaction so far. But if there is a known number of interactions between a pair of individuals, to defect always is still evolutionarily stable and is still the only strategy which is. The reason is that defection on the last interaction would be optimal for both

[6] W. D. Hamilton, in *Man and Beast: Comparative Social Behavior* (Smithsonian Press, Washington, 1971), p. 57, R. M. Fagen [see n 2] shows some conditions for single encounters where defection is not the solution.

sides, and consequently so would defection on the next-to-last interaction, and so on back to the first interaction.

Our model is based on the more realistic assumption that the number of interactions is not fixed in advance. Instead, there is some probability, $w$, that after the current interaction the same two individuals will meet again. Factors that affect the magnitude of this probability of meeting again include the average lifespan, relative mobility, and health of the individuals. For any value of $w$, the strategy of unconditional defection (ALL D) is evolutionarily stable; if everyone is using this strategy, no mutant strategy can invade the population. But other strategies may be evolutionarily stable as well. In fact, when $w$ is sufficiently great, there is no single best strategy regardless of the behavior of the others in the population.[7] Just because there is no single best strategy, it does not follow that analysis is hopeless. On the contrary, we demonstrate not only the stability of a given strategy, but also its robustness and initial viability.

Before turning to the development of the theory, let us consider the range of biological reality that is encompassed by the game theoretic approach. To start with, an organism does not need a brain to employ a strategy. Bacteria, for example, have a basic capacity to play games in that (i) bacteria are highly responsive to selected aspects of their environment, especially their chemical environment; (ii) this implies that they can respond differentially to what other organisms around them are doing; (iii) these conditional strategies of behavior can certainly be inherited; and (iv) the behavior of a bacterium can affect the fitness of other organisms around it, just as the behavior of other organisms can affect the fitness of a bacterium.

While the strategies can easily include differential responsiveness to recent changes in the environment or to cumulative averages over time, in other ways their range of responsiveness is limited. Bacteria cannot "remember" or "interpret" a complex past sequence of changes, and they probably cannot distinguish alternative origins of adverse or beneficial changes. Some bacteria, for example, produce their own antibiotics, bacteriocins; those are harmless to bacteria of the producing strain, but destructive to others. A bacterium might easily have production of its own bacteriocin dependent on the perceived presence of like hostile products in its environment, but it could not aim the toxin produced toward an offending initiator. From existing evidence, so far from an individual level, discrimination seems to be by species rather even than variety. For example, a *Rhizobium* strain may occur in nodules which it causes on the roots of many species of leguminous plants, but it may fix nitrogen for the benefit of the plant in only a few of these species [13]. Thus, in many legumes the *Rhizobium* seems to be a pure parasite. In the light of theory to follow, it would be interesting to know whether these parasitized legumes are perhaps less beneficial to free living *Rhizobium* in the surrounding soil than are those in which the full symbiosis is established. But the main point of concern here is that such discrimination by a *Rhizobium* seems not to be known even at the level of varieties within a species.

---

[7] For a formal proof, see R. Axelrod, *Am. Political Sci. Rev.*, in press. For related results on the potential stability of cooperative behavior see R. D. Luce and H. Raiffa, *Games and Decisions* (Wiley, New York, 1957), p. 102; M. Taylor, *Anarchy and Cooperation* (Wiley, New York, 1976); M. Kurz, in *Economic Progress, Private Values and Public Policy*, B. Balassa and R. Nelson, Eds. (North-Holland, Amsterdam, 1977), p. 177.

As one moves up the evolutionary ladder in neural complexity, game-playing behavior becomes richer. The intelligence of primates, including humans, allows a number of relevant improvements: a more complex memory, more complex processing of information to determine the next action as a function of the interaction so far, a better estimate of the probability of future interaction with the same individual, and a better ability to distinguish between different individuals. The discrimination of others may be among the most important of abilities because it allows one to handle interactions with many individuals without having to treat them all the same, thus making possible the rewarding of cooperation from one individual and the punishing of defection from another.

The model of the iterated Prisoner's Dilemma is much less restricted than it may at first appear. Not only can it apply to interactions between two bacteria or interactions between two primates, but it can also apply to the interactions between a colony of bacteria and, say, a primate serving as a host. There is no assumption of commensurability of payoffs between the two sides. Provided that the payoffs to each side satisfy the inequalities that define the Prisoner's Dilemma (Fig. 1), the results of the analysis will be applicable.

The model does assume that the choices are made simultaneously and with discrete time intervals. For most analytic purposes, this is equivalent to a continuous interaction over time, with the time period of the model corresponding to the minimum time between a change in behavior by one side and a response by the other. And while the model treats the choices as simultaneous, it would make little difference if they were treated as sequential.[8]

Turning to the development of the theory, the evolution of cooperation can be conceptualized in terms of three separate questions:

1 *Robustness.* What type of strategy can thrive in a variegated environment composed of others using a wide variety of more or less sophisticated strategies?
2 *Stability.* Under what conditions can such a strategy, once fully established, resist invasion by mutant strategies?
3 *Initial viability.* Even if a strategy is robust and stable, how can it ever get a foothold in an environment which is predominantly noncooperative?

## Robustness

To see what type of strategy can thrive in a variegated environment of more or less sophisticated strategies, one of us (R.A.) conducted a computer tournament for the Prisoner's Dilemma. The strategies were submitted by game theorists in economics, sociology, political science, and mathematics [14]. The rules implied the payoff matrix

---

[8] In either case, cooperation on a tit-for-tat basis is evolutionarily stable if and only if $w$ is sufficiently high. In the case of sequential moves, suppose there is a fixed chance, $p$, that a given interactant of the pair will be the next one to need help. The critical value of $w$ can be shown to be the minimum of the two side's value of $A/p(A + B)$ where $A$ is the cost of giving assistance, and $B$ is the benefit of assistance when received. See also P. R. Thompson, *Soc. Sci. Info.* **19**, 341 (1980).

shown in Fig. 1 and a game length of 200 moves. The 14 entries and a totally random strategy were paired with each other in a round robin tournament. Some of the strategies were quite intricate. An example is one which on each move models the behavior of the other player as a Markov process, and then uses Bayesian inference to select what seems the best choice for the long run. However, the result of the tournament was that the highest average score was attained by the simplest of all strategies submitted: TIT FOR TAT. This strategy is simply one of cooperating on the first move and then doing whatever the other player did on the preceding move. Thus TIT FOR TAT is a strategy of cooperation based on reciprocity.

The results of the first round were then circulated and entries for a second round were solicited. This time there were 62 entries from six countries.[9] Most of the contestants were computer hobbyists, but there were also professors of evolutionary biology, physics, and computer science, as well as the five disciplines represented in the first round. TIT FOR TAT was again submitted by the winner of the first round, Professor Anatol Rapoport of the Institute for Advanced Study (Vienna). It won again. An analysis of the 3 million choices which were made in the second round identified the impressive robustness of TIT FOR TAT as dependent on three features: it was never the first to defect, it was provocable into retaliation by a defection of the other, and it was forgiving after just one act of retaliation [15].

The robustness of TIT FOR TAT was also manifest in an ecological analysis of a whole series of future tournaments. The ecological approach takes as given the varieties which are present and investigates how they do over time when interacting with each other. This analysis was based on what would happen if each of the strategies in the second round were submitted to a hypothetical next round in proportion to its success in the previous round. The process was then repeated to generate the time path of the distribution of strategies. The results showed that, as the less successful rules were displaced, TIT FOR TAT continued to do well with the rules which initially scored near the top. In the long run, TIT FOR TAT displaced all the other rules and went to fixation (24). This provides further evidence that TIT FOR TAT's cooperation based on reciprocity is a robust strategy that can thrive in a variegated environment.

## Stability

Once a strategy has gone to fixation, the question of evolutionary stability deals with whether it can resist invasion by a mutant strategy. In fact, we will now show that once TIT FOR TAT is established, it can resist invasion by any possible mutant strategy provided that the individuals who interact have a sufficiently large probability, $w$, of meeting again. The proof is described in the next two paragraphs.

As a first step in the proof we note that since TIT FOR TAT "remembers" only one move back, one C by the other player in any round is sufficient to reset the situation as it was at the beginning of the game. Likewise, one D sets the situation to what it was at the

---

[9] In the second round, the length of the games was uncertain, with an expected probability of 200 moves. This was achieved by setting the probability that a given move would not be the last at $w = .99654$. As in the first round, each pair was matched in five games (24).

second round after a D was played in the first. Since there is a fixed chance, $w$, of the interaction not ending at any given move, a strategy cannot be maximal in playing with TIT FOR TAT unless it does the same thing both at the first occurrence of a given state and at each resetting to that state. Thus, if a rule is maximal and begins with C, the second round has the same state as the first, and thus a maximal rule will continue with C and hence always cooperate with TIT FOR TAT. But such a rule will not do better than TIT FOR TAT does with another TIT FOR TAT, and hence it cannot invade. If, on the other hand, a rule begins with D, then this first D induces a switch in the state of TIT FOR TAT and there are two possibilities for continuation that could be maximal. If D follows the first D, then this being maximal at the start implies that it is everywhere maximal to follow D with D, making the strategy equivalent to ALL D. If C follows the initial D, the game is then reset as for the first move; so it must be maximal to repeat the sequence of DC indefinitely. These points show that the task of searching a seemingly infinite array of rules of behavior for one potentially capable of invading TIT FOR TAT is really easier than it seemed: if neither ALL D nor alternation of D and C can invade TIT FOR TAT, then no strategy can.

To see when these strategies can invade, we note that the probability that the $n^{\text{th}}$ interaction actually occurs is $w^{n-1}$. Therefore, the expression for the total payoff is easily found by applying the weights $1, w, w^2 \ldots$ to the payoff sequence and summing the resultant series. When TIT FOR TAT plays another TIT FOR TAT, it gets a payoff of $R$ each move for a total of $R + wR + w^2 R \ldots$, which is $R/(1 - w)$. ALL D playing with TIT FOR TAT gets $T$ on the first move and $P$ thereafter, so it cannot invade TIT FOR TAT if

$$\frac{R}{(1 - w)} \geq T + \frac{wP}{(1 - w)}$$

Similarly when alternation of D and C plays TIT FOR TAT, it gets a payoff of

$$T = wS + w^2 T + s^3 S \ldots$$
$$= \frac{(T + wS)}{(1 - w^2)}$$

Alternation of D and C thus cannot invade TIT FOR TAT if

$$\frac{R}{(1 - w)} \geq \frac{(T + wS)}{(1 - w^2)}$$

Hence, with reference to the magnitude of $w$, we find that neither of these two strategies (and hence no strategy at all) can invade TIT FOR TAT if and only if both

$$w \geq \frac{(T - R)}{(T - P)}$$

and

$$w \geq \frac{(T - R)}{(R - S)} \tag{1}$$

This demonstrates that TIT FOR TAT is evolutionarily stable if and only if the interactions between the individuals have a sufficiently large probability of continuing.

## Initial Viability

TIT FOR TAT is not the only strategy that can be evolutionarily stable. In fact, ALL D is evolutionarily stable no matter what is the probability of interaction continuing. This raises the problem of how an evolutionary trend to cooperative behavior could ever have started in the first place.

Genetic kinship theory suggests a plausible escape from the equilibrium of ALL D. Close relatedness of interactants permits true altruism – sacrifice of fitness by one individual for the benefit of another. True altruism can evolve when the conditions of cost, benefit, and relatedness yield net gains for the altruism-causing genes that are resident in the related individuals [16]. Not defecting in a single-move Prisoner's Dilemma is altruism of a kind (the individual is foregoing proceeds that might have been taken) and so can evolve if the two interactants are sufficiently related. In effect, recalculation of the payoff matrix in such a way that an individual has a part interest in the partner's gain (that is, reckoning payoffs in terms of inclusive fitness) can often eliminate the inequalities $T > R$ and $P > S$, in which case cooperation becomes unconditionally favored [17]. Thus it is possible to imagine that the benefits of cooperation in Prisoner's Dilemma-like situations can begin to be harvested by groups of closely related individuals. Obviously, as regards pairs, a parent and its offspring or a pair of siblings would be especially promising, and in fact many examples of cooperation or restraint of selfishness in such pairs are known.

Once the genes for cooperation exist, selection will promote strategies that base cooperative behavior on cues in the environment [3]. Such factors as promiscuous fatherhood [18] and events at ill-defined group margins will always lead to uncertain relatedness among potential interactants. The recognition of any improved correlates of relatedness and use of these cues to determine cooperative behavior will always permit advance in inclusive fitness [3]. When a cooperative choice has been made, one cue to relatedness is simply the fact of reciprocation of the cooperation. Thus modifiers for more selfish behavior after a negative response from the other are advantageous whenever the degree of relatedness is low or in doubt. As such, conditionality is acquired, and cooperation can spread into circumstances of less and less relatedness. Finally, when the probability of two individuals meeting each other again is sufficiently high, cooperation based on reciprocity can thrive and be evolutionarily stable in a population with no relatedness at all.

A case of cooperation that fits this scenario, at least on first evidence, has been discovered in the spawning relationships in a sea bass [19]. The fish, which are hermaphroditic, form pairs and roughly may be said to take turns at being the high investment partner (laying eggs) and low investment partner (providing sperm to fertilize eggs). Up to ten spawnings occur in a day and only a few eggs are provided each time. Pairs tend to break up if sex roles are not divided evenly. The system appears to allow the evolution of much economy in the size of testes, but Fischer [19] has suggested that the testis condition may have evolved when the species was more sparse and inclined to inbreed. Inbreeding would imply relatedness in the pairs and this initially may have transferred the system to attractance of tit-for-tat cooperation – that is, to cooperation unneedful of relatedness.

Another mechanism that can get cooperation started when virtually everyone is using ALL D is clustering. Suppose that a small group of individuals is using a strategy such as TIT FOR TAT and that a certain proportion, $p$, of the interactions of members of this cluster are with other members of the cluster. Then the average score attained by the members of the cluster in playing the TIT FOR TAT strategy is

$$p\left[\frac{R}{(1-w)}\right] + (1-p)\left[\frac{S+wP}{(1-w)}\right]$$

If the members of the cluster provide a negligible proportion of the interactions for the other individuals, then the score attained by those using ALL D is still $P/(1-w)$. When $p$ and $w$ are large enough, a cluster of TIT FOR TAT individuals can then become initially viable in an environment composed overwhelmingly of ALL D.

Clustering is often associated with kinship, and the two mechanisms can reinforce each other in promoting the initial viability of reciprocal cooperation. However, it is possible for clustering to be effective without kinship [2].

We have seen that TIT FOR TAT can intrude in a cluster on a population of ALL D, even though ALL D is evolutionarily stable. This is possible because a cluster of TIT FOR TAT's gives each member a nontrivial probability of meeting another individual who will reciprocate the cooperation. While this suggests a mechanism for the initiation of cooperation, it also raises the question about whether the reverse could happen once a strategy like TIT FOR TAT became established itself. Actually, there is an interesting asymmetry here. Let us define a nice strategy as one, such as TIT FOR TAT, which will never be the first to defect. Obviously, when two nice strategies interact, they both receive $R$ each move, which is the highest average score an individual can get when interacting with another individual using the same strategy. Therefore, if a strategy is nice and is evolutionarily stable, it cannot be intruded upon by a cluster. This is because the score achieved by the strategy that comes in a cluster is a weighted average of how it does with others of its kind and with the predominant strategy. Each of these components is less than or equal to the score achieved by the predominant, nice, evolutionarily stable strategy, and therefore the strategy arriving in a cluster cannot intrude on the nice, evolutionarily stable strategy. This means that when $w$ is large enough to make TIT FOR TAT an evolutionarily stable strategy it can resist intrusion by any cluster of any other strategy. The gear wheels of social evolution have a ratchet.

The chronological story that emerges from this analysis is the following. ALL D is the primeval state and is evolutionarily stable. This means that it can resist the invasion of any strategy that has virtually all of its interactions with ALL D. But cooperation based on reciprocity can gain a foothold through two different mechanisms. First, there can be kinship between mutant strategies, giving the genes of the mutants some stake in each other's success, thereby altering the effective payoff matrix of the interaction when viewed from the perspective of the gene rather than the individual. A second mechanism to overcome total defection is for the mutant strategies to arrive in a cluster so that they provide a nontrivial proportion of the interactions each has, even if they are so few as to provide a negligible proportion of the interactions which the ALL D individuals have. Then the tournament approach demonstrates that once a variety of strategies is present, TIT FOR TAT is an extremely robust one. It does well in a wide range of circumstances and gradually displaces all other strategies in a simulation of a great variety of more or less sophisticated decision rules. And if the probability that interaction between two individuals will continue is great enough, then TIT FOR TAT is itself evolutionarily stable. Moreover, its stability is especially secure because it can resist the intrusion of whole clusters of mutant strategies. Thus cooperation based on reciprocity can get started in a predominantly noncooperative world, can thrive in a variegated environment, and can defend itself once fully established.

## Applications

A variety of specific biological applications of our approach follows from two of the requirements for the evolution of cooperation. The basic idea is that an individual must not be able to get away with defecting without the other individuals being able to retaliate effectively.[10] The response requires that the defecting individual not be lost in an anonymous sea of others. Higher organisms avoid this problem by their well-developed ability to recognize many different individuals of their species, but lower organisms must rely on mechanisms that drastically limit the number of different individuals or colonies with which they can interact effectively. The other important requirement to make retaliation effective is that the probability, $w$, of the same two individuals' meeting again must be sufficiently high.

When an organism is not able to recognize the individual with which it had a prior interaction, a substitute mechanism is to make sure that all of one's interactions are with the same interactant. This can be done by maintaining continuous contact with the other. This method is applied in most interspecies mutualism, whether a hermit crab and his sea-anemone partner, a cicada and the varied microorganismic colonies housed in its body, or a tree and its mycorrhizal fungi.

The ability of such partners to respond specifically to defection is not known but seems possible. A host insect that carries symbionts often carries several kinds (for example, yeasts and bacteria). Differences in the roles of these are almost wholly obscure [20]. Perhaps roles are actually the same, and being host to more than one increases the security of retaliation against a particular exploitative colony. Where host and colony are not permanently paired, a method for immediate drastic retaliation is sometimes apparent instead. This is so with fig wasps. By nature of their remarkable role in pollination, female

---

[10] For economic theory on this point see G. Akerlof, *Q. J. Econ.* **84**, 488 (1970); M. R. Darby and E. Karni, *J. Law Econ.* **16**, 67 (1973); O. E. Williamson, *Markets and Hierarchies* (Free Press, New York, 1975).

fig wasps serve the fig tree as a motile aerial male gamete. Through the extreme protogyny and simultaneity in flowering, fig wasps cannot remain with a single tree. It turns out in many cases that if a fig wasp entering a young fig does not pollinate enough flowers for seeds and instead lays eggs in almost all, the tree cuts off the developing fig at an early stage. All progeny of the wasp then perish.

Another mechanism to avoid the need for recognition is to guarantee the uniqueness of the pairing of interactants by employing a fixed place of meeting. Consider, for example, cleaner mutualisms in which a small fish or a crustacean removes and eats ectoparasites from the body (or even from the inside of the mouth) of a larger fish which is its potential predator. These aquatic cleaner mutualisms occur in coastal and reef situations where animals live in fixed home ranges or territories [3]. They seem to be unknown in the free-mixing circumstances of the open sea.

Other mutualisms are also characteristic of situations where continued association is likely, and normally they involve quasi-permanent pairing of individuals or of endogamous or asexual stocks, or of individuals with such stocks [5, 21]. Conversely, conditions of free-mixing and transitory pairing conditions where recognition is impossible are much more likely to result in exploitation – parasitism, disease, and the like. Thus, whereas ant colonies participate in many symbioses and are sometimes largely dependent on them, honeybee colonies, which are much less permanent in place of abode, have no known symbionts but many parasites [22]. The small fresh-water animal *Chlorohydra viridissima* has a permanent stable association with green algae that are always naturally found in its tissues and are very difficult to remove. In this species the alga is transmitted to new generations by way of the egg. *Hydra vulgaris* and *H. attenuata* also associate with algae but do not have egg transmission. In these species it is said that "infection is preceded by enfeeblement of the animals and is accompanied by pathological symptoms indicating a definite parasitism by the plant".[11] Again, it is seen that impermanence of association tends to destabilize symbiosis.

In species with a limited ability to discriminate between other members of the same species, reciprocal cooperation can be stable with the aid of a mechanism that reduces the amount of discrimination necessary. Philopatry in general and territoriality in particular can serve this purpose. The phrase stable territories means that there are two quite different kinds of interaction: those in neighboring territories where the probability of interaction is high, and strangers whose probability of future interaction is low. In the case of male territorial birds, songs are used to allow neighbors to recognize each other. Consistent with our theory, such male territorial birds show much more aggressive reactions when the song of an unfamiliar male rather than a neighbor is reproduced nearby [23].

Reciprocal cooperation can be stable with a larger range of individuals if discrimination can cover a wide variety of others with less reliance on supplementary cues such as location. In humans this ability is well developed, and is largely based on the recognition of faces. The extent to which this function has become specialized is revealed by a brain disorder called prosopagnosia. A normal person can name someone from facial features alone, even if the features have changed substantially over the years. People with prosopagnosia are not able to make this association, but have few other neurological symptoms

---

[11] C. M. Yonge [*Nature (London)* **134**, 12 (1979)] gives other examples of invertebrates with unicellular algae.

other than a loss of some part of the visual field. The lesions responsible for prosopagnosia occur in an identifiable part of the brain: the underside of both occipital lobes, extending forward to the inner surface of the temporal lobes. This localization of cause, and specificity of effect, indicates that the recognition of individual faces has been an important enough task for a significant portion of the brain's resources to be devoted to it [24].

Just as the ability to recognize the other interactant is invaluable in extending the range of stable cooperation, the ability to monitor cues for the likelihood of continued interaction is helpful as an indication of when reciprocal cooperation is or is not stable. In particular, when the value of $w$ falls below the threshold for stability given in condition (1), it will no longer pay to reciprocate the other's cooperation. Illness in one partner leading to reduced viability would be one detectable sign of declining $w$. Both animals in a partnership would then be expected to become less cooperative. Aging of a partner would be very like disease in this respect, resulting in an incentive to defect so as to take a onetime gain when the probability of future interaction becomes small enough.

These mechanisms could operate even at the microbial level. Any symbiont that still has a transmission "horizontally" (that is, infective) as well as vertically (that is, transovarial, or more rarely through sperm, or both) would be expected to shift from mutualism to parasitism when the probability of continued interaction with the host lessened. In the more parasitic phase it could exploit the host more severely by producing more infective propagules. This phase would be expected when the host is severely injured, contracted some other wholly parasitic infection that threatened death, or when it manifested signs of age. In fact, bacteria that are normal and seemingly harmless or even beneficial in the gut can be found contributing to sepsis in the body when the gut is perforated (implying a severe wound) [25]. And normal inhabitants of the body surface (like *Candida albicans*) can become invasive and dangerous in either sick or elderly persons.

It is possible also that this argument has some bearing on the etiology of cancer, insofar as it turns out to be due to viruses potentially latent in the genome [26]. Cancers do tend to have their onset at ages when the chances of vertical transmission are rapidly declining [27]. One oncogenic virus, that of Burkitt's lymphoma, does not have vertical transmission but may have alternatives of slow or fast production of infectious propagules. The slow form appears as a chronic mononucleosis, the fast as an acute mononucleosis or as a lymphoma [28]. The point of interest is that, as some evidence suggests, lymphoma can be triggered by the host's contracting malaria. The lymphoma grows extremely fast and so can probably compete with malaria for transmission (possibly by mosquitoes) before death results. Considering other cases of simultaneous infection by two or more species of pathogen, or by two strains of the same one, our theory may have relevance more generally to whether a disease will follow a slow, joint-optimal exploitation course ("chronic" for the host) or a rapid severe exploitation ("acute" for the host). With single infection the slow course would be expected. With double infection, crash exploitation might, as dictated by implied payoff functions, begin immediately, or have onset later at an appropriate stage of senescence.[12]

Our model (with symmetry of the two parties) could also be tentatively applied to the increase with maternal age of chromosomal nondisjunction during ovum formation

---

[12] See also I. Eshel, *Theoret. Pop. Biol.* 11, 410 (1977) for a related possible implication of multiclonal infection.

(oogenesis) [29]. This effect leads to various conditions of severely handicapped offspring, Down's syndrome (caused by an extra copy of chromosome 21) being the most familiar example. It depends almost entirely on failure of the normal separation of the paired chromosomes in the mother, and this suggests the possible connection with our story. Cell divisions of oogenesis, but not usually of spermatogenesis, are characteristically unsymmetrical, with rejection (as a so-called polar body) of chromosomes that go to the unlucky pole of the cell. It seems possible that, while homologous chromosomes generally stand to gain by steadily cooperating in a diploid organism, the situation in oogenesis is a Prisoner's Dilemma: a chromosome which can be "first to defect" can get itself into the egg nucleus rather than the polar body. We may hypothesize that such an action triggers similar attempts by the homolog in subsequent meioses, and when both members of a homologous pair try it at once, an extra chromosome in the offspring could be the occasional result. The fitness of the bearers of extra chromosomes is generally extremely low, but a chromosome which lets itself be sent to the polar body makes a fitness contribution of zero. Thus $P > S$ holds. For the model to work, an incident of "defection" in one developing egg would have to be perceptible by others still waiting. That this would occur is pure speculation, as is the feasibility of self-promoting behavior by chromosomes during a gametic cell division. But the effects do not seem inconceivable: a bacterium, after all, with its single chromosome, can do complex conditional things. Given such effects, our model would explain the much greater incidence of abnormal chromosome increase in eggs (and not sperm) with parental age.

## Conclusion

Darwin's emphasis on individual advantage has been formalized in terms of game theory. This establishes conditions under which cooperation based on reciprocity can evolve.

*References*

1  G. C. WILLIAMS, *Adaptations and Natural Selection* (Princeton Univ. Press, Princeton, 1966); W. D. HAMILTON, in *Bisocial Anthropology*, R. Fox, Ed. (Malaby, London, 1975), p. 133.
2  W. D. HAMILTON, *J. Theoret. Biol.* **7**, 1 (1964).
3  R. TRIVERS, *Q. Rev. Biol.* **46**, 35 (1971).
4  R. DAWKINS, *The Selfish Gene* (Oxford Univ. Press, Oxford, 1976).
5  W. D. HAMILTON, *Annu. Rev. Ecol. Syst.* **3**, 193 (1972).
6  D. H. JANZEN, *Evolution* **20**, 249 (1966).
7  J. T. WIEBES, *Gard. Bull. (Singapore)* **29**, 207 (1976); D. H. JANZEN, *Annu. Rev. Ecol. Syst.* **10**, 31 (1979).
8  J. MAYNARD SMITH and G. R. PRICE, *Nature (London)* **246**, 15 (1973); J. MAYNARD SMITH and G. A. PARKER, *Anim. Behav.* **24**, 159 (1976); G. A. PARKER, *Nature (London)* **274**, 849 (1978).
9  J. ELSTER, *Ulysses and the Sirens* (Cambridge Univ. Press, London, 1979).
10  S. T. EMLEN, in *Behavioral Ecology: An Evolutionary Approach*, J. Krebs and N. Davies, Eds. (Blackwell, Oxford, 1978), p. 245; P. B. STACEY, *Behav. Ecol. Sociobiol,* **6**, 53 (1979).
11  A. H. HARCOURT, *Z. Tierpsychol.* **48**, 401 (1978); C. PACKER, *Anim. Behav.* **27**, 1 (1979); R. W. WRANGHAM, *Soc. Sci. Info.* **18**, 335 (1979).
12  J. D. LIGON and S. H. LIGON, *Nature (London)* **276**, 496 (1978).

13  M. ALEXANDER, *Microbial Ecology* (Wiley, New York, 1971).

14  R. AXELROD, *J. Conflict Resolution* **24**, 3 (1980).

15  R. AXELROD, *J. Conflict Resolution* **24**, 379 (1980).

16  R. A. FISHER, *The Genetical Theory of Natural Selection* (Oxford Univ. Press, Oxford, 1930); J. B. S. HALDANE, *Nature (London) New Biol.* **18**, 34 (1955); W. D. HAMILTON, *Am. Nat.* **97**, 354 (1963).

17  M. J. WADE and F. BREDEN, *Behav. Ecol. Sociobiol*, in press.

18  R. D. ALEXANDER, *Annu. Rev. Ecol. Syst.* **5**, 325 (1974).

19  E. FISCHER, *Anim. Behav.* **28**, 620 (1980); E. G. LEIGH, JR., *Proc. Natl. Acad. Sci. U.S.A.* **74**, 4542 (1977).

20  P. BUCHNER, *Endosymbiosis of Animals with Plant Microorganisms* (Interscience, New York, 1965).

21  W. D. HAMILTON, in *Diversity of Insect Faunas*, L. A. Mound and N. Waloff, Eds. (Blackwell, Oxford, 1978).

22  E. O. WILSON, *The Insect Societies* (Belknap, Cambridge, Mass., 1971); M. TREISMAN, *Anim. Behav.* **28**, 311 (1980).

23  E. O. WILSON. *Sociobiology* (Harvard Univ. Press, Cambridge, Mass., 1975), p. 273.

24  N. GESCHWIND, *Sci. Am.* **241**, (No. 3), 180 (1979).

25  D. C. SAVAGE, in *Microbial Ecology of the Gut*, R. T. J. Clarke and T. Bauchop, Eds. (Academic Press, New York, 1977), p. 300.

26  J. T. MANNING, *J. Theoret. Biol.* **55**, 397 (1975); M. J. ORLOVE, *ibid.* **65**, 605 (1977).

27  W. D. HAMILTON, *ibid.* **12**, 12 (1966).

28  W. HENLE, G. HENLE, E. T. LENETTE, *Sci. Am.* **241** (No. 1), 48 (1979).

29  C. STERN, *Principles of Human Genetics* (Freeman, San Francisco, 1973).

# TWENTY-FIVE

# This Tax Amnesty Will Work Only Once

ROBERT J. BARRO AND ALAN STOCKMAN

*Source*: *Wall Street Journal*, August 7, 1986.

Tax amnesties have become popular with state governments, and may also be enacted at the federal level. These programs generate revenues in the short run by promising a temporary period of reduced punishment for prior tax evasions. But this attraction is offset by people's expectations that new amnesties will occur later. These expectations lower the penalties that people anticipate for future tax evasions, which reduces the government's tax revenues later on. To counter these beliefs, governments often announce that the amnesty is a one-time happening – in fact, they typically couple the amnesty with a promise of increased enforcement and penalties for future offenses. But why would anyone believe these announcements? After all, if an amnesty generated a lot of revenue once and was therefore attractive to politicians, why would it not prove to be attractive again in the future? Then it is reasonable for people to believe that tax amnesties will recur from time to time, and hence that the penalties for evading taxes will be less than they used to be. This means that amnesties would generate a lot of revenue when they were in effect – at which times they would be applauded as successes by politicians and some of the media – but would lower tax collections at other times (and probably reduce the take overall). But since it would be hard to prove that the reductions in revenues had something to do with amnesties, the popularity of the program might remain intact.

The general problem is a familiar one to economists and, in fact, fills a whole literature (referred to as time-inconsistency problems of government policy). It comes up, for example, with patents. It is appealing to abolish all existing patents in order to increase competition, except that the expectation of future abolitions deters people from inventing things. Similarly, it looks attractive today to tax old investments (or old oil) at higher rates than new ones, except that people are smart enough to figure out that new things eventually become old. As another example, it may look great to default on old public debts (perhaps through surprise inflation), as long as potential debt-holders do not realize that the government's new obligations will later be old ones.

Clearly a tax-amnesty program will be most successful if the government can somehow convince people that it would never effect another amnesty in the future. Since simple promises would carry no weight, we suggest the following plan. First, announce that a tax amnesty will be in effect for the next year. Then, after the amnesty ends, the government should announce that it was only kidding. All those who came forward with past tax offenses will be punished as if the amnesty had not existed. This proposal has the following advantages: First, it collects more revenue in the short run than a usual amnesty because the government gets more fines from those who came forward. Second, it avoids the moral dilemma of allowing criminals to escape scot-free. Third, it has no adverse consequences for future tax collections because people have no reason to think that a future amnesty would be enacted. In fact – as is desirable here – the government would have no way ever to convince people that a future amnesty was for real.

Now some people may object that the failure to follow through on the amnesty is dishonorable. But that is backward. It is the amnesty itself that proposes to ignore the rules for awhile. Reneging on the amnesty is merely a reconfirmation that the government would stick to its own rules. Thus, by reneging, the government encourages people to take rules seriously, whereas by following through, the government might make people doubt all sorts of rules.

The only problem with our plan (which surely can be applied to crimes more serious than tax evasion) is that, in phase I, the tax cheaters must be unaware that phase II entails reneging on the amnesty. This probably would have worked out better if we had not published our plan in *The Wall Street Journal*.

# TWENTY-SIX

# Fare Warning: How Airlines Trade Price Plans

Asra Q. Nomani

*Source*: *Wall Street Journal*, October 9, 1990.

A short-term fare cut suddenly appears in an airline industry computer network. To the traveler, the lower price looks like a lucky break. But is the change actually a secret message to rival airlines?

Carriers publicly deny discussing their price intentions. Last week, however, one of the industry's most respected pricing executives testified that airlines do communicate through a computer network, conducting back-and-forth exchanges regarding fares. In an otherwise obscure federal court case in Minneapolis, Steven B. Elkins, senior director of marketing systems development for NWA Inc.'s Northwest Airlines, gave an inside account of how airlines sometimes send messages to each other to fend off fare cuts in their most valuable markets, giving an example of an episode involving Northwest and Continental Airlines. Northwest viewed fare wars as an "atomic bomb," and Mr. Elkins said the airline followed a "golden rule" to try to head them off. Although Mr. Elkins didn't acknowledge any wrongdoing by Northwest, his testimony is sure to stir further controversy over the way airlines set fares.

The alleged practice of "signaling" is at the heart of the debate over airline pricing. Signals are said to be included in the thousands of fare changes submitted daily to a computer network run by Airline Tariff Publishing Co., a Washington clearinghouse. Critics express concern that these signals, which take various forms, may amount to price fixing by airlines. The Justice Department is examining this in connection with several investigations into possible price fixing by carriers and possible efforts by airlines to create monopolies in certain markets.

Mr. Elkins's testimony came during cross-examination by an attorney for International Travel Arrangers, which sued Northwest in 1986. The wholesale tour firm's suit charges that the carrier conspired to restrain trade and to monopolize the Minneapolis-St. Paul airport, where Northwest controls 80 percent of the market. Northwest declined to comment for this article, citing the pending suit. During his testimony, Mr. Elkins cited an example in which Northwest lowered fares on night flights that were flying with empty seats in a number of routes from Minneapolis and Upper Midwest cities to various West Coast cities. He said Continental swiftly responded by cutting prices in important Northwest markets. Mr. Elkins said Continental reduced all of its Minneapolis fares and some

Upper Midwest prices to Northwest's night fare levels. But the Continental fares were slated to expire one or two days after they were introduced, he said. "And we felt that what they were doing was trying to send us a message that they didn't want us setting reduced night coach fares in those markets," he testified. "We didn't think it particularly appropriate for Continental to be telling us that we shouldn't be offering reduced fares to people in Minneapolis and the Upper Midwest, and so we essentially tried to tell them to knock it off and leave us alone." To do that, he said Northwest then sent its own message. It filed into the Airline Tariff Publishing network new cheap fares from Houston to the West Coast, again with short expiration dates. Houston is a critical base for Continental, a unit of Continental Airlines Holdings Inc.

Mr. Elkins denied that Northwest was trying to deter competition. He said Northwest lowered the Houston fares "so that [Continental] would stop trying to undermine our attempt to compete by offering lower fares on specific flights." He said the short lifespan of Continental's fares "told us that they weren't serious about wanting to sell those fares.... We told them that we didn't think that their signal was appropriate."

Such back-and-forth exchanges by airlines are viewed as normal competitive activity by some economists and antitrust attorneys. And consumers often temporarily benefit from the lower fares that result. Still, the issue is controversial. Critics of the practice believe that, eventually, consumers pay higher prices because airlines end up using such tactics to negotiate air fares and stifle competition. They charge that the only difference between this and traditional anti-competitive behavior is that the negotiating no longer takes place in smoke-filled rooms. The most controversial aspect of this is when carriers slash fares to "discipline" each other – and particularly when large carriers do it in an effort to stop smaller carriers from offering discounts.

Mr. Elkins's testimony, which was interrupted and scheduled to continue Nov. 13, is likely to add fuel to the debate because he is considered one of the leading experts in airline yield management, the business of pricing tickets to get as much revenue as possible. His 14-year career has included stints in the pricing departments of Trans World Airlines, Continental, Western Airlines and Republic Airlines. Mr. Elkins testified that Northwest preferred not to lower fares in the Chicago market, dominated by UAL Corp.'s United and AMR Corp.'s American, because those rivals were sure to retaliate with cheap prices in Minneapolis, with "devastating" consequences. He said this is essentially why Northwest lived by the golden rule. The phrase appeared in an internal pricing memo he wrote in 1986 that surfaced during the trial. The memo and a 1988 deposition were submitted as evidence but neither is yet public, a court official said. Mr. Elkin's memo advises Northwest pricing analysts: "We Will Live by the Golden Rule!" In his testimony, he explained that "the golden rule in that context was that I did not want my pricing analyst initiating actions in another carrier's market like Chicago for fear of what that other carrier might do to retaliate." When asked in court if the golden rule was an attempt to shield Northwest from having to match fare cuts by rivals in Minneapolis or its other hubs, Mr. Elkins responded, "Yeah." Mr. Elkins's memo also said this was motivated, in part, by an effort to avert the fare wars that have hurt industry profits in the past. At one point in his memo, he refers to pricing as an "atomic bomb" potentially "so dangerous that none of us can permit our competitors to wield it unchallenged."

In his view, the most frequent cause of these battles is when one carrier tries to invade a hub dominated by another carrier. Unable to offer as much direct service, the invading carrier tries to compete by offering discount prices on connecting flights through its own hub. In his memo, he advised his pricing analysts not to "initiate such beggar thy neighbor pricing in other carriers' nonstop markets without provocation. Such pricing initiatives are the number one cause of fare wars and I am determined that Northwest will not be blamed for them this winter."

Mr. Elkins also addressed the use of fare expiration dates as signals in his memo. Should a competitor set a fare to run through December, for instance, a matching fare might be set – but to expire in October. Fares that a carrier doesn't want to offer "should almost always have an expiration date on them in the hopes the competition will eventually wake up and match," he wrote. In parentheses, he added: "There are ways to get their attention."

Justice Department officials appear interested in just those techniques. In one civil investigative demand, issued in June to the airlines, they requested information about how Airline Tariff Publishing can be used to influence rivals' fare changes. Industry experts privately say that virtually every airline signals others electronically. After outlining his policies on pricing, Mr. Elkins closed his memo with this: "I am confident that you will find from your own experience that these are universal truths that are equally applicable to Northwest, Republic, Western, Continental, TWA or any other domestic airline."

# TWENTY-SEVEN

# Starting Research Early

HARRY V. ROBERTS AND ROMAN L. WEIL

*Source*: Unpublished notes, University of Chicago Graduate School of Business, August 14, 1970.

After entrance in the School, doctoral students typically take courses and general examinations over a period of three years or more. When the last exam hurdle has been leaped, they turn to research for the first time. An acceptable research topic seldom appears quickly, and many students find that time and money have run out before they have more than a vague notion of the research they want to do or about how to do it. The full-time job they flee to proves to be more demanding than they thought; the dissertation languishes. It turns out to be very hard to do research without the close contact with faculty supervisors that is possible when the student is still in residence. An occasional ten-minute conversation every few days is much more helpful than a hectic visit once a year. Hence, many students don't finish at all; others finish only after years of spasmodic effort and oppressive anxiety.

The trouble is that the student uses his time in furthering his already high proficiency in taking courses and exams, but failed to learn very much about what research is or how to do it.

In general, students ought to regard courses as only one part of the training for the goal of research. How to do research must be learned in large part from experience, much as learning to ride a bicycle. Imagine trying to ride a bicycle with no other preparation than years of courses in the theory of cycling; you would have a set of hints to work from, but you still have to climb on and probably fall down a few times before you become proficient. You can learn by yourself but an instructor makes the learning easier and less painful.

The time to start research is as early in your graduate study as possible – now, for instance. Our purpose in preparing this document is to give you some hints on how to do this.

Our views on research versus courses and exams are not held by all nor even necessarily by a majority of the faculty. Some faculty members place a higher priority than we do on formal classwork. But we believe that our position is sufficiently well supported by experience and logic to be worthy of your serious consideration.

## Why start research early?

Courses are only one form of preparation for the goal of research, and you are likely to be judged fundamentally on your achievement of the goal. Evidence suggests that the discerning part of the academic marketplace pays more attention to the quality of your predoctoral and doctoral research than to your grades and courses. When we interview a faculty prospect here, we seldom ask him about what courses he took or what grades he received, although we may ask him about the things that interested him most or the courses he is not interested in teaching. We always ask what research he has done and what he plans to do. By the time his promotion decision comes up, his performance in courses during graduate study is no longer even a part of his record.

The frame of mind with which you approach courses and exams has been with you for 16 years or so of formal schooling. During that time you have become wary about making mistakes or saying foolish things, because these tend to lower your grade. In research, by contrast, you need a certain brashness and willingness to say and do things, even though you know that a certain fraction of the things you say and do will turn out in retrospect to have been foolish. You and your teachers and fellow students will catch and correct, it is hoped, most of your errors before they are widely disseminated, but the only sure way of prevention is to abstain from doing research.

## How to start

It's tempting to give an almost absolute priority to courses and general exams during the first two years of doctoral study. Everyone tends to respond to explicit, fixed, short deadlines and to put off the others. In particular, programmed work – reading assignments, problem sets – tends to push aside unprogrammed work – search for a problem, problem definition, general reflection.

But remember that the number of hours per day that you can spend on effective, concentrated study is limited. There's plenty of time left over for getting started on your research.

A pervasive illusion is that you must be fully tooled up for all contingencies before you begin your research. The fact is that you never will feel that you know enough mathematics, economics, statistics, accounting, or whatever to do justice to a research project. You will always find yourself thinking, "Another course in multivariate methods [fill in another title at will, if you wish] and I'll be able to crack the topic wide open." A better strategy – in fact, almost the only feasible strategy – is to define your problem, draw on what you already know, and try to learn a little about other tools that appear promising for your particular problem. The tools that may turn out to have been most valuable may not have even been taught in the courses that were available to you.

## Hints on choosing a topic

Do not think of your predoctoral and doctoral research as your life's supreme effort. (Only a handful of Nobel prizes have ever been awarded on the basis of a dissertation; offhand we can only think of two, and these examples are over 50 years old.) With rare exceptions, the dissertation occupies this position only for those who gave up further research because of the trauma of the dissertation. There is no need to be afraid to tackle big or ambitious topics. Simply be prepared to do only manageable parts of such a topic for your dissertation. The highest tribute to a dissertation is likely to be given by the further work it leads to, by the author and others. Your "suggestions for further research" should not be an empty formality.

Try to emphasize subject matter over technique. Don't emulate the man who has just mastered linear programming (or whatever) and is looking around for a problem to solve with it. Try to find tools that will fit the problem rather than to distort or invent a problem in order to demonstrate the tool.

Resign yourself to the fact that luck and chance play a role in research as in everything else. If you are lucky, you may find a natural topic that will virtually develop itself, receive acclaim, and lead to further fruitful research after the completion of your dissertation. But you may not be so lucky; you may have to settle for something more mundane and frustrating. If after a reasonable search for a topic, you have something solid but not spectacular, don't procrastinate until the ideal topic comes along. You may be luckier on your next research project. Don't be deterred by dogmatic views of research that picture the process as a verification of an hypothesis or else a bust. Good research can be useful and meaningful even if it didn't come out with the results you were hoping for. In statistical lingo the real question is, "What is the expected value of sample information from a proposed study?" (See G. William Walster and T. Anne Cleary, "A Proposal for a New Editorial Policy in the Social Sciences," *The American Statistician*, 24, 2, 1970, 16–18.)

For most people theoretical research is to empirical research as poetry is to prose, namely, much more difficult to carry off successfully. Moreover, in most areas of inquiry the easiest theoretical problems have often been solved. Theoretical research can be superb, but you are more likely to finish your dissertation if you choose an empirical question to answer, except possibly in management science, where a "new algorithm for X" is likely to be useful yet within the ability of many doctoral students.

Be sensitive to currently promising types of research. Current hot topics include cost/benefit and cost/effectiveness studies. But if you are really convinced you have a novel investigation of merit, and can convince at least three faculty members of it, the gamble may be worth taking.

### Hints on initial search

Expose yourself to lots of research: workshops, journals, preprints, etc. But don't feel that you have to master each such paper or presentation with the thoroughness that you would give to a section of a course upon which you would be examined. Browse, question, discuss! Occasionally you should try to delve deeply into a paper, and you should force yourself to do so from time to time. One financially rewarding way to give yourself an incentive to do this is to work for one of the many abstracting services, such as Executive Sciences Institute of Whippany, New Jersey, which pay a nominal fee for two or three page abstracts of articles from the professional literature. (See Weil for more information.) If you sign up to do abstracting in areas of interest to you, you will find the deadlines just as oppressive (and therefore compelling) as those for courses. More about deadlines follows.

Another possibility for intensive work on a paper might be worked out with faculty members who frequently referee manuscripts. Your willingness to serve as a supplementary referee might lead to interesting experiences and give you less awe about academic standards.

But the best object of all for thorough study is a paper that is closely related to your own research project, and this is still another reason for trying to latch onto such a topic as early as possible.

Talk to faculty members about tentative ideas; ask them for suggestions about others. Some faculty members are especially receptive to this kind of discussion; pester them. Some are even happy to suggest good topics that they do not expect to find time to pursue directly themselves.

Talk to your fellow students. You have much to learn from them. (Allen Wallis claims that he learned more from his fellow students than from the faculty, although in candor we must report that his fellow students included Milton Friedman, George Stigler, and Paul Samuelson.)

Insofar as you have free course choice, emphasize courses that require research papers. You may have to do a little informal research to find out just which ones these are.

### The mechanics of research

Write down your tentative ideas and keep revising them as they develop. Keep a journal or at least a file. Until you have written down an idea clearly, you probably have not understood it clearly or seen its full implications. Most of the students we have talked with have not learned this simple truth unless they have actually tried the suggestion. Moreover, by writing something down, you tend to overcome inhibitions about writing – related to the above-discussed fear of making errors – that may delay your start on serious research. Finally, many faculty members can help you more effectively if they can refer to a short written statement of your ideas and work, even though the statement be very tentative.

Set deadlines and stick to them. If you set and stick to a reasonable set of deadlines, or even if you fail to meet some of them by a few days, your tendency to procrastinate will be largely overcome. Moreover, the habit of setting deadlines helps you avoid the multiple and impossible network of commitments that are so common in the academic world.

## Dissertations with Fewer Tears

### Some unofficial tips for doctoral candidates in the School of Business [by] Harry Roberts

By casual empiricism over the last few years I have arrived at a few maxims that seem worth recording in the hopes of helping doctoral candidates to produce better dissertations more efficiently and quickly.

1. *A dissertation should resemble a good journal article rather than an encyclopedia.* Twenty-five to seventy-five double-spaced pages, supplemented by technical appendices if appropriate, will usually do the job. At most, one year's full-time work rather than a half-lifetime of procrastination should suffice. Quality counts.

Write up your study clearly and honestly, with necessary supporting data. "Survey the literature" insofar as it contains essential background, but keep the survey brief. Present a well-chosen bibliography rather than a long discourse of your own.

2. *Do not wait until all other requirements have been discharged before beginning to think seriously of your dissertation topic.*

3. *In seeking dissertation topics, hound the faculty as much as possible.* Once you get a few ideas, try them out on faculty members who might be interested. Don't expect to be spoon fed but don't feel that the whole burden rests on you alone. Most faculty members have pet ideas for research that they haven't had time to try out, and all will try to be helpful in reacting to your ideas. They also can frequently suggest journals and unpublished work that may give hints. Acquire the journal-reading habit early. Remember that almost every study concludes with "suggestions for further research." Some of these may be worth following up.

Frequent, short discussions spaced over a period of time are most likely to produce results.

4. *Seek an empirical study rather than a theoretical study, unless you are very confident of your theoretical competence and creativity.*

5. *An empirical study can focus on hypotheses to be tested, but most likely it won't.* In fields with a highly developed theoretical structure – especially the natural sciences – it is reasonable to expect that most empirical studies will have at least some sharp hypotheses to be tested. This is not true for many areas of business interest, and attempts to force research into this mould are both deceitful and stultifying. "Hypotheses" are likely to be no more than hunches as to where to look for sharper hypotheses, in which case the study might be described as an intelligent fishing trip. Descriptive research is not necessarily inappropriate nor useless: there is room, for example, even for case studies. Empirical work that reveals something worthwhile about the efficiency of measurement techniques is appropriate, either as a major or subsidiary purpose.

Even if you have an hypothesis to test, don't forget to look for the unexpected.

Don't overlook the possibility of special analysis of data collected for some other purpose.

6. *Get statistical help in the design phase of your study, and as often as necessary thereafter.* Few candidates will have enough theoretical and practical training in statistics to dispense with this step. Consulting with all doctoral candidates who seek help is a standing assignment of Harry Roberts.

7. *When you have tentatively decided on a topic, tell the director which faculty people you have found to be most interested in your topic.* He can then consider this information in forming your committee.

8. *When your topic is approved, impose a schedule, with iron deadlines, upon yourself.* And stick to it. It's better to go (relatively) hungry during a few months of full-time work than to try to fit the project into your spare moments over the next decade. In particular, don't think that dissertation-writing will harmonize with a teaching job. If you must do your

work part-time, keep in touch with your committee. Don't simply send them a completed draft after years of silence.

If you must leave the University before you finish your dissertation, be sure that you have faculty approval for the details of your study, insofar as they can be foreseen.

9. *Modify your topic as progress dictates, but do it after discussion with your committee.* Most topics – even approved ones – are too ambitious and need to be trimmed down. Often unexpected opportunities are discovered. If you wish to modify your proposal, discuss your ideas with your committee. Sometimes the original topic turns out to be totally unsuitable for some reason. Don't be afraid to face up to this and make a change.

10. *Try to pick a topic that you like, but don't be discouraged if you eventually find yourself hating it.* This happens to almost everyone, but it's worst for the part-timers (see 8, above). The feeling usually passes if you keep going.

11. *Send a copy of your draft to each member of your committee, and invite him [or her] to scribble the margins black, if he has time.*

12. *In preparing for your oral exam, try to think of important ramifications of your study so that you won't be totally surprised if someone on the examining committee brings one up.*

13. *In your oral exam, don't apologize and don't bluff.*

14. *Suggestions for further reading;*

- *Essays in Positive Economics*, Milton Friedman, Chap. 1.
- *Statistics: A New Approach*, Wallis and Roberts, Chaps. 1–6.
- *Say it with Figures*, Hans Zeisel, (Fourth Edition, 1957).

## Dissertations with Fewer Tears: II

### *How to write by Harry Roberts*

Many years ago Jim Lorie used to deliver a five-minute pep talk on writing style. Unlike most talks it often had an immediate and drastic effect: incoherent students became coherent virtually overnight. I tried delivering the lecture and found that it worked for me, too. Over the years I have added some embellishments learned from Allen Wallis and Jimmie Savage. In the hope that two hours' work now may save me many five-minute lectures in the future, I have tried to set all this down for the benefit of incoherent doctoral students and others.

I begin with an example of good expository writing:

This summer I raised a black swallowtail butterfly. It all started when we found a little caterpillar. We found it on a carrot top so I fed it carrot tops. Four days later it shed its skin and became a larger striped caterpillar. I kept on feeding it fresh carrot tops each day. It grew bigger and bigger. Two weeks later it stopped eating and got smaller. Then it spun a tread and hung itself on a stem. The next day it shed its skin and turned into a chrysalis, still attached to the carrot stem. Eight days later when we came to breakfast we found instead of a chrysalis a female black swallowtail butterfly.[1]

The author of this passage had a great advantage over most who will read this: he was only eight years old. His writing style, I confidently predict, will steadily deteriorate as his schooling progresses. Whether by design or not, our educational system encourages, develops and rewards poor writing.

Why is this good writing? It employs all the simple Lorie rules. The sentences are short, simple, declarative sentences. Each sentence gets over a point. The point of one sentence leads to the point of the next sentence. There are no useless words. There are no vague, abstract words and only one "big" word, "chrysalis." ("The pupa state of certain insects, especially of butterflies, from which the perfect insect emerges.") The big word is not there for show: it is the *right* word. The result is a clear, vivid, and concise exposition.

An acceptable prose style requires nothing more than application of these simple rules. Any intelligent person can write acceptable exposition once he understands them. Good creative writing requires genius. A distinctive style of expository writing requires practice and some talent. Acceptable exposition demands only intelligence and determination, and this will do for doctoral dissertations.

The danger for most of us is saturation with academic jargon and double-talk. Jargon is insidious, for it soon robs us of our ability to use our intelligence. We think we are saying something and we are not, or at best we are saying something that we do not intend. Words displace thought, and the weight of words makes it hard for the reader to see that no, or little, thought is present. I once saw Lorie reduce a four-page dissertation proposal to the single sentence: "Sales response depends on sales effort."

You will find it helpful to study carefully academic writing of good style. Pick up anything written by Henry Simons, Dennis H. Robertson, or Paul Halmos, and study a haphazardly chosen paragraph. (My friends Lorie, Wallis, and Savage, mentioned in the first paragraph, will do just as well.) These men are real stylists and you – or I – will never touch them, but we can learn much from them. They write as well as John Erickson, and about more difficult things.

For contrast, pick haphazardly chosen paragraphs from academic journals, especially in psychology. Try putting them in English to see what they really say: boil them down, cut out the repetition, replace the jargon and clichés with plain language, straighten out the logical structure. Then pick up something that you yourself have written and do the same thing. Whenever you write anything in the future, keep revising it in just this way until you are satisfied or exhausted.

You must care about the kinds of words and sentences you write. You must realize that you can learn to write. After that it takes only hard work.

The next lesson concerns logical structure for a longer piece of work, like a proposal or a dissertation. Here the job is to fit paragraphs into a larger structure. An outline is helpful, whether you write it down or keep it in your head. Whether or not you use an outline, however, your paragraphs should effectively create one as you go. You should ask yourself: What does this paragraph add? How does it fit in? What does it lead to? You

---

[1] John Erickson, *Junior Natural History* (Vol. 24, 1959), p. 19.

should fight the easy acceptance of the first organization of ideas that you set down on paper.

I find the advice of this last paragraph much harder to execute than that of the previous ones, and I do not hold out hope of overnight improvement here. Again, however, I have faith that determination and intelligence will help, once the need is seen.

# TWENTY-EIGHT

# Einstein Discovers that Time is Actually Money

GARY LARSON

Einstein Discovers that Time is Actually Money.

# PART SIX

# Dynamic Games with Incomplete Information

# Introduction

The discovery of how incomplete information could be incorporated into games resulted in a rush of important articles in the early 1980s. The "Gang of Four" was made up of David Kreps, Paul Milgrom, John Roberts, and Robert Wilson, who co-authored the included 1982 paper. All were prominent in the field, and had a very good year in 1982. The same issue of the *Journal of Economic Theory* which contained the article on the repeated prisoner's dilemma also included two papers showing how the idea could be applied to well-known problems in industrial organization: David Kreps and Robert Wilson, "Reputation and Imperfect Information," *Journal of Economic Theory* 27: 253–79 (August 1982); and Paul Milgrom and John Roberts, "Predation, Reputation, and Entry Deterrence," *Journal of Economic Theory* 27: 280–312 (August 1982). Together, the group published four other important papers in the same year, David Kreps and Robert Wilson, "Sequential Equilibria," *Econometrica* 50: 863–94 (July 1982); Paul Milgrom and Robert Weber, "A Theory of Auctions and Competitive Bidding," *Econometrica* 50: 1089–122 (September 1982); Paul Milgrom and John Roberts, "Limit Pricing and Entry under Incomplete Information: An Equilibrium Analysis," *Econometrica* 50: 443–59 (March 1982); and Paul Milgrom and Nancy Stokey, "Information, Trade and Common Knowledge," *Journal of Economic Theory* 26: 17–27 (February 1982). Be on the lookout for theoretical breakthroughs: a new tool makes for a rush of new applications, and such moments are not common.

One of the puzzling phenomenon of games of incomplete information that was discovered around that time, but which is still not understood in a fully satisfactory way is "cheap talk," costless, nonbinding, statements that nonetheless can affect the equilibrium. Joseph Farrell's article lays out some of what can happen with cheap talk in a simple model of natural monopoly.

The excerpt from Nicholas Pileggi's *Wise Guy* (later made into the 1990 Scorsese/De Niro movie *Goodfellas*) is about asymmetric information towards the end of a repeated game. The Mafia and other formalized criminal gangs rely heavily on repeated interactions, but the threat of violent termination of the relationship always hangs in the air. In this excerpt, the narrator of this true-crime book has been caught trading in heroin by the police, and the evidence against him is so overwhelming that he will go to prison for many years unless he enters the Witness Protection Program and testifies against his Mafia associates. He intends to testify and disappear, but first he wants to collect some heroin and some debts. His associates see him released, and wonder whether to kill him. The rest of the book is equally gripping and contains many other insights into illegal business practices, as does Pileggi's other book, *Casino: Love and Honor in Las Vegas*, New York: Simon & Schuster (1995), also made into a movie by Scorcese and De Niro, in 1995.

The cartoon, "Say, I think I see where we went off...," is for comic relief after you pore over the Gang of Four paper. That paper is short, but dense, which makes it good material for the exercise of really trying to understand an intricate game theory proof. Usually even in my Ph.D. classes I do not go over difficult proofs, but I have used this one on occasion just to show an example of how to work through them. Do remember the lesson of the cartoon in long proofs, though. If the author of the proof is working efficiently, any flaw in it is equally likely to be found in the arithmetic as in the differential topology. That is because he should devote more effort to the hard parts, so that the marginal return to error checking is the same for the easy parts as the hard parts. If people do not understand this, though, then mistakes in the easy parts are more embarrassing, which would alter the efficient allocation of effort.

# TWENTY-NINE

# Rational Cooperation in the Finitely Repeated Prisoners' Dilemma

DAVID M. KREPS, PAUL MILGROM, JOHN ROBERTS, AND ROBERT WILSON

Source: *Journal of Economic Theory* 27, 1982, pp. 245–52. © 1982 Academic Press. Reprinted by permission of the publisher.

A common observation in experiments involving finite repetition of the prisoners' dilemma is that players do not always play the single-period dominant strategies ("finking"), but instead achieve some measure of cooperation. Yet finking at each stage is the only Nash equilibrium in the finitely repeated game. We show here how incomplete information about one or both players' options, motivation or behavior can explain the observed cooperation. Specifically, we provide a bound on the number of rounds at which Fink may be played, when one player may possibly be committed to a "Tit-for-Tat" strategy. *Journal of Economic Literature* Classification Numbers: 026, 213.

The purpose of this note is to demonstrate how reputation effects due to informational asymmetries can generate cooperative behavior in finitely repeated versions of the classic prisoners' dilemma. The methods employed are those developed in our work on the chain-store paradox (Kreps and Wilson [2], Milgrom and Roberts [4]). We refer the reader to those papers for motivation, formal definitions, and interpretation.

The basic game that we consider consists of $N$ repetitions of the following two person, bimatrix, stage game:

| | COL | |
|---|---|---|
| *ROW* | Fink | Cooperate |
| Fink | 0, 0 | *a, b* |
| Cooperate | *b, a* | 1, 1 |

We require $a > 1$, $b < 0$, and $a + b < 2$.[1] At each stage, each of the two players, ROW and COL, recalls his previous actions and is informed about those of his opponent. The

---

[1] If $a + b > 2$, then the strategy of both cooperating at each stage is Pareto-dominated by alternating between fink–cooperate and cooperate–fink. Much of our analysis can be adapted to handle this case.

players move simultaneously at each stage. Payoffs in the overall game are the (undiscounted) sums of the stage payoffs.

This game has a unique Nash equilibrium path, which involves each player choosing to fink at every stage. The logic is similar to Selten's backwards induction in the chain-store game (although the argument there shows the uniqueness of the perfect equilibrium). In the final stage (which we call stage 1), finking strongly dominates cooperating, and so must ensue. Then, in the penultimate stage, finking does better than cooperating in terms of the current stage, while the choice at this stage cannot affect the outcome in stage 1. Thus finking will again be adopted by both players. And so on, for any finite $N$.[2] This outcome is clearly and dramatically inefficient.

This uniqueness result is disturbing in light of experiments with this game, of which there have been a very large number. (See Axelrod [1] and Smale [5] for references.) A common pattern in these experiments is that, at least for some time, both players cooperate and, in the process, end up with payoffs that are strictly greater than they would obtain under equilibrium play. The issue then is whether this puzzle can be resolved in the context of rational, self-interested behavior. The approach we adopt is to admit a "small amount" of the "right kind" of incomplete information.

In fact, we are able to show that certain kinds of informational asymmetries *must* yield a significant measure of cooperation in equilibrium, and that other plausible asymmetries may produce cooperation as well. Throughout, the equilibrium concept is that of sequential equilibrium (Kreps and Wilson [3]). Sequential equilibrium in a game of incomplete information requires that the action taken by any player at any point in the game tree must be part of an optimal strategy from that point forward, given his beliefs about the evolution of the game to this point (which must, to the extent possible, be consistent with Bayesian updating on the hypothesis that the equilibrium strategies have been used to date) and given that future play will be governed by the equilibrium strategies. The various models we use parallel those in [2, 4]. Each involves some element of uncertainty in the mind of (at least) one player about the other, and they can all be viewed in terms of a lack of common knowledge (between ROW and COL) that both are rational players playing precisely the game specified above. The possibilities for more detailed analysis of this model and its application in economic, political, and military contexts appear to be very rich. Various combinations of the authors hope to report on such work in the future.

## Model 1: ROW Might Play Tit-for-Tat

The first approach we consider supposes that, when the game begins, one of the players (say COL) is not absolutely certain that the other (ROW) will play "rationally" according to the payoffs specified above. Specifically, COL assigns probability $1 - \delta$ to the possibility of a "rational" opponent, and he allows a (very small) chance, $\delta$, that ROW has

---

[2] Note the sharp contrast with the infinitely repeated case, where any average payoff vector in the intersection of the positive orthant and the convex hull of the four possible stage payoff vectors can be achieved through a perfect equilibrium. Note also that in the finitely repeated case, Nash equilibrium behavior *off* the equilibrium path may involve some cooperation. But finking is required *everywhere* in any perfect equilibrium.

available only the Tit-for-Tat strategy.[3] The Tit-for-Tat strategy requires the player using it to begin by cooperating and then to cooperate at stage $n - 1$ if and only if his opponent cooperated at the preceding stage, $n$. It is worth noting that this strikingly simple and quite natural strategy emerged as the winner in Axelrod's prisoners' dilemma tournament [1].

To present a sequential equilibrium in full detail for this game is difficult. There is no question that such equilibria exist: See Kreps and Wilson [3, Prop. 1]. But the "end play" of such equilibria are very complex. So we shall be content here to prove that in any sequential equilibrium, the number of stages where one player or the other finks is bounded above by a constant depending on $\delta$ but independent of $N$. Further, if we restrict attention to sequential equilibria that are not Pareto-dominated by any other sequential equilibria, then there is cooperation in all but the last "few" stages.

We prove these statements in a number of steps. The statement of each step except the last should be prefaced: In every sequential equilibrium...

Step 1   ...if it becomes common knowledge[4] before some stage that ROW is rational, then both ROW and COL fink at this and every succeeding stage, and their payoffs from the remainder of the game are zero.

The proof is by induction on the number of stages remaining. It is apparent if there is only one stage remaining. Suppose that it is true if there are $n - 1$ or fewer stages to go. Then with $n$ stages remaining, the rational ROW must foresee that his present choice of action cannot influence the future course of the game, since it will remain common knowledge that he is rational when stage $n - 1$ arrives. Therefore he will maximize his immediate payoff, which means finking. Similarly, COL anticipates that no matter what he does at this stage, finking will occur at all later stages. In this round, finking is strictly better, so COL finks as well. Since both sides fink, their payoffs are each zero, and the induction is complete.

Step 2   ...if COL finks at stage $n + 1$, then ROW finks at stage $n$ with probability one.

If ROW did cooperate in these circumstances, it would become common knowledge that he was rational. (The "Tit-for-Tat" ROW does not have this action available.) Thus cooperation nets zero in the continuation game. But finking can do no worse than zero in the continuation game and it is strictly dominant in the stage game. Thus finking does strictly better overall. This means that ROW must fink with probability one.

---

[3] An alternative way to model this is to assume that ROW has available *all* the strategies above, but that with probability $\delta$, ROW's payoffs are not as above but rather make playing Tit-for-Tat strongly dominant. The results given below can be proved for this alternative model, although the simple "common knowledge" arguments that we use are no longer available, and slightly more complex arguments are required. An advantage of this alternative model is that it eases interpretation of the probability assessed by COL that ROW is the Tit-for-Tat player as ROW's "reputation."

[4] It is common knowledge that ROW is rational if both players know this, both know that both know this, *ad infinitum*. More formally, an event $E$ is common knowledge between two individuals at a state $\omega \in \Omega$ if there is some $A$ in the finest common coarsening (meet) of their information partitions with $\omega \in A \subseteq E$. The crucial role of common knowledge will be illustrated shortly.

STEP 3    ...starting from any point in the game tree (i), where COL assesses probability $q$ that ROW is the Tit-for-Tat player, (ii), where there are $n$ stages to go, and (iii), where COL *cooperated* on the previous stage, the expected payoff to COL for the remainder of the game is at least $qn + b$.

To show this, consider the strategy for COL of cooperating until the next time that ROW finks, and then finking ever after. Against the Tit-for-Tat player, this yields a payoff of $n$. Against the rational ROW, it yields no worse than $b$. Thus it yields an expected payoff that is at least $qn + (1 - q) b \geq qn + b$, and any equilibrium strategy must do at least as well.

STEP 4    ...starting from any point in the game tree (i), where COL assesses probability $q$ that ROW is the Tit-for-Tat player, (ii), where there are $n$ stages to go, and (iii), where COL *finked* on the previous stage, the expected payoff to COL for the remainder of the game is at least $q(n - 1) + 2b$.

Because ROW is sure to fink (see step 2), COL knows that his assessment in the subsequent stage will again be $q$. So by cooperating at this stage. COL gets $b$ immediately and at least $q(n - 1) + b$ in the continuation game. His overall expected payoff can be no worse than the sum of these, or $q(n - 1) + 2b$.

STEP 5    ...starting at a point in the game tree (i), where COL assesses probability $q$ that ROW is the Tit-for-Tat player, and (ii), where there are $n$ stages to go, the expected payoff to the rational ROW player is no less than $q(n - 1) + 3b - a$.

Note first that COL will do no worse if the rational ROW plays Tit-for-Tat than if the rational ROW plays his equilibrium strategy. This is easily verified inductively, using steps (1) and (2). Thus the bounds obtained in steps (3) and (4) apply equally well if the rational ROW were to play Tit-for-Tat. And by playing Tit-for-Tat, the rational ROW nets within $b - a$ of whatever COL gets, path by path. This gives us the bound on ROW's payoff stated above.

STEP 6    ...if COL assesses probability $q$ that ROW is the Tit-for-Tat player, and if there are more than $(2a - 4b + 2q)/q$ stages left to go, then ROW plays the Tit-for-Tat strategy with probability one. Thus along the equilibrium path, until the first stage less than $(2a - 4b + 2\delta)/\delta$, COL infers nothing from the observed behavior of ROW, and COL's assessment that ROW is the Tit-for-Tat player remains at $\delta$.

In light of Step 2, all that is needed here is to show that ROW cooperates if COL has just cooperated in these circumstances. (The second part of the statement follows trivially from the first.) If ROW were to fink, it would become common knowledge that ROW is rational. Thus the total payoff from finking cannot exceed $a$ – ROW gets at most $a$ immediately (if COL cooperates) and then zero in the continuation game (by Step 1)). By cooperating, ROW will do no worse than $b$ in this round (if COL finks) and, by Step 5, $q(n - 2) + 3b - a$ in the continuation game, where $n$ is the number of stages remaining. If $n$ exceeds $(2a - 4b + 2q)/q$, then cooperating is strictly better.

STEP 7    ...the total number of stages where one side or the other finks is bounded above by

$$\frac{2a - 4b + 2\delta}{\delta} \cdot \left[ 1 + \frac{2}{\min\{2 - a - b, 1\}} \right]$$

As seen in Step 6, ROW plays Tit-for-Tat until stage $(2a - 4b + 2\delta)/\delta$. If COL cooperates until ROW finks and then finks thereafter, his payoff must be at least $N - (2a - 4b + 2\delta)/\delta$. If COL finks before this date, then in that stage he gets $a$. If he then returns $m$ stages later to cooperating, he gets $b$ in the stage where he cooperates and zero in between. Thus he gives up $1 + m - a - b$ in this circumstance. A string of finks costs him $1 + (1 - (a + b))/m$ per round in comparison to cooperating. Thus, each time COL finks it costs him at least $\min\{2 - a - b, 1\}$. If he finks $k$ times prior to stage $(2a - 4b + 2\delta)/\delta$, his payoff cannot exceed $N - k \cdot \min\{2 - a - b, 1\}$. These two bounds on COL's payoffs yield $k \leq (2a - 4b + 2\delta)/(\delta \cdot \min\{2 - a - b, 1\})$. Each such act of finking by COL provokes a Tit-for-Tat response from ROW in the next round, so there are at most $2k$ rounds before stage $(2a - 4b + 2\delta)/\delta$ when finking occurs. Thus the maximum number of rounds with finking is that given above.

STEP 8    In any sequential equilibrium that is not Pareto-dominated by some other sequential equilibrium, there is no finking along the equilibrium path when more than $1 + (2a - 4b + 2\delta)/\delta$ stages remain.

For any equilibrium where there is finking before this date, a Pareto-superior equilibrium consists of not having that finking, and then continuing to play the game as if it had occurred.

Note that these bounds are not tight: If $\delta = 1$ they yield $n = 10$ in Step 8 for $a = 1.5$ and $b = -1$, yet in this circumstance one should see finking only in the last period. The looseness of these bounds suggests the need for further work.

The Tit-for-Tat theme can also be developed so as to further emphasize the role of lack of common knowledge. This development is in the spirit of Milgrom and Roberts [4, Appendix B].

Suppose that there are three states of the world. In state 1, ROW is the Tit-for-Tat player; in stages 2 and 3 he is rational. ROW learns whether he is Tit-for-Tat or not – his information partition (at the outset) is {1}, {2, 3}. COL, on the other hand, is given the information partition {1, 2}, {3}: In state 3 he knows whether ROW is the Tit-for-Tat player; in state 2 he does not. Suppose that state 3 prevails with very high probability. Then with very high probability, Row is not Tit-for-Tat, and COL *knows* that ROW is not Tit-for-Tat. But ROW is not sure that COL knows this, and one can show that the qualitative results proved for model 1 hold here. ROW will play Tit-for-Tat until near the end of the game, hoping that COL will be "deceived." And COL will pretend to be "deceived" even if he is not, as this improves his lot as well.

Or consider a four state case. In state 1 ROW is the Tit-for-Tat player – in states 2, 3 and 4 he is not. ROW is endowed with the information partition {1}, {2, 3}, {4}; COL with {1, 2}, {3, 4}. State 4 prevails with probability close to one. Then with probability close to one, ROW is not Tit-for-Tat, COL knows that this is so, ROW knows that COL knows this, but COL is not sure that ROW knows that COL knows. Once more the qualitative results for the original model hold up – ROW tries to "deceive" COL, knowing full well that COL will not be deceived but will act as if he is, and COL will do this in the hope that ROW may be unaware that is COL is not being deceived. One could go on like this forever: The general structure is that ROW's information partition should involve sets $\{1\}, \{2, 3\}, \ldots, \{2m, 2m + 1\}, \ldots$ and COL's should involve $\{1, 2\}, \{3, 4\}, \ldots, \{2m + 1, 2m + 2\}, \ldots$ (with termination eventually). The point is simply that so long as it is not common knowledge that ROW is not Tit-for-Tat, cooperation until near the end of the game will be rational.

## Model 2: Two-Sided Uncertainty about the Stage Payoffs

In Model 1, COL entertains a hypothesis about ROW's behavior that cannot be generated if ROW is rational and has some stage game payoffs that he sums to arrive at his overall payoff. That is, COL's hypothesis, in terms of ROW's "true" utility function, necessarily involves payoffs for ROW that cut across stages. We might then wonder: Can long-run cooperation be attained if the only alternative hypotheses that are allowed (besides the hypothesis that the player is rational with the given stage payoffs) involve changes in the stage game payoffs? (This approach is used in [2].) The answer is a qualified yes.

Suppose that *each* player originally assesses a small probability that his opponent "enjoys" cooperation when it is met by cooperation. Given our zero-one normalization, we model this by assuming that COL assigns a small probability $\delta > 0$ that $a < 1$ for ROW, and ROW entertains a similar hypothesis about COL. We can then produce a sequential equilibrium wherein each side cooperates until the last few stages of the game, although again the end-game play is rather complex. In this equilibrium, if either side ever fails to cooperate, then the other side takes this as a sure sign that the defector has stage game payoffs with $a > 1$, and the noncooperative equilibrium ensues. As the details of this equilibrium are quite complex, we refrain from giving them here. Note, however, that if we move directly to a continuous-time formulation of this game, as in Kreps and Wilson [2, Sect. 4], then one equilibrium has cooperation throughout.

There are two qualifications to be made. First, two-sided uncertainty is required. If ROW, say, is uncertain about COL's stage payoffs, but it is common knowledge that $a > 1$ for ROW, then the only sequential equilibrium has finking throughout. (This is true for any "incomplete information" about one player's stage payoffs.) The second qualification, and certainly the more important, is that this game admits sequential equilibria in which long-run cooperation does not ensue, unlike the game with a Tit-for-Tat possibility. This is true even if we make a "plausibility" restriction on beliefs off the equilibrium path in the spirit of Section 3 of Kreps and Wilson [2]. Cooperation here requires a "bootstrapping" operation: Even if each side is *certain* that the other has $a < 1$, cooperation ensues only if each side hypothesizes that the other side will cooperate. (This is a fancy way of saying: If both sides have payoffs with $a < 1$, then there are two Nash equilibria in the stage game.) One might justify the cooperative equilibrium on "efficiency" grounds, but one cannot guarantee that cooperation will prevail in every sequential equilibrium.

## References

1 R. Axelrod, The emergence of cooperation among egoists, *Amer. Pol. Sci. Rev.* 75 (1981), 306–18.

2 D. Kreps and R. Wilson, Reputation and imperfect information. *J. Econ. Theory* 27 (1982), 253–79.

3 D. Kreps and R. Wilson, Sequential equilibrium, *Econometrica*, in press.

4 P. Milgrom and J. Roberts, Predation, reputation and entry deterrence. *J. Econ. Theory* 27 (1982), 280–312.

5 S. Smale, The prisoner's dilemma and dynamical systems associated to non-cooperative games, *Econometrica* 48 (1980), 1617–34.

# THIRTY

# Cheap Talk, Coordination, and Entry

Joseph Farrell

Source: *Rand Journal of Economics* 18(1) Spring, 1987, pp. 34–9.

We show how costless, nonbinding, nonverifiable communication (cheap talk) can achieve partial coordination among potential entrants into a natural-monopoly industry, where the payoffs are qualitatively like the "battle of the sexes." The analysis would apply equally in other economic situations with such payoffs, for example, bargaining under complete information or choosing compatibility standards. While cheap talk helps achieve asymmetric coordination in a symmetric mixed-strategy equilibrium, it cannot achieve complete coordination if the game involves even a small amount of conflict.

## 1. Introduction

When a number of firms contemplate entering an industry that can profitably accommodate only some of them, how many of them will enter? The traditional answer is that just enough enter so that the addition of one more would cause all (or at least the additional one) to lose money. This is a natural answer – it is generically the unique perfect equilibrium – if the firms decide sequentially whether to enter, and for some markets it may be the right answer. In others, however, it is more natural to model the entry decisions as simultaneous. In such a model one could continue to believe the traditional answer, since it remains a Nash equilibrium. In this author's view, however, the problem demands further analysis, because such an asymmetric Nash equilibrium of the symmetric simultaneous-move game represents a considerable feat of coordination. How might such asymmetric coordination be achieved?

Dixit and Shapiro (1986) address this problem by analyzing the symmetric mixed-strategy equilibrium of a game in which firms can revise their entry decisions if it turns out that an insufficient number or an excessive number have entered. In equilibrium asymmetric coordination is achieved in the long run through reactions to short-run failures of coordination. In many markets we do seem to observe such short-run disequilibrium, and Dixit and Shapiro are right to emphasize it.

In other markets, however, sunk costs of entry are so important that firms have strong incentives to learn their rivals' plans and to communicate their own, before committing the entry costs. Dixit and Shapiro's (1986) model of reentry and reexit is unconvincing when sunk costs are very important – for example, in the markets for computer software, for telephone switching equipment (where much of the cost is in software development), or for nationwide fiberoptic telephone networks. In such markets we often observe firms announcing "plans" to enter (or not) long before final entry decisions are made. In this article we analyze a stylized model of such announcements, with a view to understanding when and to what extent they can help achieve coordination.

One way to model the effects of announcements would be to suppose that a false announcement is costly: for instance, one might well argue that firms would lose credibility in the future if they announced that they would enter, but then did not. If so, then announcements would "signal" true intentions. One could build a model (very similar to Dixit and Shapiro's) on the basis of that assumption. An alternative approach, which we adopt here, is to focus on a mechanism that does not require that a false announcement be costly, or indeed that announcements have any direct costs or benefits. To make that point clearly, we assume that announcements are "cheap talk:" they do not directly affect payoffs at all.

If announcements are cheap talk, it might seem that they should not affect the outcome. Certainly, there is an equilibrium in which they do not: if everyone believes that cheap talk will be ignored, then it is optimal (among other things) for each player to make his claims uncorrelated with his actions, and then everyone's skepticism about the claims is warranted. But this is not the only equilibrium; we focus on another that seems more appealing, and in which cheap talk is not ignored.

Suppose that players' announced plans would, if actually played, constitute a Nash equilibrium. Then, we suggest, that equilibrium becomes focal. Moreover, if everyone expects such equilibria always to be followed once announced, then cheap talk can help coordinate behavior to produce asymmetric equilibria. In this article we shall suppose that if players' announced plans ever constitute a Nash equilibrium, then they are followed. Using that assumption, we show how cheap talk can achieve some degree of coordination.

Formally, we analyze the symmetric mixed-strategy equilibrium (satisfying that assumption) of the following game. In each of $T$ rounds of communication, each of two firms nonbindingly states whether it "intends" to enter a natural-monopoly industry that either or both could enter. After the $T$ rounds, the firms must make their actual entry decisions. We show that in our equilibrium the firms achieve more coordination than they do in the symmetric equilibrium (as analyzed by Dixit and Shapiro (1986)) of the game without communication: that is, it is more likely that exactly one firm enters. Moreover, as $T$ increases, coordination improves. Even in the limit as $T$ increases without bound, however, some failures of coordination remain; we show that this is so since each firm prefers to be the entrant.

One critical assumption deserves prominent disclosure. We assume that each firm prefers, if it does not enter, that the other should enter. If not, then it would always be a dominant strategy (if announcements were given any credence) to announce "In." Our assumption is meant to reflect the fact that potential entrants to a new market are often established firms in a complementary-good market, and therefore they do not wish to see the new market unserved. For instance, telephone companies are prominent in the switching-equipment market, and computer manufacturers may consider developing new microprocessors or software. In markets without such complementarity, cheap-talk announcements cannot work as described here.

Two other applications of our method come to mind. The first is the problem of bargaining under complete information. In this problem two players (buyer and seller) wish to agree on a mutually beneficial trading price, but the seller wants a high price and the buyer a low one. A second application is the choice of industry standards. In industries with benefits from compatibility (telecommunications or computing, for instance), industry standards are often negotiated among industry participants with different firms' proposing their own technologies. Although each firm may wish above all that standardization will be achieved, each hopes that its own standard will be chosen.

This article considers the role of cheap talk in coordinating actions in a game of complete information. A different but related role is to communicate private information. Here, the seminal work is that of Crawford and Sobel (1982), who showed how the effectiveness of such talk in transmitting information depends on the degree to which players' preferences coincide. Applications of this idea include Farrell and Saloner (1985) and Farrell and Gibbons (1986). In the present article there is no private information, but the degree to which preferences coincide also determines the effectiveness of communication.

## 2.  The Model

First, we describe the last round, in which the directly payoff-relevant choices are made. Each of two firms, aiming to maximize expected profit, chooses either to enter ("In") or not to enter ("Out") a natural-monopoly market. If both enter, each loses $L$; if neither enters, each gets zero (a normalization). If just one enters, it earns profits $M$, while the other gets a surplus $B$, which we take to be positive but less than $M$. We can summarize this information in a payoff matrix:

|     | In | Out |
| --- | --- | --- |
| In | $(-L, -L)$ | $(M, B)$ |
| Out | $(B, M)$ | $(0, 0)$ |

This entry game has three Nash equilibria. In one firm 1 plays "In" and firm 2 plays "Out." In the second the roles are reversed. In the third each plays a mixed strategy, in which the probability $p$ of entry makes the other player indifferent between "In" and "Out:"

$$p(-L) + (1 - p)M = pB \tag{1}$$

or

$$p = \frac{M}{B + L + M} \tag{2}$$

We shall refer to this third equilibrium as "the Dixit-Shapiro equilibrium." If the players are identical, then, as Dixit and Shapiro (1986) argue, it is reasonable to think that, absent any coordination mechanism, they will play the symmetric equilibrium.

Next, we describe the game with one round of communication. Communication consists of each firm's saying "In" or "Out." Then they play the entry game, and payoffs are just as described above – that is, the messages sent in communication do not themselves directly affect payoffs.

There are many equilibria of this game, but we focus on the (unique) equilibrium with the following properties.

1  It is symmetric in that both firms play the same (mixed) normal-form strategy in the two-stage game. (We are concerned with the problem of how initially symmetric firms achieve asymmetric coordination: it would be begging the question to have them use asymmetric strategies.)
2  If one firm says "In" while the other says "Out," then the first firm will choose "In" in the subsequent entry game. (Because there are no payoff links between the two periods, this is an assumption. It seems a reasonable one: once an equilibrium of the original entry game becomes focal through being "agreed on," it will be followed.)
3  If both firms say "In" or if both say "Out," then they play the Dixit–Shapiro strategy in the subsequent entry game.

We look for an equilibrium with properties (1)–(3), and in which each firm announces "In" with probability $q_1$ in the communication round. Since $q_1 = 1$ or $q_1 = 0$ cannot be an equilibrium if properties (1)–(3) hold, $q_1$ must be such that each player is indifferent between his messages:

$$q_1 u_1 + (1 - q_1)M = q_1 B + (1 - q_1)u_1 \qquad (3)$$

where $u_1$ is the expected payoff in the Dixit-Shapiro (1986) equilibrium. This yields

$$
\begin{aligned}
q_1 &= \frac{M - u_1}{M - 2u_1 + B} \\
&= \frac{M - pB}{M - 2pB + B}
\end{aligned}
\qquad (4)
$$

by substituting from (2). From (4) we obtain

$$1 - q_1 = \frac{B}{M - 2pB + B}(1 - p) \qquad (5)$$

Equation (5) and the fact that $M > 2pB$ show that $q_1$ is closer to 1 than is $p$. If, as we might expect, $M \gg B$, then $q_1$ is very close to 1. In this sense, the outcome is "almost" that each firm claims that it will enter, and then randomizes. But the probability of a failure of coordination (both enter or neither enters) has fallen, if only a little, from

$[p^2 + (1 - p)^2]$ to $[p^2 + (1 - p)^2][q_1^2 + (1 - q_1)^2]$. This raises the question of what happens if we allow more rounds of communication. If each round reduced that probability by a constant factor, then many rounds of communication would essentially eliminate such failures. But that is not the case, as we now show.

Consider the $(T + 1)$-stage game in which in each of the first $T$ stages the strategies available are merely to say "In" or to say "Out," while the last stage is the entry game itself. We seek a symmetric mixed-strategy equilibrium, such that if at any stage the firms make different announcements, then they will in fact do what they have announced. If after $S \leq T$ stages they have not "reached an agreement," then they play the game with $(T - S)$ rounds of communication as if the first $S$ rounds had not happened.[1]

Writing $u_{T+1}$ for the expected payoff in that equilibrium (so that $u_2$, for example, describes the value given in (3)), we have recurrence equations:

$$u_{T+1} = q_T u_T + (1 - q_T)M = q_T B + (1 - q_T)u_T \tag{6}$$

where $q_T$ is the probability of saying "In" in the first round of the $(T + 1)$-stage game. Since $u_1 = pB < B$, and since (6) tells us that $u_{T+1}$ is a weighted average between $u_T$ and $B$, we know by induction that $u_t \leq B$ for all $t$. Note that this shows that a firm that just said "Out" and whose opponent said "In" is not tempted to deviate by unexpectedly saying "In" in the next round. This would give him $u_{t-1}$, compared with his equilibrium payoff $B$. This comparison (and other similar ones) show that our equilibrium is subgame-perfect.

From (6), since $u_t \leq B$, the sequence of $u$'s is increasing: $u_{t+1} \geq u_t$. In fact, $u_t \to B$. To see this, note that the alternative is for $u_t$ to converge to some limit $u < B$. For any $\epsilon > 0$, there would be $T(\epsilon)$ such that $|u_t - u| < \epsilon$ for all $t \geq T(\epsilon)$. For $t > T(\epsilon)$, (6) then implies that $q_t(B - u) < 2\epsilon$. Thus, we have $q_t \to 0$. But then (6) implies that $u_t \to M$, which we know is impossible, because $u_t \leq B < M$.

Since $u_t \to B$, (6) also tells us that $q_t$ converges monotonically to 1. Thus, when there is a long horizon, equilibrium requires each potential entrant to "talk very tough," and little contribution to coordination is made by these early negotiations. This suggests that the probability of successful coordination may be bounded away from 1 as $T \to \infty$. We now show that this is so.

Consider the limiting behavior as $T \to \infty$ of the probability of a failure of coordination:

$$\phi_T = [(1 - q_T)^2 + q_T^2][(1 - q_{T-1})^2 + q_{T-1}^2] \ldots [(1 - q_1)^2 + q_1^2][(1 - p)^2 + p^2]. \tag{7}$$

---

[1] In a complete information model such as this, it is natural to think of playing the subgame as if the first $S$ periods had not occurred. In a related incomplete-information model, in which, for example, firms may differ in costs, we would find at each stage that the lower-cost firms said "In" and the higher-cost firms said "Out." Then, each firm would (in equilibrium) have learned something about the other from their $S$-fold disagreement. Nevertheless, the equilibrium cutoffs in round $(S + 1)$ would be the same as if they were beginning a $(T - S)$-round game, but one in which only those "types" that in equilibrium reach this subgame would be possible.

Whether or not $\phi_T \to 0$ is equivalent to whether the series $\sum \log[(1 - q_t)^2 + q_t^2]$ diverges to $-\infty$. Since $q_t \to 1$ in a complicated way, direct attack on the problem is difficult. But we can readily get an answer by using a different method.

By symmetry the probability $(1 - \phi_T)$ of successful coordination is split equally between the two eventual outcomes (In, Out) and (Out, In). With probability $\phi_T/[p^2 + (1 - p)^2]$ the firms go through all $T$ rounds of communication without reaching agreement; then with probability $p^2$ both enter, and with probability $(1 - p^2)$ neither does. Hence,

$$u_T = \frac{1}{2}(1 - \phi_T)M + \frac{1}{2}(1 - \phi_T)B + \phi_T \frac{p^2}{p^2 + (1 - p)^2}(-L) + \phi_T \frac{(1 - p)^2}{p^2 + (1 - p)^2} 0.$$
(8)

Since $u_T$ converges to $B$ as $T \to \infty$, we have in the limit

$$B = \frac{1}{2}(1 - \phi)M + \frac{1}{2}(1 - \phi)B - \phi \frac{p^2}{p^2 + (1 - p)^2} L$$

$$\phi\left(\frac{M + B}{2} + \frac{p^2 L}{p^2 + (1 - p)^2}\right) = \frac{M - B}{2},$$
(9)

which, when we substitute in for $p$ from (2), gives

$$\phi = \frac{M - B}{M + B + \frac{2M^2}{M^2 + (B+L)^2} L}.$$
(10)

Suppose that $B/M = \beta < 1$, while $L/M = \lambda$. Then (2) gives

$$p = \frac{1}{1 + \lambda + \beta}.$$
(11)

Hence, without communication, the probability of coordination failure is:

$$p^2 + (1 - p)^2 = \frac{1 + (\lambda + \beta)^2}{(1 + \lambda + \beta)^2}.$$
(12)

From (10), the corresponding probability with many rounds of communication is

$$\phi = \frac{1 - \beta}{1 + \beta + \frac{2}{1 + (\beta + \lambda)^2} \lambda} = \frac{(1 - \beta)\left[1 + (\beta + \lambda)^2\right]}{(1 + \beta)\left[1 + (\beta + \lambda)^2\right] + 2\lambda}.$$
(13)

The ratio $\phi/[p^2 + (1 - p)^2]$ is therefore

$$R \equiv \frac{(1 - \beta)}{(1 + \beta)\left[1 + (\beta + \lambda)^2\right] + 2\lambda}[1 + \lambda + \beta]^2. \tag{14}$$

As $\beta \to 1$, this ratio converges to zero: essentially the prospect of coordination failure disappears, because the conflict in the entry game vanishes when $\beta = 1$. As $\beta \to 0$, the ratio converges to 1: when $\beta = 0$, there is no reason ever to say "Out," and communication cannot help. It is easy to ascertain from (14) that $R < 1$ whenever $\beta > 0$: communication helps. But $R > 0$ whenever $\beta < 1$: the conflict that is present because $B < M$ creates inefficiencies.

Thus, we see that the symmetric equilibrium of the extended game in which we allow for nonbinding announcements involves some failure of coordination, even as the time available for reaching an agreement expands indefinitely. The equilibrium strategy is to be "very tough" early on ($q_t \simeq 1$), so that early periods contribute little to the chance of reaching agreement.

## 3.  Conclusion

We have shown how cheap talk can help coordinate firms' choices in a game of entry, when the complementarity of existing product lines makes the game qualitatively like the "battle of the sexes": both players prefer either pure-strategy equilibrium to any other outcome, but they are in conflict over which is preferable. We concluded that such talk helps achieve coordination, but that the conflict inherent in the game prevents even unlimited communication from achieving perfect coordination.

*References*

CRAWFORD, V. and SOBEL, J. (1982), "Strategic Information Transmission." *Econometrica*, 50, 1141–52.

DIXIT, A. and SHAPIRO, C. (1986) "Entry Dynamics with Mixed Strategies" in L. G. Thomas, ed., *The Economics of Strategic Planning*, Lexington: Lexington Books.

FARRELL, J. and GIBBONS, R. (1986), "Cheap Talk in Bargaining." Mimeo, Massachusetts Institute of Technology.

——and SALONER, G. (1985), "Standardization, Compatibility, and Innovation." *Rand Journal of Economics*, 16, 70–83.

# THIRTY-ONE

# Wise Guy: Life in a Mafia Family

NICHOLAS PILEGGI

*Source*: © 1985 Pileggi Literary Properties Inc. Reprinted by permission of Pocket Books, a division of Simon and Schuster, pp. 267–9.

Henry: My scheme was to play them along until I got my own head clear, got my bail reduced, and got back on the street. I knew I was vulnerable. I knew that you were vulnerable when you were worth more dead than alive. It was that simple. But I still couldn't really believe it, and I didn't really know what I was going to do. Sometimes I thought I'd just get some money and go on the lam for a while. Then I thought I might get my head clear and straighten it all out with Paulie. I kept thinking that if I watched my step, if I kept the thought of my getting whacked in the middle of my mind, I might have a chance of surviving.

In my case I knew that getting caught in the drug thing really put me in the box. Paulie had put the taboo on drugs. It was outlawed. None of us were supposed to be in drugs. It wasn't that Paulie wanted to take some moral position. That wasn't it. What Paulie didn't want to have happen is what happened to one of his best friends, Carmine Tramunti, who went away for fifteen years just because he nodded hello to Fat Gigi Inglese in a restaurant. The jury decided to believe the prosecutor that Tramunti was nodding his agreement to a drug deal. That was it. Bang. Fifteen years at the age of fifty-seven. The guy never got out. Just at a time in his life when he was going to enjoy, when it was supposed to begin to pay off, he gets sent away forever and then dies in the can. Paulie was not going to let that happen to him. He'd kill you first.

So I knew that arrest on the drug charge made me vulnerable. Maybe too vulnerable to live. There wouldn't have been any hard feelings. I was just facing too much time. The crew also knew I was snorting a lot of coke and eating Judes. Jimmy once said my brain had turned to candy. I wasn't the only guy in the crew taking drugs. Sepe and Stabile had bigger noses than mine. But I was the one who was caught and I was the one who they felt might make a deal.

The fact that I had never made a deal before, the fact that I had always been standup, the fact that I had done two years in Nassau and four years in Lewisburg standing on my head and never gave up a mouse counted for nothing. What you did yesterday doesn't count. It's what you're doing today and could do tomorrow that counts. From where my friends stood, from where Jimmy was standing, I was a liability. I was no longer safe. I didn't need pictures.

In fact, I knew it was going to be Jimmy even before the feds played me the tape of Sepe and Stabile talking about getting rid of me. I could hear them. Sepe sounded anxious to get it over with. He said that I was no good, that I was a junkie. But Jimmy was calm. He told them not to worry about it. And that was all I heard.

Sitting in my cell, I knew I was up for grabs. In the old days Jimmy would have torn Sepe's heart out for even suggesting that I get whacked. That was the main reason why I stayed inside. I had to sort it all out. And every day I was inside, Jimmy or Mickey called my wife and asked when I was getting out, and every day that she could, Karen came to the jail and told me everything they said.

If you're a part of a crew, nobody ever tells you that they're going to kill you. It doesn't happen that way. There aren't any great arguments or finger-biting curses like in Mafia movies. Your murderers come with smiles. They come as friends, people who have cared deeply about you all your life, and they always come at a time when you are at your weakest and most in need of their help and support.

But still I wasn't sure. I grew up with Jimmy. He brought me along. Paulie and Tuddy put me in his hands. He was supposed to watch out for me, and he did. He was the best teacher a guy could want. It was Jimmy who got me into cigarette bootlegging and hijackings. We buried bodies. We did Air France and Lufthansa. We got sentenced to ten years for putting the arm on the guy in Florida. He was at the hospital when Karen had the kids, and we went to birthday parties and holidays at each other's houses. We did it all, and now maybe he's going to kill me. Two weeks before my arrest I got so paranoid and stoned that Karen got me to go see a shrink. It was nuts. I couldn't tell him anything, but she insisted. I talked to him in general terms. I told him that I was trying to get away from drug people. I said I was afraid I was going to be killed. He told me to get a phone machine.

If I was going to survive, I was going to have to turn on everything I knew. The decision was almost made for me. In jail I didn't think so much about whether or not to turn as I did about exactly how I could manage to do it and still get out of jail long enough to collect the money and dope I had out on the street. I had about $18,000 in heroin stashed in the house that the cops hadn't found. I had $20,000 owed to me by Mazzei. I'd probably have to kiss that goodbye. I had about $40,000 in loan-shark money out on the street. I wanted to recoup some of that. There was money owed me by fences on some of the jewel robberies and I had money owed me from some gun deals. Added up, there was enough to risk my neck before getting arrested by the cops or killed by my friends. It was going to have to be a con, a hustle, just like everything else.

I felt drained, and nothing had helped – not the shower, not the fresh shirt Karen had ironed, not the cologne. Nothing could get the smell of the jail and fear out of my nose. Jimmy stood up. He was smiling. He opened his arms to give me a bear hug. My court papers were all over the table. Jimmy had gotten them from the lawyers. When I sat down with him, it almost felt like it was the old days.

On the surface, of course, everything was supposed to be fine. We were supposed to be discussing my drug case, just like the dozens of other cases of mine we had discussed together, but this time I knew that the thing we were really discussing was me. I knew I was hot. I was dangerous. I knew that I could give Jimmy up and cut myself a deal with the government. I could give up Lufthansa and I could give up Paulie. I could put Jimmy and Paulie behind bars for the rest of their lives. And I knew Jimmy knew it.

None of this was said, of course. In fact, almost nothing was ever really said. Even if the feds had somehow wired our table, and then played back the tape, they wouldn't have been able to make much sense out of our conversation. It was in half words.

Shrugs. We talked about this guy and the other guy and the guy from over here and the guy from over there and the guy with the hair and the guy from downtown. At the end of the conversation I would know what we talked about and Jimmy would know what we talked about, but nobody else would know.

Jimmy had been through the papers, and he said that there had been a rat in the case. I knew he meant Bobby Germaine's kid, but I tried to slough it off. I said that they hadn't found any drugs on me or in my house. I kept saying that they didn't have a strong case, but I could see Jimmy was very nervous anyway.

He wanted to know about all the people I had working for me. He wanted to know whether Robin and Judy and the rest of the people arrested knew about him. I told him they knew nothing, but I could see he didn't believe me. He wanted to know if I had talked to Paulie yet. I said no.

Jimmy was trying to look confident. He said he had some ideas about my case. I could see what he was doing. As long as I thought he was trying to help me, he knew that I'd stay close. Then, when he felt the time was right, when I was no longer dangerous to hit, he would whack me. Jimmy was biding time to make sure he could kill me without getting Paulie upset and putting his own neck on the line.

As long as Jimmy thought I didn't know what he had planned, I had a chance of copping time on the street and scooping up some money. I had to pretend to Jimmy I didn't know what he might have had planned, and he had to pretend that he had nothing but my best interests at heart.

Then he said that he wanted me to go down to Florida in a few days. He said there was some money to be made. He said he had to meet me again soon about the case. He said we should meet on Wednesday in a bar owned by Charlie the Jap, on Queens Boulevard, in Sunnyside.

I'd never heard of the place. I've been operating with Jimmy for twenty-five years. We've been in a thousand bars together in Queens, and we've spent six years in the can together, and suddenly he wants to meet me in a bar I've never seen before.

I nod yeah, sure, but I already know there's no way in the world I'm going into that bar. As soon as breakfast is over, I drive past the place. I'm not waiting till Wednesday.

It was just the kind of place Jimmy has used in the past for hits. The place was controlled by one of the crew. It had a back entrance, and there was a parking area in the rear where you could take out a body bag in a rug without anyone seeing. Forget it. If Jimmy thought I was meeting him in that place on Wednesday he was nuts.

Instead, I showed up at Jimmy's sweatshop on Liberty Avenue on Monday. I had been out all morning trying to raise money. In the afternoon I had Karen drive me over to his shop. While I waited in a bar across the street, she went inside and told him I wanted to see him.

He came right over with Karen. I could see that he was nervous and surprised. He wasn't sure what I was going to do. Then he said if he gave me the name and address of Bobby Germaine's kid in Florida, would I go down there with Anthony Stabile and whack him. This was crazy, but I wasn't going to argue. Jimmy had never asked me to do anything like that before. And he'd never asked me to do something like that in front of Karen. Never.*

---

* Editor's note: Henry does make it back to prison, testifies against Paulie and Jimmy, and helps to write *Wise Guy*.

# THIRTY-TWO

# "Say, I Think I See Where We Went Off..."

ED FISHER

*Source*: © 1954 The New Yorker Collection, Ed Fisher from cartoonbank.com. All Rights Reserved.

"Say, I think I see where we went off. Isn't eight times seven fifty-six?"

PART SEVEN

# Moral Hazard: Hidden Actions

# Introduction

I am very glad for the chance to publish this important note by Joseph Farrell, which I know about because he was on my dissertation committee at MIT when he wrote it. It uses the idea of moral hazard to address the important policy question of what is wrong with monopolies. In 1954, Arnold Harberger pointed out that the triangle allocative losses from monopoly are surprisingly small. (Arnold Harberger, "Monopoly and Resource Allocation," *American Economic Review, Papers and Proceedings* 44: 77–87 [May 1954]). Gordon Tullock later pointed out that if firms compete to become or to preserve market power, the welfare losses become rectangles instead of triangles. (Gordon Tullock, "The Welfare Costs of Tariffs, Monopolies, and Theft", *Western Economic Journal* 5: 224–32 [June 1967]. I think this is the "Stigler trapezoid" to which Farrell refers; George Stigler later wrote about it too. Yet another possible loss is the loss in productive efficiency if for some reason a monopoly slacks off and prefers "the quiet life" to profit maximization. From the point of view of the shareholders, such slacking off is implausible. There is no reason the shareholders of a monopoly would be less willing than those of a competitive firm to keep costs down; indeed, the monopoly, with 100 percent market share, has more sales and less danger of imitation, so it actually has more incentive to reduce production cost. Farrell shows why, despite this, the monopoly might be less efficient – he brings the managers into the picture.

Ariel Rubinstein's article, published and well-known, but published in an obscure place, is also about disciplining agents, but in the context of crime. Here, the principal is the government and the agents are the citizens – or, if you like, the principal is the citizens as a group and the agent is the citizen as an individual. Courts do, in practice, punish repeat offenders much more severely, and Rubinstein's article cries out for empirical work following his theoretical line. Data is all around us. To get you started, here are some excerpts from my local newspaper.

Robert Shepard III, 25, Spencer: Found guilty of violating probation on 1997 convictions for two felony counts of conspiracy to manufacture methcathinone plus one felony count of residential burglary. Sentenced by Judge E. Michael Hoff to serve six years in prison previously suspended from his 1997 convictions, with credit for 32 days already served in jail.

Timothy D. Grow Jr., 47, Spencer: Pleaded guilty to felony conspiracy to deal cocaine in October 1998. Sentenced by Hoff to six years in prison with five years suspended, three days' credit for time already served in jail, and the rest on community corrections or house arrest; assessed $625 in court costs, public defender and drug fees.

Damon Robinson, 26, 1861 Oakdale Drive East, pleaded guilty to two counts of felony theft of two diamond rings and $200 cash from two women on April 30. Sentenced by Hoff to three years in jail, all suspended, and $1\frac{1}{2}$ years on probation with 100 hours of public restitution work on country road crew duty; assessed $200 restitution for the stolen cash plus $125 court costs.

(*The Bloomington Herald-Times*, excerpts from "Court News", p. A7 [3 August 1999])

How would you assess these penalties from the point of view of principal-agent theory?

People have come up with other institutions that lie in between the penalties of firing a manager and of putting a felon in prison. The *Wall Street Journal* article discusses one of these: bonds posted for misbehavior by workers or contractors. In the absence of any of these penalties, shirking can be expected, and this is the point of the finger-flicking Dilbert cartoon.

# THIRTY-THREE

# Monopoly Slack and Competitive Rigor: A Simple Model

JOSEPH FARRELL

*Source*: MIT mimeo, February 1983.

What is the welfare loss from monopoly? Triangle allocation losses are surprisingly small. This article shows by a simple numerical example that a substantial loss in operating efficiency can arise because a monopoly cannot use tournaments between top managers to control moral hazard.

## Introduction

Professional economists and others have long worried about monopolies, and the inefficiencies supposedly produced by them. One such inefficiency is the departure of price from marginal cost in the behavior of a profit-maximizing monopolist: this generates (in many cases) a Pareto inefficiency. For many years professional economists were mainly content to describe that as "the" loss from monopoly, even though informal thinking has often laid more stress on some sort of undisciplined slackness which can find no expression in any simple model of profit-maximizing behavior. Harberger's provocative article [1954] in which he estimate the "welfare triangle" loss from monopoly in the US at 0.1% of GNP, had the effect of dividing economists concerned with industrial organization into three broad groups. First, there were/are those who noticed inadequacies in Harberger's analysis, and set to re-calculate the loss. For example, . . . (Stigler's concept of the welfare trapezoid is perhaps the most interesting of this class.) The second group consists of those who take the conclusion at face value, more or less, and stop worrying about monopoly. The third group is exploring the question: If the conventional loss is so small, are there other, more significant losses? This paper is devoted to a simple, rigorous, maximizing model of an idea which informal (and especially non-professional) thought has always stuck to: monopolies are simply *slack*. They leave opportunities unexploited, they refrain from cutting costs, they are rude to customers, they discriminate unreasonably in employment, . . . – the list is long. Most economists react to such ideas with distress and puzzlement. Why should a monopoly, any more than another firm or economic agent, willingly give up profits?

The difficulty of this problem has led some people simply to sidestep it by defining concepts such as "X-inefficiency" or "satisficing." A closer examination suggests that problems of information must be essential. Leibenstein's "Beyond Economic Man" cites, as evidence of the existence of X-inefficiency, examples of firms whose performance improved greatly after getting some management advice. This seems more consistent with a view that they simply weren't trying. Likewise, a "satisficing" firm can hardly be supposed to be indifferent to profit beyond a certain point; rather, it is a matter of not looking for the information which might enable it to do better.

Once we put the problem in those terms, the idea that it has to do with a principal-agent problem becomes appealing. Suppose that a manager finds searching for better techniques costly. The firm itself cannot reliably tell when he is searching, and so cannot reimburse him for those costs. The firm also cannot reliably tell by results whether or not the manager has been diligent. The best they can do is provide a contract with some incentive to increase profits; but the manager's risk-aversion limits the effectiveness of this. The inefficiency which results is ameliorated if more information becomes available about the manager's activities; and, if there is a competing firm, the market interaction may convey such information.

In the model presented below, shareholders set up optimal incentive contracts for their managers to induce them to examine alternatives instead of acting at random. The alternatives are the same for each of two firms, and so comparing the performance of the two gives some information about the management of each. In fact, in the simple model I present, such a comparison completely solves the moral hazard problem and the first-best can be achieved. (That is a special result, but an analogous partial effect will occur in general.)

## 2.  The Model

### 2.1   One firm (monopoly)

There are two alternative techniques, 1 and 2. The cost of production using technique $i$ is $c_i = 1$ with probability $p$, 2 with probability $(1 - p)$. There is a manager who can choose a technique at random; or at a utility cost of $s$ (see below) he can learn the value of $c_1$ or $c_2$. His reimbursement can depend on the cost of production, but not on his search strategy (which is unobservable). Assume he is paid $R_c$ if costs are $c$ ($c = 1$ or 2), giving (von Neumann-Morgenstern) utility $log(R_c)$ if he didn't search, or $log(R_c) - s$ if he did. (It should be clear that he will never choose to inspect both techniques in this simple model). The firm's gross profits, given costs of $c$, are $\pi(c)$, with $\pi(1) > \pi(2)$. The manager must receive at least $log\ v$ from his contract in expected utility.

If the shareholders decide *not* to make the manager inspect a technique, they simply pay him $v$, and get net profits (in expected value):

$$p\pi(1) + (1 - p)\pi(2) - v \tag{1}$$

If they decide to make him inspect a technique, and adopt it if its cost is 1, adopting the other if the revealed cost is 2, then they must make the rewards satisfy

$$plog(R_1) + (1 - p)log(R_2) \leq p(2 - p)log(R_1) + (1 - p)^2 log(R_2) - s \quad (2)$$

or,

$$p(1 - p)log\left(\frac{R_1}{R_2}\right) \geq s \quad (3)$$

Subject to that, and to the expected-utility constraint, they wish (if risk-neutral) to minimize the expected cost of the contract. Hence we will have (3) satisfied with equality, and:

$$p(2 - p)log(R_1) + (1 - p)^2 log(R_2) - s = log(v) \quad (4)$$

The solution is:

$$\begin{aligned} R_1 &= ve^{s/p} \\ R_2 &= ve^{-s/(1-p)} \end{aligned} \quad (5)$$

and the expected cost is:

$$v\left[p(2 - p)e^{s/p} + (1 - p)^2 ve^{-s/(1-p)}\right] \quad (6)$$

For example, $p = \frac{1}{2}$, $s = \frac{1}{2}$ gives 2.12; $p = 0.1$, $s = 1$ gives 4,180.03.

## 2.2  Duopoly

Now suppose there are two firms, whose managers do not collude on search strategy. If manager 2 is searching, then if one of the techniques is low-cost ($c = 1$) he will get a low-cost technique; so will manager 1 if he searches. On the other hand, if 2 searches while 1 does not, there is positive probability that 1 will have $c = 2$, while 2 has $c = 1$. Accordingly, if manager 2 is searching (with positive probability as perceived by manager 1), the shareholders in firm 1 can make their manager search at no cost in equilibrium, by promising dire penalties if their firm ends up with high costs while their competitor has low costs. Notice that this depends on the simplicity of the example, but also more fundamentally that it depends on the fact that both managers are searching in the same set of techniques. There is not point comparing a manager's results to those of another manager in an unrelated industry: this is the "sufficient statistic theorem" of principle-agent analysis: see Holmstrom (1979).

Accordingly, the (expected) cost to the firm of paying the manager so that he searches is just $ve^s$, provided the other manager is expected to search. (If the penalty for bringing up the rear is sufficiently severe, the managers will plausibly go to the Nash equilibrium where both search, rather than that where neither does.) In the two examples calculated above, we compare:

$p = \frac{1}{2}$, $s = \frac{1}{2}$ gives 1.65 – some saving;
$p = 0.1$, $s = 1$ gives 2.72 – a dramatic saving;

In consequence, certain values of $\pi(1) - \pi(2)$ will lead shareholders in the monopoly case to refrain from trying to get their managers to search (since it is so expensive), while even though the profit difference may be smaller, shareholders of the duopoly firms will cause their managers to search. The result is that ex-post it will happen (with positive probability) that the monopoly is producing at cost 2, even though a cost-1 technique is available; moreover, it would have been worthwhile (ex-ante) for the monopoly to search; were it not for the unobservability of search. A duopoly structure, by contrast, may avoid this problem.

Notice moreover that in this model a duopolist faced with an "inefficient" (nonsearching) competitor can still get its manager to search at no excess cost. I suspect that, in a more general model, the "efficiency" of a competitor will affect the possibilities for a given firm's incentive contracts. This raises the interesting prospect of multiple equilibria, so that, of two ex-ante identical industries with oligopolistic structure, one may be generally efficient and the other generally inefficient. The idea is that, if others are searching effectively (and especially if there are many others), at least one firm will discover "the best technique." Thus a manager can be induced to search thoroughly by threats of severe penalties if the firm falls behind "best practice." (I suspect this is related to the fact that a principal who can observe the output of many agents solving the same problem can achieve the first-best solution.) It is less clear that, if the optimum is for the manager to search "somewhat but not exhaustively," this can be sustained. Indeed, in general that will not be true.

### References

Harberger, Arnold (1954) "Monopoly and Resource Allocation," *The American Economic Review, Papers and Proceedings*, 44, May, 77–87.
Holmstrom, Bengt (1979) "Moral Hazard and Observability," *Bell Journal of Economics*, 10, Spring, 74–91.
Leibenstein, Harvey (1976) *Beyond Economic Man: A New Foundation for Microeconomics*. Cambridge, Mass.: Harvard University Press.

# THIRTY-FOUR

# An Optimal Conviction Policy for Offenses that May Have Been Committed by Accident

ARIEL RUBINSTEIN

Source: *Applied Game Theory: Proceedings of a Conference at the Institute for Advanced Studies, Vienna, June 13–16, 1978*, edited by S. J. Brams, A. Schotter, and G. Schwödiauer, pp. 406–13. © Physica-Verlag, Wurzburg, Germany.

When the tax authorities discover that a taxpayer has failed to report a certain part of his income, they cannot tell whether this is the result of deliberate tax evasion or, perhaps, the result of an innocent oversight. Penalties must be designed so as to apply whenever mis-reporting is discovered, but society may very well wish to distinguish between a deliberate offense and an offense that has been committed by accident and to be more lenient in the latter case. However, leniency will encourage people to commit the offense deliberately. In a one-shot game, equilibrium consists of society picking severe penalties and innocent offenders being hit hard. However, in the repeated game, there exists an equilibrium in which the optimal penalties imposed by society on people with a "reasonable" record are lenient and the optimal strategy for the individuals is to refrain from deliberate offenses.

## 1. Introduction

In almost all criminal proceedings, some doubt remains as to the guilt of the accused. Often the factual element (actus reus) is not completely conclusive and even if it is, the mental element necessary in order for an act to become a crime in law (mens rea) is also frequently questionable.

Examples are numerous; here is a short list:

1  The windscreen of a car in a parking lot carries a parking permit with yesterday's date. The owner claims it has been backdated by mistake.
2  A source of income which does not appear in the appropriate income tax return is discovered. The declarer swears that he had omitted it out of forgetfulness, despite his efforts to give a true account of his earnings.

3  One of the headlights of a car is unlit. Conceivably it had just failed, and the driver
   who had checked the headlights before driving away, had found it to be in working
   order.
4  A person is caught leaving a supermarket with unpaidfor merchandise in his
   possession. Two doubts may arise; perhaps the person was confused or possibly
   someone else might have placed the merchandise where it was found without the
   person's knowledge.

In these cases, a complete dispelling of the doubt is almost impossible and the legal
system is faced with a dilemma; conviction may risk injustice whereas acquittal may open
the door to widespread breach of the law.

As far as once-and-for-all situations are concerned (as for example in cases of crimes like
murder) the law has no alternative but to consider which is more unpalatable: A possible
miscarriage of justice or a weakening of the deterrent effect of the penalty. However, for
offenses which an individual might commit periodically, a wide range of conviction and
punishment policies, built around the offender's record, are possible.

In this paper, I shall consider a simple situation which has at its core the social dilemma
described above. It will be described as a game in section 2. In section 3 I shall discuss the
corresponding repeated game in order to examine the possible policies which the legal
system may adopt. The main result (presented in section 4) is that in the repeated game,
there exists a pair of strategies, one for the penal system and one for the individual, which
are jointly optimal and which have the following structure: In any period, if the individual
is discovered as having committed the offense, then he is penalized only if his long-run
record is "unreasonably" bad; as for the individual, his optimal strategy is to refrain from
committing the offense deliberately.

## 2.  The Isolated Game

Consider the following two-person game whose players are society (player 1) and a typical
member of society (player 2).

The individual has to choose between two kinds of behaviour:

$B$ – Committing a given act which is advantageous to himself but harmful to society at
    large
$G$ – Refraining from this act

Even if the individual chooses $G$, the act may still be committed, by a cause outside
his control. Let us think of this unintentional committing of the act as the result of a
move by a fictitious *chance player* who picks the move "+" ("commit") with a given
probability, $\alpha$, and the move "−" ("do not commit") with probability $1 - \alpha$, where
$0 < \alpha < 1$. The chance player's set of strategies, that is the set, $\{+, -\}$ will be denoted $S_c$.

Society has complete information about whether an act has or has not been committed, but
it has no way of telling whether the act was committed wilfully or accidentally. Suppose that
there are but two possible sentences which the court can pass when the act has been
committed, namely conviction with a fixed penalty, or acquittal.

Society's set of strategies – $S_1$ – contains two elements:

P – *Convict and punish the individual if the act has been committed*
NP – *Do not convict the individual even though the act has been committed*

We assume the rules of the legal system are a matter of public knowledge, i.e., player 1 announces his strategy at the beginning of the game. The individual's strategy is therefore of the form: "I will do $X$ if society chooses $P$, and $Y$ otherwise", where $X, Y \in \{B, G\}$. Let this strategy be denoted simply $XY$. Then, the individual's set of strategies – $S_2$ – contains four elements: $GG$, $GB$, $BG$ and $BB$.

The following outcomes correspond to the various choices that the players and the chance player can make:

*Outcome 1*: $(NP, G, -)$. Society is lenient and the act is not committed.
*Outcome 2*: $(P, G, -)$. Society is strict and the act is not committed.
*Outcome 3*: $(NP, G, +)$. The act is committed unintentionally and the offender is not punished.
*Outcome 4*: $(P, G, +)$. The act is committed unintentionally but the offender is punished.
*Outcome 5*: $(NP, B)$. The act is committed deliberately, but the individual is not punished.
*Outcome 6*: $(P, B)$. The act is committed deliberately, and the individual is punished.

Let the set consisting of these six outcomes be denoted $S$, and let $u_1$ and $u_2$ be respectively the utility functions of society and of the individual, with $u_1 : S \to \mathbf{R}$ $i = 1, 2$. Assume that $u_1$ and $u_2$ are given by:

$$u_1(NP, G, -) = u_1(P, G, -) = 4$$

$$u_1(NP, G, +) = 3$$

$$u_1(P, B) = a \text{ with } 1 < a < 3$$

$$u_1(NP, B) = 2$$

$$u_1(P, G, +) = 1$$

and

$$u_2(NP, B) = 4$$

$$u_2(NP, G, +) = 4$$

$$u_2(NP, G, -) = u_2(P, G, -) = 3$$

$$u_2(P, B) = 2$$

$$u_2(P, G, +) = 1.$$

The specific numbers used in these definitions of $u_1$ and $u_2$ have been picked merely for ease of exposition. The numbers as said, have no significance, and the analysis depends only on the ordinal relationships among them. As a final piece of notation, let the symbol $\oplus$ be used for probability mixtures. More precisely, if $u$ and $v$ are utility numbers and if $\alpha$ satisfies $0 \le \alpha \le 1$, then $\alpha \cdot u \oplus (1 - \alpha) \cdot v$ will stand for the lottery that yields $u$ with probability $\alpha$ and $v$ with probability $1 - \alpha$.

Now it is possible to represent the game being discussed here both in extended [Figure 1] and in normal [Figure 2] forms.

If the individual prefers the utility outcome 2 over the utility lottery $\alpha \cdot 1 \oplus (1 - \alpha) \cdot 3$, then the strategy $BB$ is the dominant strategy for the individual, and the pair $(NP, BB)$ is an equilibrium point for $a < 2$ and the pair $(P, BB)$ is an equilibrium point for $a > 2$. If the individual prefers the lottery $\alpha \cdot 1 \oplus (1 - \alpha) \cdot 3$ to the utility outcome 2, then punishment is a deterrent factor, and the strategy $GB$ will be the individual's dominant strategy with the equilibrium point determined by society's preference between the lottery $\alpha \cdot 1 \oplus (1 - \alpha) \cdot 4$ and the utility outcome 2. If society is ready to take the risk of incurring injustice the act will be declared as a strict liability offense, and equilibrium will be $(P, GB)$. If not, the act will be declared legal, and equilibrium point will be $(NP, GB)$.

In all these cases the equilibrium points are also $\max_1 \max_2$ solutions. In other words, they are the outcomes of optimal legal strategies assuming the individual maximizes his utility subject to society's declared strategy. Notice that when the equilibrium points are $(P, GB)$ or $(P, BB)$ the pair $(NP, GG)$ Pareto dominates the equilibrium points.

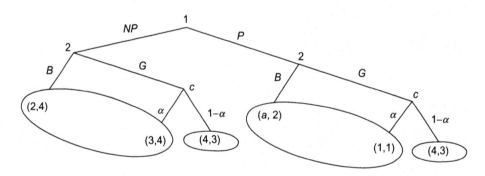

**Figure 1** Extended form

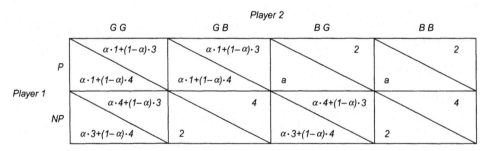

**Figure 2** Normal form

Society's most preferred pair is $(NP, GG)$. However it is not an equilibrium point in the single game. The main message of this paper is that in the repeated game, society can "enforce" this pair of strategies.

## 3. The Repeated Game

Considering offenses that the individual may repeat many times, we assume that society and the individual both expect that after each play of the game there will be more plays of the same game. The suitable concept in game theory, for analysing this situation, is the repeated game [see for example, *Luce/Raiffa*], which consists of an infinite number of plays of the single game.

This structure seems to be unrealistic. But as *Aumann* [1959] says this notion is more suitable than a repeated game consisting of any fixed number of single games. "The fact that the players know when they have arrived at the last play becomes the decisive factor in the analysis overshadowing all other considerations....*A. W. Tucker* has pointed out the condition that after each play the players expect that there will be more is mathematically equivalent to an infinite sequence of plays".

We assume that each game played at any stage of the repeated game, is identical with every other game, played at any other stage, irrespective of what had happend before.

The individual has complete information after each game. His information set is therefore

$$I_1 = \{\{(NP, B)\}, \{(NP, G, +)\}, \{(P, G, -)\}, \{(NP, G, -)\}, \{(P, G, +)\}, \{(P, B)\}\}$$

Since society cannot distinguish between deliberate and accidental acts, its information set at the end of every single game is given by

$$I_2 = \{\{(P, B), (P, G, +)\}, \{(NP, B), (NP, G, +)\}, \{(NP, G, -)\}, \{(P, G, -)\}\}$$

Both society and the individual have perfect memories. For any natural number $k$ let $I_i(k) = I_i$. Define

$$I_i^t = \mathbf{X}_{k=1}^t I_i(k)$$

In the repeated game, a strategy of a player is a sequence of the form $\{f^t\}_{t=1}^\infty$ where $f^1 \in S_1$ and $f^t: I_i^{t-1} \to S_i$. If $(\tau^1, \ldots, \tau^{t-1}) \in I_i$ is the information possessed by $i$, then $i$ will choose the strategy $f^t(\tau^1, \ldots, \tau^{t-1})$. $F_i$ denotes the set of strategies open to $i$, and $F = F_1 \times F_2$.

Let $h_i^t(f, g)$ be the random variable of the utility of player $i$ at time $t$, under the assumption that the players adopt strategies $f \in F_1, g \in F_2$. For a formal description of $h_i^t(f, g)$ see *Aumann* [1959].

As for the preferences of the players in the repeated game I assume that both society and the individual aim to maximize the limit of the long-run average utility.

If the limit

$$H_i(f,g) = \lim_{T \to \infty} \frac{1}{T} \sum_{t=1}^{T} h_i^t(f,g)$$

exists a.s., the pair $(f, g)$ will be called summable. Denote by $\tilde{F}$ the set of summable pairs of strategies.

I shall write $(f,g) >_i (\bar{f},\bar{g})$, if there exists $\epsilon > 0$ such that with positive probability there are an infinite number of $T$ for which

$$\frac{1}{T} \sum_{t=1}^{T} h_i^t(f,g) > H_i(\bar{f},\bar{g}) + \epsilon$$

DEFINITION   The pair $(f, g) \in \tilde{F}$ will be called an *equilibrium point* of the repeated game if there is no $\bar{f} \in F_1$ or $\bar{g} \in F_2$ satisfying $(\bar{f},g) >_1 (f,g)$ or $(f,\bar{g}) >_2 (f,g)$.

Let $(f,g) \in F$. The strategy $g$ is said to be $>_2$ maximal relative to $f$ if there is no $\bar{g} \in F_2$ such that $(f,\bar{g}) >_2 (f,g)$.

Now we are ready for the main definition:

DEFINITION   The pair $(f,g) \in \tilde{F}$ is a *max₁ max₂ solution* if $g$ is $>_2$ maximal relative to $f$ and there is no pair $(\bar{f},\bar{g}) \in \tilde{F}$ such that $\bar{g}$ is $>_2$ maximal relative to $\bar{f}$ and $(\bar{f},\bar{g}) >_1 (f,g)$.

## 4.  The Theorem

The main theorem asserts the optimality for society of the following legal policy: the individual will be convicted and punished at time $t + 1$ if and only if two conditions hold simultaneously: first the antisocial act is discovered to have been committed at time $t + 1$; and, second, the relative frequency of such acts having occured up to time $t$ is greater than $\alpha + \alpha_t$ where $\{\alpha_t\}$ is a sequence of positive real numbers converging to 0 "sufficiently slowly". Formally, we have –

*Theorem*: Let $k > 1$ and $\alpha_t = \sqrt{2k\,\alpha(1 - \alpha)\,\ln\,\ln\,t}/\sqrt{t}$.
Let
$\hat{f} = \{\hat{f}^t\}$ be the following social strategy:
$\hat{f}^1 = NP$

$$\hat{f}^{t+1}(\tau^1, \ldots, \tau^t) = \begin{cases} P \text{ if} & \left| \left\{ s \leq t \,\middle|\, \begin{matrix} \tau^s = \{(P,B),(P,G,+)\} \text{ or} \\ \tau^s = \{(NP,B),(NP,G,+)\} \end{matrix} \right\} \right| \geq t(\alpha + \alpha_t) \\ NP \text{ otherwise} \end{cases}$$

Let $\hat{g} = \{\hat{g}^t\}$ be the strategy of the individual where he always adopts $G$. Then:

(a)   $H_1(\hat{f},\hat{g}) = 4 \cdot (1 - \alpha) + 3\alpha$
and
$H_2(\hat{f},\hat{g}) = 3 \cdot (1 - \alpha) + 4\alpha.$

b)  $(\hat{f}, \hat{g})$ is an equilibrium point of the repeated game.
c)  $(\hat{f}, \hat{g})$ is a $\max_1 \max_2$ solution.

**Proof a)**  Let $D_t$ be the random variable which assumes the value 1 if the chance player causes the act to occur at time $t$, and assumes the value 0 otherwise.

From the law of the iterated logarithm [see, for example, *Lamperti*] we have that with probability 1 there exists $T_0$ such that for all $T \geq T_0$

$$\frac{1}{T} \sum_{t=1}^{T} D_t - \alpha < \alpha_T.$$

Therefore almost surely society will choose strategy $P$ only a finite numbers of times and with probability 1

$$\frac{1}{T} \sum_{t=1}^{T} h_1^t(\hat{f}, \hat{g}) \to 4 \cdot (1 - \alpha) + 3\alpha$$

and

$$\frac{1}{T} \sum_{t=1}^{T} h_2^t(\hat{f}, \hat{g}) \to 3 \cdot (1 - \alpha) + 4\alpha.$$

**b)–c)**  The ideal combination of strategies from society's point of view is the pair $(NP, GG)$ to be repeated forever. But even this pair will only yield a utility for society of $4 \cdot (1 - \alpha) + 3\alpha$. Therefore in order to prove that $(\hat{f}, \hat{g})$ is an equilibrium point in the repeated game and also $\max_1\max_2$ solution, it suffices to show that there does not exist a $g \in F_2$ with $(\hat{f}, g) >_2 (\hat{f}, \hat{g})$. Let $g \in F_2$ and let $\epsilon > 0$. We now show the emptiness of the event: for infinitely many $T$,

$$\frac{1}{T} \sum_{t=1}^{T} h_2^t(\hat{f}, g) > H_2(\hat{f}, \hat{g}) + \epsilon$$

Let $\{w_t\}$ be a sequence of the individual's utilities obtained from $(\hat{f}, g)$. Denote

$$\bar{w}_T = \frac{1}{T} \sum_{t=1}^{T} w_t$$

Let $N$ be the minimal natural number for which $\alpha_N + 4/N < \epsilon$. Our claim is that only for a finite number of times $T$, $\bar{w}_T > 4\alpha + 3(1 - \alpha) + \epsilon$. The claim is applied easily from the following three assertions:

For any $t > N$:

1.  if $\bar{w}_t > 4(\alpha + \alpha_N) + 3(1 - \alpha - \alpha_N)$ then $\bar{w}_{t+1} < \bar{w}_t - \alpha/(t+1)$.

2.  if $\bar{w}_t \leqslant 4\,(\alpha + \alpha_N) + 3\,(1 - \alpha - \alpha_N)$ then $\bar{w}_{t+1} < 4\alpha + 3\,(1 - \alpha) + \epsilon$.
3.  there is $T > N$ such that $\bar{w}_T \leqslant 4\,(\alpha + \alpha_N) + 3\,(1 - \alpha - \alpha_N)$.

PROOF OF ASSERTION 1
For any $t > N$ if $\bar{w}_t > 4\,(\alpha + \alpha_N) + 3\,(1 - \alpha - \alpha_N)$ then also

$$\bar{w}_t > (\alpha + \alpha_t) + 3\,(1 - \alpha - \alpha_t).$$

The relative frequency of the forbidden acts is greater than $\alpha + \alpha_t$ and therefore society's strategy at time $t + 1$ is $P$.
   Now $w_{t+1} \leq 3$ and

$$\bar{w}_{t+1} \leqslant \frac{t \cdot \bar{w}_t + 3}{t + 1} \leqslant \bar{w}_t + \frac{3 - \bar{w}_t}{t + 1} \leqslant \bar{w}_t - \frac{\alpha + \alpha_t}{t + 1} < \bar{w}_t - \frac{\alpha}{t + 1}$$

PROOF OF ASSERTION 2
If $\bar{w}_t \leqslant 4(\alpha + \alpha_N) + 3\,(1 - \alpha - \alpha_N)$ then

$$\bar{w}_{t+1} \leqslant \frac{[4\,(\alpha + \alpha_N) + 3\,(1 - \alpha - \alpha_N)]t + 4}{t + 1} = [4\alpha + 3\,(1 - \alpha)]\frac{t}{t + 1} +$$
$$+ \frac{t \cdot \alpha_N + 4}{t + 1} < 4\alpha + 3\,(1 - \alpha) + \alpha_N + \frac{4}{N} < 4\alpha + 3\,(1 - \alpha) + \epsilon$$

PROOF OF ASSERTION 3    The harmonic series diverges and therefore assertion 1) implies 3.

*Remark*:   If we replace the sequence $\{\alpha_t\}$ with the sequence $\alpha_t \equiv \epsilon > 0$, the previously optimal strategy is no longer optimal since the individual may deviate with relative frequency of say $\epsilon/2$, which would result almost surely in being punished only a finite number of times.
   If society convicts the accused whenever the frequency of the harmful act exceeds $\alpha$ (i.e. if we let $\alpha_t \equiv 0$) then the individual will be punished infinitely many times (almost surely) even if he consistently adopts the strategy $G$. The same result is true if we choose $k < 1$ in the definition of $\{\alpha_t\}$ [see *Lamperti*]. However any sequence that tends to 0 more slowly than our sequence is suitable for a definition of an optimal strategy.

*Remark*:   Some of the assumptions made above may be dropped or relaxed. For example, we can remove our assumption that committal of a forbidden act is always found out by society if we introduce a chance player representing the chance of discovery. Society's information set is represented here [in Figure 3] by loops.
   In a way similar to the main theorem we can prove that there is a positive sequence $\beta_n \to 0$ and an optimal policy which punishes the individual if the frequency of his offences in the past is greater than $\alpha \cdot \beta + \beta_n$, where $\beta$ is the probability of discovery.

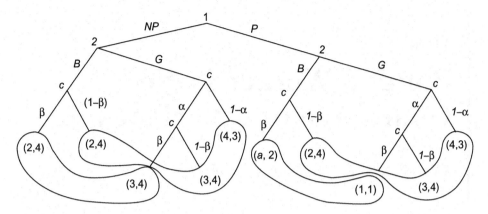

**Figure 3**

*References*

AUMANN, R. J. (1959), "Acceptable Points in General Cooperative *n*-person Game. In A. W. Tucker and R. C. Luce (eds.), *Contributions to the Theory of Games IV. Annals of Math. Studies*, 40, Princeton, N. J., 287–324.

LAMPERTI, J. (1966), *Probability*. New York.

LUCE, R. P., and H. RAIFFA (1957), *Games and Decisions*. New York.

# THIRTY-FIVE

# Bonded Worker is No Guarantee of a Perfect Job

TERI AGINS

*Source*: *Wall Street Journal*, September 30, 1985.

The words "licensed and bonded" are supposed to inspire confidence. They mean a contractor has been sanctioned by a local authority and is insured in case of badly flawed work. But those assurances fell short in the case of a New York couple whose contractor botched a bathroom remodeling job. It took the couple six months to get the contractor's full bond coverage of $5,000, and that was $838 short of what it cost to redo the work.

Licenses and bonds aren't guarantees that work will be done correctly or that a consumer will be fully reimbursed for mistakes. But regulatory agencies advise people to hire only bonded contractors because they have been investigated by both licensing and bonding agencies and are easily traceable if complaints arise. Unfortunately, the bonds that most states require licensed contractors, like plumbers and electricians, to have offer only limited protection, typically from $1,000 to $10,000. They also guarantee only that the contractor will complete the job according to standards set by the municipality. "This sometimes means that if the plumber stopped the leak, but you don't like the way he left the wall behind the sink, you don't have a claim," says Bill Kelly, surety manager for Surety Association of America, a bonding-company trade association in Iselin, N.J.

If a job doesn't meet local standards, collecting on the contractor's bond can take some time. Bonds are issued directly to local licensing authorities, which investigate claims and pay the settlements. In New York, the city must actually revoke a contractor's license before it can collect on a bond and pay the proceeds to the aggrieved customer. Typically, this process takes five to six months, according to the New York City Department of Consumer Affairs. And if several claims are pending against a contractor, all the victims of his bad work may have to share the proceeds of one $5,000 bond.

For costly projects like room additions or new roofing, a contractor can be bonded for a higher amount than that required by law. This extra protection comes in the form of so-called performance and payment bonds, which cover specific projects and ensure that work is completed on time, according to specifications and at the contractual cost. If the contractor fails to comply, the customer can file a claim directly with the bonding company. The premium, typically about 1 percent of the value of the contract, is paid by the customer. Performance and payment bonds also protect a homeowner if the contractor skips town without paying subcontractors or suppliers. Without a bond covering such payments, the unpaid suppliers and subcontractors may be able to enforce a lien on the customer's home. Unexpected damages are also covered by these bonds. "We see messes," says Dan Kirby, counsel for Western Surety Co. of Sioux Falls, S. D. "The roof that the contractor was supposed to fix will continue to leak, and then the leak seeps through the wall tiles, rots the walls and ruins the carpet." Such a bond would cover all the damage.

A third kind of bond, the fidelity bond, covers losses and damage by employees of gardening, maid, carpet-cleaning, exterminating and other service businesses. For example, Merry Maids Inc., an Omaha, Neb., franchiser of 250 cleaning businesses, covers its franchisees' employees with a fidelity bond for theft losses and damages of up to $500,000. To collect on a fidelity bond, customers should report a theft to the police, get a copy of the police report and then file the claim. Like most homeowner insurance policies, these fidelity bonds won't cover "mysterious disappearance" of valuables. Most underwriters require solid evidence – such as a conviction or written admission – that a covered employee was guilty. And as with other types of insurance claims, keeping good records will improve a person's chance of collecting on fidelity bonds. When an employee is suspected of stealing, there's almost always a "dispute on facts," says Gary Walker of New York's consumer affairs department. "Your ability to document your side of the case with receipts, witnesses and contracts will help tip the scales in your favor."

# THIRTY-SIX

# "Look, Ted! We Get Paid the Same as You but All We're Doing is Standing Around and Flicking our Fingers"

SCOTT ADAMS

*Source*: © United Media, courtesy of Knight Features, London.

# PART EIGHT
# Further Topics in Moral Hazard

# Introduction

Moral hazard is important enough to deserve two chapters. The excerpt from Adam Smith's *Wealth of Nations* with which we begin is part of his discussion of why wages differ. He begins with obvious determinants such as the skill needed for the work, but eventually he comes to the reason in the passage here: that some jobs require extra trust, and if the worker is paid a higher wage, he will be more reluctant to abuse his trust for fear of losing his good wage. That is the idea of the efficiency wage.

The examples of plea bargains are taken from an article I wrote on a very specialized point of law, whether suspects should be allowed to bargain away their right, under federal US law, to keep discussions with the police out of their trials if they cannot come to an agreement of the kind in the Pileggi book excerpted in Chapter 31. These agreements are often very one-sided. Why? The answer may help us to understand why many contracts between employers and workers or between companies and consumers are one-sided. It may have something to do with the fact that one side of the transaction has a valuable reputation, but the other does not.

The newspaper article on interplant rivalry is an example of a tournament. Does the situation of the auto unions remind you of cartels? Tournaments have much in common with product competition. What are the differences? The situation in the Dilbert cartoon, "The vacation in Aruba," is more complicated, but it, too has a tournament in the background. What are the players, actions, payoffs, and information in that game?

# THIRTY-SEVEN

# Wealth of Nations

ADAM SMITH

*Source*: *An Inquiry into the Nature and Causes of the Wealth of Nations*, Book 1, Chapter 10 (extract). First edition printed for W. Strahan and T. Cadell, London, 1776.

## Of Wages and Profit in the Different Employments of Labour and Stock

Fourthly, the wages of labour vary accordingly to the small or great trust which must be reposed in the workmen.

The wages of goldsmiths and jewellers are everywhere superior to those of many other workmen, not only of equal, but of much superior ingenuity, on account of the precious materials with which they are intrusted.

We trust our health to the physician: our fortune and sometimes our life and reputation to the lawyer and attorney. Such confidence could not safely be reposed in people of a very mean or low condition. Their reward must be such, therefore, as may give them that rank in the society which so important a trust requires. The long time and the great expense which must be laid out in their education, when combined with this circumstance, necessarily enhance still further the price of their labour.

When a person employs only his own stock in trade, there is no trust; and the credit which he may get from other people depends, not upon the nature of his trade, but upon their opinion of his fortune, probity, and prudence. The different rates of profit, therefore, in the different branches of trade, cannot arise from the different degrees of trust reposed in the traders.

THIRTY-EIGHT

# Examples of Plea Bargains

Eric Rasmusen

*Source*: Mezzanatto and the Economics of Self Incrimination, *Cardozo Law Review* (May 1998), pp. 1541–84.

An example of this third type of waiver is the following excerpt from an agreement under which the true-life organized crime figure portrayed in the movie *Goodfellas* agreed to testify against his associates:

> In addition, in the event that you do not fully comply with all the other terms of this understanding (immediate full and truthful disclosure, testimony, etc.), this agreement will be nullified. Should this occur, the Government will be free to prosecute you with regard to any and all violations of the federal criminal law in which you may have participated, and to use against you any and all statements made by you and testimony you have given prior and subsequent to the date of this agreement.[1]

The standard agreement in use in the Eastern District of New York is quite similar to the one in *Stirling*:

> If the Office determines that [the cooperator] has cooperated fully, provided substantial assistance to law enforcement authorities and otherwise complied with the terms of this agreement, the Office will file a motion with the sentencing court setting forth the nature and extent of [his] cooperation.... In this connection it is understood that the Office's determination of whether [the cooperator] has cooperated fully and provided substantial assistance, and the Office's assessment of the value, truthfulness, completeness and accuracy of the cooperation, shall be binding upon [him].... Should it be judged by the Office that [the cooperator] has failed to cooperate fully, or has intentionally given false, misleading or incomplete information or testimony...[he] shall thereafter be subject to prosecution for any federal criminal violation of which the Office has knowledge, including, but not limited to, perjury and obstruction of justice.[2]

---

[1] Nicholas Pileggi, *Wise Guy* 283 (1985).
[2] Graham Hughes, Agreements for Cooperation in Criminal Cases, 45 *Vand. L. Rev.* 1, 41 (1992), at 38.

# THIRTY-NINE

# Unions Say Auto Firms Use Interplant Rivalry to Raise Work Quotas

DALE D. BUSS

*Source*: *Wall Street Journal*, November 8, 1983.

Detroit – The United Auto Workers is accustomed to threats that US auto makers will give their jobs to low-wage workers in other countries. But recently, the companies have quietly been using a more effective tactic to push the union into cutting labor costs: pitting workers against their fellow UAW members right here in the US.

"Whipsawing," union officials call it, and it's devastatingly simple.

Take General Motors Corp.'s efforts at its six Fisher Body division "hardware" plants, which make small parts like seat belts and car-door hinges. To get GM to reverse the planned closing of two of the plants, the UAW agreed to boost hourly worker output at them by 20% early last year. Soon GM demanded matching gains at the four other hardware plants, threatening to close at least one of them if they didn't go along. Worried about big job losses, local UAW officials acceded even though some workers pleaded that they wouldn't be able to keep up with the faster production lines. The result: Fisher Body cut costs significantly without actually shutting any plants.

## End of an Era

But as potent as it is, the practice is casting a shadow over what has been touted as an era of enlightenment in auto-industry labor relations. For the auto makers and the UAW, "cooperation" is supposed to be the new motto, and the two sides have recently taken steps to imitate the less-adversarial Japanese approach. Many workers and union officials, however, assert that whipsawing is simply a reversion to the confrontational tactics of old.

"They're trying to have it both ways," complains Stanley Marshall, director of a Michigan UAW region where GM has been applying the technique frequently. "It makes it awfully hard to really try to work together with the companies when they do this," he adds.

Adds Virgil Gralton, shop chairman at a GM plant in Livonia, Mich.: "They're trying to whip us into some position we can't ever get in – how can all of the plants be Number One? It's an unattainable goal, but the competition is never-ending."

Auto makers are using the tactic simply because they see it as their only choice if they are to keep the Japanese industry's huge, persistent labor-cost advantage from widening. With industry profits rising, the UAW isn't likely to accept further major curbs in wages and benefits. Thus, though the practice incenses the union, whipsawing nevertheless represents one of the companies' best hopes for slashing labor costs in the near future, with the potential for helping to save billions of dollars in manufacturing costs. One industry cost expert estimates auto makers could slash $50 to $200 off the cost of building each car from workrule changes alone.

## Too Much Capacity

Continuing capacity surpluses, notably at parts facilities, at GM and Ford Motor Co. should give them the club they need to make the practice effective for some time. The companies can also lean on balking UAW locals with the related threat of "outsourcing" production to lower-wage, non-union contractors in the US and abroad. The union's concessionary agreement with the proposed GM-Toyota Motor Corp. joint venture might give the companies an additional wedge.

"Auto makers are just using the tremendous tactical advantage they hold these days," says Arnold Weber, president of the University of Colorado and a labor economist. "It's the flipside, really, of what the UAW" sometimes does, "such as shutting down an entire corporation by striking just one or two plants."

GM – as the largest and most vertically integrated of American auto makers – is most devoted to the tactic, UAW officials say; they also cite some incidents at Ford. Industry manufacturing experts say that although the companies have engaged in the tactic for years, plant-against-plant competition has never been more effective.

Officials at both companies insist they don't deliberately play off UAW locals against each other. They won't allow plant managers to comment. But Alfred S. Warren, GM's vice president of industrial relations, says the company does encourage managers to "do the best job they can to make their plants competitive and get work" for them.

## Cost-Cutting Drive

GM began a huge push to make its factories leaner last year after signing a new, $2\frac{1}{2}$-year national contract with the UAW that is saving the auto maker an estimated $2.5 billion to $3 billion in wage-and-benefit concessions. The union also agreed to consider new local contracts at GM plants, so company officials began trying to get workrule changes and other factory-floor efficiency measures that were to save additional hundreds of millions of dollars.

Originally, GM said it would pit its workers and plants against outside suppliers to judge necessary cost savings. But when workers and union officials have resisted concessions; playing them off against one another instead has often been instrumental in bringing locals into line. At Fisher Body's Chicago stamping plant, for example, the stubborn workforce acceded to givebacks last spring – but only after the division had stripped it of at least two major jobs, laid off close to 200, handed the plant's work to plants that had already agreed to concessions, and threatened further such actions.

Auto makers aren't restricting the practice to contract bargaining. Supervisors' shop-floor comments make the rank-and-file keenly aware of the competition with their counterparts at other plants, workers say. In some plants, they maintain, managers exploit new UAW-company programs that are supposedly meant to improve workers' satisfaction with their jobs. Such techniques motivate workers, all right, by making them fear increasingly for their jobs, union officers complain.

## Haranguing Workers

Managers at Fisher Body's Livonia trim plant, for instance, use so-called "quality-of-worklife" meetings largely to harangue workers for trailing the division's other trim plant in attendance, quality and other measuring sticks, UAW officials charge. And at some of Ford's stamping plants, managers regularly let UAW officials and workers know where their plants stand against others in meeting cost budgets and warn that the company may close one or more of the highest-cost plants.

"The company is giving us all sorts of information they never did before, but all they use it for is to tell us how badly we're doing against other plants," says Raymond Plock, president of the union local at the Chicago stamping plant.

At Fisher Body's Flint, Mich., hardware plant, management issues a weekly newsleter that includes a chart tracking labor costs at the plant compared with those at other divisional hardware plants. Quarterly, the newsletter also discloses how the plant's quality audit stacks up against the others.

The message, as interpreted by many workers, isn't very subtle. "It's divide and conquer," says James Moore, a 34-year-old worker on the window-regulator line. He says he appreciates knowing where his plant stands, "but we get to developing grudges against people at plants that are doing better than us. We shouldn't be falling into that — they're trying to keep their jobs just like we are."

## Impact at Lordstown

The most startling illustration of the effectiveness of the auto makers' toughminded tactics is the turn of events at GM's Lordstown, Ohio, car-assembly plant. The UAW local there had long been the *enfant terrible* of the industry, a radical group whose strikes and general rabble-rousing became union legend in the 1970s. But in the 1980s, recession and big layoffs have mellowed the Lordstown rebels significantly.

Just how much was indicated last winter, when sales of its J-body subcompact cars had improved so much that GM decided to add second work turns at the three plants that build them. The most cooperative, productive and quality-conscious of the three would be awarded the first new work turn, rescuing 2,500 or more workers from long layoffs.

UAW officials at Lordstown linked arms with management to win the competition. They allowed GM to increase the line speed in the body shop and to make jobs more strenuous throughout the plant. Hundreds of lingering grievances also were quickly settled. The result: Lordstown was awarded a second work turn last spring, while unemployed workers at GM's Janesville, Wis., and Leeds, Mo, assembly plants had to wait three months and seven months, respectively, to get their jobs back.

Lordstown's new attitude impresses some UAW officials as kowtowing. "We can't just take care of ourselves," complains a union officer at the Janesville plant. "We're still a *union*, and we have to rely on people in other plants to keep it that way."

## Two Possibilities

But Rudy Gasparek, president of the Lordstown local, doesn't apologize for beating other UAW locals to the prize. He boasts of the plant's high quality rating as his predecessors might have talked up a wildcat strike. "Is it being a good union brother to be hard-nosed and keep half your people on the street without jobs?" he says, "Bringing your laid-off people back to work is what's going to make us stronger, not giving the impression of strong unionism while we're eroding underneath. That's idiocy."

Such strains have split many a telling seam in UAW "solidarity" lately. In Detroit recently, meeting with Robert Stempel, general manager of the Chevrolet division, local officials from GM engine plants openly bickered over which plants should get preference for future work, "falling right into management's trap," as one official in at tendance put it. GM recently decided to close one of the plants.

One UAW officer from a Ford stamping plant says that when he meets with his counterparts from other stamping plants these days, "We can only hope we're being honest. You never know if someone isn't telling you something in order to undermine you."

Workers at the Flint Fisher Body hardware plant were the last holdouts against the division's demands for a 20% output boost last year. But while union officials were trying to bargain a lesser line speedup, some workers on the seatbelt line voluntarily began producing more belts just to show plant managers they were up to it. The fear of losing work to other plants was "so tremendous that the workers pulled the rug right out from under us," says Michael Bennett, president of the local.

## Plant Closings

The UAW is helpless to withstand whipsawing mainly because GM and Ford still have plenty of extra capacity across many of their manufacturing lines, according to industry experts. Ford has closed seven major plants in the last four years, and a Ford executive recently said that the auto maker probably won't reopen any of them. GM has permanently shut five and announced the planned closure of at least three more. Although some car assembly lines are approaching 100% of capacity, auto makers will continue to trim or cut away component operations as they deploy more computerbased automation and as front-wheel-drive and other innovations in car design sweep across the industry.

Some plants get hit by the changes seemingly all at once. The work force at GM's Bay City, Mich., parts plant is already reeling from the loss of 300 jobs due to the introduction of a highly automated manufacturing line in one part of the plant and from the news that nearly 600 workers on the carburetor line will be tossed out of jobs beginning next year; UAW officials say GM plans to phase out use of carburetors in favor of fuel-injection systems, which will be made elsewhere.

Now GM is warning local union officials to "get competitive" in the cost of making several other components and is pressing for concessions. "We don't have any choice but to go along or this plant could disappear" along with its 2,200 jobs, says a union source.

GM managers at Bay City refuse to identify the sources of the plant's competition, union officers say, so that the local's members can't be sure in which instances they are battling fellow UAW members for work and in which they are pitted against outside concerns. Losing work to lower-cost, non-union manufacturers here and abroad is another big problem for many UAW locals.

## The GM-Toyota Venture

Some local union officials fear that the car companies may soon have another big weapon: the understanding reached between the UAW and the proposed GM-Toyota joint venture. The venture would implement Japanese manufacturing techniques that are more productive and demanding on workers, possibly setting off efforts by GM and other US auto makers to get the UAW to agree to the same sort of system at all American plants.

Whether to acquiesce to such tactics or to fight them is a big part of the union's soul-searching on how to set its course these days. Top UAW leaders acknowledge US auto makers' cost problems and say the union wants to help. And in fact, as GM's Mr. Warren notes, the UAW to some degree has actually brought the use of whipsawing and other practices onto itself; the 1982 GM-UAW contract, in a statement titled "Job Security and the Competitive Edge," states that "there is an unprecedented need for change" in order to make the company competitive. The contract supports "mutually agreeable and beneficial change on the local level" toward that end.

But many rank-and-file workers and lower-level union officials remain deeply suspicious of any efforts to ease things for management, and they are pressuring the UAW to get tough on whipsawing. One alternative UAW leaders are considering: insisting next year, in its next round of bargaining with GM and Ford, on insertion of another layer of bargaining between national-contract talks and local negotiations so that plants making the same components can't as easily be pitted against one another.

"They had better hustle to do as much whipsawing as they can now," promises one member of the union's executive board. "We're going to slam the door on it next year."

FORTY

# "Dilbert, I Want You to Manage Wally's Project While He's on Vacation in Aruba"

SCOTT ADAMS

*Source*: © United Media, courtesy of Knight Features, London.

# Adverse Selection

# Introduction

George Akerlof may well win the Nobel Prize one of these days for his "Lemons" article. Published in 1970, it was first submitted in July 1967, to the *American Economic Review*, but was rejected there and at the *Review of Economic Studies* as trivial and at the *Journal of Political Economy* as unrealistic. Joshua Gans and George Shepherd tell the story in "How Are the Mighty Fallen: Rejected Classic Articles by Leading Economists," *The Journal of Economic Perspectives* 8: 165–79 (Winter 1994). See also George Shepherd (Editor) *Rejected: Leading Economists Ponder the Publication Process*, Thomas Horton (1994). The article is indeed a strange one, which is why it is worth including here. By the year 2000, we have better ways of presenting a model like this, but it is worth reading the original article for its insight into how an intelligent person first thought of this idea, and to view it outside the useful blinders we now employ. The article is a good example of what Robert Fogel once told me: "Only your home runs count." For Old World readers: in the American game of baseball, a home run is achieved by swinging a wooden bat very hard – a risky approach which usually leads to the utter failure known as a "strikeout."

The Bagehot article is not as well known as it should be, and it is another example of an idea published long before its time. I came across it in a course taught by Fischer Black, who said that "Bagehot" was a pseudonym for Jack Treynor, one of the formulators of the CAPM theory of asset pricing. The idea in the paper gave rise to the market micro-structure literature of the 1980s and 1990s.

One solution to adverse selection is for the informed player, the agent, to pay the cost of informing the uninformed player, the principal. Advertising does this; the player trying to sell something pays the cost of providing information to potential buyers. But some cost does remain for the buyer: the cost of reading the advertising. The *Wall Street Journal* article on paying viewers shows how this final barrier can be removed. The *Far Side* cartoon, "Frank's Neurosurgery," on the other hand, shows how not to sell a product of unknown quality. How many causes to be suspicious about Frank's skills can you spot in the picture?

The remaining selection in this chapter, "The Creation of New Mathematics," is an internal dialog illustrating the creative process in mathematics, a process much the same as in economics. Karl Popper proposed that scientific theorizing worked by proposing "falsifiable" theories, theories which had implications that could be tested so that, if the theory failed the test, it could be rejected. (Karl Popper, *The Logic of Scientific Discovery*, New York, Basic Books [1959], first published in German as *Logik Der Forschung*, Vienna: Springer [1934].) Milton Friedman is known for his influential application of the idea to economics in "The Methodology of Positive Economics," pp. 3–46 of *Essays in Positive Economics*, Chicago: University of Chicago Press (1953). Imre Lakatos proposed a different process, in which the theory itself is not fully formed until it is tested, and the theory evolves along with the testing. He published his views in the form of a dialog between a teacher and students discussing a mathematical theorem, with copious footnotes by Lakatos in his own person. (Imre Lakatos, *Proofs and Refutations: The Logic of Mathematical Discovery*. Cambridge: Cambridge University Press [1976].) The selection here is a short dialog in imitation of Lakatos.

# FORTY-ONE

# The Market for "Lemons": Quality Uncertainty and the Market Mechanism

GEORGE A. AKERLOF

Source: *Quarterly Journal of Economics* 84(3), 1970, pp. 488–500. © by the President and Fellows of Harvard College.

## 1. Introduction

This paper relates quality and uncertainty. The existence of goods of many grades poses interesting and important problems for the theory of markets. On the one hand, the interaction of quality differences and uncertainty may explain important institutions of the labor market. On the other hand, this paper presents a struggling attempt to give structure to the statement: "Business in under-developed countries is difficult"; in particular, a structure is given for determining the economic costs of dishonesty. Additional applications of the theory include comments on the structure of money markets, on the notion of "insurability," on the liquidity of durables, and on brand-name goods.

There are many markets in which buyers use some market statistic to judge the quality of prospective purchases. In this case there is incentive for sellers to market poor quality merchandise, since the returns for good quality accrue mainly to the entire group whose statistic is affected rather than to the individual seller. As a result there tends to be a reduction in the average quality of goods and also in the size of the market. It should also be perceived that in these markets social and private returns differ, and therefore, in some cases, governmental intervention may increase the welfare of all parties. Or private institutions may arise to take advantage of the potential increases in welfare which can accrue to all parties. By nature, however, these institutions are non-atomistic, and therefore concentrations of power – with ill consequences of their own – can develop.

The automobile market is used as a finger exercise to illustrate and develop these thoughts. It should be emphasized that this market is chosen for its concreteness and ease in understanding rather than for its importance or realism.

## 2.  The Model with Automobiles as an Example

### 2.1  The automobiles market

The example of used cars captures the essence of the problem. From time to time one hears either mention of or surprise at the large price difference between new cars and those which have just left the showroom. The usual lunch table justification for this phenomenon is the pure joy of owning a "new" car. We offer a different explanation. Suppose (for the sake of clarity rather than reality) that there are just four kinds of cars. There are new cars and used cars. There are good cars and bad cars (which in America are known as "lemons"). A new car may be a good car or a lemon, and of course the same is true of used cars.

The individuals in this market buy a new automobile without knowing whether the car they buy will be good or a lemon. But they do know that with probability $q$ it is a good car and with probability $(1 - q)$ it is a lemon; by assumption, $q$ is the proportion of good cars produced and $(1 - q)$ is the proportion of lemons.

After owning a specific car, however, for a length of time, the car owner can form a good idea of the quality of this machine; i.e., the owner assigns a new probability to the event that his car is a lemon. This estimate is more accurate than the original estimate. An asymmetry in available information has developed: for the sellers now have more knowledge about the quality of a car than the buyers. But good cars and bad cars must still sell at the same price – since it is impossible for a buyer to tell the difference between a good car and a bad car. It is apparent that a used car cannot have the same valuation as a new car – if it did have the same valuation, it would clearly be advantageous to trade a lemon at the price of new car, and buy another new car, at a higher probability $q$ of being good and a lower probability of being bad. Thus the owner of a good machine must be locked in. Not only is it true that he cannot receive the true value of his car, but he cannot even obtain the expected value of a new car.

Gresham's law has made a modified reappearance. For most cars traded will be the "lemons," and good cars may not be traded at all. The "bad" cars tend to drive out the good (in much the same way that bad money drives out the good). But the analogy with Gresham's law is not quite complete: bad cars drive out the good because they sell at the same price as good cars; similarly, bad money drives out good because the exchange rate is even. But the bad cars sell at the same price as good cars since it is impossible for a buyer to tell the difference between a good and a bad car; only the seller knows. In Gresham's law, however, presumably both buyer and seller can tell the difference between good and bad money. So the analogy is instructive, but not complete.

### 2.2.  Asymmetrical information

It has been seen that the good cars may be driven out of the market by the lemons. But in a more continuous case with different grades of goods, even worse pathologies can exist. For it is quite possible to have the bad driving out the not-so-bad driving out the medium driving out the not-so-good driving out the good in such a sequence of events that no market exists at all.

One can assume that the demand for used automobiles depends most strongly upon two variables – the price of the automobile $p$ and the average quality of used cars traded, $\mu$, or $Q^d = D(p, \mu)$. Both the supply of used cars and also the average quality $\mu$ will depend upon the price, or $\mu = \mu(p)$ and $S = S(p)$. And in equilibrium the supply must equal the demand for the given average quality, or $S(p) = D(p, \mu(p))$. As the price falls, normally the quality will also fall. And it is quite possible that no goods will be traded at any price level.

Such an example can be derived from utility theory. Assume that there are just two groups of traders: groups one and two. Give group one a utility function

$$U_1 = M + \sum_{i=1}^{n} x_i$$

where $M$ is the consumption of goods other than automobiles, $x_i$ is the quality of the $i$th automobile, and $n$ is the number of automobiles.

Similarly, let

$$U_2 = M + \sum_{i=1}^{n} \frac{3}{2} x_i$$

where $M$, $x_i$ and $n$ are defined as before.

Three comments should be made about these utility functions:

1 Without linear utility (say with logarithmic utility) one gets needlessly mired in algebraic complication.
2 The use of linear utility allows a focus on the effects of asymmetry of information; with a concave utility function we would have to deal jointly with the usual risk-variance effects of uncertainty and the special effects we wish to discuss here.
3 $U_1$ and $U_2$ have the odd characteristic that the addition of a second car, or indeed a $k$th car, adds the same amount of utility as the first. Again realism is sacrificed to avoid a diversion from the proper focus.

To continue, it is assumed

1 that both type one traders and type two traders are von Neumann-Morgenstern maximizers of expected utility;
2 that group one has $N$ cars with uniformly distributed quality $x$, $0 \leq x \leq 2$, and group two has no cars;
3 that the price of "other goods" $M$ is unity.

Denote the income (including that derived from the sale of automobiles) of all type one traders as $Y_1$ and the income of all type two traders as $Y_2$. The demand for used cars will be the sum of the demands by both groups. When one ignores indivisibilities, the demand for automobiles by type one traders will be

$$D_1 = \frac{Y_1}{p} \qquad \frac{\mu}{p} > 1$$

$$D_1 = 0 \qquad \frac{\mu}{p} < 1$$

And the supply of cars offered by type one traders is

$$S_2 = \frac{pN}{2} \qquad p \leqq 2 \tag{1}$$

with average quality

$$\mu = \frac{p}{2} \tag{2}$$

(To derive (1) and (2), the uniform distribution of automobile quality is used.)
Similarly the demand of type two traders is

$$D_2 = \frac{Y_2}{p} \qquad \frac{3\mu}{2} > p$$

$$D_2 = 0 \qquad \frac{3\mu}{2} < p$$

and

$$S_2 = 0$$

Thus total demand $D(p, \mu)$ is

$$D(p, \mu) = \frac{(Y_2 + Y_1)}{p} \quad \text{if } p < \mu$$

$$D(p, \mu) = \frac{Y_2}{p} \qquad \text{if } \mu < p < \frac{3\mu}{2}$$

$$D(p, \mu) = 0 \qquad \text{if } p > \frac{3\mu}{2}$$

However, with price $p$, average quality is $p/2$ and therefore at no price will any trade take place at all: in spite of the fact that *at any given price* between 0 and 3 there are traders of type one who are willing to sell their automobiles at a price which traders of type two are willing to pay.

## 2.3.  Symmetric information

The foregoing is contrasted with the case of symmetric information. Suppose that the quality of all cars is uniformly distributed, $0 \leq x \leq 2$. Then the demand curves and supply curves can be written as follows:

Supply

$$S(p) = N \qquad p > 1$$

$$S(p) = 0 \qquad p < 1$$

And the demand curves are

$$D(p) = \frac{(Y_2 + Y_1)}{p} \qquad p < 1$$

$$D(p) = \left(\frac{Y_2}{p}\right) \qquad 1 < p < \frac{3}{2}$$

$$D(p) = 0 \qquad p > \frac{3}{2}$$

In equilibrium

$$p = 1 \qquad \text{if } Y_2 < N \tag{3}$$

$$p = \frac{Y_2}{N} \qquad \text{if } \frac{2Y_2}{3} < N < Y_2 \tag{4}$$

$$p = \frac{3}{2} \qquad \text{if } N < \frac{2Y_2}{3} \tag{5}$$

If $N < Y_2$ there is a gain in utility over the case of asymmetrical information of $N/2$. (If $N > Y_2$, in which case the income of type two traders is insufficient to buy all $N$ automobiles, there is a gain in utility of $Y_2/2$ units.)

Finally, it should be mentioned that in this example, if traders of groups one and two have the same probabilistic estimates about the quality of individual automobiles – though these estimates may vary from automobile to automobile – (3), (4), and (5) will still describe equilibrium with one slight change: $p$ will then represent the expected price of one quality unit.

## 3.  Examples and Applications

### 3.1.  Insurance

It is a well-known fact that people over 65 have great difficulty in buying medical insurance. The natural question arises: why doesn't the price rise to match the risk?

Our answer is that as the price level rises the people who insure themselves will be those who are increasingly certain that they will need the insurance; for error in medical check-ups, doctors' sympathy with older patients, and so on make it much easier for the applicant to assess the risks involved than the insurance company. The result is that the average medical condition of insurance applicants deteriorates as the price level rises – with the result that no insurance sales may take place at any price.[1] This is strictly analogous to our automobiles case, where the average quality of used cars supplied fell with a corresponding fall in the price level. This agrees with the explanation in insurance textbooks (Dickerson, 1959, p. 333):

> Generally speaking policies are not available at ages materially greater than sixty-five.... The term premiums are too high for any but the most pessimistic (which is to say the least healthy) insureds to find attractive. Thus there is a severe problem of adverse selection at these ages.

The statistics do not contradict this conclusion. While demands for health insurance rise with age, a 1956 national sample survey of 2,809 families with 8,898 persons (Anderson with Feldman, 1956) shows that hospital insurance coverage drops from 63 per cent of those aged 45 to 54, to 31 per cent for those over 65. And surprisingly, this survey also finds average medical expenses for males aged 55 to 64 of $88, while males over 65 pay an average of $77. While noninsured expenditure rises from $66 to $80 in these age groups, insured expenditure declines from $105 to $70. The conclusion is tempting that insurance companies are particularly wary of giving medical insurance to older people.

The principle of "adverse selection" is potentially present in all lines of insurance. The following statement appears in an insurance textbook written at the Wharton School (Denenberg et al., 1964, p. 446):

> There is potential adverse selection in the fact that healthy term insurance policy holders may decide to terminate their coverage when they become older and premiums mount. This action could leave an insurer with an undue proportion of below average risks and claims might be higher than anticipated. Adverse selection "appears (or at least is possible)

---

[1] Arrow's (1963) fine article, does not make this point explicitly. He emphasizes "moral hazard" rather than "adverse selection." In its strict sense, the presence of "moral hazard" is equally disadvantageous for both governmental and private programs; in its broader sense, which includes "adverse selection," "moral hazard" gives a decided advantage to government insurance programs.

whenever the individual or group insured has freedom to buy or not to buy, to choose the amount or plan of insurance, and to persist or to discontinue as a policy holder."

Group insurance, which is the most common form of medical insurance in the United States, picks out the healthy, for generally adequate health is a precondition for employment. At the same time this means that medical insurance is least available to those who need it most, for the insurance companies do their own "adverse selection."

This adds one major argument in favor of medicare.[2] On a cost benefit basis medicare may pay off: for it is quite possible that every individual in the market would be willing to pay the expected cost of his medicare and buy insurance, yet no insurance company can afford to sell him a policy – for at any price it will attract too many "lemons." The welfare economics of medicare, in this view, is *exactly* analogous to the usual classroom argument for public expenditure on roads.

## 3.2. The employment of minorities

The Lemons Principle also casts light on the employment of minorities. Employers may refuse to hire members of minority groups for certain types of jobs. This decision may not reflect irrationality or prejudice – but profit maximization. For race may serve as a good *statistic* for the applicant's social background, quality of schooling, and general job capabilities.

Good quality schooling could serve as a substitute for this statistic; by grading students the schooling system can give a better indicator of quality than other more superficial characteristics. As T. W. Schultz (1964, p. 42) writes, "The educational establishment *discovers* and cultivates potential talent. The capabilities of children and mature students can never be known until *found* and cultivated." (Italics added.) An untrained worker may have valuable natural talents, but these talents must be certified by "the educational establishment" before a company can afford to use them. The certifying establishment, however, must be credible; the unreliability of slum schools decreases the economic possibilities of their students.

This lack may be particularly disadvantageous to members of already disadvantaged minority groups. For an employer may make a rational decision not to hire any members of these groups in responsible positions – because it is difficult to distinguish those with good job qualifications from those with bad qualifications. This type of decision is clearly what George Stigler (1962, p. 104) had in mind when he wrote, "in a regime of ignorance Enrico Fermi would have been a gardener, Von Neumann a checkout clerk at a drugstore."

---

[2] The following quote, again taken from an insurance textbook, shows how far the medical insurance market is from perfect competition:

"...insurance companies must screen their applicants. Naturally it is true that many people will voluntarily seek adequate insurance on their own initiative. But in such lines as accident and health insurance, companies are likely to give a second look to persons who voluntarily seek insurance without being approached by an agent." (Angell, 1957, pp. 8–9.)

This shows that insurance is *not* a commodity for sale on the open market.

As a result, however, the rewards for work in slum schools tend to accrue to the group as a whole – in raising its average quality – rather than to the individual. Only insofar as information in addition to race is used is there any incentive for training.

An additional worry is that the Office of Economic Opportunity is going to use cost–benefit analysis to evaluate its programs. For many benefits may be external. The benefit from training minority groups may arise as much from raising the average quality of the group as from raising the quality of the individual trainee; and, likewise, the returns may be distributed over the whole group rather than to the individual.

### 3.3.   The costs of dishonesty

The Lemons model can be used to make some comments on the costs of dishonesty. Consider a market in which goods are sold honestly or dishonestly; quality may be represented, or it may be misrepresented. The purchaser's problem, of course, is to identify quality. The presence of people in the market who are willing to offer inferior goods tends to drive the market out of existence – as in the case of our automobile "lemons." It is this possibility that represents the major costs of dishonesty – for dishonest dealings tend to drive honest dealings out of the market. There may be potential buyers of good quality products and there may be potential sellers of such products in the appropriate price range; however, the presence of people who wish to pawn bad wares as good wares tends to drive out the legitimate business. The cost of dishonesty, therefore, lies not only in the amount by which the purchaser is cheated; the cost also must include the loss incurred from driving legitimate business out of existence.

Dishonesty in business is a serious problem in underdeveloped countries. Our model gives a possible structure to this statement and delineates the nature of the "external" economies involved. In particular, in the model economy described, dishonesty, or the misrepresentation of the quality of automobiles, costs $\frac{1}{2}$ unit of utility per automobile; furthermore, it reduces the size of the used car market from $N$ to 0. We can, consequently, directly evaluate the costs of dishonesty – at least in theory.

There is considerable evidence that quality variation is greater in underdeveloped than in developed areas. For instance, the need for quality control of exports and State Trading Corporations can be taken as one indicator. In India, for example, under the Export Quality Control and Inspection Act of 1963, "about 85 per cent of Indian exports are covered under one or the other type of quality control" *The Times of India*, November 10, 1967, p. 1. Indian housewives must carefully glean the rice of the local bazaar to sort out stones of the same color and shape which have been intentionally added to the rice. Any comparison of the heterogeneity of quality in the street market and the canned qualities of the American supermarket suggests that quality variation is a greater problem in the East than in the West.

In one traditional pattern of development the merchants of the pre-industrial generation turn into the first entrepreneurs of the next. The best-documented case is Japan,[3] but this also may have been the pattern for Britain and America (Kindleberger, 1958, p. 86). In *our* picture the important skill of the merchant is identifying the quality of merchandise; those who can identify used cars in our example and can guarantee the quality may profit by as

---

[3] See Levy (1955).

much as the difference between type two traders' buying price and type one traders' selling price. These people are the merchants. In production these skills are equally necessary – both to be able to identify the quality of inputs and to certify the quality of outputs. And this is one (added) reason why the merchants may logically become the first entrepreneurs.

The problem, of course, is that entrepreneurship may be a scarce resource; no development text leaves entrepreneurship unemphasized. Some treat it as central.[4] Given, then, that entrepreneurship is scarce, there are two ways in which product variations impede development. First, the pay-off to trade is great for would-be entrepreneurs, and hence they are diverted from production; second, the amount of entrepreneurial time per unit output is greater, the greater are the quality variations.

## 3.4. Credit markets in underdeveloped countries

Credit markets in underdeveloped countries often strongly reflect the operation of the Lemons Principle. In India a major fraction of industrial enterprise is controlled by managing agencies (according to a recent survey (Government of India, 1964, p. 44) these "managing agencies" controlled 65.7 per cent of the net worth of public limited companies and 66 per cent of total assets). Here is a historian's account of the function and genesis of the "managing agency system" (Tinker, 1966, p. 134):

> The management of the South Asian commercial scene remained the function of merchant houses, and a type of organization peculiar to South Asia known as the Managing Agency. When a new venture was promoted (such as a manufacturing plant, a plantation, or a trading venture), the promoters would approach an established managing agency. The promoters might be Indian or British, and they might have technical or financial resources or merely a concession. In any case they would turn to the agency because of its reputation, which would encourage confidence in the venture and stimulate investment.

In turn, a second major feature of the Indian industrial scene has been the dominance of these managing agencies by caste (or, more accurately, communal) groups. Thus firms can usually be classified according to communal origin.[5] In this environment, in which outside investors are likely to be bilked of their holdings, either

1  firms establish a reputation for "honest" dealing, which confers upon them a monopoly rent insofar as their services are limited in supply, or
2  the sources of finance are limited to local communal groups which can use communal – and possibly familial – ties to encourage honest dealing *within* the community.

---

[4] For example, see Lewis (1955, p. 196).

[5] The existence of the following table (and also the small per cent of firms under mixed control) indicates the communalization of the control of firms. Also, for the cotton industry see Fukuzawa (1965).

It is, in Indian economic history, extraordinary difficult to discern whether the savings of rich landlords failed to be invested in the industrial sector

1  because of a fear to invest in ventures controlled by other communities,
2  because of inflated propensities to consume, or
3  because of low rates of return.[6]

At the very least, however, it is clear that the British-owned managing agencies tended to have an equity holding whose communal origin was more heterogeneous than the Indian-controlled agency houses, and would usually include both Indian and British investors.

A second example of the workings of the Lemons Principle concerns the extortionate rates which the local moneylender charges his clients. In India these high rates of interest have been the leading factor in landlessness; the so-called "Cooperative Movement" was meant to counteract this growing landlessness by setting up banks to compete with the local moneylenders.[7] While the large banks in the central cities have prime interest rates of 6, 8, and 10 per cent, the local moneylender charges 15, 25, and even 50 per cent. The answer to this seeming paradox is that credit is granted only where the granter has

1  easy means of enforcing his contract or
2  personal knowledge of the character of the borrower.

The middleman who tries to arbitrage between the rates of the moneylender and the central bank is apt to attract all the "lemons" and thereby make a loss.

[5]  cont'd

Distribution of industrial control by community

|               | 1911 | 1931 | 1951 |
|---------------|------|------|------|
|               |      | (number of firms) |      |
| British       | 281  | 416  | 382  |
| Parsis        | 15   | 25   | 19   |
| Gujartis      | 3    | 11   | 17   |
| Jews          | 5    | 9    | 3    |
| Muslims       | –    | 10   | 3    |
| Bengalis      | 8    | 5    | 20   |
| Marwaris      | –    | 6    | 96   |
| Mixed control | 28   | 28   | 79   |
| Total         | 341  | 510  | 619  |

*Source*: Mehta (1955, p. 314)

[6]  For the mixed record of industrial profits, see Buchanan (1966).

[7]  The leading authority on this is Sir Malcolm Darling. See his (1932) *Punjabi Peasant in Prosperity and Debt*. The following table may also prove instructive:

This interpretation can be seen in Sir Malcolm Darling's (1932, p. 204) interpretation of the village moneylender's power:

> It is only fair to remember that in the Indian village the money-lender is often the one thrifty person amongst a generally thriftless people; and that his methods of business, though demoralizing under modern conditions, suit the happy-go-lucky ways of the peasant. He is always accessible, even at night; dispenses with troublesome formalities, asks no inconvenient questions, advances promptly, and if interest is paid, does not press for repayment of principal. He keeps in close personal touch with his clients, and in many villages shares their occasions of weal or woe. *With his intimate knowledge of those around him he is able, without serious risk, to finance those who would otherwise get no loan at all.* [Italics added.]

Or look at Barbara Ward's (1960, p. 142) account:

> A small shopkeeper in a Hong Kong fishing village told me: "I give credit to anyone who anchors regularly in our bay; but if it is someone I don't know well, then I think twice about it unless I can find out all about him."

Or, a profitable sideline of cotton ginning in Iran is the loaning of money for the next season, since the ginning companies often have a line of credit from Teheran banks at the market rate of interest. But in the first years of operation large losses are expected from unpaid debts – due to poor knowledge of the local scene.[8]

[7] cont'd

|                   | Secured loans (per cent) | Commonest rates for unsecured loans (per cent)                              | Grain loans (per cent) |
|-------------------|--------------------------|----------------------------------------------------------------------------|------------------------|
| Punjab            | 6 to 12                  | 12 to 24 ($18\frac{3}{4}$ commonest)                                       | 25                     |
| United Provinces  | 9 to 12                  | 24 to $37\frac{1}{2}$                                                      | 25 (50 in Oudh)        |
| Bihar             |                          | 18 3/4                                                                      | 50                     |
| Orissa            | 12 to $18\frac{3}{4}$    | 25                                                                         | 25                     |
| Bengal            | 8 to 12                  | 9 to 18 for "respectable clients" 18 3/4 to $37\frac{1}{2}$ (the latter common to agriculturalists) | 25                     |
| Central Provinces | 6 to 12                  | 15 for proprietors 24 for occupancy tenants $37\frac{1}{2}$ for ryots with no right of transfer | 25                     |
| Bombay            | 9 to 12                  | 12 to 25 (18 commonest)                                                    |                        |
| Sind              |                          | 36                                                                         |                        |
| Madras            | 12                       | 15 to 18 (in insecure tracts 24 not uncommon)                             | 20 to 50               |

*Source*: Darling (1932, p. 190).

[8] Personal conversation with mill manager, April 1968.

## 4.  Counteracting Institutions

Numerous institutions arise to counteract the effects of quality uncertainty. One obvious institution is guarantees. Most consumer durables carry guarantees to ensure the buyer of some normal expected quality. One natural result of our model is that the risk is borne by the seller rather than by the buyer.

A second example of an institution which counteracts the effects of quality uncertainty is the brand-name good. Brand names not only indicate quality but also give the consumer a means of retaliation if the quality does not meet expectations. For the consumer will then curtail future purchases. Often too, new products are associated with old brand names. This ensures the prospective consumer of the quality of the product.

Chains – such as hotel chains or restaurant chains – are similar to brand names. One observation consistent with our approach is the chain restaurant. These restaurants, at least in the United States, most often appear on interurban highways. The customers are seldom local. The reason is that these well-known chains offer a better hamburger than the *average* local restaurant; at the same time, the local customer, who knows his area, can usually choose a place he prefers.

Licensing practices also reduce quality uncertainty. For instance, there is the licensing of doctors, lawyers, and barbers. Most skilled labor carries some certification indicating the attainment of certain levels of proficiency. The high school diploma, the baccalaureate degree, the Ph.D., even the Nobel Prize, to some degree, serve this function of certification. And education and labor markets themselves have their own "brand names."

## 5.  Conclusion

We have been discussing economic models in which "trust" is important. Informal unwritten guarantees are preconditions for trade and production. Where these guarantees are indefinite, business will suffer – as indicated by our generalized Gresham's law. This aspect of uncertainty has been explored by game theorists, as in the Prisoner's Dilemma, but usually it has not been incorporated in the more traditional Arrow–Debreu approach to uncertainty (Radner, 1967). But the difficulty of distinguishing good quality from bad is inherent in the business world; this may indeed explain many economic institutions and may in fact be one of the more important aspects of uncertainty.

*References*

ANDERSON, O. W. (with FELDMAN, J. J.) (1956): *Family Medical Costs and Insurance*. New York: McGraw-Hill.

ANGELL, F. J. (1957): *Insurance, Principles and Practices*. New York: The Ronald Press.

ARROW, K. (1963): "Uncertainty and the Welfare Economics of Medical Care," *American Economic Review*, 53 (5), 941–73.

BUCHANAN, D. H. (1966): *The Development of Capitalist Enterprise in India*. New York: Kelley (reprinted).

DARLING, Sir M. (1932): *Punjabi Peasant in Prosperity and Debt*, 3rd edn. London: Oxford University Press.

DENENBERG, H. S., EILERS, R. D., HOFFMAN, G. W., KLINE, C. A., MELONE, J. J. and SNIDER, H. W. (1964): *Risk and Insurance*. Englewood Cliffs, New Jersey: Prentice Hall.

DICKERSON, O. D. (1959): *Health Insurance*. Homewood, Ill.: Irwin.

FUKUZAWA, H. (1965): "Cotton Mill Industry," in V. B. Singh (ed.), *Economic History of India, 1857–1956*, Bombay: Allied Publishers, 223–59.

GOVERNMENT OF INDIA PLANNING COMMISSION (1964): *Report of the Committee on the Distribution of Income and Levels of Living, Part 1*, February, 44.

KINDLEBERGER, C. P. (1958): *Economic Development*. New York: McGraw-Hill.

LEVY, M. J., Jr. (1955): "Contrasting Factors in the Modernization of China and Japan," in S. Kuznets, W. E. Moore and J. J. Spengler (eds), *Economic Growth: Brazil, India, Japan*, Durham, N.C.: Duke University Press, 496–536.

LEWIS, W. A. (1955): *The Theory of Economic Growth*. Homewood, Ill.: Irwin.

MEHTA, M. M. (1955): *Structure of Indian Industries*. Bombay: Popular Book Depot.

RADNER, R. (1967): "Equilibre de Marchés à Terme et au Comptant en Cas d'Incertitude," *Cahiers d'Econometrie*, 12, November. Paris: Centre National de la Recherche Scientifique.

SCHULTZ, T. W. (1964): *The Economic Value of Education*. New York: Columbia University Press.

STIGLER, G. J. (1962): "Information in the Labor Market," *Journal of Political Economy*, 70, October, Supplement, 94–105.

*The Times of India* (1967): November 10, 1.

TINKER, H. (1966): *South Asia: A Short History*. New York: Praeger.

WARD, B. (1960): "Cash or Credit Crops," *Economic Development and Cultural Change*, 8 (12), January, 148–63. Reprinted in G. Foster, J. M. Potter and M. N. Diaz (eds) 1967: *Peasant Society, A Reader*, Boston: Little Brown and Company, 142.

## FORTY-TWO

# The Only Game in Town

### Walter Bagehot (Pseudonym for Jack Treynor)

Source: *Financial Analysts Journal* 27 (March–April), 1971, pp. 12–14, 22.

It has been pointed out by Colyer Crum and others that financial institutions are dominated by organizational goals other than investment performance. George Goodman argued in his book, "The Money Game" that the securities business is an emotional business with a high degree of entertainment value for at least some of the participants. If Crum and Goodman are right, people presumably participate in the stock market because, like parlor games and sports, it offers the opportunity to win more dramatically and more concretely than is possible in ordinary workaday life.

On the other hand, academic studies (in particular the studies of Professor Michael Jensen of the University of Rochester) of professionally managed portfolios have shown not only that professional investors as a group fail to perform better than amateurs, but that it is even difficult to find individual portfolios which have achieved performance significantly better than neutral. On the basis of this kind of evidence it would appear that if participants in the stock market play to get the experience of winning, then the securities business is a very poor game indeed. Why does anybody choose to play the stock market game?

Another closely related question is why we observe wide swings in the enthusiasm with which people play the stock market game. The turnover rate on the New York Stock Exchange in 1968 was roughly twice what it was as recently as 1962. Every time one investor benefits from a trade, after all, another loses. If enthusiasm for the game is influenced by past successes or failures one would expect that, aggregated across the entire investing population, the level of enthusiasm as manifested in trading volume (or better yet, in turnover volume) would be very stable.

And, finally, why is it that among professional portfolio managers yesterday's heroes are so often today's goats?

The answer to all three questions lies, I believe, in a widespread confusion between market gains (and losses) and trading gains (and losses). It is, of course, possible to diversify a portfolio so completely that essentially the only investment risk remaining is market risk – that is, uncertainty regarding whether the market as a whole will move up or down. If the market moves up then investors in general will benefit from the market movement whether they are trading securities or merely holding what they have. But if they are trading while the market moves up, they are very likely to attribute the increase in their wealth to their trading activity rather than to the fact that the market has moved up. This is what I mean by confusion of trading gains with market gains.

The effect of the confusion is particularly noticeable in portfolios that are unusually sensitive to market movements. Portfolios invested in small, growing, highly levered companies, for example, are often so sensitive to market movements that a 10 per cent rise (or fall) in the general market level will cause a 20 per cent rise (or fall) in the value of the portfolio. When one manages this kind of portfolio it is very easy to convince oneself (and others) that one is a trading genius when the market is going up, and this is precisely what happened to a number of widely publicized mutual fund portfolios in the period between 1957 and 1965. On balance the market rose sharply in this period and the value of portfolios that were especially sensitive to changes in market level rose much more sharply. But their gains were market gains, not trading gains. Because these funds were trading actively during this period, however, their gains were attributed to trading and many other portfolio managers who had previously traded less actively began to emulate them.

The result was that beginning around 1964 and 1965 many types of equity portfolios that had previously traded very little suddenly perked up and began to trade very actively. A review of trading volume figures for individual investors will show that they behaved very similarly. If people confused market gains with trading gains it is easy to understand why they continued to play the stock market game even though their trading performance rarely departed from neutral.

## The Market Maker – Key to the Stock Market Game

Investors persist in trading despite their dismal long-run trading record partly because they are seduced by the argument that because prices are as likely to go up as down (or as likely to go down as up), trading based on purely random selection rules will produce neutral performance; therefore, trading based on any germ of an idea, any clue or hunch, will result in a performance better than neutral. Apparently this idea is alluring; nonetheless it is wrong.

The key to understanding the fallacy is the market maker. The market maker is the exchange specialist in the case of listed securities and the over-the-counter dealer in the case of unlisted securities. The role of the market maker is, of course, to provide liquidity by stepping in and transacting whenever equal and opposite orders fail to arrive in the market at the same time. In order to perform this function the market maker stands ready to transact with anyone who comes to the market.

One can discuss the economics of market making in terms of three kinds of transactors who confront the market maker: one, transactors possessing special information; two, "liquidity-motivated" transactors who have no special information but merely want to convert securities into cash or cash into securities; three, transactors acting on information which they believe has not yet been fully discounted in the market price but which in fact has.

The market maker always loses to transactors in the first category. A wide spread between the market maker's bid and asked prices will discourage transactors from trading on any special information that implies only a small change in equilibrium price; but because these transactors have the option of not trading with the market maker in such circumstances, he will never gain from them – unless of course they have misappraised their special information. It is evident that transactors with special information are playing a "heads I win, tails you lose" game with the market maker.

On the other hand the market maker always gains in his transactions with liquidity-motivated transactors. The essence of marketmaking, viewed as a business, is that in order for the market maker to survive and prosper, his gains from liquidity-motivated transactors must exceed his losses to information motivated transactors. To the market maker, the two kinds of transactors are largely indistinguishable. The spread he sets between his bid and asked price affects both: the larger the spread, the less money he loses to information-motivated transactors and the more he makes from liquidity-motivated transactors (assuming that a wider spread doesn't discourage the latter transactions).

Unfortunately, the liquidity of a market is inversely related to the spread. The smallest spread a market maker can maintain and still survive is inversely related to the average rate of flow of new information affecting the value of the asset in question, and directly related to the volume of liquidity-motivated transactions. This is where the third kind of transactor comes in: from the market maker's point of view, his effect is identical to the liquidity motivated transactor's. The market maker naturally welcomes the cooperation of wire houses and information services like the *Wall Street Journal* that broadcast information already fully discounted since many investors are easily persuaded to transact based on that information, hence enable the market maker to maintain substantially smaller spreads than would be possible without their trading activity.

## The Market Consensus

It is well known that market makers of all kinds make surprisingly little use of fundamental information. Instead they observe the relative pressure of buy and sell orders and attempt to find a price that equilibrates these pressures. The resulting market price at any point in time is not merely a consensus of the transactors in the market place, it is also a consensus of their mistakes. Under the heading of mistakes we may include errors in computation, errors of judgment, factual oversights and errors in the logic of analysis. Unless these errors are in some sense systematic across the population of investors – or, to put it the other way around, to the extent that the commission of these errors is more or less statistically independent one investor from another – market price is virtually unaffected by these errors. This is a consequence of the law of large numbers: because the number of individual transactors is large and because their mistakes of judgment and estimation are likely to be independent, one transactor from another, the net effect of their mistakes on the equilibrium price is likely to be miniscule.

If, instead of seeking out the market price that equilibrates buying and selling pressures based on these appraisals, the market maker imposed his own judgment of what a security was worth, he would be risking an error of his own of the same order of magnitude as the errors committed by other investors. It is not surprising in this light that market makers generally have so little use for fundamental considerations in their work. This observation also points up the futility of trying to trade profitably by making unusually conscientious, thorough or sophisticated security analyses. The ultimate in sophisticated analysis is not likely to improve on the accuracy of the market consensus.

When the role of the market maker is as described here, the market maker can be viewed as a conduit through which money flows from liquidity-motivated transactors to transactors with special information. This result follows directly from the original observation that in order to stay in business the market maker must earn more from liquidity-motivated transactors than he loses to transactors with special information. Every time one transacts against the market maker he incurs a "spread cost" in addition to any explicit brokerage commission. The size of the effective spread on listed stocks is hidden because oscillations between "bid" and "asked" are camouflaged by the constant fluctuations in the equilibrium value of the stock. If trading volume is small, and insiders' profits are large, the spread cost incurred in transacting is necessarily large, however. Whereas it is indeed true that the transactor is as likely to gain as lose from fluctuations in equilibrium value, what he loses in trading against the spread must be large enough to provide insiders with their profits, and hopefully leave something for the market maker besides. This is why trading on hunches or rumors is more likely to degrade performance than improve it.

## Coppering the Public

The question is sometimes asked, if trading by the general public is so futile then why isn't trading against the public consistently profitable? The answer lies in the special manner, just described, in which the public loses. If all trading took place between those who got information early and those who got it late, then one could make money by trading against those who get it late. But if our picture is accurate, those who get information early make their profits from the market makers, who in turn make *their* profits from those who trade without genuinely new information. If the public traded directly against insiders, one could deduce which way insiders were trading by observing which way the public was trading (as, for example, with odd-lot information). It is true that the public loses quite consistently on its trading (as opposed to investing – as we noted, it is entirely possible to remain invested without trading), but it loses because it is trading against the market maker's spread. The public would lose just as much if at every point in time the direction of its trading were the reverse of what it actually is; hence there is no value in coppering the public.

This argument exaggerates the "spread" problem for those listed stocks that have an active auction market. How active the auction markets for NYSE stocks are can be judged, however, from the fact that in recent years Exchange members were transacting for their own accounts on one side or the other of two out of three transactions.

FORTY-THREE

# Are Advertisers Ready to Pay Their Viewers?

BART ZIEGLER

*Source*: *Wall Street Journal*, November 14, 1996. © 1997 Dow Jones & Company, Inc. All Rights Reserved.

Would people like advertising better if they were paid to look at it? That concept is being tested on the Internet by a start-up called CyberGold, whose founders include advertising legend Jay Chiat and Silicon Valley marketer Regis McKenna. CyberGold has devised a way to give people 50 cents to a few dollars to click through an ad on the World Wide Web. The venture, marketing executives say, is either a clever way to use the Web's interactive capabilities – or a desperate gimmick that shows how the ad industry is struggling to find its place on-line.

For advertisers, the Internet's ability to target "content" to certain audiences should be a dream, addressing an age-old problem: how to ensure that ads reach the right people. The Internet's interactive capabilities, meanwhile, hold the promise of allowing advertisers to track who sees ads. But on-line advertising has been a disappointment so far. Few Web ads are as enticing as the average TV spot, and the Internet's technology is still too crude to target ads and monitor who sees them.

CyberGold hopes to address at least some of these problems. Its software gathers valuable demographic data from Web users who reveal their interests on a form, and then offers them individual menus of ads on CyberGold's Web site at http://www.cybergold.com. Users must peruse each Web ad to its last page, then click on a special symbol to receive credit. Once the credit amount reaches $20, the company offers to send money – by check or transfers to an on-line bank account – or to apply the payment toward frequent-flier miles, a product purchase or a charitable donation. "Attention is becoming the scarce and valued commodity," says Nat Goldhaber, who founded Cyber-Gold along with Messrs. Chiat and McKenna. "If an advertiser would like to convey a message to a targeted customer, then that customer should be compensated," Mr. Gold-haber says. He contends it's no different from a research firm including a dollar bill when it sends a survey form to consumers.

Advertisers will pay CyberGold at least 50 cents for each ad that a consumer reads to the end, in addition to what the companies pay ad readers. Eventually, the Berkeley, Calif., company hopes to get such ads sprinkled throughout the Internet. CyberGold has attracted about 140 trial advertisers that created spots for the current test of the system, including *Nissan Motor*, *J. C. Penney* and *Pacific Telesis Group*'s Pacific Bell, and about

Winner!
**Click here** for
MyPoints cybergold
experience

**Featured Offers**

Welcome To MyPoints® Cybergold®

Make $ Join more than 9 million MyPoints®
Cybergold® members and get CASH for having fun.
Visit Web sites, sign up for free stuff, enjoy great offers
and more.

Shop & Save $ Shop here and save! Get up to 10%
cash back when you shop with more than 130 top
brand-name merchants.

Cash Out $ Spend the cash you make here on MP3
music, e-books, lifestyle gear, and more. Or donate it!
You can even transfer your cash into your checking
account or onto your credit card.

**New Offers**

**◆ Sprint.**

Get $15.00
Listen up!
Here's a great
deal on long
distance phone
rates.
Tell a Friend

**half.com**

Get $2.00
Pssst! FREE $5
instant coupon
and 50-90% off
your CDs,
DVDs, books.
Tell a Friend

**GLAMOUR**

GET $1.50
Try Glamour
Risk-FREE!
Tell a Friend

**CyberRebate**

Get 5% off
Get great deals
on thousands of
products and
get over 800
items absolutely
FREE.
Tell a Friend

**OmniChoice**

Get $2.00
OmniChoice.com
finds the best
utility plans for
you, absolutely
FREE.
Tell a Friend

**Science Fiction**

Get $10.00
Join the Science
Fiction Book
Club® and get
5 books for $1
plus an extra
book absolutely
FREE!
Tell a Friend

Powered by Magna Cash

3,000 Web cruisers have been given password-controlled access to the test site. But most of these advertisers haven't paid anything – testers now are paid out of CyberGold's marketing budget – and only a handful have agreed to continue with the service when it goes live early next year.

Paying people to read ads raises a host of questions: Won't some people click through ads just to get paid, even if they aren't interested in the products? Are the people most likely to try the plan – students and others for whom a small payment means something – really the ones advertisers are interested in reaching? And won't some people find the whole idea, well, a bit tacky?

CyberGold is a case of "the right problem, wrong answer," says John Uppgren, vice president of technology marketing at Gage Marketing Group Inc. in Minneapolis. "It's getting tougher to reach people," Mr. Uppgren says, but "if I've got to pay consumers to look at my advertising I've got a serious problem. A buck and a half to five bucks probably won't capture the most important consumers they're going after, the high-income, high-demographic consumers." The people it may attract, he says, are hackers bent on making money by cheating the system.

Many high-end consumers, Mr. Uppgren says, would pay money not to be subjected to ads. He adds that advertising on the Web is about developing "negotiated relationships" with consumers: "They're going to come to see you when they're interested and ready" for the product an advertiser is pushing, not because they receive a token fee. Then there's the added cost of CyberGold's system for advertisers. "How much money can you afford to give somebody to look at your advertising?" asks Kent Valandra, director of new media at Western International Media, a big media buyer.

But some marketing experts say that Web cruisers who fill out the surveys are uniquely qualified to receive ads. "I think it's very clever," says Steve Dapper, CEO of Rapp Collins Worldwide, a New York direct-marketing concern owned by Omnicom Group. Just by filling out CyberGold's on-line form these consumers "have raised their hand and made a conscious decision to come on board," making them a much better audience than someone just randomly surfing the Net. CyberGold says all information gathered from the surveys is for its own use only. Mr. Dapper also dismisses the concern that offering a small payment might attract the wrong consumers. "Coupons have worked for a long time in this world, and that's people attracted to 50 cents [off] or a dollar as well," he says.

CyberGold's Mr. Goldhaber, who once ran the Kaleida Labs software venture of Apple Computer and International Business Machines, admits that cash-strapped students may find the system appealing, but says advertisers still covet them as consumers and trendsetters. And in focus groups CyberGold conducted, no one seemed to find the concept objectionable. Other Internet entrepreneurs are, in effect, already paying people to look at ads, such as the Juno electronic-mail service, which is provided free but displays ads that are targeted at users who fill out a form. But despite his enthusiasm, even Mr. Goldhaber admits he is entering unknown territory. "It will either work or it won't," he says.

# FORTY-FOUR

# The Creation of New Mathematics: An Application of the Lakatos Heuristic

PHILIP J. DAVIS, REUBEN HERSH, AND ELENA MARCHISOTTO

*Source*: *The Mathematical Experience*. New York: Springer-Verlag Inc., 1981, pp. 291–8.

In *Proofs and Refutations*, Imre Lakatos presents a picture of the "logic of mathematical discovery." A teacher and his class are studying the famous Euler–Descartes formula for polyhedra

$$V - E + F = 2$$

In this formula $V$ is the number of vertices of a polyhedron, $E$, the number of its edges, and $F$, the number of its faces. Among the familiar polyhedra, these quantities take the following values:

|                    | $V$ | $E$ | $F$ |
|--------------------|-----|-----|-----|
| tetrahedron        | 4   | 6   | 4   |
| (Egyptian) pyramid | 5   | 8   | 5   |
| cube               | 8   | 12  | 6   |
| octahedron         | 6   | 12  | 8   |

(See also Chapter 7, Lakatos and the Philosophy of Dubitability [Davis, Hersh, and Marchisotto, 1981].)

The teacher presents the traditional proof in which the polyhedron is stretched on the plane. This "proof" is immediately followed by a barrage of counterexamples presented by the students. Under the impact of these counterexamples, the statement of the theorem is modified, the proof is corrected and elaborated. New counterexamples are produced, new adjustments are made.

This development is presented by Lakatos as a model for the development of mathematical knowledge in general.

The Lakatos heuristic example of proofs and refutations which was formulated for the mathematical culture at large can of course be applied by the individual in his attempt to

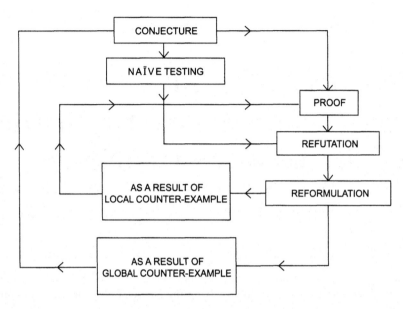

Simplified Lakatos model for the heuristics of mathematical discovery

create new mathematics. The writer has used the method with moderate success in his classes. The initial shock of presenting students not with a fixed problem to be cracked, but with an open-ended situation of potential discovery, must and can be overcome. The better students then experience a sense of exhilaration and freedom in which they are in control of the material.

I shall illustrate the method with a little example from the elementary theory of numbers.

I begin with an initial statement which I shall call the "seed." The seed statement should be an interesting one, quite simple. The object of the exercise is for the student to water the seed so that it grows into a sturdy plant. I usually present the class with a variety of seeds and they select them for watering, depending upon their experience.

## Act I

*Seed:*  "If a number ends in 2, it is divisible by 2."

*Examples:*  42 ends in and is divisible by 2. 172 ends in and is divisible by 2.

*Proof:*  A number is even if and only if it ends in 0, 2, 4, 6, 8. All even numbers are divisible by 2. In particular, those that end in 2 are divisible by 2.

*Proof:*  (more sophisticated): If the number, in digit form, is $ab \ldots c2$, then it is clearly of the form $(ab \ldots c0) + 2$, hence of the form $10Q + 2 = 2(5Q + 1)$.

*Conjectural Leap:*  If a number ends in $N$ it is divisible by $N$.

*Comment:*  Be bold and make the obvious generalization. The heavens won't fall in if it turns out to be false.

*Example:*  If a number ends in 5 it is divisible by 5. Sure: 15, 25, 128095, etc. But, alas,

*Counterexample:*   If a number ends in 4 is it divisible by 4? Is 14 divisible by 4? No. Too bad.

*Objection:*   But some numbers that end in 4 *are* divisible by 4:24. Some numbers ending in 9 *are* divisible by 9:99.

*Recap of Experience:*   The numbers 1, 2,..., 9 seem to be divisible into two categories. *Category I:* The digits $N$ such that when a number ends in $N$ it is divisible by $N$, always. *Category II:* The digits $N$ such that when a number ends in $N$ it is divisible by $N$ only occasionally.

*Category I:*   1, 2, 5.

*Category II:*   3, 4, 6, 7, 8, 9.

*Point of Order:*   What about numbers that end in 0? Are they divisible by 0? No. But they are divisible by 10. Hmm. We may have to watch this. This phenomenon doesn't fit in with the form of the seed.

*Definition:*   Let's call the numbers in Category I "magic numbers." They have a delightful property.

*Tentative Theorem:*   The numbers 1, 2 and 5 are magic numbers. They are the only magic numbers.

*Counterexample:*   What about the number 25? Isn't it magic? If a number ends in 25 it is divisible by 25. For example: 225, or 625.

*Objection:*   We thought you were talking about single-digit numbers.

*Rebuttal:*   Well, we were originally. But the 25 phenomenon is interesting. Let's open up the original inquiry a bit.

*Reformulation:*   Let $N$ now represent not necessarily a single digit but a whole group of digits like 23, 41, 505, etc. Make the definition that $N$ is magic if a number that ends with the digit group $N$ is divisible by $N$. Does this extended definition make sense?

*Examples:*   Yes it does. 25 is magic. 10 is magic. 20 is magic. 30 is magic.

*Counterexample:*   30 isn't magic. 130 is not divisible by 30. Come to think of it, how do you know 25 is magic?

*Theorem:*   25 is a magic number.

*Proof:*   If a number ends in 25 it is of the digital form $abc\ldots e25 = abc\ldots e00 + 25$, hence of the form $100Q + 25 = 25(4Q + 1)$.

*Reformulation of Goal:*   Find all the magic numbers.

*Accumulation of Experience:*   1, 2, 5, 10, 25, 50, 100, 250, 500, 1000 are all magic numbers.

*Observation:*   All the magic numbers we have been able to find seem to be products of 2's and 5's. Certainly the ones in the above list are.

*Conjecture:*   Any number $N$ of the form $N = 2^p \cdot 5^q$ where $p \geq 0, q \geq 0$ is a magic number.

*Comment:*   Seems reasonable. What have we got to lose?

*Counterexample:*   Take $p = 3, q = 1$. Then $N = 2^3 \cdot 5 = 40$. Is a number that ends in 40 always divisible by 40? No. E.g., 140.

*Reformulation:*   How about the other way around, though? All the magic numbers we have found are of the form $2^p \cdot 5^q$. Perhaps all magic numbers are of that form.

*Objection:*   Isn't that what you just proposed?

*Rebuttal:*   No, what was proposed was the other way around: a number of the form $2^p \cdot 5^q$ is magic. See the difference?

*Theorem:*  If $N$ is a magic number then $N = 2^p \cdot 5^q$.

*Proof:*  Let a number end in $N$ (recall: in this statement $N$ is acting as a group of digits.) Then the number looks like $abc \ldots eN$, digitwise. We would like to split it up, as before. Therefore, let $N$ have $d(N)$ digits. Then the number $abc \ldots eN$ is really $abc \ldots e00 \ldots 0 + N$ where there are $d(N)$ 0's at the end. Therefore the number is of the form $Q \cdot 10^{d(N)} + N$. (Try this out when $d(N) = 2, 3$, etc.) All numbers that end with $N$ are of this form. Conversely, if $Q$ is any number whatever then the number $Q \cdot 10^{d(N)} + N$ ends with $N$. Now if $N$ is magic it always divides $Q \cdot 10^{d(N)} + N$. Since $N$ divides $N$, it must always divide $Q \cdot 10^{d(N)}$ for all $Q$. But $Q$ might be the simple number 1, for example. Therefore $N$ must divide $10^{d(N)}$. Since $10^{d(N)} = 2^{d(N)} \cdot 5^{d(N)}$ is a prime factorization, it follows that $N$ must itself factor down to a certain number of 2's and 5's.

*Current Position:*  We now know that a magic number is one of the form $N = 2^p \cdot 5^q$ for some integers $p, q \geq 0$. We would like to turn it around. Then we should have a necessary and sufficient condition for magicality.

*Refocussing of Experience:*  Since we know that all magic numbers are of the form $N = 2^p \cdot 5^q$, the problem comes down to: what must be asserted about $p$ and $q$ to make the resulting $N$ magic?

*Conjecture:*  $p \leq q$?

*Counterexample:*  $p = 0, q = 4, N = 2^0 \cdot 5^4 = 625$. Is 625 magic? No: 1625 doesn't divide by 625.

*Conjecture:*  $p = q$?

*Objection:*  Then $N = 2^p 5^p = 10^p$ or $1, 10, 100, \ldots$. O.K. But there are other magic numbers.

*Conjecture:*  $p \geq q$?

*Counterexample:*  $p = 3, q = 1, N = 2^3 \cdot 5^1 = 40$. This is not magic.

*Observation:*  Hmm. Something subtle at work here. This brings down the curtain on Act I. The process goes on for those with sufficient interest and strength.


# Act II

(In this act, the heuristic line is severely abbreviated in the write-up.)

*Strategy Conference:*  Let's go back to the proof of the necessity of the form $N = 2^p \cdot 5^q$. We found that if $N$ is magic it divides $10^{d(N)}$. Recall that $d(N)$ stands for the number of digits in the group of digits $N$. Perhaps this is sufficient as well? Aha! A breakthrough?

*Theorem:*  $N$ is magic if and only if it divides $10^{d(N)}$.

*Proof:*  The necessity has already been proved. If a number ends in $N$, then, as we know, it is of the form $Q \cdot 10^{d(N)} + N$. But $N$ divides $N$ and $N$ is assumed to divide $10^{d(N)}$. Therefore it surely divides $Q \cdot 10^{d(N)} + N$.

*Aesthetic Objection:*  While it is true that we now have a necessary and sufficient condition for magicality, this condition is on $N$ itself and not on its factored form $2^p \cdot 5^q$.

*Conference:*  When does $N = 2^p \cdot 5^q$ divide $10^{d(N)}$? Well, $10^{d(N)} = 2^{d(N)} \cdot 5^{d(N)}$, so that obviously a necessary and sufficient condition for this is $p \leq d(N), q \leq d(N)$. But this is equivalent to $\max(p, q) \leq d(N)$. We still have the blasted $d(N)$ to contend with. We don't want it. We'd like a condition on $N$ itself, or possibly on $p$ and $q$. How can we convert $\max(p, q) \leq d(N) = d(2^p \cdot 5^q)$ into a more convenient form? As we know, $p = q$ is O.K. Let's see this written in the new form: $p = \max(p, p) \leq d(2^p \cdot 5^p) = d(10^p)$. Now the number of digits in $10^p$ is $p + 1$. So this is saying $p \leq p + 1$ which is O.K. What if, in the general case, we "even out" the powers of 2 and the powers of 5? Write $q = p + h$ where $h > 0$. (Aha!)

*Objection:*   What if $p > q$ so that $q = p + h$ is impossible with $h > 0$?

*Rebuttal:*   Treat that later.

*Conference:*   $\max(p, p + h) \leq d(2^p \cdot 5^{p+h}) = d(2^p \cdot 5^p \cdot 5^h) = d(10^p \cdot 5^h)$.   Now   since $h > 0, \max(p, p + h) = p + h$. Also, the number of digits in $10^p \cdot Q$ where $Q$ is any number $= p +$ number of digits in $Q$. Therefore $p + h \leq p + d(5^h)$ or: $h \leq d(5^h)$.

*Query:*   When is it true that $h > 0$ and $h \leq d(5^h)$?

*Experimentation:*   $h = 1: 1 \leq d(5^1)$ O.K. $h = 2: 2 \leq d(5^2)$ O.K. $h = 3: 3 \leq d(5^3)$ O.K. $h = 4: 4 \leq d(5^4) = d(625) = 3$. No good. $h = 5: 5 \leq d(5^5) = d(3125) = 4$. No good.

*Conjecture:*   $h \leq d(5^h)$ if and only if $h = 1, 2, 3$.

*Proof:*   Omitted.

*Reprise:*   What about $p > q$?

*Conference:*   Set $p = q + h$, $h > 0$. $q + h = \max(q + h, q) \leq d(2^{q+h} \cdot 5^q) = d(10^q \cdot 2^h) = q + d(2^h)$, or $h \leq d(2^h)$. When is $h \leq d(2^h)$?

*Experimentation:*   $h = 1: 1 \leq d(2^1)$ O.K. $h = 2: 2 \leq d(2^2)$ No good.

*Conjecture:*   $h \leq d(2^h)$ if and only if $h = 1$.

*Proof:*   Omitted.

*Theorem:*   $N$ is magic if and only if it equals a power of ten times 1, 2, 5, 25, or 125.

*Proof:*   Omitted.

In anticipation of further developments we might like to write this theorem in a different way.

*Theorem:*   $N$ is magic if and only if $N = 2^p \cdot 5^q$, where $0 \leq q - p + 1 \leq 4$.

*Proof:*   Omitted.

Act III might begin by asking what would happen if we wrote our numbers in some base other than 10. What about a prime base, or a base equal to a power of a prime?

### Further Readings

Gardner, M. 1978: *Aha! Insight*. San Francisco: W. H. Freeman.

Grevandes U. 1979: *Mathematical Experiments on the Computer Division of Applied Mathematics*, Brown University.

Lakatos, I. 1976: *Proofs and Refutations*. Cambridge: Cambridge University Press.

FORTY-FIVE

# Frank's Neurosurgery

## Gary Larson

*Source*: The Far Side by Gary Larson. © 1982 Far Works, Inc. Used with permission. All Rights Reserved.

PART TEN

# Mechanism Design in Adverse Selection and in Moral Hazard with Hidden Information

# Introduction

The *Harvard Business Review* is, like the *Financial Analysts Journal*, a practitioner journal, a good place to find relatively nontechnical write-ups of research results that are useful for businessmen. The article here shows how to use the idea of mechanism design to extract information from salesmen about the quality of their territories. Bargaining is another common application for mechanism design, as in the Myerson–Satterthwaite model. A way to avoid having to rely on one's own bargaining skills is to hire an agent, which is the subject of the *Wall Street Journal* article for this chapter. You may also find it interesting to read Ian Ayres' article on his car bargaining experiments, in which he gave testers a uniform algorithm to follow in trying to buy a particular type of car in order to discover the effect of the race and gender of customer and car salesman. Ian Ayres, "Fair Driving: Gender and Race Discrimination in Retail Car Negotiations," *Harvard Law Review* 104: 817–72 (February 1991). Cars seem to attract shady practices, perhaps because they are valuable, are owned by unsophisticated as well as sophisticated people, and they break down sooner or later. The cartoon, "Of course that's only an estimate..." points to a common difficulty in translating the messages of car mechanics.

Hal Varian is an excellent all-round economist best known for his doctoral textbook, *Microeconomic Analysis*, New York: W. W. Norton (1st edn 1978, 2nd edn 1987, 3rd edn, 1992). He surprised everyone by becoming the dean of Berkeley's School of Information Management and Systems (the library school), but it fits his research interest in information and his polymath character. If you find his essay appealing, try his website at http://www.sims.berkeley.edu/~hal/. His essay is perhaps the best of the many good essays on doing research in the excellent book, *Passion and Craft*. Other favorites of mine in that book are the essays by William Landes, Paul Krugman, and Avinash Dixit.

# FORTY-SIX

# Tie Salesmen's Bonuses to Their Forecasts

JACOB GONIK

*Source*: *Harvard Business Review* 56 (May–June), 1978, pp. 116–23. © 1978 the President and Fellows of Harvard College. All Rights Reserved. Reprinted by permission of Harvard Business Review.

John and Peter are two salesmen for the XYZ corporation.
John sells twice as much as Peter.
John earns twice as much as Peter, right?
Wrong, John may even earn less.

The XYZ corporation's sales compensation plan is not unique in the modern business world. In the past decade many companies have turned to sophisticated incentive plans that seem to challenge Darwin's law of survival. Throughout the years sales people have been paid by either fixed salaries or variable incentives such as commissions and shares in profits. Other forms of payment are expense accounts and fringe benefits such as paid insurance and vacations, but these are never used alone and can be set aside when discussing the motivational aspects of compensation plans.

Most companies use a combination of straight salary and commissions. By including both a fixed monthly wage and a sales percentage bonus, managements seek to secure company control as well as provide salesmen with ample motivation. For example, at XYZ John and Peter will each earn $10,000 a year guaranteed, plus another $10,000 in bonuses which depend directly on their results. How, though, can Peter sell less and still earn more than John even though they sell the same piece of machinery for XYZ?

The dilemma is resolved if one takes into consideration how management measures John's and Peter's performance.

In this article I describe a sales compensation system which, unlike most incentive plans, rewards salespeople not only for their actual results but also for their effort and ability to forecast accurately. Before describing that system, however, let us take a look at the two basic compensation systems from which all others spring.

## Basic Compensation Systems

Many years ago a manager's payroll slogan was quite straightforward: "Bring me more revenue and I will pay you more!" A salesperson's commissions were proportional to his or her sales. The proportion could vary from product to product, but in the end the salesperson's reward was linked to the benefit he or she brought to the company. This is a system set up to reward results.

## Achievement system

Under this system, every salesman had a yearly quota, that is, a standard by which he could measure his performance on December 31, but the achievement of which brought no extra money at all. The prize and motivation to achieve that quota was often a trip to a winner's convention plus, of course, an opportunity for a promotion. But the quota had no links to earnings.

After World War I when business boomed so quickly, the flaws in the straight achievement system revealed themselves. Companies using it found that they were paying huge unexpected commissions to some salesmen for the same effort they had made before. And these sudden commissions created enormous differences in earnings between salesmen owing to inequitable territories.

In addition, as products became more and more complex, companies needed more and more investments for longer periods. Because one single product could require five years to be developed and a small mistake could turn into a big loss, planning became a fundamental business effort. Sales forecasting and quota setting became major disciplines and activities, and reaching the quota became even more important since it meant achieving the overall goal of the company.

The need to tie quota objectives to salesmen's earnings was a natural consequence of this panorama, and many different sales compensation plans sprang to life. Commissions might be paid for quota completion only, or just for sales in excess of quota. Complex payment curves were built to sharpen the importance of achieving the preset goal. The most imaginative method rewards salesmen for achieving a company's objectives.

## Objective-achievement system

Ed and Charles are two factory workers and use the same type of tools for punching the same kind of holes in a television chassis. They are paid by the number of holes they punch a day. Since Ed is more experienced and quicker than Charles, he punches more holes and gets more money.

One day their manager calls Ed and tells him that since he is more experienced than Charles, it is absolutely normal that he punches more holes. From that day on, therefore, he will earn the same as Charles for doing twice as much. One can imagine the look on Ed's face.

When applied to sales effort the objective-achievement system is not as absurd as it looks in the factory case. Say a TV set manufacturing company determines each salesman's bonus according to his experience, time with the company, and merit. Frank, for instance, qualifies for a $15,000 bonus, while Steve for only $12,000. Their bonuses have no relation to their territories or objectives.

Next, let us assume that their manager has a sales quota of 700 TV units which he must split between the two of them. The manager decides that Frank has a "better" territory – i.e., one with more market potential – and should get an objective of 500 units. The remaining units he assigns to Steve. Frank and Steve each sell 200 units, but while Steve

Exhibit I   Objective-achievement system results

|         | Possible bonus | Objective | Achievement | Percent of objective | Actual bonus |
|---------|----------------|-----------|-------------|----------------------|--------------|
| Frank   | $15,000        | 500       | 200         | 40%                  | $6,000       |
| Steve   | 12,000         | 200       | 200         | 100                  | 12,000       |

makes 100 percent of his quota and gets the full bonus, Frank reaches just 40 percent of his objective and thus only 40 percent of his bonus. *Exhibit I* shows how objectives and actual achievements were calculated for Frank and Steve. Although Steve did a better job because of the toughness of his territory, under the old achievement system both would have received the same amount.

Using the objective-achievement approach all managers can shuffle territories and salesmen around without the salesmen complaining. Those who must spend time on assisting customers in installing complex machinery receive a smaller sales quota. Salesmen with good sales prospects get higher objectives; thus they neither frustrate other salesmen nor eat up the company's sales budget.

The system is not only fair to salesmen but also fits into operational plans. All quotas add up to the company's total objective, or nearly. It is quite simple. Simple but tricky. The whole concept depends on a precise forecasting technique. Up to now nobody has ever invented such a precise forecasting method, particularly when dealing with the small figures of a one-man territory.

In many cases, the objective-achievement system has more holes in it than Ed and Charles will ever make in the TV sets at their plant. For instance, Mary is a young saleswoman for an air-conditioning manufacturer. She sells air conditioners to any prospective customers within a given geographic territory. She works with a list of potential buyers given to her by the headquarters staff.

In September, Mary is asked to update the prospects list, indicating how many units each customer might buy in the following year. This does not make her happy because she knows that her information will be used to set up her next year's quota which will limit her gains. Mary sees the forecasting process as an enemy.

Although every month she prepares a 90-day sales forecast pinpointing the hot prospects, near the end of the year Mary does not enhance the list with new names. The company understands that she is concentrating on the most probable buyers and does not have time to open new accounts. On December 31 the 90-day forecast is near zero. The new year rewinds everyone's production clock. Mary is back to zero sales, and ready to get a new quota, which she hopes will be low.

The board of directors, however, wants growth – a 20 percent increase over last year's results. The branch offices receive the same percentage increase, so do the sales managers, and so does Mary who ends with a higher objective despite her forecast. Slow learns that the company had not trusted her forecast anyway. It looks like it is a mutual cheating system.

Since Joe, another salesman, is supposed to spend his year assisting old customers, he gets half of Mary's quota. Life goes on. Mary has a tough year barely reaching 100 percent of her objective, while she watches Joe get 300 percent of his quota, because of an unexpected order from a big builder in his territory and, therefore, 300 percent of his bonus.

Managers also see quota setting as an annoyance. Although the company's yearly objective is rather easy to decide on, splitting it equitably among sales people remains difficult at best. Even if the distribution looks fair in January, so many new facts take place during 12 months that, in the end, it is never equal.

Let us stop here to recall the objectives all managers are shooting for in a complex sales environment. First, they want to pay salesmen for their absolute sales volume. Second, they want to pay them for their effort, even if they are in tough areas where they will sell less. Third, they want good and fresh field information on market potential for planning and control purposes.

In the achievement system, salesmen are paid only according to actual sales volume. Since they are not paid extra if they achieve their quota, salesmen simply do not care and forecast poorly. The achievement system, therefore, satisfies only the first objective (volume), and works only in businesses where the second and third objectives (payment for effort and planning) are not pursued.

The objective-achievement system does not stress the first objective. Salesmen are paid by the percentage of their quota that they achieve and not by absolute results. Unfortunately, for payment to be based on quota achievement there must be good forecasting. This dependency is exactly what acts against the system. To ensure reaching their quota, salesmen try to provide the lowest possible forecast, which affects the company's overall plan and could eventually kill the chances for a perfect quota distribution.

In spite of this deficiency, however, this system can be used successfully in all cases where management has certain quota-fixing flexibility, and where the company's planning cycle does not depend deeply on the salesmen's forecast.

In any case, analysis of these two systems shows that there is still substantial room for improvement. This is why we at IBM Brazil have developed a system which includes all three objectives and which was successfully tested in a very important contest for salespeople.

## Measuring the "OFA" System

Through a new approach, which is known as the "OFA" system, earnings are based on a combination of three different measurements:

1  The objective, O, or quota the company chooses.
2  The forecast, F, the salesman provides.
3  The actual, A, results the salesman achieves.

*Exhibit II* displays the grid and formulas on which the OFA system is based. After receiving his objective, O, a salesman must turn in his forecast, F; F divided by O determines the column in which the salesman's bonus percentage will fall. For instance, the 1.0 column represents a forecast equal to the quota, the 0.5 column means the forecast is half the objective, and the 1.5 column indicates a forecast 50 percent larger than the objective. The letter "A" stands for actual sales results. Thus A divided by O and multiplied by 100 is the percentage of the objective that was actually achieved by the

Exhibit II   The OFA system grid and formulas

| | | F/O (Forecast divided by objective) | | | | | | | | | | |
|---|---|---|---|---|---|---|---|---|---|---|---|---|
| A/O ×100 | | 0 | 0.5 | 1.0 | 1.5 | 2.0 | 2.5 | 3.0 | 3.5 | 4.0 | 4.5 | 5.0 |
| (Actual results | 0 | – | – | – | – | – | – | – | – | – | – | – |
| divided by | 50 | 30 | 60 | 30 | – | – | – | – | – | – | – | – |
| objective, then | 100 | 60 | 90 | 120 | 90 | 60 | 30 | – | – | – | – | – |
| multiplied by | 150 | 90 | 120 | 150 | 180 | 150 | 120 | 90 | 60 | 30 | – | – |
| 100) | 200 | 120 | 150 | 180 | 210 | 240 | 210 | 180 | 150 | 120 | 90 | 60 |
| | 250 | 150 | 180 | 210 | 240 | 270 | 300 | 270 | 240 | 210 | 180 | 150 |
| | 300 | 180 | 210 | 240 | 270 | 300 | 330 | 360 | 330 | 300 | 270 | 240 |
| | 350 | 210 | 240 | 270 | 300 | 330 | 360 | 390 | 420 | 390 | 360 | 330 |
| | 400 | 240 | 270 | 300 | 330 | 360 | 390 | 420 | 450 | 480 | 450 | 420 |
| | 450 | 270 | 300 | 330 | 360 | 390 | 420 | 450 | 480 | 510 | 540 | 510 |
| | 500 | 300 | 330 | 360 | 390 | 420 | 450 | 480 | 510 | 540 | 570 | 600 |

Calculation of grid numbers
If F equal to A then OFA $= 120 \times$ F/O
If F smaller than A then OFA $= 60 \times (A + F)/O$
If F bigger than A then OFA $= 60 \times (3A - F)/O$

salesman; 100 percent means full achievement of the company's objective, not of the salesman's forecast.

Now let us see how it works. John sells photographic equipment. His quota is 500 cameras. Let us assume that John fully agrees to his quota and turns in a 500-units forecast. (On the grid, F/O equals 1.0.) If John sells 500 cameras, he makes 100 percent of his objective and is entitled to 120 percent of his bonus. In other words, he gets a 20 percent premium for his good planning capability. How much that represents in dollars depends on John's personal value, namely, his experience, time with the company, and merit.

If John sells 750 cameras, which is 150 percent of his objective, he is entitled to 150 percent of his bonus; the more he sells the more he earns. But now John realizes that if his forecast had been 750 instead of 500 units (1.5 on the grid), then he would have received 180 percent of his bonus instead of 150 percent. Bad planning on his part has deprived him of a good chunk of money. If John had sold 250 units, half of his objective, he would have earned just 30 percent of his incentive. Here again, John sees that it would have been better to have forecasted 250 instead of 500 for his earnings would have been 60 percent.

In other words, the best earnings lie in the diagonals that goes down from left to right in the grid. For a given result, A, the more precise John's forecast is, the higher his earnings. But John will always earn most if his forecast is perfect.

After being introduced to the grid, John goes back to study his territory. This time he does not want to return a faulty forecast – his earnings are at stake. He may still complain that the objective set up by his manager is too high – there is no solution to that – but for the first time he can enhance his earnings through a good work plan. If he comes in with a low forecast, he may damage his earnings in exchange for safety. On the other hand, a high forecast may plunge him into trouble if his sales are too low. John understands that he must be precise. This is exactly what his manager is waiting for.

From that moment on, John becomes committed to the number he forecasts. The grid tells him that his sales should be equal to or higher than the forecast in order for his earnings to increase. Soon, John sees that, because of the new interactive approach, the headquarters staff begins to really understand the market and sets sales objectives that approach his own forecast. Total accuracy will never happen, but for practical purposes the three main objectives of the system – sales volume, payment for performance, and good field information for planning – will be brought about.

## Putting the System to Work

The OFA system is a new idea. IBM has tried it successfully two times in its Brazilian operations during 1975 and 1976. Both times the OFA supplemented IBM Brazil's regular incentive programs. (See the Appendix for a description of how IBM Brazil adopted the system. A description of how the system might be applied to accounts receivable is included [on page 237].)

Clearly, however, there will be hitches in actually using the system that do not appear when one considers it in the abstract. For instance, it is difficult for salesmen to present good forecasts one year in advance. Because of this, in most cases the bonus can be an average between the monthly and yearly objectives.

For example, Sherm sells tractors. His quota of 1,200 units a year means he must sell 100 a month. But Sherm knows the true opportunities of his territory and is shooting for higher gains. He forecasts 1,800 tractors for the coming year, that is, 150 for each month.

The company asks him also for a monthly forecast. Sherm thinks that 50 is a good number for January. Unfortunately, he sells only 25. With the help of the OFA grid, let us see how much he will earn, assuming his incentive bonus is $24,000 a year, or $2,000 a month.

Since $F/O = 150/100 = 1.5$, Sherm's yearly forecast falls in the 1.5 column of the grid. In January he sold 25 units. Therefore, according to the grid formula (see *Exhibit II*):

$$OFA = 60 \times (3 \times 25 - 150)/100$$

The result is zero bonus. Since $F/O = 50/100 = 0.5$, Sherm's monthly forecast falls in the 0.5 column of the grid. F is still bigger than A, so the same formula applies:

$$OFA = 60 \times (3 \times 25 - 50)/100 = 15\%$$

The average between the yearly and the monthly calculation is 7.5 percent. Sherm receives $150 which is 7.5 percent of his monthly bonus.

In any traditional approach, forecasts would not have been considered, and Sherm would have received a quarter of his bonus, $500. Under the OFA system, Sherm was penalized for reaching only half of his forecast as well as for his low sales.

Let us keep in mind the whole concept. The company wants Sherm to sell 100 tractors a month as an average. He foresaw potential sales of 150 units by month, and decided to shoot for the 1.5 grid column which could give him 180 percent of his bonus. Because of his own choice, if he sells just 100, which *is* what the company wants, he gets only 90 percent of his bonus.

Sherm's January forecast and results did not help him. In February, however, Sherm forecasts that he will sell 200 tractors, which puts him in the 2.0 column of the grid, and he meets his forecast. Let us compute his earnings.

Sherm's yearly forecast, of 150 tractors a month, is smaller than his February achievement of 200. Therefore, he receives:

$$OFA = 60 \times (150 + 200)/100 = 210\%$$

For the monthly bonus, Sherm's forecast, 200, was equal to sales, so he gets:

$$OFA = 120 \times 200/100 = 240\%$$

Sherm's average is $(210 + 240)/2 = 225$ percent; his bonus value is \$4,500.

For January *and* February, Sherm got 232.5 percent of his monthly incentive (7.5% + 225%). He sold a total of 225 tractors against a forecast of 300 and a company objective of 200. In any traditional system he would have received 225 percent of his bonus (225/100). With OFA, his February planning was so good that it compensated for January's failure and provided him with an additional premium.

Sherm's company decided to use a direct average between monthly and yearly forecasts. Say Company B decides to weight them differently, considering the yearly forecast two times more important than the monthly one. Working for Company B, Sherm would have received slightly less money in February since the weighted calculation would have been

$$(2 \times 210\% + 1 \times 240\%)/3 = 220\%$$

Size, number of salesmen, and market type are some of the aspects to be taken into consideration when deciding the weighting factor.

## *Penalties for delays*

No matter how rough the waves, the surfing expert will manage to find the best path. While the corporation is working out a compensation system that will pay for high quality work and foster precise forecasting, its salesmen will try to uncover the best way to earn the most out of, or beat, the system.

Sherm, our brightest tractor salesman, for instance, finds out that whenever he receives a customer order that is bigger that his monthly forecast, it pays to hold it for the next month. In March, Sherm forecasts 50 tractors but he gets an unexpected 100-unit order. By the grid, his bonus will by 90 percent. If he holds the order until April, and then forecasts 100, his payment will go up to 120 percent.

Clearly, this absurdity is not supposed to be part of the OFA system, but Sherm's cleverness allows me to introduce a major piece of the OFA concept: the tool for penalizing the salesman for any delay in achieving the objectives set up by the corporation.

The problem is not new. How can we make the sales uniform throughout the year instead of having the usual peaks and lows? How can we avoid the traditional downturn during the first months of a new year? How can we avoid intentional or unintentional delays? The OFA system provides a clue. Sherm's company set his objective at 1,200 units a year. *We* immediately assumed 100 tractors a month and started to measure Sherm's results against this standard. But that assumption was wrong.

In the OFA system *every objective must include a piece of the previous unfulfilled objective.* If Sherm sells 100 or more tractors in January, then his February objective would also be 100 units. But if his January sales fall short of 100 units, then his February objective should be immediately raised. Since Sherm sold only 25 tractors in January, his new monthly objective should be between 100 and 175 units, depending on how tough with sales delays his company wants to be.

With an 80 percent penalty factor, Sherm's February quota would be 160 (80 percent of 175) instead of 100. Since he forecasted and sold 200 tractors, Sherm's final monthly percentage would be

$$\text{OFA} = 120 \times 200/160 = 150\%$$

At this point, Sherm will think twice before he holds up a customer order until the following month. Better than that, Sherm will rush ahead to reach his forecast as soon as possible.

Every objective must be attainable. The company ought to decide on a penalty that fits the type of business and not set up impossible goals for its sales force. A certain level of delays will always exist and should be accepted.

When preparing a sales incentive plan, the management team needs to understand that it will not be doing a good job if in the end the salesmen do not come out with a fair dollar share of the business.

## The OFA system for accounts receivable

Professional collectors and even branch office managers can work under the OFA incentive system. Because of cash flow problems, good forecasting is as vital in accounts receivable as it is for sales figures.

To start with, the objective should be divided into short periods, weeks if possible, and the collectors should visit customers before the actual collection in order to add pressure and improve their input to the accounts receivable department.

Sticking to the OFA concept that every objective must include a piece of the previous unfulfilled objective, the collector's weekly quota should equal the current debt, plus a percentage of the overdue at the beginning of the period under consideration.

A collector who turns back a low collection forecast is doing a good job by informing the company in advance of any problems in cash availability. But he is not free of his responsibility to improve that situation. The OFA system pays him a premium for his correct information, but it also penalizes him for staying under his objective. On the other hand, those that collect much more than they have forecasted cannot earn as much as those who really know what is going on in their territory.

## Appendix: The IBM Brazil Sales Contest

In designing a special sales contest to achieve $7 million revenue from a certain product in 1975, the IBM Brazil headquarters' staff had a number of concerns. It wanted to reward salespeople for good performance, given different territories, and at the same time it wanted to make sure the company achieved its objectives.

Management divided the total sales potential into three segments – A, B, and C – each group representing a different customer size and, thus, different degrees of difficulty. The relationship among the groups as to sales effort was 1 to 2.5 to 4.0. Each branch office, and so every salesman in it, was then assigned to one of the three groups.

In addition to regular incentives, top management selected $20,000 as the bonus base for $7 million in sales.

Management assessed the overall marketing opportunities for the three groups, based on historical data, and made the following sales prognoses:

| | | |
|---|---|---|
| Group A (small) | $ 500,000 | (7 percent of the total objective) |
| Group B (medium) | 2,800,000 | (40 percent of the total objective) |
| Group C (large) | 3,700,000 | (53 percent of the total objective) |

In addition to requiring four times less effort than Group A customers, Group C could also absorb over seven times more sales.

The salesmen were not given management's sales forecast by group. Yet it provided us with the major tool to compute the index or objective by salesman, as follows:

$$\$500/1 + \$2,800/2.5 + \$3,700/4 = \$2,545$$

Assuming that a salesman receives a $100 bonus for attaining his objective, then for a salesman in Group A, the objective would be figured as follows:

$$\$100 \times \$2,545,000/\$20,000 = \$12,725 \text{ (rounded to } \$12,700)$$

The final figures for the objectives were:

| | |
|---|---|
| For a Group A salesman: | $12,700 |
| For a Group B salesman: | $12,700 \times 2.5 = \$31,750$ |
| For a Group C salesman: | $12,700 \times 4.0 = \$50,800$ |

When the contest and objectives were made public, not one salesman complained about the effort relationship and its effect on the objectives. The distribution was considered fair, a very uncommon reaction.

If actual results had been precisely as planned, the bonus payment would have been as shown in *Table A*. Since we expected salesmen to be 80 percent precise in their forecasting, we figured the final bonus should be $19,238 (0.8 × $24,048).

At the end of the year, we achieved $8 million in sales, almost 15 percent over plan. Of the total sales force, 33 percent provided forecasts, and 3 percent received orders which, on the average, amounted to 85 percent of their forecasts. These orders represented 35 percent of the $8 million. Nine other orders came from nonforecasted customers and represented the other 65 percent of the total achievement.

**Table A**  Sales contest objectives by sales group

|  | Group A | Group B | Group C | Total |
|---|---|---|---|---|
| Objective by salesman | $ 12,700 | 31,750 | 50,800 | – |
| Expected sales | $500,000 | 2,800,000 | 3,700,000 | $ 7,000,000 |
| Total objectives to sell | 39.37 | 88.19 | 72.83 | |
| Bonus by objectives | $    100 | 100 | 100 | |
| Bonus for perfect forecast | $  4,725 | 10,583 | 8,740 | $ 24,048 |
| Bonus for no forecast | $  2,362 | 5,292 | 4,370 | $ 12,024 |

**Table B**  Result of sales contest by sales group

|  | Group A | Group B | Group C | Total |
|---|---|---|---|---|
| Plan | $500,000 | 2,800,000 | 3,700,000 | $7,000,000 |
| Actual results | $400,000 | 4,100,000 | 3,500,000 | $8,000,000 |
| Percentage of salesmen | 36% | 44 | 19 | 100% |
| Percentage of salesmen with orders | 2% | 4 | 2 | 8% |
| Total bonus paid | $ 2,350 | $ 10,370 | $ 4,040 | $ 16,760 |

The actual results by market group are shown in *Table B*.

Sales by group, as projected by the headquarters staff, were extraordinarily precise for Groups A and C, but underestimated for Group B. On the whole, despite the $1 million extra revenue, IBM spent less in bonuses than expected ($16,760 against $19,238).

Satisfaction at the salesmen level was high. Over $5 million came from nonforecasted orders, which showed that the usual sales drive was not disturbed; quite possibly it was enhanced by the payment for performance concept. All salesmen who closed orders were clearly pleased with the level of their bonuses.

The fact that only 8 percent of the salesmen got any orders means that a traditional quota distribution system (where everyone receives a quota objective) would have upset over 90 percent of the salesmen. On the other hand, if we had used a pure objective system, assuming that the same results could have been achieved, which is questionable, we would have paid around $23,000 ($20,000 × 8/7), about 50 percent more.

In addition to the $8 million achieved in 1975, another $7 million of possible sales were identified, which represented significant revenue potential for 1976. The overall result of the program, therefore, totaled $15 million.

For 1976, however, a new objective of $16 million was set for the same product. Once again, the company decided to use the OFA system exclusively for this bonus, as well as the regular incentive program.

For 1976, 95 percent of all salesmen submitted forecasts, and 40 percent succeeded. The final achievement was $30 million, with the following distribution:

| | | |
|---|---|---|
| 1976 sales from sales identified in 1975 | $ 4.6 | million |
| 1976 sales never forecasted | 6.7 | million |
| 1976 sales forecasted by salesmen | 18.7 | million |
| Total | $30.0 | million |

The most impressive fact was that in March 1976 (i.e., seven months before closing their orders), the salesmen who brought in those $18.7 million of forecasted orders had told the company that they expected to sell $18 million. They reached 104 percent of their forecast in only the second year of the experiment with the OFA system. This precision proved that a forecasting system with salesmen participation under the OFA grid would work and was efficient.

Once again, additional possible customers were identified and sales calls started. This time, a potential revenue of $18 million passed to 1977, and management felt that a new contest in 1977 was, therefore, not needed.

It is important to point out that IBM Brazil's success with OFA also has been dependent on other factors, such as strong central coordination, an effective education program, and accurate responses to customers' needs. The bonus was part of a complete marketing program.

The most important feature introduced by the system was undoubtedly the participation of the employees in creating their own objectives, which enhanced their overall motivation toward attaining the company's goals. The OFA system does not ignore the company's goals; on the contrary, it stresses their importance by setting them as the main objective in the bonus calculation.

# FORTY-SEVEN

# Car-Buying Services Can Save Money, Especially for Those who Hate Haggling

Melinda Grenier Guiles

*Source*: *Wall Street Journal*, April 23, 1985.

Bruce Entin of San Jose, Calif., had trouble finding the car he wanted at a price he thought was reasonable. On a friend's recommendation, he turned to a local auto broker, who got him his Toyota Cressida for about $2,000 less than the best deal he could negotiate on his own. "Going to dealers was one frustration after another," he says. "Using a broker was a lot less expensive and it was troublefree. There was no negotiating and I didn't have to run all over town."

Not everyone can save $2,000 by using a broker or car-buying service when they need a new car or light-duty truck. Not everyone will have a trouble-free experience. But brokers and buying services can save money in many instances and they could save time and aggravation if shopping showrooms or haggling with dealers doesn't sound like fun. It's important to pick carefully, however. New-car brokers and buying services come in all sizes – from large, well-established national companies to individuals working out of their basements. Their fees range from less than $10 to more than $200. Their services vary from selling a computerized price list to arranging the purchase and financing and demonstrating the radio. It's also important to be realistic about what the service or broker can do. The savings claimed is a relative term; most people can negotiate something off the sticker price of an average model. But Richard White, a spokesman for the American Automobile Association, which offers its own buying service, says: "Sharp bargainers are few and far between. The car salesman does this every day so he has an edge. The car-buying service cuts that edge a bit in favor of the customer."

The so-called full-service brokers will handle virtually every aspect of the deal, including helping sell the buyer's used car and arranging financing for the new model. Buyers usually go to the dealership only to sign the necessary papers. This type of service generally charges the highest fee. Automotive Search Inc., in Rockville, Md., which mainly serves Washington, D.C.-area residents, charges $190 for, among other things, evaluating the prospective buyer's travel and driving habits. Accident-prone drivers shouldn't buy cars with metallic paints, for example, because these paints are hard to match, says Alin H. Jacobs, president. The company then finds the car that the buyer wants and negotiates a price with the dealer. Depending on the specific model, customers pay an average of about $100 over the dealer's invoice on domestic cars and up to about

$1,000 over invoice on imported cars, Mr. Jacobs says. He claims he can save customers "a couple hundred dollars" on average, even after his fee.

Nationwide Auto Brokers Inc., of Southfield, Mich., charges $6.95 for a detailed comparison of the dealer's invoice price and retail prices. The price of a car bought through Nationwide includes a mark up ranging from less than 1 percent on some domestic models to as much as 8 percent on some imported models. That compares with an average mark up in the manufacturer's suggested retail price ranging from 12 percent to 18 percent over dealer invoice, plus any additional dealer mark up on popular models. For example, a $12,968 Nationwide price quote for a 1985 model Oldsmobile Cutlass Supreme Brougham Coupe includes a wide range of options, such as air conditioning and rustproofing, a $75 mark up that goes to Nationwide and a $75 dealer preparation charge. The manufacturer's suggested list price for the same car is about $14,600, without rustproofing.

Both Nationwide and Automotive Search say they can negotiate lower prices because they have arranged to buy large numbers of vehicles from dealers.

Buyers willing to do some of the work themselves can use buying or referral services that provide names of dealers who have arranged with the service to sell cars at a specific dollar or percentage level under the manufacturer's suggested retail price. While generally less expensive than the full-service brokers, these services require a buyer to negotiate prices on dealer-installed options like rustproofing and trim stripes. The buyer must also set up financing and handle any trade in. Car/Puter International Corp., based in Brooklyn, N. Y., provides referrals to more than 450 dealers for a $20 fee, which includes a detailed price comparison. These dealers have agreed to sell domestic cars for an average of $50 to $200 over invoice price and imported cars for $400 to $1,200 over invoice, says Arnold W. Wonsever, Car/Puter president.

Some buying services are limited to geographic areas or groups of people. USAA Cardeal, for example, offers its referral service only to certain military or ex-military personnel. For $50, the San Antonio, Texas-based firm supplies the name of a dealer who will sell a car, truck or van for 1 percent to 5 percent over the dealer invoice cost. United Buying Service of Colorado Inc., which restricts its service to certain groups and companies, will recommend one of about 17 Denver-area car dealers who have agreed to sell at about 2 percent to 4 percent above invoice on American cars.

Meanwhile, buyers willing to do almost all the work themselves can obtain guidance about a fair price from the Nationwide or Car/Puter price lists or one sold by Consumer Reports for $10. The lists give a detailed breakdown of the dealer's invoice price for a particular model, including prices of options and destination charges. Detailed price lists also are available in paperback book form, but these mightn't be as up-to-date as the computer lists.

Even when using a broker, it's a good idea to check the price guides first. A USAA Cardeal ad says it will save a buyer $3,774.91 on a Cadillac Eldorado, but that savings is on the top-of-the-line model with a sunroof, anti-theft system and the most expensive sound system. The savings probably wouldn't be as big on a less option-laden model. Another potential problem is that many brokers and buying services don't handle imported cars and some can't get discounts on certain popular models. Car buyers might also find that sales people aren't eager to handle customers referred by a buying service because they don't make as much money on those deals.

It's especially important to make sure the broker or company is reputable. A history of unresolved complaints might show up at Better Business Bureaus and the consumer fraud or consumer protection division of the district attorney's office or attorney general's office in the city or state where the service is based. Some states require brokers or buying services to be licensed or bonded. That could be helpful to consumers if a company keeps a customer's fee and any deposit without providing any service. In 1982, for example, Michigan sued two car brokers following charges by consumers that they had made deposits on cars but never received them or a refund.

# FORTY-EIGHT

# How to Build an Economic Model in Your Spare Time

Hal R. Varian

Source: *Passion and Craft: Economists at Work*, Michael Szenberg (ed.), Ann Arbor: University of Michigan Press, 1999.

Most of my work in economics involves constructing theoretical models. Over the years, I have developed some ways of doing this that may be worth describing to those who aspire to practice this art. In reality the process is much more haphazard than my description would suggest – the model of research that I describe is an idealization of reality, much like the economic models that I create. But there is probably enough connection with reality to make the description useful – which I hope is also true for my economic models.

## 1. Getting Ideas

The first step is to get an idea. This is not all that hard to do. The tricky part is to get a *good* idea. The way you do this is to come up with lots and lots of ideas and throw out all the ones that aren't good.

But where to get ideas, that's the question. Most graduate students are convinced that the way you get ideas is to read journal articles. But in my experience journals really aren't a very good source of original ideas. You can get lots of things from journal articles – technique, insight, even truth. But most of the time you will only get someone else's ideas. True, they may leave a few loose ends lying around that you can pick up on, but the reason they are loose is probably that the author thought about them a while and couldn't figure out what to do with them or decided they were too tedious to bother with – which means that it is likely that you will find yourself in the same situation.

My suggestion is rather different: I think that you should look for your ideas outside the academic journals – in newspapers, in magazines, in conversations, and in TV and radio programs. When you read the newspaper, look for the articles about economics...and then look at the ones that aren't about economics, because lots of the time they end up being about economics too. Magazines are usually better than newspapers because they go into issues in more depth. On the other hand, a shallower analysis may be more stimulating: there's nothing like a fallacious argument to stimulate research.[1]

Conversations, especially with people in business, are often very fruitful. Commerce is conducted in many ways, and most of them have never been subjected to a serious economic analysis. Of course you have to be careful not to *believe* everything you hear – people in business usually know a set of rules that work well for running their own business, but they often have no idea of where these rules come from or why they work, and this is really what economists tend to find interesting.

In many cases your ideas can come from your own life and experiences. One of my favorite pieces of my own work is the paper I wrote on "A Model of Sales". I had decided to get a new TV so I followed the ads in the newspaper to get an idea of how much it would cost. I noticed that the prices fluctuated quite a bit from week to week. It occurred to me that the challenge to economics was not why the prices were sometimes low (i.e., during sales) but why they were ever high. Who would be so foolish as to buy when the price was high since everyone knew that the item would be on sale in a few weeks? But there must be such people, otherwise the stores would never find it profitable to charge a high price. Armed with this insight, I was able to generate a model of sales. In my model there were two kinds of consumers: informed consumers who read the ads and uninformed consumers who didn't read the ads. The stores had sales in order to price discriminate between the informed and uninformed consumers.

Once I developed the model I had a research assistant go through a couple of years' worth of the *Ann Arbor News* searching for the prices of color TVs. Much to my delight the general pattern of pricing was similar to that predicted by the model. And, yes, I did manage to get a pretty good deal on the TV I eventually bought.

## 2.   Is your Idea Worth Pursuing?

So let's assume (a favorite word of economists) that you have an idea. How do you know if it is any good? The first test is to try to phrase your idea in a way that a non-economist can understand. If you can't do this it's probably not a very good idea. If you can phrase it in a way that a noneconomist can understand, it still may be a lousy idea, but at least there's hope.

Before you start trying to decide whether your idea is correct, you should stop to ask whether it is interesting. If it isn't interesting, no one will care whether it is correct or not. So try it out on a few people – see if they think that it is worth pursuing. What would follow from this idea if it is correct? Would it have lots of implications or would it just be a dead end? Always remember that working on this particular idea has an opportunity cost – you could be spending your time working on a different idea. Make sure that the expected benefits cover that opportunity cost. One of the primary purposes of economic theory is to generate insight. The greatest compliment is "Ah! So that explains it!" That's what you should be looking for – forget about the "nice solid work" and try to become a Wizard of Ahs.

---

[1] But which sources to read? I read the *New York Times*, the *Wall Street Journal* and the *Economist*; these are probably good places to start.

## 3.  Don't Look at the Literature Too Soon

The first thing that most graduate students do is they rush to the literature to see if someone else had this idea already. However, my advice is to wait a bit before you look at the literature. Eventually you should do a thorough literature review, of course, but I think that you will do much better if you work on your idea for a few weeks before doing a systematic literature search. There are several reasons for delay.

First, you need the practice of developing a model. Even if you end up reproducing exactly something that is in the literature already you will have learned a lot by doing it – and you can feel awfully good about yourself for developing a publishable idea! (Even if you didn't get to publish it yourself...)

Second, you might come up with a different approach than is found in the literature. If you look at what someone else did your thoughts will be shaped too much by their views – you are much more likely to be original if you plunge right in and try to develop your own insights.

Third, your ideas need time to incubate, so you want to start modeling as early as possible. When you read what others have done their ideas can interact with yours and, hopefully, produce something new and interesting.

## 4.  Building your Model

So let's skip the literature part for now and try to get to the modeling. Lucky for you, all economics models look pretty much the same. There are some economic agents. They make choices in order to advance their objectives. The choices have to satisfy various constraints so there's something that adjusts to make all these choices consistent. This basic structure suggests a plan of attack: Who are the people making the choices? What are the constraints they face? How do they interact? What adjusts if the choices aren't mutually consistent?

Asking questions like this can help you to identify the pieces of a model. Once you've got a pretty good idea of what the pieces look like, you can move on to the next stage. Most students think that the next stage is to prove a theorem or run a regression. No! The next stage is to work an example. Take the simplest example – one period, 2 goods, 2 people, linear utility – whatever it takes to get to something simple enough to see what is going on.

Once you've got an example, work another one, then another one. See what is common to your examples. Is there something interesting happening here? When your examples have given you an inkling of what is going on, *then* you can try to write down a model. The critical advice here is KISS: keep it simple, stupid. Write down the simplest possible model you can think of, and see if it still exhibits some interesting behavior. If it does, then make it even simpler.

Several years ago I gave a seminar about some of my research. I started out with a very simple example. One of the faculty in the audience interrupted me to say that he had worked on something like this several years ago, but his model was "much more complex". I replied "My model was complex when I started, too, but I just kept working on it till it got simple!"

And that's what you should do: keep at it till it gets simple. The whole point of a model is to give a simplified representation of reality. Einstein once said "Everything should be as simple as possible ... but no simpler." A model is supposed to reveal the essence of what is going on: your model should be reduced to just those pieces that are required to make it work.

This takes a surprisingly long time – there are usually lots of false starts, frustrating diversions, and general fumbling around. But keep at it! If it were easy to do, it would have already been done.

## 5. Generalizing your Model

Suppose that you've finally made your model as simple as possible. At this point your model is probably *too* simple to be of much interest: it's likely just an example or a special case. But if you have made your model as simple as possible, it will now be much easier to see how to generalize it since you know what the key pieces are that make the model work.

Here is where your education can be helpful. At last you can use all those techniques you learned in graduate school. Most of the time you were a student you probably studied various canonical models: things like consumer choice, and producer choice, general equilibrium, game theory and so on. The professor probably told you that these were very general models that could encompass lots of special cases.

Well, it was all true. Over the last fifty years economists have come up with some very general principles and models. Most likely your model is a special case of one of these general models. If so you can immediately apply many of the results concerning the general model to your special case, and all that technique you learned can help you analyze your model.

## 6. Making Mistakes

This process – simplify to get the result, complexify to see how general it is – is a good way to understand your model. Most of the time that I spend modeling is involved in this back- and-forth process. Along the way, I make a lot of mistakes. As Piet Hein puts it:

> The road to wisdom? We'll it's plain
> and simple to express:
> Err
> and err
> and err again
> but less
> and less
> and less.

This back-and-forth iteration in building a model is like sculpting: you are chipping away a little bit here, and a little bit there, hoping to find what's really inside that stubborn block of marble. I choose the analogy with sculpting purposely: like sculpture most of the work in building a model doesn't consists of adding things, it consists of subtracting them.

This is the most fun part of modeling, and it can be very exciting when the form of the idea really begins to take shape. I normally walk around in a bit of a daze at this stage; and I try not to get too far away from a yellow pad. Eventually, if you're lucky, the inner workings of your model will reveal itself: you'll see the simple core of what's going on and you'll also understand how general the phenomenon really is.

## 7.  Searching the Literature

At this point you can start doing your literature search. Tell your professors about what you've discovered – nine times out of ten they'll tell you to look in the "1983 *AER*" or "*Econometrica* 77" or some textbook (maybe even one of mine). And lots of the time they'll be right. You'll look there and find "your" model – but it will be much better done, much more fully developed, and much clearer.

Hey, no one said research would be easy. But this is a point where you really have a chance to learn something – read the article(s) carefully and ask yourself "Why didn't I do that?" If someone started with the same idea as you and carried it further, you want to see what you missed.

On the other hand, if you really followed the advice I gave you above to keep it simple, you may have come up with something that is much clearer than the current treatments. Or, maybe you've found something that is more general. If so, you may have a worthwhile insight. Go back to your advisor and tell him or her what you have found. Maybe you've got a new angle on an old idea that is worth further exploration. If so, congratulations – you would never have found this if you did the literature search right away.

Maybe what you've figured out is not already in the literature. The next possibility is that you are wrong. Maybe your analysis isn't right, maybe the idea is just off the wall. This is where your advisor can play a big role. If you've really made your analysis as simple as possible, it is a) less likely to contain an error, and b) any errors that remain will be easier to find.

This brings me to another common problem. When you've worked on a topic for several months – or even several weeks – you tend to lose a lot of perspective... literally. You're just too close to the work to really get a picture of what is going on. This lack of perspective takes one of two forms: first, you may think something is obvious when it really isn't. It may be obvious to *you*, but you've been thinking about this issue for several months – it probably isn't so obvious to someone who doesn't have the benefit of that experience.

The other possibility is that you may think something is complicated when it is really obvious – you've wandered into a forest via a meandering path. Maybe there's a nice clear trail just a few feet away that you've totally missed.

So at this point you've got to start getting some independent judgment of your work. Talk to your advisor, talk to your fellow students, talk to your wife, husband, girlfriend, boyfriend, neighbor, or pet... whoever you can get to listen. And here's what you'll find: they've got no idea of what you are talking about (especially your pet). So *you* have to go back to trying to figure out what you really are talking about: what *is* the fundamental idea of your model?

## 8. Giving a Seminar

After you've bored your friends, relatives and pets to death, you should give a seminar. This is a really important phase: the more you can talk about your work, the better the final paper will be. This is because a talk forces you to *get to the point*. If you want your audience to listen to you, you've got to make your idea clear, concise, and organized – and the experience that you gain by doing this is extremely useful for writing your paper.

I listen to a lot of stupid ideas – but that's what I'm paid to do. Lots of people listen to stupid ideas from me, too: my colleagues get paid to do it, and the students get examined on it. But most people don't have to listen to you. They don't have to read your paper. They won't even have to glance at the abstract unless they have a reason to.

This comes as a big shock to most graduate students. They think that just because they've put a lot of work and a lot of thought into their paper that the rest of the world is obliged to pay attention to them. Alas, it isn't so. Herb Simon once said that the fundamental scarcity in the modern world was scarcity of attention – and brother, is that the truth. There are demands for everybody's attention, and if you want someone to pay attention to you, you have to give them a reason to do so. A seminar is a way to get them to pay attention, so be sure to exploit this opportunity to get people to listen to you.

The useful thing about a seminar is that you get immediate feedback from the audience. An audience won't put up with a lot of the things that authors try to write in papers: turgid prose, complex notation, and tedious details. And, believe it or not, readers won't put up with these things either! The trick is to use the seminar to get all those things out of your paper – that way, it may actually get read.

### Controlling the audience

I've seen it claimed that one of the greatest fears that most people have is speaking before a group. I imagine that most assistant professors have this problem, but after many years of giving lectures before several hundred students it goes away.

In fact, lecturing can become downright addictive (as my family often reminds me). As the mathematician R. H. Bing once said: "When I was young, I would rather give a lecture on mathematics than listen to one. Now that I am older and more mature I would rather give *two* lectures on mathematics than listen to one." Giving lectures is a bit like eating oysters. Your first one requires some courage, but after you develop a taste for them, it can be hard to stop.

There are three parts to a seminar: the introduction, the content, and the conclusion. My advice about introductions is simple: don't have one. I have seen many seminars ruined by long, pretentious, contentless introductions. My advice: say a few sentences about the big picture and then get down to business: show them what you've got and why it's important. The primary reason to get down to business right away is that your audience will only remember about twenty minutes of your talk – and that is usually the *first* twenty minutes. So make sure that you get some useful information into that first twenty minutes.

As for conclusions, the most common problem is letting the seminar trail off into silence. This can ruin a good talk. I always like to spend the last couple of minutes summarizing what I accomplished and why the audience should care. After all, this is what they will walk away with, so you might as well tell them what they should remember rather than make them figure this out for themselves.

Nowadays everyone seems to use overheads for their lectures. The downside of this is that the seminar isn't very spontaneous – but the upside is that the seminar is usually better organized. My advice is to limit yourself to one or two slides for an introduction and one for a conclusion. That way you will be forced to get to *your* contribution sooner rather than later. And make your overheads *big*; use large type and don't try to say too much on each one.

There are two things to avoid in your presentation: don't let your audience go to sleep, and don't let them get too lively. You want the audience to hear what you have to say. They won't hear your message if they are sleeping, and they won't hear your message if they are talking more than you are. So don't lose control of your seminar!

The key to maintaining control is to establish credibility early on. The way to do that is to go into great detail in the presentation of your first result – a theorem, a regression, a diagram, whatever. Spell out each aspect of your result in excruciating detail so no one can possibly misunderstand. When you do this you will certainly get questions like "Will this generalize to $n$ agents?" or "Have you corrected for heteroskedasticity?"

If you know the answer to the question, go ahead and answer it. If you don't know the answer – or the question is totally off the wall – say "That's a good question; let me come back to that at the end of the seminar." (Of course you never will.) Don't get sidetracked: the point of going through the initial result in great detail is to establish credibility.

Once you've presented your result and you see that the audience has understood the point – their heads are nodding but not nodding off – you can go on to the generalizations and elaborations. If you've done a good job at establishing your credibility initially now the audience will believe anything you say! Of course you shouldn't abuse this trust, but it is useful to exploit it in the rest of your presentation. This is the fundamental reason for starting simple: if you start out with a delicate argument, it will be hard for the audience to understand and you will never establish trust.

When you are done with your talk you should take a few minutes to jot down some notes: what was difficult for people to understand? what questions did they ask? what suggestions did they make? what references did they give you? You may think that you will remember these points, but quite often you won't. The audience is a very useful resource for clarifying your thoughts – make sure you use it well.

## 9.   Planning your Paper

Almost everyone writes on computers these days. I know that computers are great time savers: I get almost as much work done now as I got done before I started using computers.[2]

I thought that I would spend a bit of time talking about how I use computers, not because it is all that important, but because no one else in this collection will discuss such mundane matters. Since I am well known as a computer nerd, people always ask me what I use, and I figure I can save time by pointing them to this article. Undoubtedly this will all look incredibly archaic in a few years, but that's the cost of being on the bleeding edge of technology.

I currently use a Unix machine, but most of what I say applies equally well to other environments. I have a directory on my computer called Papers and when I start to work on a new topic I create a subdirectory under papers. (For example, this paper is in a directory Papers/how-I-work.) When I create the directory I create a notes.txt file: this contains my initial ideas, a rough outline, whatever. For example, the notes.txt file for this paper initially had entries in it like:

```
*read the newspaper
*simplify
*write and talk
**if you don't grab them in the first page, they won't read it
```

I create a notes file like this when I first start to work on a topic – I jot down the initial ideas I have, which are usually pretty sketchy. In the following days and weeks I occasionally take a look at this outline. When I look at it I move things around, add material and so on. I rarely take anything out completely – I just move material to the end of the file. After all, I might want those notes again.

After organizing these ideas for several weeks or months I am ready to write the first draft of the paper. I usually try to do this in a day or two, to keep it all fresh. I normally put the notes in one window and the paper in the other and write the paper while I refer back and update the notes to keep them in sync with the paper.

Once the paper is written I put it aside for a couple of weeks. Papers need to age like fine cheese – it's true that mold might develop, but the flavor is often enhanced. More importantly, it gives your subconscious mind a chance to work on the idea – maybe it will come up with something your conscious mind has missed.

When I come back to the paper I try to read it with a fresh mind, like someone who has never seen it before.[3] On rare occasions I like what I read, but usually I have lots of criticisms. Whenever I have to pause and think "what does that mean?" I rewrite – I add more explanation, change the notation, or whatever is necessary to make the paper clearer. When I'm done with this process I have a first draft.

---

[2] If a train stops at a train station, what do you think happens at a work station?
[3] This is much easier once you reach middle age.

I next check this draft into a revision control system. This is a piece of software that keeps track of the revisions of a paper. It documents all of the changes you make and allows you to restore any previous version of a paper. I use the Unix utility rcs but I know there are many other systems available. Revision control systems are especially valuable if you are working with a coauthor since they keep track of which person made which changes when.

I then repeat the process: let the paper sit for a few more weeks or months, then come back to it, read it with a fresh mind and revise it accordingly.

It is particularly useful to do a revision right after you give a seminar. Remember those notes I told you to write after your seminar ended? Sit down with the paper and go over the questions the audience had and the suggestions they made. Can you answer their questions in your paper? Can you incorporate their suggestions? Be sure to modify the notes/outline/slides for your talk when you incorporate the audience's suggestions.

### *Bibliographic software*

One very useful computer tool is a bibliographic system. This is a piece of software designed to managed a list of references. There is a master database of references that is stored on your computer. You assign a key to each article like Arrow70 or ArrowRisk. When you want to refer to a paper you use the key, by saying something like\cite{Arrow70}. The bibliographic program then looks up the appropriate citation in your database and puts it in the list of references at the end of your article.

I use the system called BibTEX, since it works well with TEX. However, there are many other systems available that work for other wordprocessing packages. It's a good idea to get in the habit of using a system like this. Over the years you will build up a comprehensive bibliography for the areas you work in.

But where do you get your references in the first place? Well, one way is to ask people: your adviser, your colleagues, your friends, and so on. This is still one of the most reliable ways. But nowadays there are a number of computerized databases available online or on CDs that allow for easy search. You can open the CD for the *Journal of Economic Literature*, type in a few key words like "price discrimination" and get the last 10 years worth of abstracts of published articles that contain the words "price discrimination." As you look at these articles you will see a few "classic" articles cited. When you identify these classic articles go to the *Social Science Citation Index* and search for all the recent papers that have cited these classics. This process should give you an up-to-date bibliography pretty quickly. Often you can download the citations you get directly into your bibliography database program.

## 10.  The Structure of the Paper

There's an old joke about academic papers. They are all supposed to have three parts. The first part, everyone can understand. The second, only a handful of readers can understand.

The last part no one can understand – that's how the readers know it's a serious piece of work!

The big mistake that authors make these days is to leave out the first part of the paper – that part that everyone can understand. But the introduction is the most important part of the paper. You've got to grab the reader on the first page. No matter how brilliant the rest of the paper is, it won't be noticed if no one reads it. And no one will read it if you don't get their interest in the first few paragraphs. If you really know what your paper is about, you shouldn't find it hard to explain this to your readers in a couple of paragraphs.

My basic advice is to make your paper look like your talk. Get to the point. Use examples. Keep it simple. Tell people why what you did is important after you've done it. Put the tedious stuff in the appendix. End with a summary of what you have accomplished. If you have really written a good paper, people won't have to listen to your seminar to find out what you have done: they can just read it in your paper.

## 11.  When to Stop

You can tell when your work is getting ready for publication by the reactions in the seminars: people stop asking questions. (Or at least, the people who have read your paper stop asking questions.) If you've followed my advice, you've already asked their questions – and answered them – in your paper.

Once you've made your point, stop. Lots of papers drag on too long. I said earlier that people only remember about 20 minutes of your seminar (if you're lucky), and they only remember about 10 pages of your paper. You should be able to say most of what you want to say in that length.

Once your paper is written, you can submit it to a journal. I don't have too much to say about this; Dan Hamermesh has written a nice article that describes the procedure better than I can.[4] All I can say is to echo his advice that you go over the article with a fine tooth comb before sending it in. Nothing turns off an editor or a referee more than to find typos, missing references and sloppy editing in the articles they deal with.

## 12.  Writing Textbooks

Most of what I've had to say so far has to do with writing articles. But I suppose I really should say a bit about the other kind of writing I've done: textbooks.[5]

My first text, *Microeconomic Analysis* really wasn't planned; it just happened. When I first started my professional career at MIT in 1973 I was asked to teach the first year graduate micro course. The text, such as it was, consisted of about 20 pages of

---

[4] Daniel S. Hamermesh, "The Young Economist's Guide to Professional Etiquette", *Journal of Economic Perspectives*, 6: 1, 169–80.

[5] The reader may recall Disraeli's warning: "An author who speaks about his own books is almost as bad as a mother who talks about her own children."

notes written by Bob Hall, maybe 40 pages of notes from Dan McFadden and Sid Winter, and a few journal articles. The notes were awfully sketchy, and the journal articles were much too advanced for first year students. So I had to write my own notes for the students.

The first year I wrote about 50 pages; the next year another 50, and the year after that another 50. The students who used them were great. They read them carefully and told me what was wrong: where the obscurities were, where the errors were, what was too advanced, and what was too simple. I owe much of the success of that book to the fact it was class tested before a highly critical audience.

During this period I happened to meet Richard Hamming, an electrical engineer who had written several texts. He gave me a key piece of advice: "Get together the problems that you want your students to be able to solve after they've read your book – and then write the book that will teach them how to solve them."

This was great advice. I followed it to some degree with the graduate text, but later, when I wrote the undergraduate text, I followed it religiously – but more about that below.[6]

One day a publisher came into my office and asked (as they often do) "Are you writing a book?" I said that would be a silly thing for an assistant professor to do – but as a matter of fact, I did have some class notes that I had been working on for a few years.

Next thing I knew, I had several publishers interested in my notes. I spent a semester at Berkeley in 1977 and used that opportunity to hammer them into shape. Much to my surprise the notes eventually become a book and ended up being very widely used. I did a second edition in 1983 and I *should* have done a revision in 1987 or so – but instead I decided to write an undergraduate text.

I wanted to write an undergraduate book because I was fed up with the books I had been using. I had tried several different ones, but couldn't find any I really liked. I remember one semester I sat down and tried to write a midterm exam – but the book I had been using was so vapid that I couldn't think of any problems that the students could solve using the tools that had been presented in the book! At that point I figured I could produce something better.

About the same time one of my undergraduates had picked up a workbook by Marcia Stigum called, I believe, *Problems in Microeconomics*. The student found this very helpful in understanding the concepts of economics, and I remembered what Hamming had told me about how to write a textbook. So I asked my colleague Ted Bergstrom if he would like to work with me to create a serious workbook.[7] Ted created problems as the text was being written, and I had to make sure that the text contained everything necessary to solve the problems he created. I created problems too, but those were automatically coordinated with the textbook – the external stimulus imposed by Ted's problems was much more important in shaping the content of the book. If the students weren't able to solve the problems, I had to add explanations to the text until they could – and if we couldn't create

---

[6] The general principle that I followed (and still follow) with the graduate text is that it should give the student the information they need to know to read a microeconomics paper in the *American Economic Review*. Every now and then I go through a few issues of the *AER* and note topics that should go in the next edition of the book.

[7] As it turned out, it wasn't quite as serious as I had expected – in fact, I think that it is quite funny, but that is due to Ted's unique sense of humor rather than my intentions.

a problem to illustrate some point, the point probably wasn't important enough to put in the text.

It's a pity that most workbooks are created as afterthoughts. Creating the workbook really should be an integral part of the writing process, as Hamming suggested. You want the students to be able to *use* the material you teach them, so the first order of business is to figure out what it is that you want them to be able to do. The latest buzzword in education is "learning by doing" but as far as I'm concerned that's always been the only way to go.

The undergraduate text turned out to be pretty successful as well. And the workbook has ended up selling two or three times as much as any of its competitors – which goes to show that there still is a market for a quality product in the textbook market.

## 13. Summary

I said that every talk should have a summary – so I suppose I have to follow my own advice. Here are the points to take away:

- Look for ideas in the world, not in the journals.
- First make your model as simple as possible, then generalize it.
- Look at the literature later, not sooner.
- Model your paper after your seminar.
- Stop when you've made your point.

And now my points have been made, so I'm duty bound to stop. Go forth and model!

## FORTY-NINE

# "Of Course That's Only an Estimate..."

SIDNEY HOFF

"Of course that's only an estimate. The actual cost will be somewhat more."

# Signalling

# Introduction

The classic article on signaling is Michael Spence, "Job Market Signalling," *Quarterly Journal of Economics* 87: 355–74 (August 1973). I have deliberately chosen not to include it in this collection because I consider it to be a confusing presentation of the idea of signaling and neither particularly well written nor stimulating. My aim in this book is not to include the most important papers – of which this is certainly one – but those which I think are still worth not only citing, but reading. The Spence article is roughly as important as the Akerlof "lemons" article which I did include, but Spence's article is more straightforward and conventional, and so more easily replaced by textbook presentation. Instead, I have included a much later article on signaling by Bagwell and Riordan which is only moderately well known, but which I consider to be well written and representative of the mature literature on signaling.

The prospector cartoon captures the idea of signal-jamming. At the cost of a little effort to look goofy, our prospector conceals whether he made his big strike or not. Cartoons are much like models, seeking to capture the essence of a situation economically, stripping away non-essentials and needing the participation of the reader to be understood. As David Remnick says on p. iii of his preface to *The New Yorker Book of Business Cartoons*, edited by Robert Mankoff (1998), "The best cartoons have about them a sense of effortlessness, as if they were pieces of found art. They seem so stark and simple, like a small bomb. The combination of ink drawing and a few words produce a kind of explosive release – laughter – and truth all at once. Something so simple must be near impossible to do. My colleagues and I routinely give lip service to the art of concision – good taste dictates Flaubert over Hugo – but what writer isn't always *hokking* an editor for more space? As a writer, I have been guilty of it. We are road hogs, forever trying to occupy the whole highway, and so when we see the magical effects the cartoonists get with their drawings and their combustible bits of language, we begin to wonder about our own failings, the grossness of our 10,000- and 20,000-word bloviations."

As an exercise, consider another cartoon, which cost too much to include here but which is easy to describe: a lawyer is sitting behind an elegant desk dressed in a clown suit and saying to a client something like, "If I weren't a very good lawyer, could I practise law in a clown suit?" Can you construct a formal model of that situation? Could there be a pooling equilibrium in which *all* lawyers, good and bad alike, had to wear clown suits? Before you laugh, ask yourself whether there could be a pooling equilibrium in which all lawyers, good and bad alike, had to wear silk strips hanging from their necks.

My inclusion of the Davis article may strike you as odd. What is a sixty-year-old article from a practitioner law journal doing in a collection of readings in game theory? I include it because arguing cases before the Supreme Court and presenting research before I.O. economists turns out to be much the same. The speaker has limited time, he must think about the audience and not about his paper, he must make technical arguments understandable, and he should realize that questions are more important than displaying every last one of his ideas. Before one worries about such subtleties as signaling, one must worry about simply being comprehensible.

# FIFTY

# High and Declining Prices Signal Product Quality

KYLE BAGWELL AND MICHAEL H. RIORDAN*

*Source*: *The American Economic Review* 81(1) March, 1991, pp. 224–39.**

© American Economic Association. Reprinted with their permission and that of the authors.

High and declining prices signal a high-quality product. High prices are the efficient means of signaling, because the consequent loss of sales volume is most damaging for lower-cost, lower-quality products. As time passes and the number of informed consumers increases, the signaling distortion lessens, resulting in a declining price profile. The prediction of high and declining prices is robust across a variety of dynamic models and is consistent with recent empirical findings.

The marketing literature has produced various evidence on price-quality relationships. Numerous experimental studies show that consumers infer a higher quality from a higher price (Kent B. Monroe, 1973). This inference is consistent with the findings of several case studies. Such diverse products as fountain-pen ink and car wax (André Gabor and Clive Granger, 1965) and vodka, skis, and television sets (Robert D. Buzzell et al., 1972) have been successfully introduced at high prices to connote high quality. A variety of empirical data is also available. Analyses of *Consumer Reports* data yield positive price-quality rank-order correlations for many products, and particularly for consumer durables (Eitan Gerstner, 1985; Gerard J. Tellis and Birger Wernerfelt, 1987). Moreover, a recent longitudinal analysis of *Consumer Reports* data for consumer durables indicates declining trends in (a) real prices, (b) price differentials between competing brands, and (c) the rank-order correlation between price and quality (David J. Curry and Peter C. Riesz, 1988).[1]

These "stylized facts" are consistent with two important features of markets. First, firms signal high-quality new products with prices that are above full-information profit-

* Department of Economics, Northwestern University, Evanston, IL 60208, and Department of Economics, Boston University, 270 Bay State Road, Boston, MA 02215, respectively. We thank Scott Davis, Ray Deneckere, Garey Ramey, Birger Wernerfelt, two anonymous referees, and seminar participants at the Universities of California at Berkeley and Los Angeles, the University of Chicago, Northwestern University, and the 1987 Winter AEA Meeting for helpful comments. This research has been supported by the National Science Foundation through grant numbers IST-8507300 and IRI-8706150.

** Material from pages 232–7 omitted here.

[1] Curry and Riesz collected all test-study evaluations with five or more brands reported in *Consumer Reports* over a 20-year period. They retained only those durable products whose characteristics remained stable during at least three separate publication time periods.

maximizing prices. Second, over time, as information about the product diffuses, this price distortion lessens or vanishes entirely.

We demonstrate the logic and robustness of this argument in several equilibrium models of behavior by consumers and firms. The models have different assumptions about consumer information. However, all of the models possess intuitively plausible equilibria in which higher-quality products are introduced at higher prices that decline over time.

Our essential argument is outlined as follows. Consider a market in which a firm introduces a new product possessing some innovative feature of uncertain quality. Some consumers can ascertain the quality, while others cannot, but all understand that a higher-quality product is more costly to produce. The most efficient way for the firm to signal high quality is to charge a price too high to be profitable if the product were in fact of lower quality. This high-price strategy is potentially successful for two reasons. First, the consequent loss of sales volume is less damaging to a higher-cost product. Second, a lower-quality product would lose more sales from informed consumers by charging a high price. Understanding this, uninformed consumers rationally infer higher quality from the higher price.

However, as consumers gain experience with the product and information about its quality diffuses, the portion of uninformed consumers in the market declines. Consequently, it becomes even more costly for the firm to signal a higher quality falsely to the uninformed. The firm can efficiently signal a higher quality with a smaller price distortion. Thus, a high and declining price path identifies a high-quality product.

A positive correlation between price and quality follows, because higher-quality products are more costly to produce, so that signaling distorts upward the price of newly introduced high-quality products. As information diffuses, signaling distortions diminish, and the prices of newer products converge downward to those of older products of corresponding quality. An associated weakening of the correlation between price and quality can then be explained by measurement errors in the data. Thus, the theory appears to be consistent with the stylized facts.

Our conclusion that high-quality products have a downward sloping price profile differs from that of previous theoretical contributions to the economics literature. For example, Carl Shapiro (1983) shows that a monopolist charges a high and declining price if consumers optimistically overestimate product quality and charges a low introductory price if consumers pessimistically underestimate product quality. However, these conclusions depend on an assumption that consumers have adaptive expectations about product quality with no possibility of price signaling.

Paul Milgrom and John Roberts (1986) focus on the introductory phase of a nondurable product's life and argue that prices will rise over time as repeat buyers learn about their own preferences. Their analysis is similar to ours in that they also recognize the potential for high prices to signal high (expected) quality due to cost effects. However, we abstract from short-run experimental-buying effects and focus on the long-run trends associated with the signaling of product quality.[2]

---

[2] This focus seems justified given the nature of the long-run data we seek to understand (see footnote 1). Further, introductory offers to inspire repeat purchases are less relevant for consumer durables than for nondurables, because of the infrequency of consumer purchases of durable goods. For other models of introductory offers and repeat purchases that focus on different issues, see Bagwell (1987), Jacques Crémer (1984), and Joseph Farrell (1986).

In a dynamic model of consumer learning, Kenneth L. Judd and Riordan (1987) show that high-quality prices tend to rise after the introductory period. This is because signaling does not occur until after consumers have gained experience with the product, which follows from an assumption of cost parity for different-quality products. Moreover, they conjecture that, for multi-period extensions, price would eventually decline as consumers gain further experience.

John Conlisk et al. (1984) and Nancy L. Stokey (1981) have argued for a declining price path for a durable good of known quality. This path represents the firm's attempt to "skim" the market of higher-valuation buyers. Edward P. Lazear (1986) also predicts a declining price path, under the assumptions that the firm is unsure of the size of its demand and that consumers know quality. While these theories are complementary to ours, they do not provide direct insight into the relationships between price and quality described above.

Our distinction between informed and uninformed consumers is reminiscent of a related literature on product selection in which some consumers observe quality while others do not. In this context, Yuk-Shee Chan and Hayne Leland (1982), Russell Cooper and Thomas W. Ross (1984, 1985), Scott Davis (1989), Joseph Farrell (1980), Riordan (1986), and Asher Wolinsky (1983) argue that the presence of informed consumers enables high prices to signal high-quality choices. While our work is related, we take quality to be exogenous and also analyze the role of production costs in establishing high prices as signals. Indeed, we find that high prices can signal high quality even if all consumers are uninformed. Informed consumers are not necessary for the signaling of a given quality, but they do determine the size of the signaling distortion.

Finally, we note independent work by Garey Ramey (1986) and Doron Fertig (1988). They analyze a static model with a continuum of types and no informed consumers and demonstrate a unique separating equilibrium in which high prices signal quality. Our model has only two cost-quality types, introduces informed consumers, and uses the "intuitive criterion" (In-Koo Cho and David M. Kreps, 1987) to select among equilibria. Ramey and Fertig do not develop predictions about the time path of prices.[3]

The paper is organized in three sections. Our basic results are developed in a static context in Section I. Various multiperiod extensions are analyzed in Section II. Sections I and II may have methodological interest. The intuitive criterion is actively employed in each section, and the criterion is applied in Section II to dynamic signaling games with the possibility of multiple dimensions of private information. Our conclusions are summarized in Section III.

## I.  Basic Model

Consider a one-period consumer market in which a firm has introduced a new product with a novel feature of uncertain quality. For simplicity, assume that quality is either high or low: $q \in \{H, L\}$.

The production technology is common knowledge. The average cost of a high-quality product is constant and equal to $c > 0$, while low-quality production cost is normalized to zero without loss of generality.

---

[3] Also, Jean Tirole (1988 Ch. 2) has a nice expository discussion of price as a signal of quality which refers to an earlier working paper (Bagwell and Riordan, 1986), which this article supersedes.

There are many potential consumers of the new product, approximated by a continuum of mass $M$ (Judd, 1985), each with a potential demand for one unit. Consumers have a common reservation price, $P^L > 0$, for a low-quality product. On the other hand, consumers have heterogeneous reservation prices for a high-quality product, uniformly distributed between $P^L$ and $(1 + P^L)$. The uniform distribution is convenient because it generates a linear demand for a high-quality product.

Some consumers are informed about product quality, while remaining consumers believe that quality is high with probability $r$. This prior belief is common knowledge. Let $X$ denote the ratio of informed to uninformed consumers.

At the beginning of the period, the firm and informed consumers observe the true quality of the product. The firm then sets a price $P$, and uninformed consumers update their beliefs about product quality on the basis of this signal. Let $b = b(P)$ be the uninformed consumers' posterior belief that quality is high when the price is $P$. Consumers are assumed to make purchase decisions that maximize expected utility (i.e., the expected reservation price minus $P$), given beliefs. This process generates an informed demand curve, in which a fraction $1 + P^L - P$ of informed consumers buy when $P \in [P^L, 1 + P^L]$ and $q = H$, and an uninformed demand curve, characterized by a fraction $1 + (P^L - P)/b$ of uninformed consumers buying when $P \in [P^L, b + P^L]$ and quality is believed to be high with probability $b$. With these demand curves and our assumptions on cost technologies, the profit of a firm with quality $q$ and price $P$ facing uninformed consumers with belief $b$, denoted $\pi(q, b, P)$, is straightforward to define explicitly.[4] We assume that the objective of the firm is to maximize profits.

These actions and objectives define an extensive-form game of incomplete information with multiple sequential equilibria (Kreps and Robert Wilson, 1982). A sequential equilibrium requires that the firm and consumers act in a sequentially rational fashion and that uninformed consumers update beliefs using Bayes' rule on the equilibrium path. As usual, we distinguish between separating equilibria (in which high- and low-quality firms choose different prices) and pooling equilibria. However, we do restrict attention to pure-strategy equilibria.

We select plausible equilibria by imposing the "intuitive criterion" (Cho and Kreps, 1987). Consider an equilibrium in which the firm earns profits of $\pi(H)$ and $\pi(L)$ for high-and low-quality products, respectively. Then the equilibrium satisfies the intuitive criterion if there does not exist a price $P'$ such that: (a) $\pi(H, 1, P') > \pi(H)$ and (b) $\pi(L, 1, P') < \pi(L)$. Intuitively, if such a price $P'$ did exist, then uninformed consumers should believe that only a high-quality firm would charge $P'$, which by (a) causes the equilibrium to fail.[5]

Letting $P(q)$ denote the equilibrium price charged by a type-$q$ firm, we now state our first two lemmas, which are almost obvious.

---

[4] For example, if $P \in (P^L, b + P^L)$, then

$$\pi(L, b, P) = P[1 + (P^L - P)/b]M/(1 + X)$$

and

$$\pi(H, b, P) = (P - c)[(1 + P^L - P)X + (1 + (P^L - P)/b)]M/(1 + X)$$

[5] We use the intuitive criterion throughout to restrict the class of equilibria. A weaker refinement is to eliminate dominated strategies (Elon Kohlberg and Jean-Francois Mertens, 1986; Milgrom and Roberts, 1986). This refinement is sufficient for all of our results for separating equilibria and for some of our work on pooling equilibria. The intuitive criterion is necessary, however, for Theorems 3 and 6.

LEMMA 1: *In any equilibrium, $P(q) \geq P^L$ for $q \in \{H, L\}$.*

PROOF   The function $\pi(q, b(P), P)$ is strictly increasing in $P$, for all $q \in \{H, L\}$ and all functions $b(\cdot)$, when $P < P^L$. Thus, were $P(q)$ less than $P^L$, the type-$q$ firm could increase its price slightly and increase profits.

LEMMA 2: *In any separating equilibrium, $P(H) > P^L$ and $P(L) = P^L$.*

PROOF   A low-quality firm earns zero profits in a separating equilibrium if $P(L) > P^L$ and positive profits if $P(L) = P^L$. Therefore, the results follows from Lemma 1.

In a separating equilibrium, the low-quality firm charges $P^L$ and the high-quality firm charges some higher price. Moreover, it must be that $\pi(L, 0, P^L) \geq \pi(L, 1, P(H))$; otherwise, the low-quality firm would mimic its high-quality counterpart. We are thus led to consider the set

$$\{P | \pi(L, 0, P^L) = \pi(L, 1, P)\}.$$

This equation has an upper and lower root,

$$\bar{P}(X) = [(1 + P^L)/2] + \left( \left[ (1 + P^L)^2/4 \right] - P^L(1 + X) \right)^{1/2}$$

and

$$\underline{P}(X) = [(1 + P^L)/2] - \left( \left[ (1 + P^L)^2/4 \right] - P^L(1 + X) \right)^{1/2}$$

expressed as functions of $X$.

We assume that $1 > P^L$ and represent $\bar{P}(X)$ and $\underline{P}(X)$ by the upper and lower boundaries of the parabola in Figure 1.[6] These equations have no solution for values of $X > \bar{X}$. For $X \leq \bar{X}$, any price inside the parabola, $P \in (\underline{P}(X), \bar{P}(X))$, satisfies $\pi(L, 0, P^L) < \pi(L, 1, P)$; the low-quality firm would mimic any such price. This leads immediately to the following lemma.

LEMMA 3: *If $X < \bar{X}$, then in any separating equilibrium either $P(H) \geq \bar{P}(X)$ or $P(H) \leq \underline{P}(X)$.*

---

[6] If $P^L \geq 1$, then for $\epsilon = P - P^L > 0$

$$\pi(L, 1, P) = \pi(L, 0, P^L) - [P^L X + \epsilon(P^L - 1) + \epsilon^2]M/(1 + X) < \pi(L, 0, P^L)$$

so that a low-quality firm's marginal revenue for a price increase above $P^L$ is negative no matter how beliefs adjust. Thus, if $P^L \geq 1$, then mimicry is never profitable for the low-quality firm, and the problem degenerates. The following can be shown: if $P^L \geq 1 + c > 1$, then the unique equilibrium has $P(H) = P(L) = P^L$; while if $1 + c \geq P^L \geq 1$, then the unique equilibrium has $P(L) = P^L$ and $P(H) = (1 + P^L + c)/2 \equiv P^H$. $P^L < 1$ is thus the interesting case.

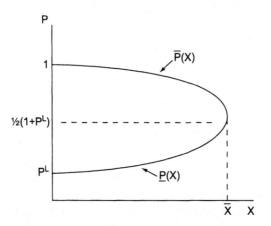

**Figure 1**   Separating prices

It is important to understand the parabola in Figure 1. By mimicking a high-quality price $P(H) > P^L$, the low-quality firm both gains and loses. It gains by tricking uninformed consumers with reservation prices at or above $P(H)$ into buying at a higher price, but it loses because all informed consumers and the remaining uninformed consumers refuse to buy at that price. The gains outweigh the losses for prices inside the parabola; for these prices, the low-quality firm finds mimicry profitable.

When all consumers are uninformed ($X = 0$), a price slightly above $P^L$ is certainly worth mimicking, as only a very few consumers refuse to buy at the higher price. It follows that the lower branch of the parabola begins at $P^L$, reflecting the fact that all uninformed consumers buy at this price regardless of beliefs. As price climbs higher, eventually sales to uninformed consumers are sufficiently restricted that mimicry becomes unattractive. The critical price marking the beginning of the upper branch of the parabola is easily shown to be 1. When the ratio of informed to uninformed consumers ($X$) rises, it becomes increasingly costly for the low-quality firm to mimic its high-quality counterpart and thereby sacrifice all informed purchases. For this reason, the parabola narrows about $(1 + P^L)/2$, the maximizer of $\pi$ (L, 1, $P$). This is the low-quality firm's monopoly price when all uninformed consumers believe it to be high-quality. For $X$ above $\bar{X}$, the low-quality firm refuses to mimic even $(1 + P^L)/2$.

The high-quality firm's full-information monopoly price is $P^H \equiv (1 + P^L + c)/2$, the maximizer of $\pi$ (H, 1, $P$). However, with uninformed consumers, the high-quality price may be distorted upward as shown in the following theorem. The theorem establishes necessary conditions for a separating equilibrium satisfying the intuitive criterion.

**Theorem 1:**   $P(H) = \max\{\bar{P}(X), P^H\}$ and $P(L) = P^L$ *are the only separating equilibrium prices satisfying the intuitive criterion.*

**Proof**   Lemma 2 implies $P(L) = P^L$, so suppose $P(H) \neq \max\{\bar{P}(X), P^H\}$ and consider Figure 2. $X^H$ satisfies $\bar{P}(X^H) = P^H$. For $X > X^H$, the intuitive criterion fails by setting

$P' = P^H$. For $X \leq X^H$, Lemma 3 rules out $P(H) \in (\underline{P}(X), \bar{P}(X))$. Moreover, the intuitive criterion fails for $P' \in (\bar{P}(X), P(H))$ if $P(H) > \bar{P}(X)$, and for $P' \in (P(H), \underline{P}(X))$ if $P(H) < \underline{P}(X)$. This leaves the possibility that $P(H) = \underline{P}(X)$, but it is straightforward to show that $c > 0$ implies $\pi(H, 1, \bar{P}(X)) > \pi(H, 1, \underline{P}(X))$, from which it follows that $P' = \bar{P}(X) + \epsilon$ violates the intuitive criterion for sufficiently small $\epsilon$.

Theorem 1 identifies two cases. If $P^H \geq \bar{P}(X)$, then the separating equilibrium has $P(H) = P^H$ and $P(L) = P^L$. This is because the low-quality firm is unwilling to mimic the high-quality firm's favorite price. The more interesting case emerges when $P^H < 1$, or equivalently $P^L + c < 1$, and separation is potentially costly for the high-quality firm. In this case, a supramonopoly price is charged if the ratio of informed to uninformed consumers is small.

COROLLARY 1:  *If $P^H < 1$ and $X$ is sufficiently small, $P(H) = \bar{P}(X) > P^H$ and $P(L) = P^L$ are the only separating equilibrium prices satisfying the intuitive criterion.*

For expositional reasons, we assume henceforth that $P^H < 1$.

Figure 2 illustrates the prices charged in a separating equilibrium satisfying the intuitive criterion (the parabola is the same as in Fig. 1). It may seem surprising that a high-quality firm separates with $\bar{P}(X)$ instead of a lower price $\underline{P}(X)$, when $X$ is small. However, a simple intuition underlies this result. Because high-quality production is costly ($c > 0$), the full-information monopoly price $P^H$ is closer to $\bar{P}(X)$ than to $\underline{P}(X)$.[7] Put differently,

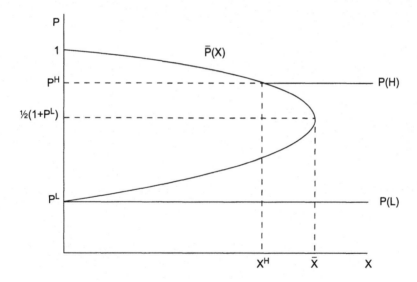

**Figure 2**  Equilibrium separating prices

---

[7] The assumption that higher-quality firms have at least somewhat higher costs of production is crucial. As the cost asymmetry between qualities diminishes, the high-quality firm's preferred separating price, $\bar{P}(X)$, remains constant; that is, $\bar{P}(X)$ is independent of $c$. In the limiting case when $c = 0$, prices corresponding to the lower branch of the parabola also satisfy the intuitive criterion. This is because the high-quality firm is then indifferent between $\bar{P}(X)$ and $\underline{P}(X)$. We believe $c > 0$ to be a realistic case.

the high price is the efficient means of separation because the forgone profit from a lost customer is less for the high-quality firm (Milgrom and Roberts, 1986). Thus, the high-quality firm prefers to separate with the high price.

So far we have characterized necessary conditions for a separating equilibrium. We now turn to existence.

Separation can occur only if the high-quality firm chooses not to monopolize informed consumers at the expense of losing uninformed consumers. Such a deviation is potentially attractive only if separation is costly for the high-quality firm, that is, when $X < X^H$ (see Fig. 2) in which case $P(H) = \bar{P}(X) > P^H$. Prices that might then increase high-quality profit must be inside the parabola and thus must also be prices that could increase low-quality profit. The intuitive criterion does not restrict beliefs for such prices, and at worst a deviation in this range could induce the belief of certain low quality. The high-quality firm will thus charge the price $P(H) = \bar{P}(X)$ when $X < X^H$ in a separating equilibrium if and only if $\pi(H, 1, \bar{P}(X)) \geq \pi(H, 0, P^H)$.[8] Setting $\pi(H, 1, P) = \pi(H, 0, P^H)$ when $X < X^H$ defines a "no-defect" root,

$$P^\dagger(X) = P^H + [(1 + P^L - c)(1 + X)^{-1/2}/2]$$

which begins at $(1 + P^L)$ for $X = 0$ and asymptotically declines to $P^H$, as shown in Figure 3. The high-quality firm has no incentive to defect if and only if $P(H) \leq P^\dagger(X)$. Since "intuitive" beliefs can entail $b(P') = 0$ for all $P' \in (\underline{P}(X), \bar{P}(X))$, it is easily established

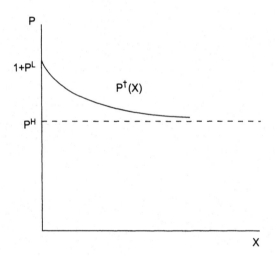

**Figure 3**   No-defect prices

---

that the low-quality firm is also unwilling to defect from the proposed separating equilibrium. We thus have the following existence theorem.

THEOREM 2: *A separating equilibrium satisfying the intuitive criterion exists if and only if* $X \geq \bar{X}$ *or if* $X < \bar{X}$ *and*

$$\Delta(X) \equiv P^\dagger(X) - \bar{P}(X) \geq 0.$$

Two observations are in order, which we state below as corollaries. First, a separating equilibrium always exists if the ratio of informed to uninformed consumers is small because $\Delta(0) \equiv P^L > 0$. Second, it can be shown numerically that a separating equilibrium exists for any value of $X$ unless $P^L$ and $c$ are small; Figure 4 illustrates parameter values for which separating equilibria fail to exist for some intermediate $X$.

COROLLARY 2: *A separating equilibrium satisfying the intuitive criterion exists if* $X$ *is sufficiently small.*

COROLLARY 3: *A separating equilibrium satisfying the intuitive criterion exists if* $P^L$ *or* $c$ *is sufficiently large.*

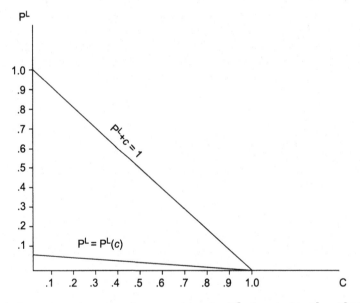

**Figure 4** Parameter values suporting separations: for $(P^L, c)$ such that $P^L > P^L(c)$, a unique separating equilibrium satisfying the intuitive criterion exists; if instead $P^L < P^L(c)$, a separating equilibrium may fail to exist for intermediate values of X

We next turn to pooling equilibria. The following theorem establishes that, if the percentage of informed consumers is sufficiently small, then the only equilibrium satisfying the intuitive criterion is a separating equilibrium. In other words, when the market is very uninformed, there always exists a high price at which the high-quality firm can profitably distinguish itself.

THEOREM 3: *If $X$ is sufficiently small, then no pooling equilibrium satisfies the intuitive criterion.*

PROOF   We prove the result for $X = 0$; the result follows for $X$ close to 0 by continuity. Let $Q(P, b) \equiv [1 - (P - P^{\mathrm{L}})/b]M$ denote the quantity of sales at a price $P$ when consumers believe high quality with probability $b$. In a pooling equilibrium, $P(\mathrm{H}) = P(\mathrm{L}) = P^*$, and $b(P^*) = r$. The high- and low-quality firms earn profits $\pi(\mathrm{H}) \equiv (P^* - c)Q(P^*, r)$ and $\pi(\mathrm{L}) \equiv P^*Q(P^*, r)$, respectively. Clearly $1 + r > P^* \geq \max\{P^{\mathrm{L}}, c\}$; otherwise, one or the other type of firm would defect. Thus, $\pi(\mathrm{L}) > \pi(\mathrm{H}) \geq 0$. Since $P^*Q(P^*, 1) > \pi(\mathrm{L})$, there exists $P'' > P^*$ such that $\pi(\mathrm{L}, 1, P'') \equiv P''Q(P'', 1) = \pi(\mathrm{L})$ and $\pi(\mathrm{H}, 1, P'') = \pi(\mathrm{H}) + c[Q(P^*, r) - Q(P'', 1)] > \pi(\mathrm{H})$. Moreover, $PQ(P, 1)$ is decreasing in $P$ at $P''$. Therefore, $P' \equiv P'' + \epsilon$ violates the intuitive criterion for $\epsilon > 0$ sufficiently small.

Pooling is therefore impossible if $X$ is sufficiently small. Similarly, if the market is sufficiently well informed that $X$ is large, then pooling is impossible to maintain, as each firm type prefers to deviate and monopolize informed consumers. For example, if $X \geq \bar{X}$ (see Fig. 1), then pooling is clearly impossible, because the low-quality firm would not select $P > P^{\mathrm{L}}$ even if it were then believed to certainly have a high-quality product. The critical $X$ beyond which pooling is impossible is actually smaller than $\bar{X}$, since pooling only generates the belief $b(P(\mathrm{L})) = r$. This point is stated in the following theorem, as is the related point that pooling is impossible when consumers' prior belief of high quality is pessimistic and, correspondingly, the profits from pooling are low.[9]

THEOREM 4:   *If $r \leq \max\{P^{\mathrm{L}}, c - P^{\mathrm{L}}\}$ or $X \geq (r - P^{\mathrm{L}})^2/4rP^{\mathrm{L}}$, then no pooling equilibrium exists satisfying the intuitive criterion.*

PROOF   By Lemma 1, pooling can never occur at $P < P^{\mathrm{L}}$. Moreover, since $1 > P^{\mathrm{L}}$, pooling at $P = P^{\mathrm{L}}$ violates the intuitive criterion as the high-quality firm would deviate to $\bar{P}(X)$. A necessary condition for pooling at $P$ is $\pi(\mathrm{L}, r, P) \geq \pi(\mathrm{L}, 0, P^{\mathrm{L}})$. Suppose pooling occurs at $P > P^{\mathrm{L}} \geq r$. Let $M/(1 + X)$ denote the stock of uninformed consumers and let $\epsilon \equiv P - P^{\mathrm{L}} > 0$. Then

$$\pi(\mathrm{L}, r, P) = \pi(\mathrm{L}, 0, P^{\mathrm{L}}) - [\epsilon(P^{\mathrm{L}} - r)/r + \epsilon^2/r]M/(1 + X) < \pi(\mathrm{L}, 0, P^{\mathrm{L}})$$

---

[9] By Theorems 2, 3, and 4 and Corollary 2, pure-strategy sequential equilibria satisfying the intuitive criterion might not exist if $r$ is small and $X$ is in an intermediate range. However, equilibria do exist satisfying the intuitive criterion in which the high-quality firm selects a price $P(\mathrm{H}) > P^{\mathrm{L}}$, the low-quality firm mixes between $P(\mathrm{H})$ and $P^{\mathrm{L}}$ with weights $\lambda$ and $1 - \lambda$, and uninformed consumers believe high quality with probability $b$, where $P(\mathrm{H})$, $\lambda$, and $b$ satisfy $b = r/[r + (1 - r)\lambda]$, $\pi(\mathrm{H}, b, P(\mathrm{H})) = \pi(\mathrm{H}, 0, P^{\mathrm{H}})$, and $\pi(\mathrm{L}, b, P(\mathrm{H})) = \pi(\mathrm{L}, 0, P^{\mathrm{L}})$.

a contradiction. Suppose next that pooling occurs when $r \leq c - P^L$. Pooling at $P$ requires $P \geq c$ and $P < r + P^L$ (lest the low-quality firm deviate to $P^L$), which is contradictory. Finally, suppose $r > \max\{P^L, c - P^L\}$. Then it is easy to show that $X \geq (r - P^L)^2/4rP^L$ implies that at $P > P^L$, $\pi(L, r, P) \leq \pi(L, r, (r + P^L)/2) < \pi(L, 0, P^L)$, a contradiction.

Finally, if $r$ is big and $X$ is intermediate, pooling equilibria satisfying the intuitive criterion may exist. The possible prices for such equilibria are easily restricted. First, pooling at or below $P^L$ is inconsistent with the intuitive criterion, as argued in the proof of Theorem 4. Second, given that pooling must occur above $P^L$, the pooling price must certainly be inside the parabola, or the low-quality firm would deviate to $P^L$. In fact, since pooling only gives the belief $b(P(L)) = r$, a tighter bound can be found. Setting $\pi(L, r, P) = \pi(L, 0, P^L)$ gives the prices at which the low-quality firm is just willing to pool. The corresponding roots are

$$\bar{P}_r(X) = [(r + P^L)/2] + \left( \left[ (r + P^L)^2/4 \right] - rP^L (1 + X) \right)^{1/2}$$

$$\underline{P}_r(X) = [(r + P^L)/2] - \left( \left[ (r + P^L)^2/4 \right] - rP^L (1 + X) \right)^{1/2}.$$

As shown in Figure 5, a "pooling parabola" inside the initial (separating) parabola is thus defined. The pooling parabola is drawn under the assumption that $r > P^L$ and is not defined for $X \geq (r - P^L)^2/4rP^L$, as suggested by Theorem 4. Any price outside of the pooling parabola has $\pi(L, r, P) < \pi(L, 0, P^L)$ and therefore cannot be supported as a pooling equilibrium. We thus have the following necessary condition for pooling.

THEOREM 5: *In any pooling equilibrium satisfying the intuitive criterion,* $\underline{P}_r(X) \leq P(H) = P(L) \leq \bar{P}_r(X)$.

Therefore, if an intuitive pooling equilibrium does exist, then $r$ must be large, $X$ must be intermediate, and the pooling price must be lower than the intuitive separating price for high quality. [...]

## III. Conclusions

A high-quality good will be introduced at a high price that is lowered over time toward the full-information monopoly price. The high introductory price signals high quality, because a high-cost firm is more willing to restrict sales volume than is a low-cost firm. Furthermore, a low-quality firm loses greater sales volume from a high price, since informed consumers refuse to buy at such a price. As information about product quality diffuses and more consumers become more informed, it therefore becomes easier for a high-quality firm to signal its quality. High-quality prices thus decline as the market matures.

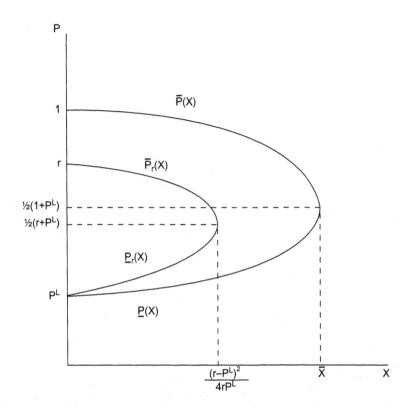

**Figure 5**    The pooling parabola

Our prediction of high and declining prices is consistent with the stylized facts of the marketing literature.[10] In particular, our model provides an explanation for the declining trends in consumer durables of real prices, price differentials between competing brands, and the rank-order correlation between price and quality.

The prediction is robust to a variety of assumptions about consumer information. Whether or not uninformed consumers know past prices and firm age, intuitively plausible equilibria exist in which high-quality products have high and declining prices.

Our model relies on many special features that can be relaxed. For example, linear demands and costs are not crucial for our conclusions.[11] The two-period framework is also easily extended into a many-period setting.

Many interesting extensions do remain. It would be worthwhile to study an explicit model of word-of-mouth communication. Further empirical work might investigate how price-quality relationships depend on the amount and type of consumer information. One intriguing possibility is to interpret the publication of a *Consumer Reports* evaluation of a

---

[10] It should be noted, however, that at least some of our "stylized facts" are in fact controversial (Valarie A. Zeithaml, 1988).

[11] Bagwell (1990) establishes that high prices signal a high-quality product in a model that allows for a general demand function and product quality choice.

product group as a proxy for an increase in the "fraction of informed consumers." This suggests the empirical test that a *Consumer Reports* publication should itself lower the relative price of high-quality items and weaken price-quality correlation.

[Appendix omitted]

*References*

BAGWELL, KYLE, "Introductory Price as a Signal of Cost in a Model of Repeat Business," *Review of Economic Studies*, July 1987, *54*, 365–84.
——, "Optimal Export Policy for a New Product Monopoly," Northwestern University Discussion Paper 898, 1990.
—— and RIORDAN, MICHAEL H., "Equilibrium Price Dynamics for an Experience Good," Northwestern University Discussion Paper 705, 1986.
BUZZELL, ROBERT D, NOURSE, ROBERT E. M., MATTHEWS, JOHN B. and LEVITT, THEODORE, *Marketing: A Contemporary Analysis*, New York: McGraw-Hill, 1972.
CHAN, YUK-SHEE and LELAND, HAYNE, "Prices and Qualities in Markets with Costly Information," *Review of Economic Studies*, October 1982, *49*, 499–516.
CHO, IN-KOO, "A Refinement of Sequential Equilibrium," *Econometrica*, November 1987, *55*, 1367–90.
—— and KREPS, DAVID M., "Signaling Games and Stable Equilibria," *Quarterly Journal of Economics*, May 1987, *102*, 179–221.
CONLISK, JOHN, GERSTNER, EITAN and SOBEL, JOEL, "Cyclic Pricing by a Durable Goods Monopolist," *Quarterly Journal of Economics*, August 1984, *99*, 489–505.
COOPER, RUSSELL and ROSS, THOMAS W., "Prices, Product Qualities and Asymmetric Information: The Competitive Case," *Review of Economic Studies*, April 1984, *51*, 197–208.
—— and ——, "Monopoly Provision of Product Quality with Uninformed Buyers," *International Journal of Industrial Organization*, September 1985, *3*, 439–49.
CRÉMER, JACQUES, "On the Economics of Repeat Buying," *Rand Journal of Economics*, Autumn 1984, *15*, 396–403.
CURRY, DAVID J. and RIESZ, PETER C., "Prices and Price/Quality Relationships: A Longitudinal Analysis," *Journal of Marketing*, January 1988, *52*, 36–51.
DAVIS, SCOTT, *The Role of Price as a Signal of Product Quality in Monopolistic Markets*, Ph.D. Dissertation, Stanford University, 1989.
FARRELL, JOSEPH, *Prices as Signals of Quality*, Ph.D. Dissertation, Brasenose College, Oxford, 1980.
——, "Moral Hazard as an Entry Barrier," *Rand Journal of Economics*, Autumn 1986, *17*, 440–9.
FERTIG, DORON, *Advertising as a Signal of Quality*, Ph.D. Dissertation, Northwestern University, 1988.
GABOR, ANDRÉ and GRANGER, CLIVE, "The Pricing of New Products," *Scientific Business*, August 1965, *3*, 141–50.
GERSTNER, EITAN, "Do Higher Prices Signal Higher Quality?" *Journal of Marketing Research*, May 1985, *22*, 209–15.
JUDD, KENNETH L., "The Law of Large Numbers with a Continuum of IID Random Variables," *Journal of Economic Theory*, February 1985, *35*, 19–25.
—— and RIORDAN, MICHAEL H., "Price and Quality in a New Product Monopoly," mimeograph, Stanford University, 1987.
KOHLBERG, ELON and MERTENS, JEAN-FRANCOIS, "On the Strategic Stability of Equilibria," *Econometrica*, September 1986, *54*, 1003–38.
KREPS, DAVID M. and WILSON, ROBERT, "Sequential Equilibria," *Econometrica*, July 1982, *50*, 863–94.
LAZEAR, EDWARD P., "Retail Pricing and Clearance Sales," *American Economic Review*, March 1986, *76*, 14–32.

MILGROM, PAUL and ROBERTS, JOHN, "Price and Advertising Signals of Product Quality," *Journal of Political Economy*, August 1986, *94*, 796–821.

MONROE, KENT B., "Buyers' Subjective Perceptions of Price," in Harold H. Kassarjian and Thomas S. Robertson, eds., *Perspectives in Consumer Behavior*, Glenview, IL: Scott, Foresman, 1973, 23–42.

RAMEY, GAREY, "Moral Hazard, Signaling, and Product Quality," mimeograph, Stanford University, 1986.

RIORDAN, MICHAEL H., "Monopolistic Competition with Experience Goods," *Quarterly Journal of Economics*, May 1986, *101*, 255–80.

SHAPIRO, CARL, "Optimal Pricing of Experience Goods," *Bell Journal of Economics*, Autumn 1983, *14*, 497–507.

STOKEY, NANCY L., "Rational Expectations and Durable Goods Pricing," *Bell Journal of Economics*, Spring 1981, *12*, 112–28.

TELLIS, GERARD J. and WERNERFELT, BIRGER, "Competitive Price and Quality Under Asymmetric Information," *Marketing Science*, Summer 1987, *6*, 240–53.

TIROLE, JEAN, *The Theory of Industrial Organization*, Cambridge, MA: MIT Press, 1988.

WOLINSKY, ASHER, "Prices as Signals of Product Quality," *Review of Economic Studies*, October 1983, *50*, 647–58.

ZEITHAML, VALARIE A., "Consumer Perceptions of Price, Quality and Value: A Means-End Model and Synthesis of Evidence," *Journal of Marketing*, July 1988, *52*, 2–22.

# FIFTY-ONE

# The Argument of an Appeal

JOHN W. DAVIS

*Source*: *American Bar Association Journal* 26 (December), 1940, pp. 895–909. Reprinted with permission.

If a lecture on the well worn subject assigned to me is to be given in this series, no one knows better than the Chairman of your Committee on Post-Admission Legal Education[1] that he and not I should be the person to give it. This is true in the first place because of the fact that in his lecture on Summary Judgment he has given the perfect example of what these lectures ought to be – informative, scholarly, helpful – and has set a standard which it is unfair to ask others to rival. And in the second place a discourse on the argument of an appeal would come with superior force from a judge who is in his judicial person the target and the trier of the argument than from a random archer like myself. Or, supposing fishes had the gift of speech, who would listen to a fisherman's weary discourse on flycasting, the shape and color of the fly, the size of the tackle, the length of the line, the merit of different rod makers and all the other tiresome stuff that fishermen talk about, if the fish himself could be induced to give his views on the most effective methods of approach. For after all it is the fish that the angler is after and all his recondite learning is but the hopeful means to that end.

I hope I may not be charged with levity or disrespect in adopting this piscatorial figure. I do not suggest any analogies between our reverend masters on the Bench and the finny tribe. God forbid! Let such conceits tempt the less respectful. Yet it is true, is it not, that in the argument of an appeal the advocate is angling, consciously and deliberately angling, for the judicial mind. Whatever tends to attract judicial favor to the advocate's claim is useful. Whatever repels it is useless or worse. The whole art of the advocate consists in choosing the one and avoiding the other. Why otherwise have argument at all?

I pause for definition. Argument, of course, may be written as well as oral, and under our modern American practice written argument has certainly become the most extended if not always the weightier of the two. As our colleague, Joseph H. Choate, Jr., recently remarked, "we have now reached the point where we file our arguments in writing and deliver our briefs orally." But it was not always so and in certain jurisdictions it is not so today. In England, for instance, where many, perhaps most cases are decided as soon as

---

[1] Hon. Bernard L. Shienntag, Justice, Supreme Court, New York City.

the argument is closed, counsel are not expected to speak with one strabismic eye upon the clock and the other on the court.

I recall that I once visited the chambers of the Privy Council in London hoping to hear a Canadian friend argue a Canadian appeal. When I arrived his adversary had the floor and was laboriously reading to the Court from the open volumes, page by page and line by line, the reported cases on which he relied. Said I to the Clerk, "How long has he been speaking and when will So-and-So come on?" "He has now been speaking," said the Clerk, "for six consecutive days and I doubt if he concludes today." I picked up my hat and sadly departed, realizing into what an alien atmosphere I had wandered.

In the old days, when not only courts but lawyers and litigants are reputed to have had more time at their disposal, similar feats were performed at the American Bar. It has been stated, for instance, that the arguments of Webster, Luther Martin and their colleagues in *McCulloch v. Maryland* consumed six days, while in the *Girard* will case Webster, Horace Binney and others, for ten whole days assailed the listening ears of the Court.

Those days have gone forever; and partly because of the increased tempo of our times, partly because of the increase of work in our appellate tribunals, the argument of an appeal, whether by voice or pen, is hedged about today by strict limitations of time and an increasing effort to provoke an economy of space. The rules of nearly every court give notice that there is a limit to what the judicial ear or the judicial eye is prepared to absorb. Sometimes the judges plead, sometimes they deplore, sometimes they command. The bar is continuously besought to speak with an eye on the clock and to write with a cramped pen.

Observing this duty of condensation and selection I propose tonight to direct my remarks primarily to the oral argument. I begin after the briefs have all been filed; timely filed of course, for in this matter lawyers are never, hardly ever, belated. I shall assume that these briefs are models of brevity, are properly indexed, and march with orderly logic from point to point; not too little nor yet too much on any topic, even though in a painful last moment of proof-reading many an appealing paragraph has been offered as a reluctant sacrifice on the altar of condensation.

I assume also that the briefs are not overlarded with long quotations from the reported opinions, no matter how pat they seem; nor over-crowded with citations designed it would seem to certify to the industry of the brief-maker rather than to fortify the argument. A horrible example of this latter fault crossed my desk within the month in a brief which, in addition to many statutes and textwriters, cited by volume and page no less than 304 decided cases; a number calculated to discourage if not to disgust the most industrious judge.

I assume further that they are not defaced by *supras* or *infras* or by a multiplicity of footnotes which, save in the rare case where they are needed to elucidate the text, do nothing but distract the attention of the reader and interrupt the flow of reasoning. And I remark in passing that these are no more laudable in a judge's opinion than they are in a lawyer's brief.

I assume that there is not a pestilent "and/or" to be found in the brief from cover to cover; or if there is, that the court, jealous of our mother-tongue, will stamp upon the base intruder.

And finally I assume as of course that there has been no cheap effort to use variety in type to supply the emphasis that well constructed sentences should furnish for themselves. It may be taken as axiomatic that even judges, when they are so disposed, can read understandingly; and I should think that where the pages of a brief begin conversationally in small pica, nudge the reader's elbow with repeated italics, rise to a higher pitch with whole paragraphs of the text – not mere headings – in black letter, and finally shout in full capitals (and such have been observed), the judge might well consider that what was a well intentioned effort to attract his attention was in reality a reflection on his intelligence.

So it is with our briefs brought to this state of approximate perfection that we approach our oral argument. Much has been said pro and con as to the utility of this particular exercise. The appellate court which I most frequently encountered in my early days at the bar made no secret of the fact that it regarded the time spent in hearing cases as a sheer waste; and the announcement "Submitted on briefs" always won an approving nod from the bench. Fortunately, I think, that was an idiosyncrasy which has passed away even in that tribunal. There is much testimony, ancient and modern, for the contrary view.

Says Lord Coke, "No man alone with all his uttermost labors, nor all the actors in them, themselves by themselves out of a court of justice, can attain unto a right decision; nor in court without solemn argument where I am persuaded Almighty God openeth and enlargeth the understanding of those desirous of justice and right." Agreeing as we must with this pious sentiment, we lawyers sometimes think nevertheless that "God moves in a mysterious way, his wonders to perform." Judge Dillon in his lecture on the Laws and Jurisprudence of England and America, declares that as a judge he felt reasonably assured of his judgment where he had heard counsel, and a very diminished faith where the cause had not been orally argued, for says he, "Mistakes, errors, fallacies and flaws elude us in spite of ourselves unless the case is pounded and hammered at the bar." Chief Justice Hughes is on record to the effect that "The desirability of a full exposition by oral argument in the highest court is not to be gainsaid. It is a great saving of the time of the court in the examination of extended records and briefs, to obtain the grasp of the case that is made possible by oral discussion and to be able more quickly to separate the wheat from the chaff." With all this most judges. I think, will agree, always provided that the oral argument is inspired as it should be with a single and sincere desire to be helpful to the Court.

Professing no special fitness for the task, I have ventured accordingly to frame a decalogue by which such arguments should be governed. There is no mystical significance in the number ten, although it has respectable precedent; and those who think the number short and who wish to add to the roll when I have finished, have my full permission to do so.

At the head of the list I place, where it belongs, the cardinal rule of all, namely:

(1) Change places (in your imagination of course) with the Court.

Courts of appeal are not filled by Demigods. Some members are learned, some less so. Some are keen and perspicacious, some have more plodding minds. In short, they are men and lawyers much like the rest of us. That they are honest, impartial, ready and eager to reach a correct conclusion must always be taken for granted. You may rightfully expect and you do expect nothing but fair treatment at their hands.

Yet those who sit in solemn array before you, whatever their merit, know nothing whatever of the controversy that brings you to them, and are not stimulated to interest in it by any feeling of friendship or dislike to anyone concerned. They are not moved as perhaps an advocate may be by any hope of reward of fear of punishment. They are simply being called upon for action in their appointed sphere. They are anxiously waiting to be supplied with what Mr. Justice Holmes called the "implements of decision." These by your presence you profess yourself ready to furnish. If the places were reversed and you sat where they do, think what it is you would want first to know about the case. How and in what order would you want the story told? How would you want the skein unravelled? What would make easier your approach to the true solution? These are questions the advocate must unsparingly put to himself. This is what I mean by changing places with the Court.

If you happen to know the mental habits of any particular judge, so much the better. To adapt yourself to his methods of reasoning is not artful, it is simply elementary psychology; as is also the maxim not to tire or irritate the mind you are seeking to persuade. And may I say in passing that there is no surer way to irritate the mind of any listener than to speak in so low a voice or with such indistinct articulation or in so monotonous a tone as to make the mere effort at hearing an unnecessary burden.

I proceed to Rule No. 2 –

(2) State first the nature of the case and briefly its prior history.

Every Appellate Court has passing before it a long procession of cases that come from manifold and diverse fields of the law and human experience. Why not tell the Court at the outset to which of these fields its attention is about to be called? If the case involves the construction of a will, the settlement of a partnership, a constitutional question or whatever it may be, the judge is able as soon as the general topic is mentioned to call to his aid, consciously or unconsciously, his general knowledge and experience with that particular subject. It brings what is to follow into immediate focus. And then for the greater ease of the court in listening it is well to give at once the history of the case in so far as it bears on the court's jurisdiction. And sometimes there may be, I am not sure, a certain curiosity to know just whose judicial work it is that the court is called upon to review. For judges, like humbler men, judge each other as well as the law.

Next in order –

(3) State the facts.

If I were disposed to violate the rule I have previously announced against emphasis by typography, I would certainly employ at this point the largest capital type. For it cannot be too often emphasized that in an appellate court the statement of the facts is not merely a part of the argument, it is more often than not the argument itself. A case well stated is a case far more than half argued. Yet how many advocates fail to realize that the ignorance of the court concerning the facts in the case is complete, even where its knowledge of the law may adequately satisfy the proverbial presumption. The court wants above all things to learn what are the facts which give rise to the call upon its energies; for in many, probably in most, cases when the facts are clear there is no great trouble about the law. *Ex facto oritur jus*, and no court ever forgets it.

No more courteous judge ever sat on any bench than the late Chief Justice White, but I shall never forget a remark which he addressed to a distinguished lawyer, now dead, who was presenting an appeal from an order of the Interstate Commerce Commission. He had plunged headlong into a discussion of the powers of the Commission, and after he had talked for some twenty-five minutes, the Chief Justice leaned over and said in his blandest tone, "Now, Mr. So-and-So, won't you please tell us what this case is about. We could follow you so much better."

Of course there are statements and statements. No two men probably would adopt an identical method of approach. Uniformity is impossible, probably undesirable. Safe guides, however, are to be found in the three C's – chronology, candor and clarity: Chronology, because that is the natural way of telling any story, stringing the events on the chain of time just as all human life itself proceeds; candor, the telling of the worst as well as the best, since the court has the right to expect it, and since any lack of candor, real or apparent, will wholly destroy the most careful argument; and clarity, because that is the supreme virtue in any effort to communicate thought from man to man. It admits of no substitute. There is a sentence of Daniel Webster's which should be written on the walls of every law school, court room and law office: "The power of clear statement" said he, "is the great power at the bar." Purple passages can never supply its absence. And of course I must add that no statement of the facts can be considered as complete unless it has been so framed and delivered as to show forth the essential merit, in justice and in right of your client's cause.

(4) State next the applicable rules of law on which you rely.

If the statement of facts has been properly done the mind of the court will already have sensed the legal questions at issue, indeed they may have been hinted at as you proceed. These may be so elementary and well established that a mere allusion to them is sufficient. On the other hand, they may lie in the field of divided opinion where it is necessary to expound them at greater length and to dwell on the underlying reasons that support one or the other view. It may be that in these days of what is apparently waning health on the part of our old friend *Stare Decisis*, one can rely less than heretofore upon the assertion that the case at bar is governed by such-and-such a case, volume and page. Even the shadow of a long succession of governing cases may not be adequate shelter. In any event the advocate must be prepared to meet any challenge to the doctrine of the cases on which he relies and to support it by original reasoning. Barren citation is a broken reed. What virtue it retains can be left for the brief.

(5) Always "go for the jugular vein."

I do not know from what source I quote that phrase but it is of course familiar. Rufus Choate's expression was "the hub of the case." More often than not there is in every case a cardinal point around which lesser points revolve like planets around the sun, or even as dead moons around a planet; a central fortress which if strongly held will make the loss of all the outworks immaterial. The temptation is always present to "let no guilty point escape" in the hope that if one hook breaks another may hold. Yielding to this temptation is pardonable perhaps in a brief, of which the court may read as much or as little as it chooses. There minor points can be inserted to form "a moat defensive to a wall." But there is no time and rarely any occasion in oral argument for such diversions.

I think in this connection of one of the greatest lawyers, and probably the greatest case winner of our day, the late John G. Johnson of Philadelphia. He was a man of commanding physical presence and of an intellect equally robust. Before appellate courts he addressed himself customarily to but a single point, often speaking for not more than twenty minutes but with compelling force. When he had concluded it was difficult for his adversary to persuade the court that there was anything else worthy to be considered. This is the quintessence of the advocate's art.

(6) Rejoice when the Court asks questions.

And again I say unto you, rejoice! If the question does nothing more it gives you assurance that the court is not comatose and that you have awakened at least a vestigial interest. Moreover a question affords you your only chance to penetrate the mind of the court, unless you are an expert in face reading, and to dispel a doubt as soon as it arises. This you should be able to do if you know your case and have a sound position. If the question warrants a negative answer, do not fence with it but respond with a bold *thwertutnay* – which for the benefit of the illiterate I may explain as a term used in ancient pleading to signify a downright No. While if the answer is in the affirmative or calls for a concession the Court will be equally gratified to have the matter promptly disposed of. If you value your argumentative life do not evade or shuffle or postpone, no matter how embarrassing the question may be or how much it interrupts the thread of your argument. Nothing I should think would be more irritating to an inquiring court than to have refuge taken in the familiar evasion "I am coming to that" and then to have the argument end with the promise unfulfilled. If you are really coming to it indicate what your answer will be when it is reached and never, never sit down until it is made.

Do not get into your head the idea that there is a deliberate design on the part of any judge to embarrass counsel by questions. His mind is seeking help, that is all, although it may well be that he calls for help before he really needs it. You remember Bacon's admonition on the subject in his Essay on Judicature:

> "It is no grace to a judge" he says, "first to find that which he might have heard in due time from the bar, or to show quickness of conceit in cutting off evidence or counsel too short, or to prevent information by questions though pertinent."

On the other hand, Chief Justice Denison of the Supreme Court of Colorado puts the matter thus:

> "A perfect argument would need no interruption and a perfect Judge would never interrupt it; but we are not perfect. If the argument . . . discusses the truth of the first chapter of Genesis when the controlling issue is the constitutionality of a Tennessee statute it ought to be interrupted . . . It is the function of the Court to decide the case and to decide it properly . . . The Judge knows where his doubts lie, at which point he wishes to be enlightened; it is he whose mind at last must be made up, no one can do it for him, and he must take his own course of thought to accomplish it. Then he must sometimes interrupt."

Judges are sometimes more annoyed by each others' questions than counsel, I have observed. I remember a former Justice of the Supreme Court much given to interrogation, who engaged counsel in a long colloquy of question and answer at the very threshold of his argument. In a stage whisper audible within the bar Chief Justice White was heard to moan "I want to hear the argument." "So do I, damn him," growled his neighbor, Justice Holmes. Yet questions fairly put and frankly answered give to oral argument a vitality and spice that nothing else will supply.

(7) Read sparingly and only from necessity.

The eye is the window of the mind, and the speaker does not live who can long hold the attention of any audience without looking it in the face. There is something about a sheet of paper interposed between speaker and listener that walls off the mind of the latter as if it were boiler-plate. It obstructs the passage of thought as the lead plate bars the X-rays. I realize that I am taking just this risk at present, but this is not a speech or an argument, only, God save the mark, a lecture.

Of course where the case turns upon the language of a statute or the terms of a written instrument it is necessary that it should be read, always, if possible, with a copy in the hands of the court so that the eye of the court may supplement its ear. But the reading of lengthy extracts from the briefs or from reported cases or long excerpts from the testimony can only be described as a sheer waste of time. With this every appellate court of my acquaintance agrees. A sentence here or a sentence there, perhaps, if sufficiently pertinent and pithy, but not I beg of you print by the paragraph or page.

There is a cognate fault of which most of us from time to time are guilty. This arises when we are seeking to cite or distinguish other cases bearing on our claims and are tempted into a tedious recital of the facts in the cited case, not uncommonly prefaced by the somewhat awkward phrase "That was a case where," etc. Now the human mind is a pawky thing and must be held to its work and it is little wonder after three or four or half a dozen such recitals that not only are the recited facts forgotten but those in the case at bar become blurred and confused. What the advocate needs most of all is that his facts and his alone should stand out stark, simple, unique, clear.

(8) Avoid personalities.

This is a hard saying, especially when one's feelings are ruffled by a lower court or by opposing counsel, but none the less it is worthy of all acceptation, both in oral argument and in brief. I am not speaking merely of the laws of courtesy that must always govern an honorable profession, but rather of the sheer inutility of personalities as a method of argument in a judicial forum. Nor am I excluding proper comment on things that deserve reprobation. I am thinking psychologically again. It is all a question of keeping the mind of the court on the issues in hand without distraction from without.

One who criticizes unfairly or harshly the action of a lower court runs the risk of offending the quite understandable *esprit de corps* of the judicial body. Rhetorical denunciation of opposing litigants or witnesses may arouse a measure of sympathy for the persons so denounced, while controversies between counsel impose on the court the wholly unnecessary burden and annoyance of preserving order and maintaining the decorum of its proceedings. Such things can irritate, they can never persuade.

(9) Know your record from cover to cover.

This commandment might properly have headed the list for it is the *sine qua non* of all effective argument. You have now reached a point in the litigation where you can no longer hope to supply the want of preparation by lucky accidents or mental agility. You will encounter no more unexpected surprises. You have your last chance to win for your client. It is clear therefore that the field tactics of the trial table will no longer serve and the time has come for major strategy based upon an accurate knowledge of all that has occurred. At any moment you may be called on to correct some misstatement of your adversary and at any moment you may confront a question from the Court which, if you are able to answer by an apt reference to the record or with a firm reliance on a well-furnished memory, will increase the confidence with which the Court will listen to what else you may have to say. Many an argument otherwise admirable has been destroyed because of counsel's inability to make just such a response.

(10) Sit down.

This is the tenth and last commandment. In preparing for argument you will no doubt have made an outline carefully measured by the time at your command. The notes of it which you should have jotted down lie before you on the reading desk. When you have run through this outline and are satisfied that the court has fully grasped your contentions, what else is there left for you to do? You must be vain indeed to hope that by further speaking you can dragoon the Court into a prompt decision in your favor. The mere fact that you have an allotted time of one hour more or less does not constitute a contract with the Court to listen for that length of time. On the contrary, when you round out your argument and sit down before your time has expired, a benevolent smile overspreads the faces on the bench and a sigh of relief and gratification arises from your brethren at the bar who have been impatiently waiting for the moment when the angel might again trouble the waters of the healing pool and permit them to step in. Earn these exhibitions of gratitude therefore whenever you decently can, and leave the rest to Zeus and his colleagues, that is to say, to the judges on high Olympus.

Before I obey this admonition myself, may I say, Mr. Chairman, how painfully conscious I am that I have offered nothing new concerning the subject in hand. I have not even been able to cover old thoughts with new varnish. How could I have hoped to do so? The process of appeal from one tribunal to another is very old in the history of human justice. No matter in what form it is carried on the essentials of an appeal are always the same, and there is nothing very new to be said about it. The need for an appellate process arises from the innate realization of mankind that the human intellect and human justice are frail at their best. It is necessary therefore to measure one man's mind against another in order to purge the final result, so far as may be, of all passion, prejudice or infirmity. It is the effort to realize the maximum of justice in human relations; and to keep firm and stable the foundations on which all ordered society rests. There is no field of nobler usefulness for the lawyer. For him, who in the splendid words of Chancellor D'Aguesseau, belongs to an order "as old as the magistracy, as noble as virtue, as necessary as justice."

FIFTY-TWO

# "Yes, but the Trouble is he *Always* Wears that Mysterious Smile"

SIDNEY HOFF

*Source*: © The New Yorker Collection 1955 Sidney Hoff from cartoon-bank.com. All Rights Reserved.

"Yes, but the trouble is he *always* wears that mysterious smile."

PART TWELVE

# Bargaining

# Introduction

In "The Bargaining Problem," Nash invented the most important equilibrium concept in cooperative game theory, just as in the articles in Chapters 3 and 4 he invented the most important one for noncooperative games. Try comparing the two and see how different the style of approach is.

Everybody agrees that a 50–50 split is reasonable for pie division games, but the axiomatic approach of the Nash article is unsatisfactory. Rubinstein's 1982 article arrives at the same pie division but justifies it in the setting of a noncooperative game, a structural rather than a reduced-form model.

One of the objections to the axiomatic approach is that it assumes away some of the most important problems. The assumption that players arrive at an efficient solution rules out any delay in reaching a solution. Why, then, do we get strikes and wars? The UPS strike of the *Wall Street Journal* article in this Part is interesting for two reasons. First, both UPS and the labor union were willing to incur real losses in delaying agreement. Why did UPS not give in immediately, rather than wait? Second, the disagreement was not simply over whether wages would be higher or lower. Rather, the negotiations were over many different issues, including contract length, management of pension funds, wages, and employment levels. The usual answer to why strikes occur is there is incomplete information, and costly delay is necessary for a player to signal his unwillingness to accept the other side's terms. These models become very intricate very quickly, however, which is why "Whatever Happened to *Elegant* Solutions?" is an appropriate cartoon for this part of the book.

# FIFTY-THREE

# The Bargaining Problem*

JOHN F. NASH, JR.

Source: *Econometrica* 18 (April), 1950, pp. 155–62. Reprinted by permission of The Econometric Society, Evanston, Illinois.

A new treatment is presented of a classical economic problem, one which occurs in many forms, as bargaining, bilateral monopoly, etc. It may also be regarded as a nonzero-sum two-person game. In this treatment a few general assumptions are made concerning the behavior of a single individual and of a group of two individuals in certain economic environments. From these, the solution (in the sense of this paper) of the classical problem may be obtained. In the terms of game theory, values are found for the game.

## Introduction

A TWO-PERSON bargaining situation involves two individuals who have the opportunity to collaborate for mutual benefit in more than one way. In the simpler case, which is the one considered in this paper, no action taken by one of the individuals without the consent of the other can affect the well-being of the other one.

The economic situations of monopoly versus monopsony, of state trading between two nations, and of negotiation between employer and labor union may be regarded as bargaining problems. It is the purpose of this paper to give a theoretical discussion of this problem and to obtain a definite "solution" – making, of course, certain idealizations in order to do so. A "solution" here means a determination of the amount of satisfaction each individual should expect to get from the situation, or, rather, a determination of how much it should be worth to each of these individuals to have this opportunity to bargain.

This is the classical problem of exchange and, more specifically, of bilateral monopoly as treated by Cournot, Bowley, Tintner, Fellner, and others. A different approach is suggested by von Neumann and Morgenstern in *Theory of Games and Economic Behavior*[1] which permits the identification of this typical exchange situation with a nonzero-sum two-person game.

---

* The author wishes to acknowledge the assistance of Professors von Neumann and Morgenstern who read the original form of the paper and gave helpful advice as to the presentation.

[1] John von Neumann and Oskar Morgenstern, *Theory of Games and Economic Behavior*, Princeton: Princeton University Press, 1944 (Second Edition, 1947), pp. 15–31.

In general terms, we idealize the bargaining problem by assuming that the two individuals are highly rational, that each can accurately compare his desires for various things, that they are equal in bargaining skill, and that each has full knowledge of the tastes and preferences of the other.

In order to give a theoretical treatment of bargaining situations we abstract from the situation to form a mathematical model in terms of which to develop the theory.

In making our treatment of bargaining we employ a numerical utility, of the type developed in *Theory of Games*, to express the preferences, or tastes, of each individual engaged in bargaining. By this means we bring into the mathematical model the desire of each individual to maximize his gain in bargaining. We shall briefly review this theory in the terminology used in this paper.

## Utility Theory of the Individual

The concept of an "anticipation" is important in this theory. This concept will be explained partly by illustration. Suppose Mr. Smith knows he will be given a new Buick tomorrow. We may say that he has a Buick anticipation. Similarly, he might have a Cadillac anticipation. If he knew that tomorrow a coin would be tossed to decide whether he would get a Buick or a Cadillac, we should say that he had a $\frac{1}{2}$ Buick, $\frac{1}{2}$ Cadillac anticipation. Thus an anticipation of an individual is a state of expectation which may involve the certainty of some contingencies and various probabilities of other contingencies. As another example, Mr. Smith might know that he will get a Buick tomorrow and think that he has half a chance of getting a Cadillac too. The $\frac{1}{2}$ Buick, $\frac{1}{2}$ Cadillac anticipation mentioned above illustrates the following important property of anticipations: if $0 \leq p \leq 1$ and $A$ and $B$ represent two anticipations, there is an anticipation, which we represent by $pA + (1 - p)B$, which is a probability combination of the two anticipations where there is a probability $p$ of $A$ and $1 - p$ of $B$.

By making the following assumptions we are enabled to develop the utility theory of a single individual:

1 An individual offered two possible anticipations can decide which is preferable or that they are equally desirable.

2 The ordering thus produced is transitive; if $A$ is better than $B$ and $B$ is better than $C$ then $A$ is better than $C$.

3 Any probability combination of equally desirable states is just as desirable as either.

4 If $A$, $B$, and $C$ are as in assumption (2), then there is a probability combination of $A$ and $C$ which is just as desirable as $C$. This amounts to an assumption of continuity.

5 If $0 \leq p \leq 1$ and $A$ and $B$ are equally desirable, then $pA + (1 - p)C$ and $pB + (1 - p)C$ are equally desirable. Also, if $A$ and $B$ are equally desirable, $A$ may be substituted for $B$ in any desirability ordering relationship satisfied by $B$.

These assumptions suffice to show the existence of a satisfactory utility function, assigning a real number to each anticipation of an individual. This utility function is not unique, that is, if $u$ is such a function then so also is $au + b$, provided $a > 0$. Letting capital letters represent anticipations and small ones real numbers, such a utility function will satisfy the following properties:

(a)  $u(A) > u(B)$ is equivalent to $A$ is more desirable than $B$, etc.
(b)  If $0 \leq p \leq 1$ then $u[pA + (1 - p)B] = pu(A) + (1 - p)u(B)$.

This is the important linearity property of a utility function.

## Two Person Theory

In *Theory of Games and Economic Behavior* a theory of $n$-person games is developed which includes as a special case the two-person bargaining problem. But the theory there developed makes no attempt to find a value for a given $n$-person game, that is, to determine what it is worth to each player to have the opportunity to engage in the game. This determination is accomplished only in the case of the two-person zero-sum game.

It is our viewpoint that these $n$-person games should have values; that is, there should be a set of numbers which depend continuously upon the set of quantities comprising the mathematical description of the game and which express the utility to each player of the opportunity to engage in the game.

We may define a two-person anticipation as a combination of two one-person anticipations. Thus we have two individuals, each with a certain expectation of his future environment. We may regard the one-person utility functions as applicable to the two-person anticipations, each giving the result it would give if applied to the corresponding one-person anticipation which is a component of the two-person anticipation. A probability combination of two two-person anticipations is defined by making the corresponding combinations for their components. Thus if $[A, B]$ is a two-person anticipation and $0 \leq p \leq 1$, then

$$p[A, B] + (1 - p)[C, D]$$

will be defined as

$$[pA + (1 - p)C, pB + (1 - p)D].$$

Clearly the one-person utility functions will have the same linearity property here as in the one-person case. From this point onwards when the term anticipation is used it shall mean two-person anticipation.

In a bargaining situation one anticipation is especially distinguished; this is the anticipation of no cooperation between the bargainers. It is natural, therefore, to use utility functions for the two individuals which assign the number zero to this anticipation. This still leaves each individual's utility function determined only up to multiplication by a positive real number. Henceforth any utility functions used shall be understood to be so chosen.

We may produce a graphical representation of the situation facing the two by choosing utility functions for them and plotting the utilities of all available anticipations in a plane graph.

It is necessary to introduce assumptions about the nature of the set of points thus obtained. We wish to assume that this set of points is compact and convex, in the mathematical senses. It should be convex since an anticipation which will graph into any point on a straight line segment between two points of the set can always be obtained by the appropriate probability combination of two anticipations which graph into the two points. The condition of compactness implies, for one thing, that the set of points must be bounded, that is, that they can all be inclosed in a sufficiently large square in the plane. It also implies that any continuous function of the utilities assumes a maximum value for the set at some point of the set.

We shall regard two anticipations which have the same utility for any utility function corresponding to either individual as equivalent so that the graph becomes a complete representation of the essential features of the situation. Of course, the graph is only determined up to changes of scale since the utility functions are not completely determined.

Now since our solution should consist of *rational* expectations of gain by the two bargainers, these expectations should be realizable by an appropriate agreement between the two. Hence, there should be an available anticipation which gives each the amount of satisfaction he should expect to get. It is reasonable to assume that the two, being rational, would simply agree to that anticipation, or to an equivalent one. Hence, we may think of one point in the set of the graph as representing the solution, and also representing all anticipations that the two might agree upon as fair bargains. We shall develop the theory by giving conditions which should hold for the relationship between this solution point and the set, and from these deduce a simple condition determining the solution point. We shall consider only those cases in which there is a possibility that both individuals could gain from the situation. (This does not exclude cases where, in the end, only one individual could have benefited because the "fair bargain" might consist of an agreement to use a probability method to decide who is to gain in the end. Any probability combination of available anticipations is an available anticipation.)

Let $u_1$ and $u_2$ be utility functions for the two individuals. Let $c(S)$ represent the solution point in a set $S$ which is compact and convex and includes the origin. We assume:

6    If $\alpha$ is a point in $S$ such that there exists another point $\beta$ in $S$ with the property $u_1(\beta) > u_1(\alpha)$ and $u_2(\beta) > u_2(\alpha)$, then $\alpha \neq c(S)$.
7    If the set $T$ contains the set $S$ and $c(T)$ is in $S$, then $c(T) = c(S)$.

We say that a set $S$ is symmetric if there exist utility operators $u_1$ and $u_2$ such that when $(a, b)$ is contained in $S$, $(b, a)$ is also contained in $S$; that is, such that the graph becomes symmetrical with respect to the line $u_1 = u_2$.

8    If $S$ is symmetric and $u_1$ and $u_2$ display this, then $c(S)$ is a point of the form $(a, a)$, that is, a point on the line $u_1 = u_2$.

The first assumption above expresses the idea that each individual wishes to maximize the utility to himself of the ultimate bargain. The third expresses equality of bargaining skill. The second is more complicated. The following interpretation may help to show the naturalness of this assumption: If two rational individuals would agree that $c(T)$ would be a fair bargain if $T$ were the set of possible bargains, then they should be willing to make an agreement, of lesser restrictiveness, not to attempt to arrive at any bargains represented by points outside of the set $S$ if $S$ contained $c(T)$. If $S$ were contained in $T$ this would reduce their situation to one with $S$ as the set of possibilities. Hence $c(S)$ should equal $c(T)$.

We now show that these conditions require that the solution be the point of the set in the first quadrant where $u_1 u_2$ is maximized. We know some such point exists from the compactness. Convexity makes it unique.

Let us now choose the utility functions so that the above-mentioned point is transformed into the point (1, 1). Since this involves the multiplication of the utilities by constants, (1, 1) will now be the point of maximum $u_1 u_2$. For no points of the set will $u_1 + u_2 > 2$, now, since if there were a point of the set with $u_1 + u_2 > 2$ at some point on the line segment between (1, 1) and that point, there would be a value of $u_1 u_2$ greater than one (see Figure 1).

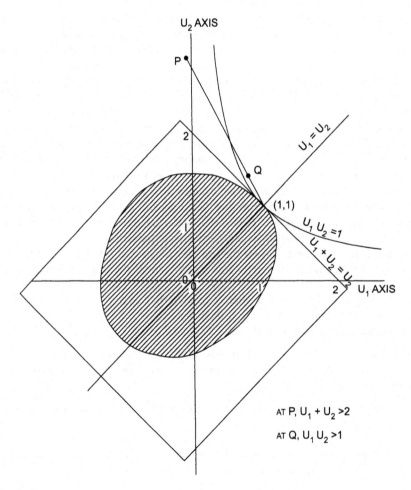

Figure 1

We may now construct a square in the region $u_1 + u_2 \leq 2$ which is symmetrical in the line $u_1 = u_2$, which has one side on the line $u_1 + u_2 = 2$, and which completely encloses the set of alternatives. Considering the square region formed as the set of alternatives, instead of the older set, it is clear that $(1, 1)$ is the only point satisfying assumptions (6) and (8). Now using assumption (7) we may conclude that $(1, 1)$ must also be the solution point when our original (transformed) set is the set of alternatives. This establishes the assertion.

We shall now give a few examples of the application of this theory.

## Examples

Let us suppose that two intelligent individuals, Bill and Jack, are in a position where they may barter goods but have no money with which to facilitate exchange. Further, let us assume for simplicity that the utility to either individual of a portion of the total number of goods involved is the sum of the utilities to him of the individual goods in that portion. We give below a table of goods possessed by each individual with the utility of each to each individual. The utility functions used for the two individuals are, of course, to be regarded as arbitrary.

| Bill's goods | Utility to Bill | Utility to Jack |
|---|---|---|
| book | 2 | 4 |
| whip | 2 | 2 |
| ball | 2 | 1 |
| bat | 2 | 2 |
| box | 4 | 1 |
| Jack's goods | | |
| pen | 10 | 1 |
| toy | 4 | 1 |
| knife | 6 | 2 |
| hat | 2 | 2 |

The graph for this bargaining situation is included as an illustration (Figure 2). It turns out to be a convex polygon in which the point where the product of the utility gains is maximized is at a vertex and where there is but one corresponding anticipation. This is:

*Bill gives Jack*: book, whip, ball, and bat,
*Jack gives Bill*: pen, toy, and knife.

When the bargainers have a common medium of exchange the problem may take on an especially simple form. In many cases the money equivalent of a good will serve as a satisfactory approximate utility function. (By the money equivalent is meant the amount of money which is just as desirable as the good to the individual with whom we are concerned.) This occurs when the utility of an amount of money is approximately a linear function of the amount in the range of amounts concerned in the situation. When we may

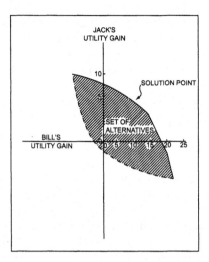

**Figure 2**   The solution point is on a rectangular hyperbola lying in the first quadrant and touching the set of alternatives at but one point.

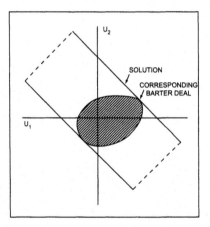

**Figure 3**   The inner area represents the bargains possible without the use of money. The area between parallel lines represents the possibilities allowing the use of money. The solution must be formed using a barter-type bargain for which $u_1 + u_2$ is at a maximum and using also an exchange of money.

use a common medium of exchange for the utility function for each individual the set of points in the graph is such that that portion of it in the first quadrant forms an isosceles right triangle. Hence the solution has each bargainer getting the same money profit (see Figure 3).

# FIFTY-FOUR

# Perfect Equilibrium in a Bargaining Model

Ariel Rubinstein*

*Source*: *Econometrica* 50 (January), 1982, pp. 97–109. Reprinted by permission of The Econometric Society, Evanston, Illinois.

Two players have to reach an agreement on the partition of a pie of size 1. Each has to make in turn, a proposal as to how it should be divided. After one player has made an offer, the other must decide either to accept it, or to reject it and continue the bargaining. Several properties which the players' preferences possess are assumed. The Perfect Equilibrium Partitions (P.E.P.) are characterized in all the models satisfying these assumptions.

Specially, it is proved that when every player bears a fixed bargaining cost for each period ($c_1$ and $c_2$), then: (i) if $c_1 < c_2$ the only P.E.P. gives all the pie to 1; (ii) if $c_1 > c_2$ the only P.E.P. gives to 1 only $c_2$.

In the case where each player has a fixed discounting factor ($\delta_1$ and $\delta_2$) the only P.E.P. is $(1 - \delta_2)/(1 - \delta_1\delta_2)$.

## 1. Introduction

When I refer in this paper to the *Bargaining Problem* I mean the following situation and question:

Two individuals have before them several possible contractual agreements. Both have interests in reaching agreement but their interests are not entirely identical. What "will be" the agreed contract, assuming that both parties behave rationally?

I begin with this clarification because I would like to prevent the common confusion of the above problem with two other problems that may be asked about the bargaining situation, namely: (i) the positive question – what is the agreement reached in practice; (ii) the normative question – what is the just agreement.

* This research was supported by the U.K. Social Sciences Research Council in connection with the project: "Incentives, Consumer Uncertainty, and Public Policy," and by the Rothschild Foundation. It was undertaken while I was a research fellow at Nuffield College, Oxford. I would like to thank J. Mirrlees and Y. Shilony for their helpful comments. I owe special thanks to Ken Binmore for his encouragement and remarks.

Edgeworth [4] presented this problem one hundred years ago, considering it the most fundamental problem in Economics. Since then it seems to have been the source of considerable frustration for Economic theorists. Economists often talk in the following vein (beginning of Cross [3]).

"Economists traditionally have had very little to say about pure bargaining situations in which the outcome is clearly dependent upon interactions among only a few individuals" (p. 67).

The "very little" referred to above is that the agreed contract is individual-rational and is Pareto optimal; i.e. it is no worse than disagreement, and there is no agreement which both would prefer. However, which of the (usually numerous) contracts satisfying these conditions will be agreed? Economists tend to answer vaguely by saying that this depends on the "bargaining ability" of the parties.

Many attempts have been made in order to get to a clear cut answer to the bargaining problem. Two approaches may be distinguished in the published literature. The first is the strategic approach. The players' negotiating maneuvers are moves in a noncooperative game and the rationality assumption is expressed by investigation of the Nash equilibria. The second approach is the axiomatic method.

"One states as axioms several properties that it would seem natural for the solution to have and then one discovers that the axioms actually determine the solution uniquely" [11, p. 129].

(For a survey of the axiomatic models of bargaining, see Roth [13].) The purpose of this approach is to bypass the difficulties inherent in the strategic approach. We make assumptions about the solution without specifying the bargaining process itself. Notice that in order to be relevant to our problem, these axioms may only either restrict the domain of the solution or be obtained from the assumption of rationality. Thus, for example, Nash's symmetry axiom can be considered as an assumption that all the differences between the players can be expressed in the set of utility pairs arising from the possible contracts and that there is no other relevant element that distinguishes between them. But, the key axiom in most axiomatizations – the "Independence of Irrelevant Alternatives" has not received a proper defense and in fact it is more suited to the normative question (see Luce and Raiffa [9] and Binmore [2]).

It was Nash himself who felt the need to complement the axiomatic approach (see [10]) with a non-cooperative game. (For a wider discussion, see Binmore [2].) In his second paper on the solution that he proposed [11], Nash proved that the solution is the limit of a sequence of equilibria of bargaining games. These models, however, are highly stylized and artificial. Among the later works, I mention here three, wherein the bargaining is represented by a multi-stage game. Ståhl [19, 20] and Krelle [7] assume the existence of a known finite number of bargaining periods and their solutions are based on dynamic programming. Rice [12] uses the notion of a differential game. The bargaining period is identified with an interval, equilibrium strategies are the limits of "step-wise" strategies, and the lengths of those steps tend to zero.

In this paper I will adopt the strategic approach. I will consider the following bargaining situation: two players have to reach an agreement on the partition of a pie of size 1. Each has to make in turn, a proposal as to how it should be divided. After one party has made such an offer, the other must decide either to accept it or to reject it and continue with the bargaining. The players' preference relations are defined on the set of ordered pairs of the type $(x, t)$ (where $0 \leqq x \leqq 1$ and $t$ is a nonnegative integer). The pair $(x, t)$ is interpreted as "1 receives $x$ and 2 receives $1 - x$ at time $t$."

This paper is limited to the investigation of a family of models in which the preferences satisfy:

(A-1)  "pie" is desirable,
(A-2)  "time" is valuable,
(A-3)  continuity,
(A-4)  stationarity (the preference of $(x, t)$ over $(y, t + 1)$ is independent of $t$),
(A-5)  the larger the portion the more "compensation" a player needs for a delay of one period to be immaterial to him.

The two elements in which the parties may differ are the negotiating order (who has "first turn") and the preferences.

Two sub-families of models to which I will refer, are:

(i)   *Fixed bargaining cost*: $i$'s preference is derived from the function $y - c_i t$, i.e. every player bears a fixed cost for each period.

(ii)  *Fixed discounting factor*: $i$'s preference is derived from the function $y \cdot \delta_i^t$, i.e. every player has a fixed discounting factor.

So my first step has been to restrict the bargaining situation to be considered. Secondly, I will give a severe interpretation to the rationality requirement by investigating *perfect equilibria* (see Selten [17, 18]). A perfect equilibrium is one where not only the strategies chosen at the beginning of the game form an equilibrium, but also the strategies planned after all possible histories (in every subgame).

Quite surprisingly[1] this leads to the isolation of a single solution for most of the cases examined here. For example, in the fixed bargaining cost model, it turns out that if $c_1 > c_2$, 1 receives $c_2$ only. If $c_1 < c_2$, 1 receives all the pie. If $c_1 = c_2$, any partition of the pie from which 1 receives at least $c_1$ is a perfect equilibrium partition (P.E.P.). In other words, a weaker player gets almost "nothing"; he can at most get the loss which his opponent incurs during one bargaining round. In the fixed discounting factor model there is one P.E.P., 1 obtaining $(1 - \delta_2)/(1 - \delta_1 \delta_2)$. This solution is continuous, monotonic in the discounting factors, and gives relative advantage to the player who starts the bargaining.

The work closest to that appearing here is that of Ingolf Ståhl[2] [19, 20]. He investigates a similar bargaining situation but which has a finite and known negotiating time horizon,

---

[1] Especially considering that the perfect equilibrium concept has been "disappointing" when applied to the supergames, see Aumann and Shapley [1], Kurz [8], and Rubinstein [14, 15, 16].

[2] I would like to thank Professor R. Selten for referring me to Ståhl's work, after reading the first version of this paper.

and in which the pie can be only partitioned discretely. Ståhl studies cases for which there exists a single P.E.P. which is independent of who has the first move.

The discussed bargaining model may be modified in numerous ways, many being only technical modifications. However I would like to point out one type of modification which I believe to be extremely interesting. A critical assumption in the model is that each player has complete information about the preference of the other. Assume on the other hand that 1 and 2 both know that 1 has a fixed bargaining cost. They both know that 2 has also a fixed bargaining cost, but only 2 knows its actual value. In such a situation some new aspects appear. 1 will try to conclude from 2's behavior what the true bargaining cost is, and 2 may try to cheat 1 by leading him to believe that he, 2, is "stronger" than he actually is. In such a situation one can expect that the bargaining will continue for more than one period. I hope to deal with this situation in another paper.

## 2. The Bargaining Model

Two players, 1 and 2, are bargaining on the partition of a pie. The pie will be partitioned only after the players reach an agreement. Each player, in turn offers a partition and his opponent may agree to the offer "$Y$" or reject it "$N$". Acceptance of the offer ends the bargaining. After rejection, the rejecting player then has to make a counter offer and so on. There are no rules which bind the players to any previous offers they have made.

Formally, let $S = [0, 1]$. A partition of the pie is identified with a number $s$ in the unit interval by interpreting $s$ as the proportion of the pie that 1 receives. Let $s_i$ be the portion of the pie that player $i$ receives in the partition $s$: that is $s_1 = s$ and $s_2 = 1 - s$.

Let $F$ be the set of all sequences of functions $f = \{f^t\}_{t=1}^{\infty}$, where $f^1 \in S$, for $t$ odd $f^t : S^{t-1} \to S$, and for $t$ even $f^t : S^t \to \{Y, N\}$. ($S^t$ is the set of all sequences of length $t$ of elements in $S$.) $F$ is the set of all strategies of the player who starts the bargaining. Similarly let $G$ be the set of all strategies of the player who in the first move has to respond to the other player's offer; that is, $G$ is the set of all sequences of functions $g = \{g^t\}_{t=1}^{\infty}$ such that, for $t$ odd $g^t : S^t \to \{Y, N\}$ and for $t$ even $g^t : S^{t-1} \to S$.

The following concepts are easily defined rigorously. Let $\sigma(f, g)$ be the sequence of offers in which 1 starts the bargaining and adopts $f \in F$, and 2 adopts $g \in G$. Let $T(f, g)$ be the length of $\sigma(f, g)$ (may be $\infty$). Let $D(f, g)$ be the last element of $\sigma(f, g)$ (if there is such an element). $D(f, g)$ is called the *partition* induced by $(f, g)$. The outcome function of the game is defined by

$$P(f,g) = \begin{cases} (D(f,g), T(f,g)), & T(f,g) < \infty, \\ (0, \infty), & T(f,g) = \infty \end{cases}$$

Thus, the outcome $(s, t)$ is interpreted as the reaching of agreement $s$ in period $t$, and the symbol $(0, \infty)$ indicates a perpetual disagreement.

For the analysis of the game we will have to consider the case in which the order of bargaining is revised and player 2 is the first to move. In this case a strategy for player 2 is an element of $F$ and a strategy for player 1 is an element of $G$. Let us define $\sigma(g, f)$,

$T(g, f)$, $D(g, f)$ and $P(g, f)$ similarly to the above for the case where player 2 starts the bargaining and adopts $f \in F$ and player 1 adopts $g \in G$.

The last component of the model is the preference of the players on the set of outcomes. I assume that player $i$ has a preference relation (complete, reflexive, and transitive) $\succsim_i$ on the set of $S \times N \cup \{(0, \infty)\}$, where $N$ is the set of natural numbers.

I assume that the preferences satisfy the following five assertions:
For all $r, s \in S, t, t_1, t_2 \in N$, and $i \in \{1,2\}$:

(A-1)   if $r_i > s_i$, then $(r, t) >_i (s, t)$;
(A-2)   if $s_i > 0$ and $t_2 > t_1$, then $(s, t_1) >_i (s, t_2) >_i (0, \infty)$;
(A-3)   $(r, t_1) \succsim_i (s, t_1 + 1)$ iff $(r, t_2) \succsim_i (s, t_2 + 1)$;
(A-4)   if $r_n \to r$ and $(r_n, t_1) \succsim_i (s, t_2)$, then $(r, t_1) \succsim_i (s, t_2)$;
         if $r_n \to r$ and $(r_n, t_1) \succsim_i (0, \infty)$, then $(r, t_1) \succsim_i (0, \infty)$;
(A-5)   if $(s + \epsilon, 1) \sim_i (s, 0)$, $(\bar{s} + \bar{\epsilon}, 1) \sim_i (\bar{s}, 0)$, and $s_i < \bar{s}_i$, then $\epsilon_i \leqq \bar{\epsilon}_i$.

From (A-3) we can use the notation $(r, T) \succsim_i (s, 0)$ and $(r, T) \precsim_i (s, 0)$ for $(r, T + t) \succsim_i (s, t)$ and $(r, T + t) \precsim_i (s, t)$, respectively.

Two families of models in which the preferences satisfy the above conditions are:

I.    *Fixed bargaining costs.* Each player $i$ has a number $c_i$ such that $(s, t_1) \succsim (\bar{s}, t_2)$ iff $(s_i - c_i \cdot t_1) \geqq (\bar{s}_i - c_i \cdot t_2)$.

II.   *Fixed discounting factors.* Each player $i$ has a number $0 < \delta_i \leqq 1$ such that $(s, t_1) \succsim_i (\bar{s}, t_2)$ iff $s_i \delta_i^{t_1} \geqq \bar{s}_i \delta_i^{t_2}$.

We reserve $\delta_i = 0$ for the lexicographic preference: $(s, t_1) \succsim_i (\bar{s}, t_2)$ if $(t_1 < t_2)$ or $(t_1 = t_2$ and $s_i \geqq \bar{s}_i)$.

REMARK:   In a more general framework of the model, player $i$ would be characterized by the sequence of preferences $\{\succsim_i^t\}$, where $\succsim_i^t$ is $i$'s preference on the outcomes assuming that the players have not reached an agreement in the first $t - 1$ periods. In fact, I assume that $\succsim_i^t \equiv \succsim_i$. This assumption precludes discussion of some interesting bargaining situation such as: (1) player $i$ has a sequence $\{c_i^t\}$ where $c_i^t$ is the cost to $i$ of the bargaining in period $t$; (2) player $i$ has a fixed bargaining cost and his utility is not linear.

## 3. Perfect Equilibrium

The ordered pair $(\hat{f}, \hat{g}) \in F \times G$ is called a *Nash Equilibrium* if there is no $f \in F$ such that $P(f, \hat{g}) >_1 P(\hat{f}, \hat{g})$ and there is no $g \in G$ such that $P(\hat{f}, g) >_2 P(\hat{f}, \hat{g})$.

The following simple proposition indicates that even after the restriction of the bargaining problem to our model, the Nash equilibrium is a "weak" concept.

PROPOSITION: *For all $s \in S$, $s$ is a partition induced by Nash equilibrium.*

PROOF   Let us define $\hat{f} \in F$ and $\hat{g} \in G$ as follows:

for $t$ odd, $\hat{f}^t \equiv s$, $\quad \hat{g}^t(s^1 \ldots s^t) = \begin{cases} Y, & s^t \leqq s, \\ N, & s^t > s; \end{cases}$

for $t$ even, $\hat{g}^t \equiv s$, $\quad \hat{f}^t(s^1 \ldots s^t) = \begin{cases} Y, & s^t \geqq s, \\ N, & s^t < s. \end{cases}$

Clearly, $(\hat{f}, \hat{g})$ is a Nash equilibrium and $P(\hat{f}, \hat{g}) = (s, 1)$.

The above equilibrium highlights the inadequacy of the concept of a Nash equilibrium in the current context. Assume 1 demands $s + \varepsilon (\varepsilon > 0)$. At this point of the game, 2 intends to insist on the original planned contract and 1 intends to agree to this offer. But if $\varepsilon$ is sufficiently small so that $(s, 1) <_2 (s + \varepsilon, 0), 2$ will prefer to agree to player 1's deviation. Thus, player 1 may carry out a manipulative maneuver and offer $s + \varepsilon$ in the certainty that 2 will agree to it.

In order to overcome this difficulty (see also Harsanyi [5]) I will use the concept of the Perfect Equilibrium following the definition of Selten (see [17, 18]). For this definition we need some additional notation. Let $s^1 \cdots s^T \in S$. Define $f|s^1 \cdots s^T$ and $g|s^1 \cdots s^T$ as the strategies derived from $f$ and $g$ after the offers $s^1 \cdots s^T$ have been announced and already rejected. (That is, for $T$ odd and $t$ odd,

$$(f|s^1 \ldots s^T)^t \ (r^1 \ldots r^{t-1}) = f^{T+1} \ (s^1 \ldots s^T, r^1 \ldots r^{t-1})$$

$$(g|s^1 \ldots s^T)^t \ (r^1 \ldots r^t) = g^{T+1} \ (s^1 \ldots s^T, r^1 \ldots r^t)$$

and so on.)

Notice that if $T$ is even it is 1's turn to propose a partition of the pie, and 2's first move is a response to 1's offer. Thus $f|s^1 \ldots s^T \in F$ and $g|s^1 \ldots s^T \in G$. If $T$ is odd, it is 2's turn to make an offer and therefore $g|s^1 \ldots s^T \in F$ and $f|s^1 \ldots s^T \in G$. And now to the central definition which, as mentioned, follows Selten's definition of subgame perfectness [17, 18] (what may at first seem to be a slightly clumsy version of Selten's idea has been chosen to prevent the use of some additional notation which would be redundant in this paper):

DEFINITION: $(\hat{f}, \hat{g})$ is *Perfect Equilibrium* (P.E.) if for all $s^1 \ldots s^T$, if $T$ is odd:

(P-1)   there is no $f \in F$ such that $P(\hat{f}|s^1 \ldots s^T, f) >_2 P(\hat{f}|s^1 \ldots s^T, \hat{g}|s^1 \ldots s^T)$;
(P-2)   if $\hat{g}^T(s^1 \ldots s^T) = Y$, there is no $f \in F$ such that $P(\hat{f}|s^1 \ldots s^T, f) >_2 (s^T, 0)$;
(P-3)   if $\hat{g}^T(s^1 \ldots s^T) = N, P(\hat{f}|s^1 \ldots s^T, \hat{g}|s^1 \ldots s^T) \gtrsim_2 (s^T, 0)$;
            and if $T$ is even:
(P-4)   there is no $f \in F$ such that $P(f, \hat{g}|s^1 \ldots s^T) >_1 P(\hat{f}|s^1 \ldots s^T, \hat{g}|s^1 \ldots s^T)$;
(P-5)   if $\hat{f}^T(s^1 \ldots s^T) = Y$, there is no $f \in F$ such that $P(f, \hat{g}|s^1 \ldots s^T) >_1 (s^T, 0)$;
(P-6)   if $\hat{f}^T(s^1 \ldots s^T) = N, P(\hat{f}|s^1 \ldots s^T, \hat{g}|s^1 \ldots s^T) \gtrsim_1 (s^T, 0)$.

(P-1) and (P-4) ensure that after a sequence of offers and rejections $s^1 \ldots s^T$ the player who has to continue the bargaining has no better strategy other than to follow the planned strategy. (P-2) and (P-5) ensure that a player who has planned to accept the offer $s^T$ has no better alternative than to accept it, and (P-3) and (P-6) ensure that if a player is expected to reject an offer, it is not better for him to accept the offer.

EXAMPLE    To clarify the notation, let us show that the pair $(\hat{f}, \hat{g})$ (with $s = 0.5$) described in the proof of the above proposition is not a perfect equilibrium for fixed bargaining cost preferences with $c_1 = 0.1$ and $c_2 = 0.2$. Player 2 plans to reject a possible offer of 0.6 by player 1: that is, $\hat{g}^1(0.6) = N$. After such a rejection the players expect to agree on 0.5: that is, $P(\hat{f}|0.6, \hat{g}|0.6) = (0.5, 1)$. Player 2 prefers $(0.6, 0)$ to $(0.5, 1)$: thus, $(\hat{f}, \hat{g})$ violates condition (P-3).

REMARK    Notice that a strategy has been defined in Section 2 as a sequence of functions which is interpreted as the player's plans after every history, including histories which are not consistent with his own plans. For example, $f^3(s^1, s^2)$ is required to be defined even where $f^1 \neq s^1$ and $f^2(s^1, s^2) = Y$. The reader is directed to Selten [17, 18], Harsanyi [5] and Harsanyi and Selten [6] for details on the significance of the requirement.

# 4.  Lemmas

In this section we have only to assume that the preferences satisfy (A-1) and (A-2). The following Lemmas establish connections between two sets: (A) the set of all P.E.P.'s in a game in which 1 starts the bargaining, that is, $\{s \in S|$ there is a P.E. $(f, g) \in F \times G$ such that $s = D(f, g)\}$; and (B) the set of all P.E.P.'s in a game in which 2 starts the bargaining, that is, $\{s \in S|$ there is a P.E. $(g, f) \in G \times F$ such that $s = D(g, f)\}$.

REMARK    In a generalized model in which the $\succsim_i^t$ are not identical the same considerations would be used to establish connections between the sets $\{A^t\}_{t=1,3,5...}$ and $\{B^t\}_{t=2,4,6,...}$ where $A^t (B^t)$ is the set of all P.E.P.'s in a game which starts at time $t$, 1(2) making the first offer.

LEMMA 1: *Let $a \in A$. For all $b \in S$ such that $b > a$, there is $c \in B$ such that $(c, 1) \succsim_2 (b, 0)$.*

REMARK    Lemma 1 states that for $a$ to be in $A$, it has to be "protected" from the possibility that 1 will demand and achieve some better contract. Player 1 will certainly do so if there is $b \in S$ satisfying $b > a$ such that 2 would accept $b$ if it were offered. Player 2 must therefore reject such an offer. In order that it be optimal for him to carry out this threat, player 2 has to expect to achieve a better partition in the future; that is, there must be a P.E.P. $c \in B$ in the subgame that takes place after 2's rejection such that $(c, 1)$ is preferred by 2 to $(b, 0)$.

PROOF    Let $(\hat{f}, \hat{g})$ be a P.E. such that $D(\hat{f}, \hat{g}) = a$. Let $b \in S$ and $b > a$. From (P-1), $\hat{g}^1(b) = N$ (otherwise if $f^1 = b$ then $P(f, \hat{g}) = (b, 1) >_1 (a, 1) \succsim_1 (a, T(\hat{f}, \hat{g})) = P(\hat{f}, \hat{g})$ in contradiction to (P-1)). From (P-3) $P(\hat{f}|b, \hat{g}|b) \succsim_2 (b, 0)$ thus, $(D(\hat{f}|b, \hat{g}|b), T(\hat{f}|b, \hat{g}|b)) \succsim_2 (b, 0)$ and by (A-2) $(D(\hat{f}|b, \hat{g}|b), 1) \succsim_2 (b, 0)$ and therefore $D(\hat{f}|b, \hat{g}|b)$ is the desirable $c$.
    Similarly, it is easy to prove the following lemma.

LEMMA 2:    *For all $a \in B$ and for all $b \in S$ such that $b < a$, there is $c \in A$ such that $(c, 1) \succsim_1 (b, 0)$.*

LEMMA 3:   *Let $a \in A$. Then for all $b$ such that $(b,1) >_2 (a,0)$ there is $c \in A$ such that $(c,1) \gtrsim_1 (b,0)$.*

REMARK   Lemma 3 states that if $a$ is a P.E.P. then 1 should have a "good reason" to reject any offer from 2 which is preferred by 2 to accepting 1's original offer. Assume that in a certain P.E., player 2 plans to agree to $a$ in the first period (case B below). Consider $b$ such that $(b,1) >_2 (a,0)$. Then, player 2 will reject $a$ if he thinks that 1 would agree to $b$. Thus player 1 must threaten to reject any such offer $b$. In order that this threat be credible there must be a P.E. in the subgame beginning with 1's offer which yields an agreement $c$ such that $(c,1) \gtrsim_1 (b,0)$. This $c$ must be a member of $A$.

PROOF   Let $(\hat{f}, \hat{g})$ be a P.E. such that $D(\hat{f}, \hat{g}) = a$.
   *Case A*: $\hat{g}^1(\hat{f}^1) = N$. Let $\hat{f}^1 = s$. Then $D(\hat{f}|s, \hat{g}|s) = a$ and $a \in B$. From (A-1) and (A-2), if $(b,2) >_2 (a,1)$ then $b < a$ and therefore from Lemma 2 there is $c \in A$ such that $(c,1) \gtrsim_1 (b,0)$.
   *Case B*: $\hat{f}^1 = a, \hat{g}^1(a) = Y$. Let $b$ satisfy $(b, 1) >_2 (a, 0)$, $\hat{f}^2(a,b) = N$, because otherwise, for any $f \in F$ satisfying $f^1 = b, P(\hat{f}|a,f) = (b,1) >_2 (a, 0)$, in contradiction to (P-2). From (P-6), $P(\hat{f}|a,b,\hat{g}|a,b) \gtrsim_1 (b, 0)$. Thus $(D(\hat{f}|a,b,\hat{g}|a,b), 1) \gtrsim_1 (b, 0)$ and $D(\hat{f}|a,b,\hat{g}|a,b) \in A$.

In a similar way it is possible to prove the following lemma.

LEMMA 4: *For all $a \in B$ and for all $b \in S$ such that $(b,1) >_1 (a,0)$ there is $c \in B$ such that $(c,1) \gtrsim_2 (b,0)$.*

## 5.   The Theorem

Let

$$\Delta = \left\{ (x,y) \in S \times S \,\middle|\, \begin{array}{l} y \text{ is the smallest number such that } (x,1) \lesssim_1 (y,0); \\ x \text{ is the largest number such that } (y,1) \lesssim_2 (x,0) \end{array} \right\},$$

$$\Delta_1 = \{x \in S | \text{there is } y \in S \text{ such that } (x,y) \in \Delta\},$$

$$\Delta_2 = \{y \in S | \text{there is } x \in S \text{ such that } (x,y) \in \Delta\}.$$

PROPOSITION 1: *If $(x,y) \in \Delta$, then $x \in A$ and $y \in B$.*

PROOF   Consider the following $(\hat{f}, \hat{g})$; for $t$ odd

$$\hat{f}^t \equiv x, \quad \hat{g}^t(s^1 \ldots s^t) = \begin{cases} N, & x < s^t, \\ Y, & s^t \le x, \end{cases}$$

and for $t$ even

$$\hat{f}^t(s^1 \ldots s^t) = \begin{cases} N, & s^t < y, \\ Y, & y \le s^t, \end{cases} \quad \hat{g} \equiv y$$

It is easy to check that $(\hat{f}, \hat{g})$ is a perfect equilibrium.

PROPOSITION 2: $\Delta \ne \phi$ (and therefore $A$ and $B$ are not empty).

PROOF Let

$$d_1(x) = \begin{cases} 0 & \text{if for all } y \; (y, 0) >_1 (x, 1), \\ y & \text{if there exists } y, (y, 0) \sim_1 (x, 1), \end{cases}$$

and

$$d_2(y) = \begin{cases} 1 & \text{if for all } x \; (x, 0) >_2 (y, 1), \\ x & \text{if there exists } x, (x, 0) \sim_2 (y, 1) \end{cases}$$

$d_1(x)$ is the smallest $y$ such that $(y, 0) \gtrsim_1 (x, 1)$ and $d_2(y)$ is the largest $x$ such that $(x, 0) \gtrsim_2 (y, 1)$. Therefore

$$\Delta = \{(x, y) | y = d_1(x) \text{ and } x = d_2(y)$$

It is easy to check that $d_1$ (and $d_2$) is well defined, continuous, increasing, and strictly increasing where $d_1(x) > 0 \; (d_2(y) < 1)$.

Let $D(x) = d_2(d_1(x))$. Thus, $\Delta = \{(x, y) | y = d_1(x) \text{ and } D(x) = x\}$. Notice that $D(1) \le 1$ and $D(0) \ge 0$. From the continuity of $D$ it follows that there exists $x_0$ such that $D(x_0) = x_0$. Thus, $(x_0, d_1(x_0)) \in \Delta$. [See Figure 1.]

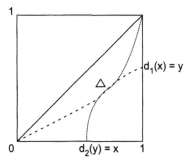

Figure 1

PROPOSITION 3: *The graph of* $\Delta$ *is a closed line segment which lies parallel to the diagonal* $y = x$.

PROOF   From the continuity of $d_1$ and $d_2$, the set $\Delta$ is closed. Notice that $x - d_1(x)$ is an increasing function. To see this, let $x_0$ satisfy $(0,0) \sim_1 (x_0, 1)$ (take $x_0 = 1$ if there is no $x$ that satisfies $(0,0) \sim_1 (x, 1)$). For $x \leq x_0$, $d_1(x) = 0$ and $x - d_1(x) = x$. For $x_1 > x_2 \geq x_0$, $(d_1(x_1), 0) \sim_1 (x_1, 1)$ and $(d_1(x_2), 0) \sim_2 (x_2, 1)$. The function $d_1$ is an increasing function. Thus, (A-5) implies $x_1 - d_1(x_1) \geq x_2 - d_1(x_2)$. Similarly, $d_2(y) - y$ is a decreasing function. We have to show that $x - y$ is constant for all $(x, y) \in \Delta$. Suppose that $x_2 < x_1$ and that $(x_1, y_1)$ and $(x_2, y_2)$ are both in $\Delta$. Then $x_1 - d_1(x_1) \geq x_2 - d_1(x_2)$ and $x_1 - y_1 \geq x_2 - y_2$.   Also $d_2(y_1) - y_1 \leq d_2(y_2) - y_2$   and   $x_1 - y_1 \leq x_2 - y_2$.   Thus $x_1 - y_1 = x_2 - y_2$.

PROPOSITION 4: *If* $a \in A$, *then* $a \in \Delta_1$, *and if* $b \in B$, *then* $b \in \Delta_2$.

PROOF   Suppose $\Delta_1 = [x_1, x_2]$ and $\Delta_2 = [y_1, y_2]$. Let $s = \sup\{a \in A\}$. Assume $x_2 < s$. Then $d_2(d_1(s)) < s$. Let $a \in A$ satisfy $r = d_2(d_1(s)) < a < s$. Let $b \in S$ satisfy $d_2^{-1}(a) > b > d_1(s)$. Then $a > d_2(b)$ and $(b, 1) >_2 (a, 0)$. From Lemma 3 there exists $c \in A$ such that $(c, 1) \gtrsim_1 (b, 0)$. Therefore there exists $c \in A$ satisfying $d_1(c) \geq b$. The facts that $d_1$ is an increasing function and that $d_1(c) \geq b > d_1(s)$ imply $c > s$ in contradiction to the definition of $s$.

Similarly, using Lemma 4 it is possible to show that $y_1 = \inf\{b \in B\}$. Using Lemmas 1 and 2 we get $x_1 = \inf\{a \in A\}$ and $y_2 = \sup\{b \in B\}$.

To summarize:

THEOREM: $A = \Delta_1 \neq \phi, B = \Delta_2 \neq \phi$. *A and B are closed intervals and there exists* $\epsilon \geq 0$ *such that* $B = A - \epsilon$.

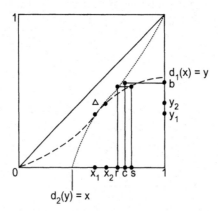

**Figure 2**

## 6. Conclusions

The following are applications of the theorem to the fixed bargaining cost and the fixed discounting factor models.

CONCLUSION 1: In the case where both the players have fixed bargaining costs, $c_1$ and $c_2$ (case I in the introduction):
(1) If $c_1 > c_2, c_2$ is the only P.E.P.
(2) If $c_1 = c_2$, every $c_1 \leqq x \leqq 1$ is a P.E.P.
(3) If $c_1 < c_2$, 1 is the only P.E.P.

PROOF   $d_1(x) = \max \{x - c_1, 0\}$ and $d_2(y) = \min \{y + c_2, 1\}$. Thus $\Delta$ is the set of all solutions to the set of equations $y = \max \{x - c_1, 0\}$ and $x = \min\{y + c_2, 1\}$. The conclusion is implied by the three diagrams of Fig. 3 related to the cases (1) $c_1 > c_2$, (2) $c_1 = c_2$, and (3) $c_1 < c_2$.

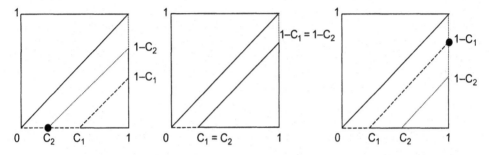

**Figure 3**

REMARK   Given a particular P.E., is agreement reached immediately after the very first offer? A positive answer results when $A \cap B = \phi$. If $(\hat{f}, \hat{g})$ is a P.E. and $T(\hat{f}, \hat{g}) > 1$, then $D(\hat{f}, \hat{g})$ is a member not only of $A$ but also of $B$. Thus in almost all cases covered by Conclusions 1 and 2 (the possible exception being the case $c_1 = c_2$ in Conclusion 1) the bargaining indeed ends in the first period.
   The following pair of strategies $(\hat{f}, \hat{g})$ is an example of a P.E. in the game where the players have fixed bargaining costs $c_1 = c_2 = c$. The pair $(\hat{f}, \hat{g})$ has the property that the negotiation ends at the second period: Let $\varepsilon(x)$ be a non-negative function defined in the unit interval such that $\varepsilon(x) \leqq \max\{0, x - c\}$. Assume $\varepsilon(x)$ attains its maximum at $x_0$ where $x_0 > 2c$ and $\varepsilon(x_0) > 2c$. Let $(\hat{f}, \hat{g})$ satisfy

$$\hat{f}^1 = x_0,$$

$$\hat{g}^1(s^1) = \begin{cases} N, & c < s^1, \\ Y, & s^1 \leqq c, \end{cases}$$

and "after," the strategies are identical to the strategies described in Proposition 1 for the partition $\varepsilon(s^1)$. The partition of this P.E. is $\varepsilon(x_0)$ (Figure 4).

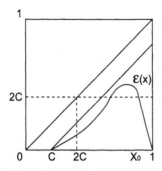

**Figure 4**

In this example the first move by player 1 serves as a signal to player 2. Player 2 interprets 1's signal $s^1$ as an agreement to continue with a pair of strategies that yields the partition $\varepsilon(s^1)$. Not every $s^1$ may serve as such a signal, since 2 will agree to every partition that gives 2 more than $1 - c$. The partition $\varepsilon(s^1)$ must give 2 at least $1 - s^1 + c$; therefore $\varepsilon(s^1)s^1 - c$. A final restriction on $\varepsilon$ is that $x_0 \geqq 2c$. Otherwise 1 would prefer to offer a partition that 2 "could not refuse" (some offer between $c$ and $x_0 - c$). This also shows that the P.E. outcome may not be Pareto optimal; both players prefer to agree to $1 - \varepsilon(x_0)$ at the beginning of the bargaining.

CONCLUSION 2:   In the case where the players have fixed discounting factors – $\delta_1$ and $\delta_2$ (Case II in the introduction) – if at least one of the $\delta_1$ is strictly less than 1 and at least one of them is strictly positive, then the only P.E.P. is $M = (1 - \delta_2)/(1 - \delta_1\delta_2)$.

REMARK   Notice that when $\delta_2 = 0$, player 2 has no threat because the pie has no worth for him after the first period. Player 1 can exploit this to get all the pie ($M = 1$). When $\delta_1 = 0$, 1 can gain $1 - \delta_2$ only, that is, the proportion of the pie that 2 may lose if he refuses 1's offer and gets 1 in the second period. When $0 < \delta_1 = \delta_2 = \delta < 1$, 1 gets $1/1 + \delta > 1/2$. As one would expect, 1's gain from the fact that he starts the bargaining decreases as $\delta$ tends to 1.

PROOF   $d_1(x) = x \cdot \delta_1$ and $d_2(y) = 1 - \delta_2 + \delta_2 \cdot y$. The conclusion follows from Figure 5 (the intersection of $d_1$ and $d_2$ is where $1 - \delta_2 + \delta_2 x \delta_1 = x$, that is where $x = M$).

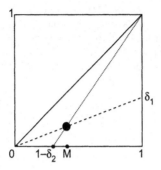

**Figure 5**

*References*

[1] AUMANN, R. J., and L. SHAPLEY: "Long Term Competition: A Game Theoretic Analysis," 1976, unpublished manuscript, Stanford University.

[2] BINMORE, K. G.: "Nash Bargaining Theory I," International Center for Economics and Related Disciplines, London School of Economics, Discussion Paper 80–09, 1980.

[3] CROSS, J. G.: "A Theory of the Bargaining Process," *American Economic Review*, 55(1965), 67–94.

[4] EDGEWORTH, F. Y.: "*Mathematical Psychics: An Essay on the Applications of Mathematics to the Moral Sciences*," L.S.E. Series of Reprints of Scarce Tracts in Economics and Political Sciences, No. 10, 1932.

[5] HARSANYI, J. C.: "A Solution Theory for Non-cooperative Games and its Implications for Cooperative Games," Center for Research in Management Science, University of California, Berkeley, CP-401, 1978.

[6] HARSANYI, J. C., and R. SELTEN: "A Generalized Nash Solution for Two Person Bargaining Games with Incomplete Information," *Management Science*, 18(1972), 80–106.

[7] KRELLE, W.: "A New Theory of Bargaining," unpublished manuscript, 1975.

[8] KURZ, M.: "Altruism as an Outcome of Social Interaction," *American Economic Review*, 68(1978), 216–222.

[9] LUCE, R. P., and H. RAIFFA: *Games and Decisions*, New York: John Wiley and Sons, 1957.

[10] NASH, J. F.: "The Bargaining Problem," *Econometrica*, 18(1950), 155–162.

[11] ———:"Two-person Cooperative Games," *Econometrica*, 21(1953), 128–140.

[12] RICE, P.: "A Note on the Hicks Theory of Strike Bargaining," *Zeitschsrift fur die Gesamte Staatswissenschaft*, 133(1977), 236–244.

[13] ROTH, A. E.: *Axiomatic Models of Bargaining*, Lecture Notes in Economics and Mathematical Systems No. 170. Berlin: Springer-Verlag, 1979.

[14] RUBINSTEIN, A.: "Equilibrium in Supergames," Center for Research in Math. Economics and Game Theory, the Hebrew University, Jerusalem, Israel, R.M. 25, 1977.

[15] ———: "Equilibrium in Supergames with the Overtaking Criterion," *Journal of Economic Theory*, 21 (1979), 1–9.

[16] ———: "Strong Perfect Equilibrium," *International Journal of Game Theory*, 9(1980), 1–12.

[17] SELTEN, R.: "Spieltheoretische Behandlung eines Oligopolmodels mit Nachfragetragheit," *Zeitschrift fur die Gesamte Staatswissenschaft*, 12(1965), 301–324 and 667–689.

[18] ——: "Re-examination of the Perfectness Concept for Equilibrium Points in Extensive Games," *International Journal of Game Theory*, 4(1975), 25–55.

[19] STÅHL, I.: *Bargaining Theory*. Stockholm: Stockholm School of Economics, 1972.

[20] ——: "An *N*-Person Bargaining Game in the Extensive Form," in *Mathematical Economics and Game Theory*, ed. by R. Henn and O. Moeschlin, Lecture Notes in Economics and Mathematical Systems No. 141. Berlin: Springer-Verlag, 1977.

# FIFTY-FIVE

# UPS Faces More Than $1 Billion a Year in New Labor Expenses: Pact Calls for Substantial Pay Increases, Full-Time Jobs and a Union Pension Plan

Douglas A. Blackmon, Martha Brannigan, Glenn Burkins, and Laura Jereski

Source: Wall Street Journal, August 20, 1997. © 1997 Dow Jones & Company Inc. All Rights Reserved.

United Parcel Service of America Inc. faces new labor costs that, within three years, will total more than $1 billion a year as a result of its tentative settlement with the Teamsters to end a 15-day strike. The new contract, which provides for substantial pay increases for full-time and part-time workers and the creation of thousands of new full-time jobs, was approved by union officials. Under the labor accord, UPS abandoned its proposal to withdraw from 21 multiemployer pension plans operated by the union. The Teamsters, in turn, agreed to a five-year contract instead of a three-year pact. The pact still faces a mail-in ratification vote by the union rank and file over the next month. But workers began returning to their jobs, and UPS hopes to restart the engines of its sprawling shipping network over the next few days.

### UPS May Have Blinked

It appeared that it was UPS that blinked in the face of revenue losses totaling more than $600 million since the start of the strike Aug. 4. As a result, the company has estimated that as many as 15,000 of the 185,000 Teamsters employed at UPS might be laid off at least temporarily if business lost to the strike isn't regained.

A blistering media campaign by the union that marshaled public opinion behind the striking workers also put pressure on the package-delivery concern. And Teamsters

President Ron Carey wasted no time after the agreement was reached late Monday to declare victory for the union and begin expanding his theme that "part-time America doesn't work." Mr. Carey said the final terms of the agreement proved that he was right last week when he refused to let union members vote on what the company was then calling it: "last, best and final offer."

"In virtually every area, this agreement is much better than the last offer before the strike," he said. Tuesday, on Mr. Carey vowed to take his campaign against part-time jobs to other big companies, including largely nonunion Federal Express Corp., where the Teamsters have been aggressively working to organize.

## "Nothing but Losers"

UPS officials spent much of Tuesday denying that the company had surrendered to Teamster demands, saying that the total cost of the deal it struck was little different from what the company offered days before the strike began. "There are nothing but losers," said UPS Chairman and Chief Executive Officer James P. Kelly. "We lost. Our people lost, and our customers lost." UPS said it hasn't yet calculated what effect the increased labor costs will have on its pricing, although analysts say the company will almost certainly be forced to raise prices in the face of the additional costs. The company traditionally raises prices at the beginning of each calendar year.

UPS says its labor costs for all employees total approximately 60 percent of annual revenue, or about $13.4 billion. The company wouldn't disclose a total value for the agreement reached with the Teamsters. However, Mr. Kelly said the new pact will add "hundreds of millions of dollars" a year in costs during the first year of the contract. That will rise to more than $500 million annually in the second year, he said, and in the final three years of the contract, the additional annual costs will exceed "perhaps a billion" dollars.

In 1996, the company's net income totaled $1.15 billion on revenue of $22.4 billion. UPS officials said the total costs of the agreement are similar to an informal proposal put on the negotiating table just before the union contract expired on July 31. When no agreement was reached on that offer, UPS says, it made a revamped "last, best" proposal and hunkered down for a long fight.

Thus, UPS executives reject the Teamsters' claim of victory, saying instead that the walkout gained little for either side, and that the same agreement could have been reached 10 days ago.

## UPS Gains Concessions

To be sure, the agreement gives concessions to UPS that are critical to its global campaign to keep in step with Federal Express, its aggressively expanding, Memphis, Tenn., rival. Wages and benefits, for instance, were held to lower levels than originally hoped for by the union. And the five-year term of the contract, called "tremendously important" by Mr. Kelly, gives UPS a free pass on Teamster negotiations into the next century. But on the issue of withdrawing from multiemployer pension funds controlled by the union, an issue on which UPS had said it wouldn't budge, the company surrendered, as it has done in each of the previous contract talks, in which the same issue was raised. Mr. Kelly called the issue the company's biggest concession.

During the height of negotiations, Mr. Kelly had described the pension issue, in which the company proposed starting its own pension program exclusively for UPS workers, as the single-biggest stumbling block separating the two sides. Tuesday, he played down its significance. "I can assure you," he said, "there was no single issue that was more important than those dozens of other issues that existed during these negotiations." UPS, which had said it would make a $700 million lump-sum contribution in order to withdraw from the multiemployer funds, said that over time, the company would have reduced its annual costs while improving the benefits paid to retired Teamsters. In the new pact, UPS agreed instead to redistribute that $700 million through wage boosts and other benefits.

UPS also gave in on the full-time-jobs issue. The tentative agreement calls for the company to create at least 10,000 full-time jobs for current part-time workers over the five-year life of the pact. UPS had proposed creating only 1,000 such jobs in its last official offer.

Here are some of the key contract provisions:

WAGES   Under the tentative accord, current full-time employees will receive raises of about $3.10 an hour, an average increase totaling 15 percent over five years, or roughly 3 percent a year, the company said. The full-time workers' wages will increase to an average of $23.11 an hour from the current $20.01 an hour, UPS said. The new contract would also raise part-time employees' wages by as much as $4.10 an hour over the life of the contract, a raise of 35 percent total, or an average of 7 percent per year. A part-time employee's wages would increase on average to $15.10 an hour, from $11 an hour currently.

The pay increases in the tentative contract are significantly higher than the company's "final" offer, which proposed to raise full-time wages by $1.50 an hour and part-time wages by at least $2.50 an hour over five years. But the tentative accord includes no profit-sharing provision. The company's proposal would have paid profit sharing of $3,060 to full-time workers and $1,530 to part-time workers in 1997, with a second installment to be paid in the year 2000 based on 1999 profit margins. Instead the funds slated for profit sharing have been folded into other wages and benefits.

FULL-TIME JOBS FOR PART-TIMERS   The tentative contract calls for creating 10,000 new full-time jobs, at an average rate of 2,000 jobs each year over the five-year contract. The company also agreed to move some 10,000 part-time workers into full-time jobs as they open up through attrition and growth. The company earlier had been offering to provide 11,000 full-time jobs over five years, but 10,000 of those positions were to come from attrition and growth and only 1,000 from newly created full-time slots.

With about 57 percent of the UPS labor force working part time, the union had said it wanted 10,000 new full-time jobs over the next four years for part-timers, many of whom have worked at the company many years but are still on a part-time status. The new full-time jobs UPS will be providing will be created by guaranteeing eight-hour workdays to employees, some of whom now work nearly full-time anyway by shuttling between two or more part-time jobs, said Ken Sternad, a UPS spokesman. For example, some workers load packages into trucks at UPS facilities and then drive a UPS air-express truck. Currently, they are paid different hourly wages for each task and aren't guaranteed a full-time work schedule.

For those new "full-time" workers doing combined tasks, the contract provides an eight-hour workday at a new wage scale that will be $15 an hour and then increase to $17.50 an hour over five years, according to Teamsters' spokesman Rand Wilson. As full-time workers, these employees will also receive better pension and health benefits, he said.

PENSION FUND  UPS will provide higher contributions to the existing Teamster-controlled pension plan. Mr. Sternad, the UPS spokesman, said it will be up to the trustees of the 21 Teamster plans to determine any improvements in benefits.

Mr. Wilson concedes that Mr. Carey, the Teamsters president, has had difficulty spurring trustees of various local and regional pension funds to improve benefits to retirees, which was one of his campaign pledges. "Mr. Carey has over the course of his reform administration wrestled with trustees to get them to increase benefits, but he's quite happy with the commitment the funds have made," Mr. Wilson said. He said the Teamsters expect to "meet or exceed" the benefit levels that UPS was offering in its proposed contract.

Even with the tentative settlement with the Teamsters, UPS still faces another worrisome labor issue. Contract talks with the Independent Pilots Association, a union representing the company's 2,100 pilots, are set to resume in the next few weeks, under the auspices of a federal mediator. The pilots, who refused to fly during the Teamsters walkout, have already authorized a strike if no accord is reached quickly. If the pilots strike, the Teamsters have pledged to back them. UPS officials won't discuss the pilot talks, but have said they are confident a strike can be avoided.

The agreement with the Teamsters should minimize the drama surrounding the quarterly meeting set for Wednesday of UPS's 13-member board of directors. The board, made up mostly of current and retired UPS executives, will set a new price for shares of UPS, which aren't publicly traded. The stock, currently priced at $30.50 per share, is owned principally by employees and retirees of the company, and its price has never been lowered. Without the strike, a UPS spokesman said, the board will discuss where the business is heading, how we're going to win back customers. There's quite a bit to address.

## The UPS Strike: What the Sides Wanted, What They Got

|  | UPS | Teamsters | Tentative 5-Year Contract |
|---|---|---|---|
| Jobs | Create 11,000 full-time jobs over five years for current part-time workers; 1,000 new, 10,000 open through attrition and growth | Create 10,000 new full-time positions over four years; open another 10,000 full-time jobs to part-timers through attrition and growth | Create 10,000 full-time jobs over five years by combining tasks currently done by part-time workers. Open another 10,000 full-time jobs to part-timers over five years, contingent on attrition and growth. The new full-time job classification for sorters, loaders, and the like, will pay less than existing full-time jobs, which are held by drivers. |
| Pension | Its own pension system, managed by both the company and union.<br>– Full-time: receive $100 a month in retirement benefits for every year of credited service<br>– Part-time: $50 a month for every year of service | Retain the current pension system, in which UPS makes contributions to 31 union-run local and regional pension funds. | Preserves current multi-employer system, with UPS providing additional contributions to the pension and health and welfare systems |
| Wages/Profit Sharing | *Pay increases over five years:*<br>– Full-time: $1.50 an hour<br>– Part-time: at least $2.50 an hourt<br><br>*Profit sharing*<br>– Full-time: installment of $3,060 in 1997, and a second installment in 2000 based on 1999 profit margins.<br>– Part-time: $1,530 upon ratification of the contract and a second payment in 2000 based on 1999 profit margins. | *Pay increases over four years:*<br>–Full-time: $2.60 an hour<br>–Part-time: $3.60 an hour; 50-cent increase in the starting rate<br><br><br><br>*No profit-sharing proposal* | *Pay increases over five years:*<br>– Full-time: $3.10 an hour, an increase of 15 percent total; boosts average driver to $23.11 an hour from $20.01<br>– Part-time: $4.10 an hour, a total of 35 percent; an increase of 50 cents an hour in the starting wage to $8.50 an hour.<br><br>*No profit-sharing provision* |

# FIFTY-SIX

# "Whatever Happened to *Elegant* Solutions?"

SIDNEY HARRIS

*Source*: © 2000 by Sidney Harris.

"Whatever happened to *elegant* solutions?"

# PART THIRTEEN
# Auctions

# Introduction

Auctions are the opposite of bargaining: in an auction, two players compete against each other, to the advantage of a player on the other side of the market. Other situations, however, are like auctions even though there is no "other side of the market." Shubik's dollar auction is a simple paradigm for this, useful in thinking about rent-seeking, patent races, and other tournaments. It also applies to arms races: see Barry O'Neill, "International Escalation and the Dollar Auction," *Journal of Conflict Resolution* 30: 33–50 (1986). Shubik discusses the problem of collusion in the dollar auction, which for that particular auction is actually to the social good, except for the seller. In most auctions, however, collusion is as pernicious as in oligopolies. The antique market is an interesting example, because antique auctions have a mix of sophisticated repeat players – the professional dealers – and unsophisticated one-time players – direct consumers.

Governments have often used auctions in procurement and in selling securities, but economists have urged them to use auctions more in sales of natural assets and privileges. The FCC airwaves auctions are the result of decades of such urging. In the *Journal of Economic Perspectives* article, McAfee and McMillan describe the choice of auction rules and the bidding that resulted. The cartoon, "The next item up for bid is the presidency of the United States . . . " raises a good question for the economist: Why not? Tax farming – the right to collect taxes – has often been sold by government in past centuries. Seats on the boards of directors of corporations are effectively sold via shares' voting rights. So why not sell off what are now elected offices?

# FIFTY-SEVEN

# The Dollar Auction Game: A Paradox in Noncooperative Behavior and Escalation

MARTIN SHUBIK

Source: *Journal of Conflict Resolution* 15 (March), 1971, pp. 109–11.
Reprinted by permission of Sage Publications Inc., Thousand Oaks.

## The Game

There is an extremely simple, highly amusing, and instructive parlor game which can be played at any party by arranging for the auction of a dollar. This game illustrates some of the difficulties with the noncooperative equilibrium concept and games in extensive form (von Neuman and Morgenstern, 1945).

The game is simplicity itself and is usually highly profitable to its promoter. The auctioneer auctions off a dollar bill to the highest bidder, with the understanding that *both* the highest bidder and the second highest bidder will pay. For example, if A has bid 10 cents and B has bid 15 cents, then the auctioneer will obtain 25 cents, pay a dollar to B, and A will be out 10 cents.

Suppose that bids must be made in multiples of 5 cents. Furthermore, suppose that the game ends if no one bids for a specific length of time. Ties are resolved in favor of the bidder closest to the auctioneer.

These rules completely specify the game except for a finite end rule; i.e., as specified, bidding could conceivably never cease. We could add an upper limit to the amount that anyone is permitted to bid. However, the analysis is confined to the (possibly infinite) game without a specific termination point, as no particularly interesting general phenomena appear if an upper bound is introduced.

In playing this game, a large crowd is desirable. Furthermore, experience has indicated that the best time is during a party when spirits are high and the propensity to calculate does not settle in until at least two bids have been made. For the purposes of the discussion and analysis, we limit ourselves to an auctioneer and two bidders, as the basic difficulties with this game can be illustrated at this level.

Let us assume that the auction has started, A has bid 5 cents and B has raised to 10 cents. By raising to 15 cents, A stands to gain 85 cents; by standing pat, he will certainly lose 5 cents. This argument holds (with modifications on gains and losses) at any stage. In particular, a turning point in the game occurs when the bidding stands with, say, A having a bid of 50 cents and B with a bid of 45 cents. At that point, it may appear to B that he should bid 55 cents and take his chances, rather than take a certain loss of 45 cents. If B bids 55 cents, then a critical zone has been passed for the auctioneer. No matter what happens to bidding, he will always make money, as the sum of the two top bids is now larger than a dollar.

The next critical zone appears in its most spectacular form when one of the bids is at a dollar. Suppose that B had bid one dollar, and A had previously bid 80 cents. At this point, A may elect to bid $1.05 rather than lose 80 cents with certainty. Beyond this point, both bidders will be losing, but still may escalate their bids in order to cut down on losses.

Once two bids have been obtained from the crowd, the paradox of escalation is real. Experience with the game has shown that it is possible to "sell" a dollar bill for considerably more than a dollar. A total of payments between three and five dollars is not uncommon.

## Some Formal Analysis

Considering the auction with an auctioneer and two bidders; this can be viewed as a three person constant-sum game. Let the auctioneer be Player 1 and the bidders, players 2 and 3. The characteristic function (von Neuman and Morgenstern, 1945) is:

$$V(1) = -95 \text{ cents}, \ V(2) = V(3) = 0;$$

$$V(1, 2) = 0, V(1, 3) = 0, V(2, 3) = 95 \text{ cents};$$

$$V(1, 2, 3) = 0.$$

The auctioneer cannot prevent a loss of 95 cents to himself if the two bidders form a coalition with one bidding 5 cents and the other refraining from bidding. Any coalition involving the auctioneer and only some bidders can obtain nothing. For any size of game, the only coalition that has a positive value is the one of all bidders.

When the auction is viewed as a cooperative game, it is evident that the auctioneer is at a disadvantage. When we switch to a noncooperative analysis, the locus of the disadvantage changes to the bidders.

There is a trivial and quite unsatisfactory noncooperative equilibrium point where the first bidder bids $1.00 as his opening bid and no one else bids. This yields a payoff of zero to all.

Another solution concept which points to a further difficulty with the equilibriums at the bid of $1.00 is that of:

$$\text{Max}-\text{Min} \ (P_A - P_B),$$

where $P_A$ and $P_B$ are the payoffs to bidders A and B respectively.

The "max–min the difference" solution can be considered in terms of a damage exchange rate. The bidders are concerned with their relative gains or losses rather than their absolute gains or losses.

Suppose that A had opened with a bid of $1.00. Then, for the cost of 5 cents, B can inflict damage of $1.00 on A by bidding $1.05. The damage exchange rate is 20 to 1. Unless there is an upper boundary to the bidding, there is no boundary to the escalation in the damage exchange rate.

## On Threats and Communication

The key to the understanding of the processes at work in this game is in communication conditions. Generally in a crowd the individuals bid independently. They do not have lengthy discussions with each other. Furthermore, they do not sign agreements and specify strategies.

If it were possible to specify one's complete strategy, the first bidder would bid 5 cents and say, "If anyone else bids, I will immediately bid $1.00 if he bids less; or I will bid 5 cents more than he, if he bids $1.00 or more." If the other bidders believe him, then this strategy will block them from bidding and he will gain 95 cents.

If there is no formal mechanism for precommitment, we would need to specify the degree of belief of the other bidders in order to check upon the stability of the market.

In fact the bidders do not communicate directly more than their immediate bid, with no contingent statement whatsoever, except whatever might be signaled by facial expression, tone of voice, or other acts associated with bidding. In this sequential process a person is required to "put your money where your mouth is." The only communication is the bid, and the only signals are the history of bidding in the auction. There is no option to go back upon your word, as you do not have a word to go back upon.

## Game Theory, Social-Psychology, Institutions and Escalation

This simple game is a paradigm for escalation. Once the contest has been joined, the odds are that the end will be a disaster to both. When this is played as a parlor game, this usually happens.

Can we generalize from this formal structure to interorganization fights or internation escalation? Only in a limited manner is the generalization useful. The internation negotiation has communication conditions considerably different from the parlor game. Signals and quasi-commitment are possible and common.

The game theory analysis of the game in extensive form shows us that the game theory model alone does not appear to be adequate. A general description of a typical play of the parlor game shows this. Why should anyone bid in the first place? Usually, it is because of fun or desire to participate in a parlor game rather than because of individualistic analysis.[1]

---

[1] Technically, it is not difficult to modify the game in such a manner that two individuals are randomly selected as having bid 5 cents and 10 cents respectively, thus starting the process.

Bidding proceeds fairly briskly until the point when the sum of the two top bids is greater than a dollar, after which a look of realization comes onto the faces of many participants. There is a pause and hesitation in the group when the bid goes through the one dollar barrier. From them on, there is a duel with bursts of speed until tension builds, bidding then slows and finally peters out.

The game's play appears to depend upon virtually only the social-psychology of the players, or other unstated factors of the environment in which it is played. It is far simpler than a real auction where the bidders need to evaluate the worth of items to themselves and others. It is even simpler than the Prisoner's Dilemma, where at least the concept of a $2 \times 2$ payoff matrix must be taught.

In bargaining between bureaucracies or nations, very often the negotiations are carried out by fiduciaries. Large time lags are present in the system. Furthermore, statements and explicit displays of intent concerning future behavior can be, and are, made. As much of the bargaining depends upon finding out one's own powers and wants as well as the powers and wants of the other side, the dynamics will be critically influenced by the perceptions and clarity of purpose of the negotiators.

There is no neat game theoretic solution to apply to the dynamics of the Dollar Auction, or to escalation between two nations *in abstracto*. The static game theory analysis is trivial, and although of some value, it is not enlightening concerning how to proceed from statics to dynamics.

The Dollar Auction is sufficiently simple that it may be a useful experimental game, as it contains an extremely simple aspect of escalation. Even were we to obtain clear results from such a study, it would be of only limited value in understanding escalation between nations. The latter requires a specific understanding of the mechanisms for the enforcement of agreement and the meaning of threat (Shubik, 1966). The game theoretic model for bargaining between nations must differ considerably from the Dollar Auction; and although a game theory analysis alone will probably never be adequate to explain such a process, it can serve to delimit the threat and enforcement possibilities.

### References

Shubik, M. Towards a theory of threats. In A. Mensch (ed.), *Proceedings of a Conference Under the Aegis of the NATO Scientific Committee, Toulon, June–July 1964*. London: English Universities Press, 1966.

von Neuman, J., and O. Morgenstern. *The Theory of Games and Economic Behavior*. Princeton, N.J.: Princeton University Press, 1945.

# FIFTY-EIGHT

# Analyzing the Airwaves Auction

## R. Preston McAfee and John McMillan

*Source*: *Journal of Economic Perspectives* 10(1), 1996, pp. 159–75. Reprinted with the permission of the authors and the American Economic Association. © American Economic Association.

Just as the Nobel committee was recognizing game theory's role in economics by awarding the 1994 prize to John Nash, John Harsanyi and Reinhard Selten, game theory was being put to its biggest use ever. Billions of dollars worth of spectrum licenses were being sold by the U.S. government, using a novel auction form designed by economic theorists. Suddenly, game theory became news. William Safire in the *New York Times* called it "the greatest auction in history." *The Economist* remarked, "When government auctioneers need worldly advice, where can they turn? To mathematical economists, of course. . . . As for the firms that want to get their hands on a sliver of the airwaves, their best bet is to go out first and hire themselves a good game theorist." *Fortune* said it was the "most dramatic example of game theory's new power. . . . It was a triumph, not only for the FCC and the taxpayers, but also for game theory (and game theorists)." *Forbes* said, "Game theory, long an intellectual pastime, came into its own as a business tool." The *Wall Street Journal* said, "Game theory is hot."[1]

The government auctioned licenses to use the electromagnetic spectrum for personal communications services (PCS): mobile telephones, two-way paging, portable fax machines and wireless computer networks. Thousands of licenses were offered, varying in both geographic coverage and the amount of spectrum covered. The bidders were the local, long-distance and cellular telephone companies, as well as paging and cable television companies and a host of smaller firms. The Federal Communications Commission (FCC) chose an innovative form of auction over the time-tested alternatives (like a sealed-bid auction), because theorists predicted it would induce more competitive bidding and a better match of licenses to firms.

The designing of the spectrum auction has been described in this journal by McMillan (1994).[2] In what follows, we examine how the auction actually worked. We describe the

---

[1] The citations for the quotations in this paragraph are *New York Times*, March 16, 1995, p. A17; *The Economist*, July 23, 1994, p. 70; *Fortune*, February 6, 1995, p. 36; *Forbes*, July 3, 1995, p. 62; *Wall Street Journal*, February 13, 1995, p. A19.

[2] For more on game theory's role in the design of the FCC auction, see Milgrom (1995). For more on auction performance and bidder strategies, see Cramton (1995a, b) and Salant (1995). On the case for using auctions to assign the spectrum, see McMillan (1995), and on the history and politics of spectrum allocation, see Hazlett (1995).

strategies used by the bidders, and analyze the success of the auction in realizing the government's goals. While theory was used in designing the auction, in turn the auction has stimulated further theorizing, as we discuss. We also propose some other potential uses of the auction form that the FCC pioneered.

## The Simultaneous Ascending Auction

In the 1993 legislation authorizing the FCC to hold auctions, Congress charged the FCC with encouraging an "efficient and intensive use of the electromagnetic spectrum." Congress also said the auction should advance various public-policy goals and in particular ensure some licenses went to minority-owned and women-owned firms. Congress said revenue raising was an aim of the auction, but gave it a low priority.

The auction the FCC adopted is a *simultaneous ascending auction*, first proposed by Paul Milgrom and Robert Wilson (consultants for Pacific Telesis) and Preston McAfee (a consultant for Air Touch Communications). Multiple licenses are open for bidding at the same time, and remain open as long as there is some bidding on any of the licenses. Bidding occurs over rounds, with the results of each round announced to the bidders before the start of the next. The auction is run by computer, with on-line bidding.

Many detailed rules are needed to support the broad principles of the simultaneous ascending auction. Months of work by FCC officials (Evan Kwerel's contribution to the design process was crucial) and the theorist-consultants (including John McMillan, who worked for the FCC) went into writing the auction rules to close any gaps that could be exploited by clever bidders: the rules, in FCC (1994), cover more than 130 pages. The most important of these details are the activity rules (devised by Milgrom and Wilson). A bidding firm might play cautiously, waiting to see how the others bid while not revealing its own intentions. If all bid in this way the auction would take inordinately long to close. The activity rules are designed to prevent the bidders from holding back, so the auction proceeds at a reasonable pace. Before the auction, each bidder must specify how many licenses it hopes to win and must post a proportionate bond. A bidder is defined to be active on a particular license if either it has the standing high bid from the previous round or it submits an acceptable bid in this round. The auction has three stages, each containing an unspecified number of bidding rounds. In the first stage a bidder must be active on licenses that add up to one-third of its desired total; in the second stage, two-thirds; and in the final stage, 100 percent. If a bidder ever falls short of the required activity level, the number of licenses it is eligible to own shrinks proportionately. There is no prespecified final round; instead, the auction closes when no one wants to continue bidding. Other rules define the size of bid increments, the penalties for bid withdrawal,[3] provisions for waivers from the activity rules, the length of time for a bidding round, and so on.

Why use a simultaneous ascending auction? Why not use the time-tested method, a sequential auction, in which the licenses are simply offered one after the other? Or why not use the quickest method, offering all the licenses simultaneously in a single round of sealed bids? The main reason is that the licenses are interdependent. For most of the

---

[3] The withdrawal penalty involved guaranteeing the price bid. If after the license was reoffered, the final price was less than the withdrawn bid, the bidder who withdrew owed a penalty equal to the difference.

licenses there is a close substitute: a twin license that covers the same region and the same amount of spectrum. Licenses are also complementary: a license may be more valuable if the holder also has the license for a contiguous region.

Efficiency in a spectrum auction – which means assigning the licenses to the firms best able to use them – requires that some bidders win multiple licenses, because of the license complementarities. The FCC did not know before the sale how the licenses should be aggregated: partly because the technology was new, but also because different bidders had different, mutually inconsistent preferred aggregations (for various reasons, such as their cellular-telephone holdings and local expertise). The simultaneous ascending auction was designed to let market processes establish the shape of the license aggregations.

Both features of the auction form – the *simultaneous* bids and the *ascending* bids – aid efficiency. The ascending bids let bidders see how highly their rivals value each license and which aggregations they are seeking. By the time equilibrium is approached, each bidding firm knows whether it is likely to be able to construct its preferred aggregation and roughly how much it is going to cost. With all licenses open for bidding simultaneously, a bidder has flexibility to seek whatever license aggregation it wishes, as well as to switch to a back-up aggregation if its first-choice aggregation becomes too expensive.

As well as aiding license aggregation, the ascending bidding, by allowing bidders to respond to each others' bids, diminishes the winner's curse: that is, the tendency for naive bidders to bid up the price beyond the license's actual value, or for shrewd bidders to bid cautiously to avoid overpaying. Also, ascending simultaneous bidding means it is likely that substitute licenses fetch similar prices, because bidders can switch across the substitutes if their bid prices differ, bidding up any lower-priced licenses.

The alternative auction forms do not assure either efficient aggregation or that similar items will fetch the same price.[4] A single-round, sealed-bid auction, for example, would almost certainly cause a poor match of licenses to firms. Bidders must bid blind, unable to know how high they must bid to win a particular license. Only by good luck would a bidding firm win all the licenses it needs for an efficient aggregation; bad luck could mean the firm wins more licenses than it needs. Also, the bidders' fear of the winner's curse induces more cautious bidding and lower prices than ascending bids would yield. The risk of winning too many licenses further induces low bidding from budget-constrained bidders. Simultaneous single-round, sealed-bid auctions were used in New Zealand for spectrum licenses and in Australia for satellite-television licenses, with disappointing results: low revenues and inefficient license allocations (McMillan, 1994).

Sequential auctions also have problems. First, identical items can sell for quite different prices: items sold later in the sequence typically fetch less than items sold earlier (Ashenfelter, 1989; McAfee and Vincent, 1993). Second, a firm might bid in a predatory manner, driving early prices unreasonably high to eliminate its budget-constrained rivals from the later bidding (Pitchik and Schotter, 1988). Third, and most important, the sequential form hinders license aggregation. In the early auctions, a firm must bid without knowing whether it will win complementary licenses offered later. Later, a firm may wish

---

[4] There was, however, considerable disagreement among the theorists involved in the design process, based on differing judgments about the sizes of various effects and the workability of the simultaneous ascending auction. Some advocated a sequential auction; others, an auction in which bidders could bid for license combinations, not just single licenses. On this debate, see McMillan's (1994) article in this journal.

to rebid on a license already sold if it discovers it needs that license to complete its set; but in a sequential auction it cannot go back. One of the pitfalls of the sequential auction is shown by the 1981 sale of seven identical licenses to use RCA's communications satellite for cable television broadcasts. Sotheby Parke Bernet ran a sequential auction. The winning bids varied widely. The highest (on the first license sold) was $14.4 million, and the lowest (the sixth license) was $10.7 million.[5] The FCC nullified the auction, saying the procedure was "unjustly discriminatory" in levying different prices for the same service, and ordered RCA to charge the same price to all. The inflexibility of the sequential auction caused the $3.7 million (or 26 percent) price difference. It would not have arisen had a simultaneous ascending auction been used, as price disparities would be bid away.[6]

After-market trading of licenses is permitted, subject to FCC approval, and such trading will assist in ultimately producing an efficient allocation of spectrum rights. But it is unrealistic to believe that the after-market can completely solve the allocation problem no matter what the initial allocation – which would mean the auction form would not matter – because it will be far from fully competitive. There will be few buyers and few sellers. Also, the firms possess private information about license values through their knowledge of customers, local conditions and technology. Modern theory shows that private information can hinder efficient trade (Akerlof, 1970; Myerson and Satterthwaite, 1983).

Persuaded of the superiority of the simultaneous ascending auction by the theorists, and of its workability by some experiments, the FCC decided to adopt it. The FCC's courage in using an untried mechanism devised by a set of mathematical economists was rewarded: the simultaneous ascending auction came to be widely regarded as a success.

## Auction Performance

Because of the logistical complexities of running a huge simultaneous auction, not all of the roughly 2,000 licenses were offered for sale at once. The FCC planned five auctions, each in the simultaneous ascending format. Three have been held at the time of this writing. The first two sold narrowband licenses, thin slivers of the spectrum to be used for paging services: nationwide licenses were sold in July 1994 and regional licenses in October 1994, covering 1.2 mHz of spectrum between them. The other auctions offer broadband licenses, which cover a wide enough slice of spectrum to be usable for voice and data mobile communications services. The third and largest auction, which ran from December 1994 to March 1995, sold 60 mHz of spectrum: two 30 mHz broadband licenses covering relatively large geographic areas (the "major trading areas," or MTAs, which divide the United States into 51 regions). The fourth and fifth auctions will each offer

---

[5] The story is told in several places: *PR Newswire*, November 9, 1981; *Christian Science Monitor*, June 29, 1982, p. 11; *Time*, December 13, 1982, p. 148.

[6] Prices sometimes rise rather than fall during a sequential auction. In Israel's 1987–1990 sequential auctions of cable television licenses, Gandal (1994) finds that the prices tended to be higher for licenses auctioned later. The competition seems to have intensified later, because by then some bidders held complementary licenses and so were willing to pay more. If a simultaneous ascending auction had been used instead, the earlier licenses may have been bid higher, and different bidders may have won the later licenses. Whether prices rise or fall, the uncertainty in a sequential auction creates difficulties for bidders, exacerbating the winner's curse and hindering efficient aggregation.

broadband licenses covering 30 mHz of spectrum over smaller areas (the "basic trading areas," or BTAs, which divide the United States into 492 regions).

The Office of Management and Budget estimated in 1993 that $10 billion would be paid for the broadband spectrum – enough to make a dent in the budget deficit. The industry's immediate response to this estimate was (possibly strategic) skepticism. BellSouth chairman John Clendenin said, "There is no rational methodology on which that $10 billion was calculated." The government estimate, he asserted, "was sort of pulled out of thin air" (and perhaps he was right). MCI chairman Bert Roberts said, "The government is smoking something to think they are going to get $10 billion for these licenses." As it turned out, however, the government's estimate was low.

"For once, the government is doing a great job of dragging money out of people," said Wayne Perry of McCaw Cellular Communications during the first auction. The two narrowband auctions raised over $1 billion, far more than most predictions. Then the broadband MTA auction attracted the big spenders: Wirelessco L.P. (a consortium of the Sprint Corp. with the cable television companies TCI, Comcast and Cox), which bid a total of $2.1 billion; the AT&T Corp., $1.7 billion; PCS Primeco L.P. (a consortium of Bell Atlantic, U.S. West, AirTouch and Nynex), $1.1 billion; and the Pacific Telesis Group (or PacTel), $0.7 billion. Selling half the 120 mHz of broadband spectrum, this auction raised $7.7 billion.[7]

The simultaneous ascending auction should yield similar prices for similar items. Did it? The nationwide narrowband auction priced similar licenses very closely (see Table 1: the five 100 kHz licenses are close substitutes, as are the three 65.5 kHz licenses and the two 50 kHz licenses). In the regional narrowband auction, prices for substitute licenses were similar, though not as close as in the nationwide auction (see Table 2: licenses 1 and 2 are substitutes, as are licenses 3, 4, 5 and 6). A price disparity existed across the two auctions, however: prices in the regional auction were higher than in the earlier nationwide auction (compare the last row of Table 2 with Table 1).

Prices were lower in the broadband MTA auction than in the narrowband auctions. The average broadband price per pop (that is, price per person covered by the license) was $15.51, which meant the price per mHz-pop was just 16 percent of the narrowband price. The lower prices had several sources. First, the broadband spectrum has intrinsically lower value, as some of it has incumbent users who will have to be moved. Second, the firms had budget constraints, the sums bid being large even for a firm as big as AT&T. Third, the competition was less intense, as the ratio of initially expressed demand to licenses for sale was just two-to-one.

The broadband prices varied greatly from license to license. The winners of the ten largest-population licenses are shown in Table 3. Highest in price per pop were Chicago ($31.90 and $30.88), Atlanta ($28.58 and $26.60) and Seattle ($27.79 and $27.48). Lowest in price per pop were Guam ($0.61 for both licenses) and Alaska ($1.82 and $3.00). Variations in price in part reflect regional variations in predicted demand for PCS services. The profitability of a license varies with income level, population density,

---

[7] The complete auction data, including round-by-round bids, can be found on the Internet at the FCC web server, www.fcc.gov. The $7.7 billion sum includes the revenue from the licenses awarded as "pioneer preferences." Before the auction the FCC awarded three MTA licenses – New York, Los Angeles and Washington D.C. – to three firms as a reward for developing new technologies. These firms paid concessionary prices based on the winning bids. (The quotations in the paragraph are from *Reuters Financial Report*, October 20, 1993, and *Wall Street Journal*, August 1, 1994, p. A1.)

predicted population growth and so on. There are also bidder-specific effects, such as home-base advantages for the local Bell companies or the ownership of a cellular license in a neighboring area. Some of the price differences, however, do not seem to be explained by value differences: for example, the Chicago price per pop is nearly twice New York and 20 percent higher than Los Angeles. Few bidders were eligible to bid on some licenses.

**Table 1**  Auction results for nationwide narrowband licenses

| Licence | Winning bid ($ millions) | Winning bidder |
|---------|--------------------------|----------------|
| 50/50 kHz | 80.0 | Paging Network of Virginia |
| 50/50 kHz | 80.0 | Paging Network of Virginia |
| 50/50 kHz | 80.0 | KDM Messaging Co. |
| 50/50 kHz | 80.0 | KDM Messaging Co. |
| 50/50 kHz | 80.0 | Nationwide Wireless Network Corp. |
| 50/12.5 kHz | 47.0 | AirTouch Paging |
| 50/12.5 kHz | 47.5 | BellSouth Wireless |
| 50/12.5 kHz | 47.5 | Nationwide Wireless Network Corp. |
| 50 kHz | 37.0 | Paging Network of Virginia |
| 50 kHz | 38.0 | Pagemart II, Inc. |
| Total | 617.0 | |

The 50/50 and 50/12.5 licenses each have two separated slices of spectrum, to allow two-way pager communication.
*Source*: FCC (1994).

**Table 2**  Auction results for regional narrowband licenses (*discounted final prices in millions and winning bidder by region and spectrum block*)

| Region/Block | 1 | 2 | 3 | 4 | 5 | 6 |
|--------------|-----|-----|--------|--------|--------|--------|
| (kHz) | (50/50) | (50/50) | (50/12.5) | (50/12.5) | (50/12.5) | (50/12.5) |
| Northeast | 17.5 | 14.9 | 9.5 | 9.0 | 8.7 | 10.3 |
|  | Pagemart | PCSD | Mobile | Am.W. | AirTouch | L.G.S. |
| South | 18.4 | 18.8 | 11.8 | 11.5 | 8.0 | 11.3 |
|  | Pagemart | PCSD | Mobile | Am.W. | Instacheck | L.G.S. |
| Midwest | 16.8 | 17.4 | 9.3 | 10.1 | 9.5 | 10.3 |
|  | Pagemart | PCSD | Mobile | Am.W. | Ameritech | L.G.S. |
| Central | 17.3 | 17.1 | 8.3 | 8.8 | 8.3 | 10.5 |
|  | Pagemart | PCSD | Mobile | Am.W. | AirTouch | Benbow |
| West | 22.6 | 22.8 | 14.9 | 14.3 | 14.3 | 10.9 |
|  | Pagemart | PCSD | Mobile | Am.W. | AirTouch | Benbow |
| Total | 92.6 | 90.9 | 53.7 | 53.6 | 48.7 | 53.2 |

Spectrum blocks 1 and 2 consisted of two 50 kHz channels; blocks 3, 4, 5 and 6 consisted of one 50 kHz and one 12.5 kHz channel. Spectrum blocks 2 and 6 had the 40 percent minority/woman credit; the prices shown for these two licenses are net of this discount. "PCSD" is the PCS Development Corp. "Mobile" is Mobilemedia, Inc. "Am.W." is American Wireless Messaging. "L.G.S." is Lisa-Gaye Shearing.
*Source*: FCC (1994).

**Table 3** Auction results for broadband MTA licenses (*top 10 licenses, winner and price bid in $ millions*)

| Region/Block | A | | B | |
|---|---|---|---|---|
| New York | [a] | | Wirelessco | 443 |
| Los Angeles | [a] | | PacTel | 494 |
| Chicago | AT&T | 373 | Primeco | 385 |
| San Francisco | Wirelessco | 207 | PacTel | 202 |
| Detroit | AT&T | 81 | Wirelessco | 86 |
| Charlotte | AT&T | 67 | BellSouth | 71 |
| Dallas | Primeco | 88 | Wirelessco | 88 |
| Boston | AT&T | 122 | Wirelessco | 127 |
| Philadelphia | AT&T | 81 | Phillieco | 85 |
| Washington | [a] | | AT&T | 212 |
| Total revenue: | $7.7 billion (including pioneer preference awards) | | | |

Wirelessco includes Sprint, TCI, Comcast and Cox. Primeco includes Bell Atlantic, US West, AirTouch and Nynex.
[a]Pioneer preference award.
*Source*: FCC (1994).

Chicago was the only license among the top ten for which all three of the big bidders competed: AT&T, Primeco and Wirelessco. Some of the price variations reflect differences in the strength of competition.

Revenue is not the only criterion for evaluating the FCC auctions; it is not even the main goal. Another criterion is whether the auctions generated an economically efficient allocation; that is, assigned the licenses to the firms best able to use them, given the complementarities among licenses and the gains from aggregations.

Only time will tell whether the auctions put the licenses into the hands of the right firms. The secondary market will give some evidence. A large number of licenses being resold would suggest that the auction had produced an inefficient allocation. Little secondary-market activity would not provide decisive evidence of efficiency, however, because the secondary market will be thin, with few players and large informational asymmetries, and cannot be expected to work smoothly. Conclusive evidence on the efficiency of the auction outcome will come only after the firms have their mobile-communications services operating, which will take several years. The bid data do, however, allow us to speculate on whether the simultaneous ascending auction allowed the bidders to construct efficient license aggregations.

For the regional narrowband auction, the FCC divided the country into five regions, with six licenses in each. Four bidders – Pagemart, PCS Development Corp., Mobilemedia, Inc., and American Wireless Messaging – assembled nationwide licenses, winning all five licenses in a particular wavelength. Also, two bidders built consistent subnational aggregations: AirTouch won three of the licenses on one waveband, and Lisa-Gaye Shearing won three on another (see Table 2). This suggests that the auction did enable the bidders to build their desired aggregations.

Did the bidders in the broadband MTA auction achieve efficient aggregations? PacTel won the aggregation that it had made no secret it was seeking: northern plus southern

California. The other three big bidders appeared to bid for the licenses that filled gaps in their cellular holdings.[8] They did not fill all of their gaps, but they came close. Of the 46 contiguous-U.S. licenses, when previous cellular holdings are added to the new PCS winnings, AT&T owns 40, Wirelessco owns 39 and Primeco owns 38. Each of these firms holds cellular or PCS licenses in each of the top ten markets (with the exception of Wirelessco's missing Chicago, since all three competed for the two Chicago licenses).

The bid data suggest, then, that the auctions facilitated license aggregation. The bidders agreed. After the broadband auction, Primeco president George F. Schmitt said his group expected to have a complete nationwide network operating within two years. Steven Hooper, chairman of AT&T's mobile-telephone subsidiary, said, "This enables us to build a nationwide network."[9]

A failure some feared for the auction appears not to have occurred. A bidder seeking a particular aggregation might unexpectedly fail to win a crucial license. Then the licenses that bidder wins might be worth less than their total price, bid in anticipation of winning the lost license. Some economists argued that, for this reason, bidders should be allowed to bid for combinations of licenses, rather than bidding license by license.[10] It does not appear, however, that bidders became exposed in this way. If they had, we would expect to see them withdrawing bids. In fact there were few withdrawals, and those that occurred did not seem to result from license aggregation failures. In the broadband MTA auction, for example, Wirelessco seemed not to change its bidding behavior after it lost the Chicago licenses. Failure to complete an aggregation might not be serious. The complementarities may not be so sizable as to generate large discontinuities in the values of aggregations. Also, substitution is possible: Wirelessco could complete its set by winning licenses in a later auction, or by forming alliances with other firms.

Congress stated a further criterion for the auction, beyond efficiency and revenue. Some licenses should go to minority- and woman-owned firms, small businesses and rural telephone companies. The initial auction design had ambitious provisions to aid these so-called "designated entities." FCC chairman Reed E. Hundt said this would be "the single most important economic opportunity made available to women and minorities in our country's history." The first two auctions ran under these rules. Then a June 1995 Supreme Court judgment that an affirmative-action program must be "narrowly tailored" to support "a compelling governmental interest" induced the FCC to scrap the race- and gender-based preferences. Some preferences remain, however. The fourth auction, offering 30 mHz (not held at the time of writing), is to be limited to entrepreneurs (defined as

---

[8] Marketing and brand-name gains come from offering nationwide mobile services. Cellular and PCS are not perfect substitutes, however, as telephones that transmit on both spectrum bands are expected to be more expensive than those specialized to a single band. The FCC's antimonopoly rules prevented a bidder from acquiring a broadband license in a region where it already held a cellular license.

[9] Reactions from a story in the *Wall Street Journal*, March 14, 1995, p. A12.

[10] Combinational bidding has some problems. Because of the huge number of license aggregations, combinational bids create impossibly complex computations. The FCC could prespecify a limited number of aggregations. But the existing theory of combinational bidding (Bernheim and Whinston, 1986, Banks, Ledyard and Porter, 1989; Branco, 1995; Rothkopf, Pekec and Harstad, 1995) offers little guidance on the effects of combinational bidding with restricted permissible aggregations. Experiments often find gains from combinational bidding; but the theory currently does not say when restricted combinational bidding would work better, for either revenue or efficiency, than the much simpler single-license bidding.

firms with less than $125 million in annual revenue and $500 million in assets) and small businesses (revenue under $40 million), with the latter receiving bid discounts.

The designated entities were eligible for a discount in the nationwide narrowband auction: if they won they would pay 25 percent less than their bid. The size of this discount was set by guesswork as, this being the first auction, there were no data from which to estimate its effects. As it turned out, 25 percent was too small for any of them to win licenses. For the second auction, the regional narrowband auction, the FCC used higher preferences. On two of the six wavebands the designated firms were offered a 40 percent discount. Minority bidders won all 10 licenses on which they were offered discounts (see Table 2). PCS Development Corp., a start-up minority company, won a nationwide aggregation. The prices on the designated licenses were bid so much higher than the other licenses that in net terms, after subtracting the discount, the designated firms paid approximately as much as the nonfavored firms. (The designated entities still received some special treatment, however, as they were permitted to pay in installments.)

Bid discounts not only address the policy goal of getting licenses into the hands of the designated firms, but also can actually boost the government's revenue (Myerson, 1981; McAfee and McMillan, 1988, 1989). The designated bidders, presumably, have a lower willingness to pay for the licenses than the nondesignated firms – otherwise preferences would not be needed. With level-playing-field bidding, they would therefore not be competitive with the nondesignated firms, who could bid low. A discount for the designated firms stimulates the bidding competition, forcing the nondesignated firms to bid higher. This may have happened in the narrowband auctions. Prices rose 12 percent higher in the regional auction than in the nationwide auction (the average price per mHz-pop was $3.10 in the nationwide auction and $3.47 net of discounts in the regional auction). Perhaps, as the theory says, the discounts did increase the bidding competition.

## Bidder Strategies

"Bidding for the PCS licenses is like playing a dozen hands of billion-dollar poker at once," said the *Wall Street Journal* (23.12.1995, p. B1). Bidder strategies can be aggressive or passive. The theorists, when designing the auction, expected that the bidders would be cagey, revealing to their rivals as little of their intentions as the auction rules permitted. As it happened, in the first two auctions many of the bidders behaved much more aggressively than this. But in the third, the broadband MTA auction, the huge amounts of money at stake induced the bidders to be circumspect, as the theorists had predicted.

Aggressive bidding took the form of "jump bidding:" entering bids that were far above the required minimum. In the nationwide narrowband auction, one spectacular jump bid was 138 percent above the previous high bid. In nine instances, bids were between 40 and 70 percent above the previous high, and in 20 cases they were 20 to 40 percent higher (minimum increments were typically 5 to 10 percent). The jump bidding occurred in the early rounds, including the opening bids. The 30 bids that beat the standing bid by 20 percent or more all came in the first 27 rounds of the auction (which took 46 rounds to close). An extreme form of jump bidding, which happened on several occasions, involved submitting a higher bid for a license on which the bidder already had the standing high bid. Jump bidding was common also in the regional narrowband auction.

Jump bidding is intended to signal the jump bidder's toughness, to try to persuade the others it is pointless to compete (Avery, 1993). Did jump bidding achieve the bidders' aims, or did it just aid the FCC by speeding up the auction? Despite jump bidding's prevalence in the two narrowband auctions, most of the jump bids were eventually overtaken. Few of the final prices were reached by a jump bid; instead, the final prices were reached gradually, by a series of minimum-increment bids. This suggests that the jump bids had little effect, for they did not deter competitors.

By the time of the third and biggest of the auctions, the broadband MTA auction, the bidders, having observed the two narrowband auctions, had apparently decided that jump bids did not work, for they mostly eschewed them. A few jump bids were used. Sometimes a bid beat the standing bid by twice the minimum increment; in round 30 ALAACR Communications, Inc., raised Pacific Telesis's $183 million bid on Los Angeles to $300 million; in round 81 Wirelessco submitted bids on four small markets that exceeded the standing bids by 10 times the minimum increment; and on a handful of occasions bidders such as SouthWest Bell and ALAACR raised their own standing bid. But most bids beat the standing bid by just the minimum increment or slightly more.

The broadband bidders bid cautiously in another way, by not bidding for more licenses than the activity rule required. The auction's pace was driven by the auction rules more than by the bidders' decisions. Total revenue rose at the rate set by the mechanism. The effect of the three stages of the activity rule is seen in Figure 1.[11] In each stage, bid activity steadily dropped off, until the imposition of the next stage (in rounds 12 and 65), with its stricter activity requirements, caused a jump in bid activity. The revenue curve is scallop shaped, steepening when a new stage starts and roughly concave within each stage.

The broadband MTA auction had few bidders relative to the number of licenses on offer. The low excess demand, just two-to-one, gave rise to fears that the bidders might collude. A drawback of the simultaneous ascending auction is that collusion is easier than under a single round of sealed bids. Through their bidding patterns in the early rounds, the bidders might in effect say to each other: "This is 'my' territory. Stay away from it, and I will stay away from 'yours.' If you ever bid on it, I will drive up the price of 'yours' in retaliation." The FCC could have hindered collusion by revealing only the bid amounts between rounds, and not the bidders' identities. It chose not to do this in the broadband auction and instead gave out full details of each round's bidding, because it judged that the risk of collusion was outweighed by benefits of the information. (Bidder identities are useful to the bidders for evaluating the meaning of others' bids, reducing the winner's curse and generally assisting sensible bidding.) Some of the firms may have tried to coordinate their bids. Primeco president George F. Schmitt was reported as saying during the broadband MTA auction: "You mess with me in Chicago, you pay."[12] Primeco won its Chicago license, however, only after a bruising three-way battle for the two licenses, involving Primeco, Wirelessco and AT&T, which drove the bids to the highest level in the nation. Schmitt's threat, if such it was, had little effect. It takes only one maverick bidder to upset an attempt at collusion. ALAACR, in particular, seems to have used a strategy of bidding on any major license that was relatively underpriced (and American Portable

---

[11] This figure was devised by Peter Cramton for the FCC.
[12] The Schmitt quotation is from the *New York Times*, March 27, 1995, p. C9.

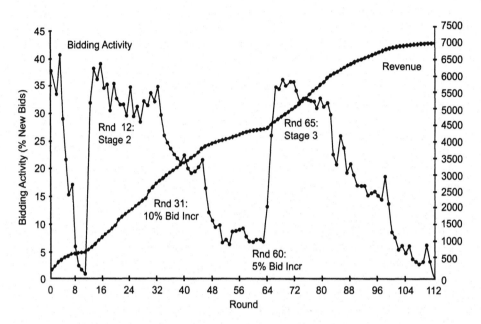

**Figure 1** Revenue and bidding activity, MTA broadband PCS auction

Telecommunications seems to have bid similarly); and this helped to keep the bidding competitive.[13]

One of the reasons for adopting the simultaneous ascending auction was to aid efficient license aggregation by allowing a bidder to switch to a back-up aggregation if the bid prices in its first-choice aggregation rose too high. The bid data contain many examples of back-up strategies. In the nationwide narrowband auction, Nationwide Wireless Network began by bidding for two of the 62.5 kHz licenses. In round 26, about the halfway point, it apparently decided that the prices were too high, and it switched to bidding for a single 100 kHz license, which is what it won. In the regional narrowband auction, Air Touch began by apparently seeking a nationwide aggregation of five licenses. Then it scaled back, and sought and won three licenses, supplementing the nationwide license it had won in the first auction. During the broadband MTA auction, firms such as GTE and Wirelessco often shifted their bidding across different license sets.

A consistent pattern of closing (especially in the narrowband auctions, but less clearly in the broadband MTA auction) was that, as equilibrium came near, the winning bidders

---

[13] ALAACR is owned by Craig McCaw, who became a billionaire by building America's leading cellular company and then, after selling it to AT&T, bid on his own account for the PCS licenses. Despite its aggressive bidding, ALAACR ended up without a single license. However, according to *Forbes* (July 3, 1995, p. 64), "McCaw had a grand time giving ulcers to the functionaries at the big bidders and adding hundreds of millions to the U.S. Treasury. 'Craig McCaw thought he was playing Nintendo. He was having the time of his life,' says Sam Ginn, chief executive of AirTouch." Incidentally, McCaw envisages novel uses of the spectrum: according to *Fortune* (December 12, 1994, p. 102), he "once suggested in all apparent seriousness – as color drained from the face of a PR man in attendance – that the FCC should reserve spectrum for telepathic communications to be made possible by brain implants he thinks will exist some day."

tended to be established first on the highest-valued licenses. Then the activity shifted progressively to lower-valued licenses, with the lowest-valued settling last.

## New Theory of Multiunit Auctions

The spectrum sale is more complicated than anything in auction theory. No theorem exists – or can be expected to develop – that specifies the optimal auction form. The auction designers based their thinking on a range of models, each of which captures a part of the issue. The basic ideas used in designing the auction and in advising the firms on bidding strategy include the way the different bidders' valuations are related – they are partly idiosyncratic and partly common, or *affiliated* – and the effects of this on bidder behavior (Milgrom and Weber, 1982); how auctions reveal and aggregate dispersed information (Wilson, 1977); and the logic of bidding in the face of the winner's curse (Wilson, 1969; Milgrom and Weber, 1982). Other ideas used include the revenue-increasing effect of bid discounts (Myerson, 1981, McAfee and McMillan, 1988, 1989) and reserve prices as substitutes for bidding competition (Myerson, 1981; Riley and Samuelson, 1981).[14]

A lesson from this experience of theorists in policymaking is that the real value of the theory is in developing intuition. The role of theory, in any policy application, is to show how people behave in various circumstances, and to identify the tradeoffs involved in altering those circumstances. What the theorists found to be the most useful in designing the auction and advising the bidders was not complicated models that try to capture a lot of reality at the cost of relying on special functional forms. Such theorizing fails to develop intuition, as it confounds the effects of the functional forms with the essential elements of the model. Instead, a focused model that isolates a particular effect and assumes few or no special functional forms is more helpful in building understanding.

The spectrum auction, itself based on theory, has in turn sparked a new wave of theorizing. Although sequential auctions and single-round simultaneous auctions had been modeled, there had been little formal work on simultaneous ascending auctions of the sort the FCC used. Most of the existing theory omitted the crucial feature of the spectrum auction: the fact that the licenses complement and substitute for each other. Prompted by the FCC auctions, theorists are beginning to address this issue, though because of the intrinsic difficulty of the question, the existing attempts are preliminary.

One promising approach is to assume away asymmetries of information and the strategic behavior they induce, in order to focus on how bidding proceeds when the goods complement and substitute for each other. Complementarities mean market-clearing prices may not exist. Equilibrium is likely to exist if the buyers have similar views about how the goods should be aggregated, whereas it may not if they disagree about what constitutes good aggregations.[15] Some recent research has identified conditions for the existence of equilibrium in this sort of auction. Gul and Stacchetti (1995a, b), for example,

---

[14] There is a direct link between game theory's Nobel laureates and the spectrum auction. The ideas with which Nash, Harsanyi and Selten are associated – Nash, Bayesian and perfect equilibrium – are the basic tools of the theory used in designing the auction.

[15] An example with no equilibrium has two items and two buyers. Buyer 1 sees the two goods as perfect substitutes, but buyer 2 sees them as perfect complements. Buyer 1 puts a value of 2 on getting either good 1 or

show that a certain kind of substitutability among goods ensures existence. Their model also yields a decentralized price-setting process in which prices rise when demand exceeds supply.

Strategic behavior in a simultaneous ascending auction is analyzed by Menezes (1995), again assuming complete information. Prices are quoted and rise until excess demand becomes zero. The bidders' game playing means there are many equilibria. On applying a natural way of selecting one of the equilibria – the iterated elimination of weakly dominated strategies – Menezes shows, remarkably, that the sale takes place at the opening prices. Bidders forecast how much they will eventually purchase and shrink the amounts they demand in the first round to this level; the consequence of iterating this logic is immediate sale. This result rests on the unrealistic assumption of complete information; but it provides a warning about the peculiar possibilities in simultaneous ascending auctions.[16]

More new theory is needed. Features of the FCC's auction should be modeled. How should the activity rule parameters be set? How do the bid withdrawal rules affect the bidding? If bidders fear being stuck holding an incomplete bundle by losing a crucial license, do they bid unduly cautiously? Is this caution lessened by the availability of substitute licenses? How does the FCC-style auction, with its single-license bidding, compare in efficiency and revenue with combinational bidding under certain prespecified permissible combinations? Together with experiments (Plott, 1994), theory will map the scope and the limits of the simultaneous ascending auction.

## Other Uses of the Simultaneous Ascending Auction

Auctions are used when the seller does not know the bidders' willingness to pay for idiosyncratic items for which there is no well-functioning market. The fundamental purpose of any auction is to reveal the bidders' valuations, thereby extracting a good price for the seller. The simultaneous ascending auction extends this notion of value-discovery to multiple items and how they fit together. The seller need not know how the items for sale complement or substitute for each other, as the auction induces the bidders to express their ideas about serviceable aggregations, and so the market process determines the outcome.

---

good 2 or both. Buyer 2 puts zero value on having either good alone, but puts a value of 3 on having both. The allocation that is efficient, and therefore the only candidate for a Walrasian equilibrium, gives buyer 2 both goods, for a value of 3. Since buyer 1 gets nothing, the price of each good must be 2, for otherwise buyer 1 would buy one of them. But buyer 2 will not buy the goods at those prices. (If buyer 2 were allowed to bid all-or-nothing for the aggregation, however, the efficient outcome would result.) For more on existence, see Bikhchandani and Mamer (1994).

[16] Krishna and Rosenthal (1995) model a simultaneous auction with bidders who are either local bidders, who want only one of the items, or global bidders, who get extra value if they acquire both, and show the global bidders' strategies may be discontinuous. Rosenthal and Wang (1995) extend this to a common-value case. In Jehiel, Moldovanu and Stacchetti (1995), one bidder's ownership has externalities for the others (for example, MCI may prefer GTE to obtain a license rather than AT&T). The negative externalities mean a bidder may pay even when the item is not sold, and the item may fail to sell even though a bidder is willing to pay more than the seller's value. Jehiel and Moldovanu (1995) add an after-market to the auction, finding that after-market trading does not ensure efficiency.

The evidence from the FCC auctions is that the simultaneous ascending auction is an effective mechanism for selling interdependent items. The simultaneous ascending auction has many other potential uses for selling multiple items that are complements or substitutes. Further possible public-sector uses include the sale of oil and mineral rights, timber and grazing rights, houses held by the Resolution Trust Corp. or the Federal Deposit Insurance Corp., and airport landing rights. The FCC might also begin selling spectrum rights to broadcasters, who currently receive a huge hidden subsidy through receiving spectrum for free. In the private sector, the simultaneous ascending auction could be used for art and real estate.

More innovative uses might also emerge. One possible use is by a firm buying inputs from other firms. Conventional procurement specifies the level of assembly at which components are to be purchased. If instead a simultaneous mechanism were used, the procuring firm could define the components finely and have the potential suppliers bid component by component, with the possibility of winning several contracts and so supplying a bundle of components. By the set of components it bid for, each supplier would reveal its economies of scope. Another possible application is in the sale of a multidivisional corporation. The simultaneous auction could allow buyers to bid division by division. The bidders could thereby express their ideas on which parts of the firm fit together and which should be spun off. The uses of this new auction have just begun.

## References and Further Reading

AKERLOF, G. A. (1970): "The Market for 'Lemons': Quality Uncertainty and the Market Mechanism," *Quarterly Journal of Economics*, 84, August, 488–500.

ASHENFELTER, O. (1989): "How Auctions Work for Wine and Art," *Journal of Economic Perspectives*, 3, Summer, 23–36.

AVERY, C. (1993): "Strategic Jump Bidding and English Auctions," discussion paper, Kennedy School of Government, Harvard University.

BANKS, J. S., LEDYARD, J. O. and PORTER, D. (1989): "Allocating Uncertain and Unresponsive Resources: An Experimental Approach." *Rand Journal of Economics*, 20, Spring, 1–22.

BERNHEIM, B. D. and WHINSTON, M. D. (1986): "Menu Auctions, Resource Allocation, and Economic Influence," *Quarterly Journal of Economics*, 101, February, 1–32.

BIKHCHANDANI, S. and MAMER, J. W. (1994): "Competitive Equilibrium in an Economy with Indivisibilities," unpublished paper, University of California, Los Angeles, October.

BRANCO, F. (1995): "Multi-Object Auctions: On the Use of Combinatorial Bids," unpublished paper, Universidade Catolica Portuguesa, April.

CRAMTON, P. C. (1995a): "Money Out of Thin Air: The Nationwide Narrowband PCS Auction," *Journal of Economics and Management Strategy*, 4, Summer, 267–343.

—— (1995b): "The PCS Spectrum Auctions: An Early Assessment," unpublished paper, University of Maryland, July.

FEDERAL COMMUNICATIONS COMMISSION (FCC), (1994): "Fifth Report and Order," FCC 94–178, Washington DC, July 15.

GANDAL, N. (1994): "Sequential Auctions of Cable Television Licenses: The Israeli Experience," working paper 31–94, Tel-Aviv University, December.

GUL, F. and STACCHETTI, E. (1995a): "English Auctions with Multiple Goods," unpublished paper Northwestern University, June.

—— and —— (1995b): "Walrasian Equilibrium without Consumption Complementarities," unpublished paper Northwestern University, June.

HAZLETT, T. W. (1995): "Assigning Property Rights to Radio Spectrum Users: Why Did FCC License Auctions Take 67 Years?", unpublished paper, University of California, Davis, July.

JEHIEL, P. and MOLDOVANU, B. (1995): "Resale Markets and the Assignment of Property Rights," discussion paper 1196, Centre for Economic Policy Research, London, June.

—— and STACCHETTI, E. (1995): "Multidimensional Mechanism Design for Auctions with Externalities," unpublished paper. Bonn University, February.

KRISHNA, V. and ROSENTHAL, R. W. (1995): "Simultaneous Auctions with Synergies," unpublished paper, Boston University, March.

MCAFEE, R. P. and MCMILLAN, J. (1987): "Auctions and Bidding," Journal of Economic Literature, 25, June, 699–738.

—— (1988): Incentives in Government Contracting. Toronto: University of Toronto Press.

—— (1989): "Government Procurement and International Trade," Journal of International Economics, 26, May, 291–308.

MCAFEE, R. P. and VINCENT, D. (1993): "The Declining Price Anomaly," Journal of Economic Theory, 60, June, 191–212.

MCMILLAN, J. (1994): "Selling Spectrum Rights," Journal of Economic Perspectives, 8, Summer, 145–62.

—— (1995): "Why Auction the Spectrum?", Telecommunications Policy, 19, April, 191–99.

MENEZES, F. (1995): "Multiple-Unit English Auctions," unpublished paper, Australian National University, May.

MILGROM, P. (1995): "Auction Theory for Privatization," draft, Stanford University.

—— and WEBER, R. J. (1982): "A Theory of Auctions and Competitive Bidding," Econometrica, 50, September, 1089–122.

MYERSON, R. (1981): "Optimal Auction Design," Mathematics of Operations Research, 6, February, 58–73.

—— and SATTERTHWAITE M. A. (1983): "Efficient Mechanisms for Bilateral Trading," Journal of Economic Theory, 29, April, 265–81.

PITCHIK, C. and SCHOTTER, A. (1988): "Perfect Equilibria in Budget-Constrained Sequential Auctions: An Experimental Study," Rand Journal of Economics, 19, Autumn, 363–88.

PLOTT, C. R. (1994): "Market Architectures, Institutional Landscapes and Testbed Experiments," Economic Theory, 4 (1), 3–10.

RILEY, J. and SAMUELSON, W. (1981): "Optimal Auctions," American Economic Review, 71, June, 381–92.

ROSENTHAL, R. W. and WANG, R. (1995): "Simultaneous Auctions with Synergies and Common Values," unpublished paper, Boston University, August.

ROTHKOPF, M. H., PEKEC, A. and HARSTAD, R. M. (1995): "Computationally Manageable Combinatorial Auctions," unpublished paper, Rutgers University, April.

SALANT, D. J. (1995): "Up in the Air: GTE's Experience in the MTA Auctions for PCS Licenses," unpublished paper, Charles River Associates, July.

WILSON, R. B. (1969): "Competitive Bidding with Disparate Information," Management Science, 15, March, 446–48.

—— (1977): "A Bidding Model of Perfect Competition," Review of Economic Studies, 44, October, 511–18.

# FIFTY-NINE

# At Many Auctions, Illegal Bidding Thrives as a Longtime Practice Among Dealers

Meg Cox

*Source: Wall Street Journal*, February 19, 1988.

So the stock market was tainted with insider trading. At least there are some unspoiled markets left, like old-fashioned auctions, where open competition sets the price. Or are there? The Justice Department, which spent the past two years investigating antique dealers in the Philadelphia area, found that dealers routinely banded together and agreed not to bid against one another at auctions, a practice called pooling. Only one dealer in a pool would bid. Later pool members would hold a private session, called a "knockout," and re-auction the goods among themselves. The extra money paid for each item would be divided among the poolers.

In one case, Margaret Hood, a widow from Chadds Ford, Pa., watched bidders go up to $1,325 for a desk she sold at a 1984 auction. She didn't learn until much later, during one dealer's trial, that the desk brought $5,000 at the knockout session. Twelve Philadelphia antique dealers were charged by the Justice Department with antitrust violations. Eleven pleaded guilty last fall and were fined between $1,000 and $50,000, and given probationary sentences up to three years. The 12th was found guilty by a jury, sentenced to 30 days of house arrest and fined $30,000.

Department officials believe illegal pooling is widespread in America's $100 billion-a-year auction markets. In pursuing the antique auction case, investigators picked up a trail that has led to others. Nineteen corporations and seventeen of their officials in six states have been indicted for pooling in machinery auctions. All but four individuals and four corporations have pleaded guilty or have had their charges dismissed. The others go to trial in federal court next month in Newark, N.J. Now the department is investigating jewelry and rug auctions in New York City. Charles F. Rule, assistant attorney general in charge of the antitrust division, says, "We've only just begun. Our objective here is to stop pooling, and we will follow it into whatever industry and state it leads."

Pooling always works to shortchange the seller. "Our records show that pooling antique dealers regularly paid 50% to 100% more at the knockouts" than at the original sale, says

Roger L. Currier, a Justice Department lawyer in Philadelphia. "Auction after auction and year after year, that adds up."

Pooling has an old if not exactly honorable history in this country, dating back at least to the turn of the century. Despite scattered court cases, mostly involving auctions of tobacco, cattle, timber and other commodities, the practice has gone practically unchallenged in art, antiques and industrial products. It has been perceived in the trade as customary and sometimes as sleazy but also inevitable. At times, dealers gathered in conspicuous clumps at auctions for rugs, jewelry and silver in New York and then were seen openly rebidding for the goods at neighborhood cafes. "It was just an accepted thing, and it still goes on," says Arthur Halpern, a New York rug dealer. "If they (other dealers) think you will bid against them and raise prices, they will always ask people to pool." "Dealers liked to pool because even if they didn't go home with any merchandise, at least they would leave with cash in their pockets," says Daniel Comly, an industrial auctioneer in Philadelphia. "I have seen pools in burlap, scrap metal and sewing machines. You can see them form up, see them watching each other (bid). My dad used to tell stories about burlap pools during the Depression."

Pooling is less likely at big auctions of widely collected objects, where large numbers of dealers and private buyers compete. It occurs more frequently at small sales of specialized goods that attract mostly dealers. Auctioneers say there isn't much they can do to combat pooling except set a secret minimum price, called a reserve. But reserve prices aren't practical at estate and bankruptcy sales where the seller wants everything sold at once.

Auctioneer Leslie Hindman recalls the first auction of estate jewelry she held after opening her Chicago auction house in 1982. "All the jewelry dealers sat together, and only one was bidding. I was 28 years old and starting out, and I was so upset," says Ms. Hindman. "I had no reserves, but I just refused to sell at those prices. I called off the auction and told the executor to sell the stuff in New York." But that countertactic isn't always possible or practical. Ms. Hindman lost her commission on a $40,000 sale.

Interviews with some of the Philadelphia dealers show just how deeply the practice is ingrained. "I pride myself in being an upstanding, law-abiding citizen who pays his taxes," says Morris Finkel, a silver-haired man who runs a quilt-filled antiques shop with his daughter, Amy. Until Federal Bureau of Investigation agents marched into his shop and asked whether he pooled, Mr. Finkel says, he had no idea the practice was illegal. "The day I was allowed to go into the pool" – in the late 1940s – "was a banner day," he says. "If you weren't in a pool, you weren't considered much of a dealer." Like many of his colleagues, Mr. Finkel kept meticulous records of his pooling activity and used checks to make the knockout payments; the biggest single one he ever received, he says, was for $1,250. "We weren't trying to hide anything," he says. But he says he pleaded guilty because "trying to fight the U.S. government was more than I could do." His sentence included $20,000 in fines, two years of probation and 500 hours of community service. Legal fees cost him $40,000.

Dealer Ronald Pook of Downington, Pa., says he also viewed his first invitation to pool, in the 1970s, as "a mark of distinction." He says that pooling comes from a tradition of business friendship, not criminal intent. "If you bid against another dealer, then he won't tell you next time a great little cupboard shows up (at auction) out his way," he says. "Would you go to an auction and bid against a friend?" Mr. Pook fought the Justice Department and took his case to a jury, but lost. Like the other dealers charged in the case, Mr. Pook says he has stopped pooling and won't ever do it again. But others say the practice will never be eliminated. "It is unpoliceable," says Beau Freeman, owner of a Philadelphia auction house.

Mr. Comly, the industrial auctioneer in Philadelphia, agrees: "Instead of quitting the practice and letting the competitive atmosphere take its course, they (dealers) are changing the routine. Maybe they will form a joint venture to buy things, which isn't illegal, and then when they sell something, they will split the profits." But the feds will be watching. If people buy together because they can't afford something alone, as museums sometimes team up at auction, that's fine, says Mr. Currier of the Justice Department. "But if they are joining together to hold down the price," he says, "that is illegal and we will treat them like felons."

# SIXTY

# "The Next Item up for Bid is the Presidency of the United States..."

ROB ROGERS

*Source*: © 1999 United Feature Syndicate, Inc., courtesy of Knight Features, London.

# Pricing

# Introduction

Francis Edgeworth was, befitting someone with the middle name "Ysidro," an unusually original thinker, much like George Akerlof. What he is best known for, besides the Edgeworth box, is the Edgeworth Paradox, that price competition between two firms with capacity constraints or upward sloping marginal cost curves can result in no equilibrium in pure strategies. He first wrote this up in a now-lost English version translated into Italian as "La Teoria Pura del Monopolio," *Giornale degli Economisti* (1897), which was translated back into English as "The Pure Theory of Monopoly," pp. 111–42 of Volume I of his *Papers Relating to Political Economy*, London: Macmillan (1925). Pages 117–21 of that article deal with the Edgeworth Paradox with capacity constraints, and much of the rest is concerned with the effect of taxes. I have chosen instead to include a 1922 version of the paradox, a numerical example with upward sloping marginal cost. Note that, in both articles, Edgeworth also considers the case of differentiated products.

Harold Hotelling, however, is the man who published the seminal article in the economics of differentiated products. Like Edgeworth, he made important contributions to both economics and statistics in a time when the fields were much more sharply differentiated than they are today. In economics, he is best known for "Stability in Competition," for the equally seminal "The Economics of Exhaustible Resources," *Journal of Political Economy* 39: 139–75 (1931), and for being Kenneth Arrow's dissertation advisor. See Adrian Darnell, "Harold Hotelling: 1895–1973," *Statistical Science* 3: 7–62 (February 1988) for an interesting view of a many-faceted scholar.

This classic paper, however, like a number of other classics, has a mistake. Can you find it? If not, look at pp. 323–34 of William Vickrey, *Microstatics*, New York: Harcourt, Brace and World (1964), or at Claude D'Aspremont, J. Gabszewicz, and Jacques Thisse, "On Hotelling's Stability of Competition," *Econometrica* 47: 1145–50 (September 1979), which independently found the mistake, or Martin Osborne and Carolyn Pitchik, "Equilibrium in Hotelling's Model of Spatial Competition," *Econometrica* 55: 911–22 (July 1987), which solves for the correct equilibrium as best as our current mathematics can manage.

Hotelling did not consider the case when three firms simultaneously choose their locations, though he mentions what happens when a third firm unexpectedly shows up after the first two have already fixed their locations. Perhaps he avoided that case because one of his points was that oligopoly can be more stable than Edgeworth thought, and with three firms choosing location, there is no equilibrium in pure strategies. In the *Journal of Industrial Economics* article that I have included here, Avner Shaked solves for the equilibrium in mixed strategies that does exist.

In thinking about pricing, it is important not to forget the importance of collusion, tacit or explicit. The article, "Busting a Trust," is a reminder that despite the complexity of some antitrust cases like those involving Microsoft or Intel, the bread and butter of an antitrust agency is still simple price fixing and merger for market power. The cartoon, "Isn't it great...," makes the same point: consumers may complain about having too much choice between different deals or too many differentiated products, but too little choice is much worse.

# SIXTY-ONE

# Stability in Competition

HAROLD HOTELLING

*Source*: *Economic Journal* 39 (March), 1929, pp 41–57.

After the work of the late Professor F. Y. Edgeworth one may doubt that anything further can be said on the theory of competition among a small number of entrepreneurs. However, one important feature of actual business seems until recently to have escaped scrutiny. This is the fact that of all the purchasers of a commodity, some buy from one seller, some from another, in spite of moderate differences of price. If the purveyor of an article gradually increases his price while his rivals keep theirs fixed, the diminution in volume of his sales will in general take place continuously rather than in the abrupt way which has tacitly been assumed.

A profound difference in the nature of the stability of a competitive situation results from this fact. We shall examine it with the help of some simple mathematics. The form of the solution will serve also to bring out a number of aspects of a competitive situation whose importance warrants more attention than they have received. Among these features, all illustrated by the same simple case, we find (1) the existence of incomes not properly belonging to any of the categories usually discussed, but resulting from the discontinuity in the increase in the number of sellers with the demand; (2) a socially uneconomical system of prices, leading to needless shipment of goods and kindred deviations from optimum activities; (3) an undue tendency for competitors to imitate each other in quality of goods, in location, and in other essential ways.

Piero Sraffa has discussed[1] the neglected fact that a market is commonly subdivided into regions within each of which one seller is in a quasi-monopolistic position. The consequences of this phenomenon are here considered further. In passing we remark that the asymmetry between supply and demand, between buyer and seller, which Professor Sraffa emphasises is due to the condition that the seller sets the price and the buyers the quantities they will buy. This condition in turn results from the large number of the buyers of a particular commodity as compared with the sellers. Where, as in new oil-fields and in agricultural villages, a few buyers set prices at which they will take all that is offered

---

[1] "The Laws of Returns Under Competitive Conditions," *Economic Journal*, Vol. XXXVI, pp. 535–550, especially pp. 544 ff. (December 1926).

and exert themselves to induce producers to sell, the situation is reversed. If in the following pages the words "buy" and "sell" be everywhere interchanged, the argument remains equally valid, though applicable to a different class of businesses.

Extensive and difficult applications of the Calculus of Variations in economics have recently been made, sometimes to problems of competition among a small number of entrepreneurs.[2] For this and other reasons a re-examination of stability and related questions, using only elementary mathematics, seems timely.

Duopoly, the condition in which there are two competing merchants, was treated by A. Cournot in 1838.[3] His book went apparently without comment or review for forty-five years until Walras produced his *Théorie Mathématique de la Richesse Sociale*, and Bertrand published a caustic review of both works.[4] Bertrand's criticisms were modified and extended by Edgeworth in his treatment of duoply in the *Giornale degli Economisti* for 1897,[5] in his criticism of Amoroso,[6] and elsewhere. Indeed all writers since Cournot, except Sraffa and Amoroso,[7] seem to hold that even apart from the likelihood of combination there is an essential instability in duopoly. Now it is true that such competition lacks complete stability; but we shall see that in a very general class of cases the independent actions of two competitors not in collusion lead to a type of equilibrium much less fragile than in the examples of Cournot, Edgeworth and Amoroso. The solution which we shall obtain can break down only in case of an express or tacit understanding which converts the supposed competitors into something like a monopoly, or in case of a price war aimed at eliminating one of them altogether.

Cournot's example was of two proprietors of mineral springs equally available to the market and producing, without cost, mineral water of identical quality. The demand is elastic, and the price is determined by the total amount put on the market. If the respective quantities produced are $q_1$ and $q_2$ the price $p$ will be given by a function

$$p = f(q_1 + q_2).$$

The profits of the proprietors are respectively

$$\pi_1 = q_1 f(q_1 + q_2)$$

and

[2] For references to the work of C. F. Roos and G. C. Evans on this subject see the paper by Dr. Roos, "A Dynamical Theory of Economics," in the *Journal of Political Economy*, Vol. XXXV. (1927), or that in the *Transactions of the American Mathematical Society*, Vol. XXX. (1928), p. 360. There is also an application of the Calculus of Variations to depreciation by Dr. Roos in the *Bulletin of the American Mathematical Society*, Vol. XXXIV, (1928), p. 218.

[3] *Recherches sur les Principes Mathématiques de la Théorie des Richesses*. Paris (Hachette). Chapter VII. English translation by N. T. Bacon, with introduction and bibliography by Irving Fisher (New York, Macmillan, 1897 and 1927).

[4] *Journal des Savants* (1883), pp. 499–508.

[5] Republished in English in Edgeworth's *Papers Relating to Political Economy* (London, Macmillan, 1925), Vol. I, pp. 116–26.

[6] *Economic Journal*, Vol. XXXII, (1922), pp. 400–7.

[7] *Lezioni di Economia Mathematica* (Bologna, Zanichelli, 1921).

$$\pi_2 = q_2 f(q_1 + q_2).$$

The first proprietor adjusts $q_1$ so that, when $q_2$ has its current value, his own profit will be as great as possible. This value of $q_1$ may be obtained by differentiating $\pi_1$, putting

$$f(q_1 + q_2) + q_1 f_1(q_1 + q_2) = 0.$$

In like manner the second proprietor adjusts $q_2$ so that

$$f(q_1 + q_2) + q_2 f_2(q_1 + q_2) = 0.$$

There can be no equilibrium unless these equations are satisfied simultaneously. Together they determine a definite (and equal) pair of values of $q_1$ and $q_2$. Cournot showed graphically how, if a different pair of $q$'s should obtain, each competitor in turn would readjust his production so as to approach as a limit the value given by the solution of the simultaneous equations. He concluded that the actual state of affairs will be given by the common solution, and proceeded to generalise to the case of $n$ competitors.

Against this conclusion Bertrand brought an "objection péremptoire." The solution does not represent equilibrium, for either proprietor can by a slight reduction in price take away all his opponent's business and nearly double his own profits. The other will respond with a still lower price. Only by the use of the quantities as independent variables instead of the prices is the fallacy concealed.

Bertrand's objection was amplified by Edgeworth, who maintained that in the more general case of two monopolists controlling commodities having correlated demand, even though not identical, there is no determinate solution. Edgeworth gave a variety of examples, but nowhere took account of the stabilising effect of masses of consumers placed so as to have a natural preference for one seller or the other. In all his illustrations of competition one merchant can take away his rival's entire business by undercutting his price ever so slightly. Thus discontinuities appear, though a discontinuity, like a vacuum, is abhorred by nature. More typical of real situations is the case in which the quantity sold by each merchant is a continuous function of two variables, his own price and his competitor's. Quite commonly a tiny increase in price by one seller will send only a few customers to the other.

# I

The feature of actual business to which, like Professor Sraffa, we draw attention, and which does not seem to have been generally taken account of in economic theory, is the existence with reference to each seller of groups of buyers who will deal with him instead of with his competitors in spite of a difference in price. If a seller increases his price too far he will gradually lose business to his rivals, but he does not lose all his trade instantly when he raises his price only a trifle. Many customers will still prefer to trade with him because they live nearer to his store than to the others, or because they have less freight to pay from his warehouse to their own, or because his mode of doing business is more to their liking, or because he sells other articles which they desire, or because he is a relative or a fellow Elk or Baptist, or on account of some difference in service or quality, or for a combination of reasons. Such circles of customers may be said to make every entrepreneur a monopolist within a limited class and region – and there is no monopoly which is not confined to a limited class and region. The difference between the Standard Oil Company in its prime and the little corner grocery is quantitative rather than qualitative. Between the perfect competition and monopoly of theory lie the actual cases.

It is the gradualness in the shifting of customers from one merchant to another as their prices vary independently which is ignored in the examples worked out by Cournot, Amoroso and Edgeworth. The assumption, implicit in their work, that all buyers deal with the cheapest seller leads to a type of instability which disappears when the quantity sold by each is considered as a continuous function of the differences in price. The use of such a continuous function does, to be sure, seem to violate the doctrine that in one market there can at one time be only one price. But this doctrine is only valid when the commodity in question is absolutely standardised in all respects and when the "market" is a point, without length, breadth or thickness. It is, in fact, analogous to the physical principle that at one point in a body there can at one time be only one temperature. This principle does not prevent different temperatures from existing in different parts of a body at the same time. If it were supposed that any temperature difference, however slight, necessitates a sudden transfer of all the heat in the warmer portion of the body to the colder portion – a transfer which by the same principle would immediately be reversed – then we should have a thermal instability somewhat resembling the instability of the cases of duopoly which have been discussed. To take another physical analogy, the earth is often in astronomical calculations considered as a point, and with substantially accurate results. But the precession of the equinoxes becomes explicable only when account is taken of the ellipsoidal bulge of the earth. So in the theory of value a market is usually considered as a point in which only one price can obtain; but for some purposes it is better to consider a market as an extended region.

Consider the following illustration. The buyers of a commodity will be supposed uniformly distributed along a line of length $l$, which may be Main Street in a town or a transcontinental railroad. At distances $a$ and $b$ respectively from the two ends of this line are the places of business of A and B (Fig. 1). Each buyer transports his purchases home at a cost $c$ per unit distance. Without effect upon the generality of our conclusions we shall suppose that the cost of production to A and B is zero, and that unit quantity of the commodity is consumed in each unit of time in each unit of length of line. The demand is thus at the extreme of inelasticity. No customer has any preference for either seller except on the ground of price plus transportation cost. In general there will be many causes leading particular classes of buyers to prefer one seller to another, but the ensemble of such consideration is here symbolised by transportation cost. Denote A's price by $p_1$, B's by $p_2$, and let $q_1$ and $q_2$ be the respective quantities sold.

**Figure 1**   Market of length $l = 35$. In this example $a = 4, b = 1, x = 14, y = 16$.

Now B's price may be higher than A's, but if B is to sell anything at all he must not let his price exceed A's by more than the cost of transportation from A's place of business to his own. In fact he will keep his price $p_2$ somewhat below the figure $p_1 + c(l - a - b)$ at which A's goods can be brought to him. Thus he will obtain all the business in the segment of length $b$ at the right of Fig. 1, and in addition will sell to all the customers in a segment of length $y$ depending on the difference of prices and lying between himself and A. Likewise A will, if he sells anything, sell to all the buyers in the strips of length $a$ at the left and of length $x$ to the right of A, where $x$ diminishes as $p_1 - p_2$ increases.

The point of division between the regions served by the two entrepreneurs is determined by the condition that at this place it is a matter of indifference whether one buys from A or from B. Equating the delivered prices we have

$$p_1 + cx = p_2 + cy$$

Another equation between $x$ and $y$ is

$$a + x + y + b = l$$

Solving we find

$$x = \frac{1}{2}\left(l - a - b + \frac{p_2 - p_1}{c}\right),$$

$$y = \frac{1}{2}\left(l - a - b + \frac{p_1 - p_2}{c}\right)$$

so that the profits are

$$\pi_1 = p_1 q_1 = p_1(a + x) = \frac{1}{2}(l + a - b)p_1 - \frac{p_1^2}{2c} + \frac{p_1 p_2}{2c}$$

and

$$\pi_2 = p_2 q_2 = p_2(b + y) = \frac{1}{2}(l - a + b)p_2 - \frac{p_2^2}{2c} + \frac{p_1 p_2}{2c}$$

If $p_1$ and $p_2$ be taken as rectangular co-ordinates, each of the last equations represents a family of hyperbolas having identical asymptotes, one hyperbola for each value of $\pi_1$ or $\pi_2$. Some of these curves are shown in Fig. 2, where (as also in Fig. 1) we have taken $l = 35, a = 4, b = 1, c = 1$.

Each competitor adjusts his price so that, with the existing value of the other price, his own profit will be a maximum. This gives the equations

$$\frac{\partial \pi_1}{\partial p_1} = \frac{1}{2}(l + a - b) - \frac{p_1}{c} + \frac{p_2}{2c} = 0$$

$$\frac{\partial \pi_2}{\partial p_2} = \frac{1}{2}(l - a + b) + \frac{p_1}{2c} - \frac{p_2}{c} = 0$$

from which we obtain

$$p_1 = c\left(l + \frac{a - b}{3}\right)$$

$$p_2 = c\left(l - \frac{a - b}{3}\right)$$

and

$$q_1 = a + x = \frac{1}{2}\left(l + \frac{a - b}{3}\right)$$

$$q_2 = b + y = \frac{1}{2}\left(l - \frac{a - b}{3}\right)$$

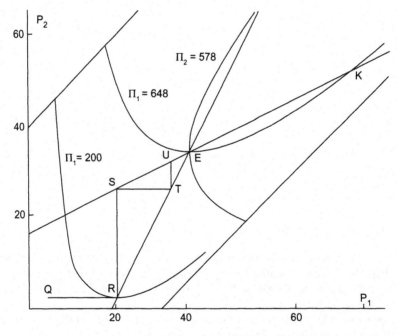

**Figure 2**  Conditions of competition for the market of Fig. 1. The co-ordinates represent the prices at A's and B's shops for the same article. The straight lines through $E$ are the two lines of maximum profit. On one of the curves through $E$, A's profit is everywhere 648; on the other, B's is 578. The lower curve is the locus on which A's profit is 200.

The conditions $\partial^2\pi_1/\partial p_1^2 < 0$ and $\partial^2\pi_2/\partial p_2^2 < 0$, sufficient for a maximum of each of the functions $\pi_1$ and $\pi_2$, are obviously satisfied.

If the two prices are originally the co-ordinates of the point $Q$ in Fig. 2, and if A is the more alert business man of the two, he will change his price so as to make his profit a maximum. This is represented graphically by a horizontal motion to the point $R$ on the line $\partial\pi_1/\partial p_1 = 0$. This line has the property that every point on it represents a greater profit for A than any other point having the same ordinate. But presently B discovers that his profits can be increased by a vertical motion to the point $S$ on his own line of maximum profit. A now moves horizontally to $T$. Thus there is a gradual approach to the point $E$ at the intersection of the two lines; its co-ordinates are given by the values of $p_1$ and $p_2$ found above. At $E$ there is equilibrium, since neither merchant can now increase his profit by changing his price. The same result is reached if instead of $Q$ the starting point is any on the figure.[8]

Now it is true that prices other than the co-ordinates of the equilibrium point may obtain for a considerable time. Even at this point one merchant may sacrifice his immediate income to raise his price, driving away customers, in the hope that his rival will do likewise and thus increase both profits. Indeed if A moves to the right from $E$ in Fig. 2 he may reasonably expect that B will go up to his line of maximum profit. This will make A's profit larger than at $E$, provided the representing point has not gone so far to the right as $K$. Without this proviso, A's position will be improved (and so will B's as compared with $E$) if only B will sufficiently increase $p_2$. In fact, since the demand is inelastic, we may imagine the two alleged competitors to be amicably exploiting the consumers without limit by raising their prices. The increases need not be agreed upon in advance but may proceed by alternate steps, each seller in turn making his price higher than the other's, but not high enough to drive away all business. Thus without a formal agreement the rivals may succeed in making themselves virtually a monopoly. Something of a tacit understanding will exist that prices are to be maintained above the level immediately profitable in order to keep profits high in the long run.

But understandings between competitors are notoriously fragile. Let one of these business men, say B, find himself suddenly in need of cash. Immediately at hand he will have a resource: Let him lower his price a little, increasing his sales. His profits will be larger until A decides to stop sacrificing business and lowers his price to the point of maximum profit. B will now be likely to go further in an attempt to recoup, and so the

---

[8] The solution given above is subject to the limitation that the difference between the prices must not exceed the cost of transportation from A to B. This means that $E$ must lie between the lines $p_1 - p_2 = \pm c(l - a - b)$ on which the hyperbolic arcs shown in Fig. 2 terminate. It is easy to find values of the constants for which this condition is not satisfied (for example, $l = 20, a = 11, b = 8, c = 1$). In such a case the equilibrium point will not be $E$ and the expressions for the $p$'s, $q$'s and $\pi$'s will be different; but there is no essential difference either in the stability of the system or in the essential validity of the subsequent remarks. A's locus of maximum profit no longer coincides with the line $\partial\pi_1/\partial p_1 = 0$, but consists of the portion of this line above its intersection with $p_1 - p_2 = c(l - a - b)$, and of the latter line below this point. Likewise B's locus of maximum profit consists of the part of the line $\partial\pi_2/\partial p_2 = 0$ to the right of its intersection with $p_2 - p_1 = c(l - a - b)$, together with the part of the last line to the left of this point. These two loci intersect at the point whose co-ordinates are, for $a > b$,

$$p_1 = c(3l - 3a - b), p_2 = 2c(l - a)$$

and the type of stability is the same as before.

system will descend to the equilibrium position $E$. Here neither competitor will have any incentive to lower his price further, since the increased business obtainable would fail to compensate him.

Indeed the difficulties of maintaining a price-fixing agreement have often been remarked. Not only may the short-sighted cupidity of one party send the whole system crashing through price-cutting; the very fear of a price cut will bring on a cut. Moreover, a price agreement cannot be made once for all; where conditions of cost or of demand are changing the price needs constant revision. The result is a constant jarring, an always obvious conflict of interests. As a child's pile of blocks falls to its equilibrium position when the table on which it stands is moved, so a movement of economic conditions tends to upset quasi-monopolistic schemes for staying above the point $E$. For two independent merchants to come to an agreement of any sort is notoriously difficult, but when the agreement must be made all over again at frequent intervals, when each has an incentive for breaking it, and when it is frowned upon by public opinion and must be secret and perhaps illegal, then the pact is not likely to be very durable. The difficulties are, of course, more marked if the competitors are more numerous, but they decidedly are present when there are only two.

The details of the interaction of the prices and sales will, of course, vary widely in different cases. Much will depend upon such market conditions as the degree of secrecy which can be maintained, the degree of possible discrimination among customers, the force of habit and character as affecting the reliance which each competitor feels he can put in the promises of the other, the frequency with which it is feasible to change a price or a rate of production, the relative value to the entrepreneur of immediate and remote profits, and so on. But always there is an insecurity at any point other than the point $E$ which represents equilibrium. Without some agreement, express or tacit, the value of $p_1$ will be less than or equal to the abscissa of $K$ in Fig. 2; and in the absence of a willingness on the part of one of the competitors to forgo immediate profits in order to maintain prices, the prices will become the co-ordinates of $E$.

One important item should be noticed. The prices may be maintained in a somewhat insecure way *above* their equilibrium values but will never remain *below* them. For if either A or B has a price which is less than that satisfying the simultaneous equations it will pay him *at once* to raise it. This is evident from the figure. Strikingly in contrast with the situation pictured by Bertrand, where prices were for ever being cut below their calculated values, the stabilising effect of the intermediate customers who shift their purchases gradually with changing prices makes itself felt in the existence of a pair of minimum prices. For a prudent investor the difference is all-important.

It is, of course, possible that A, feeling stronger than his opponent and desiring to get rid of him once for all, may reduce his price so far that B will give up the struggle and retire from the business. But during the continuance of this sort of price war A's income will be curtailed more than B's. In any case its possibility does not affect the argument that there is stability, since stability is by definition merely the tendency to return after *small* displacements. A box standing on end is in stable equilibrium, even though it can be tipped over.

## II

Having found a solution and acquired some confidence in it, we push the analysis further and draw a number of inferences regarding a competitive situation.

When the values of the $p$s and $q$s obtained on p. 350 are substituted in the previously found expressions for the profits we have

$$\pi_1 = \frac{c}{2}\left(l + \frac{a-b}{3}\right)^2, \quad \pi_2 = \frac{c}{2}\left(l - \frac{a-b}{3}\right)^2$$

The profits as well as the prices depend directly upon $c$, the unit cost of transportation. These particular merchants would do well, instead of organising improvement clubs and booster associations to better the roads, to make transportation as difficult as possible. Still better would be their situation if they could obtain a protective tariff to hinder the transportation of their commodity between them. Of course they will not want to impede the transportation of the supplies which come to them; the object of each is merely to attain something approaching a monopoly.

Another observation on the situation is that incomes exist which do not fall strictly within any of the commonly recognised categories. The quantities $\pi_1$ and $\pi_2$ just determined may be classified as monopoly profits, but only if we are ready to extend the term "monopoly" to include such cases as have been considered, involving the most outright competition for the marginal customer but without discrimination in his favour, and with no sort of open or tacit agreement between the sellers. These profits certainly do not consist of wages, interest or rent, since we have assumed no cost of production. This condition of no cost is not essential to the existence of such profits. If a constant cost of production per unit had been introduced into the calculations above, it would simply have been added to the prices without affecting the profits. Fixed overhead charges are to be subtracted from $\pi_1$ and $\pi_2$, but may leave a substantial residuum. These gains are not compensation for risk, since they represent a minimum return. They do not belong to the generalised type of "rent," which consists of the advantage of a producer over the marginal producer, since each makes a profit, and since, moreover, we may suppose $a$ and $b$ equal so as to make the situation symmetrical. Indeed $\pi_1$ and $\pi_2$ represent a special though common sort of profit which results from the fact that the number of sellers is finite. If there are three or more sellers, income of this kind will still exist, but as the number increases it will decline, to be replaced by generalised "rent" for the better-placed producers and poverty for the less fortunate. The number of sellers may be thought of as increasing as a result of a gradual increase in the number of buyers. Profits of the type we have described will exist at all stages of growth excepting those at which a new seller is just entering the field.

As a further problem, suppose that A's location has been fixed but that B is free to choose his place of business. Where will he set up shop? Evidently he will choose $b$ so as to make

$$\pi_2 = \frac{c}{2}\left(l + \frac{b-a}{3}\right)^2$$

as large as possible. This value of $b$ cannot be found by differentiation, as the value thus determined exceeds $l$ and, besides, yields a minimum for $\pi_2$ instead of a maximum. But for all smaller values of $b$, and so for all values of $b$ within the conditions of the problem, $\pi_2$ increases with $b$. Consequently B will seek to make $b$ as large as possible. This means that he will come just as close to A as other conditions permit. Naturally, if A is not exactly in the centre of the line, B will choose the side of A towards the more extensive section of the market, making $b$ greater than $a$.[9]

This gravitation of B towards A increases B's profit at the expense of A. Indeed, as appears from the expressions on p. 350, if $b$ increases so that B approaches A, both $q_2$ and $p_2$ increase while $q_1$ and $p_1$ diminish. From B's standpoint the sharper competition with A due to proximity is offset by the greater body of buyers with whom he has an advantage. But the danger that the system will be overturned by the elimination of one competitor is increased. The intermediate segment of the market acts as a cushion as well as a bone of contention; when it disappears we have Cournot's case, and Bertrand's objection applies. Or, returning to the analogy of the box in stable equilibrium though standing on end, the approach of B to A corresponds to a diminution in size of the end of the box.

It has become common for real-estate subdividers in the United States to impose restrictions which tend more or less to fix the character of future businesses in particular locations. Now we find from the calculations above that the total profits of A and B amount to

$$\pi_1 + \pi_2 = c\left[l^2 + \left(\frac{a-b}{3}\right)^2\right]$$

Thus a landlord or realtor who can determine the location of future stores, expecting to absorb their profits in the sales value of the land, has a motive for making the situation as unsymmetrical as possible; for, the more the lack of symmetry, the greater is $(a-b)^2$, which appears in the expression above for $\pi_1 + \pi_2$.

Our example has also an application to the question of capitalism v. socialism, and contributes an argument to the socialist side. Let us consider the efficiency of our pair of merchants in serving the public by calculating the total of transportation charges paid by consumers. These charges for the strip of length $a$ amount to

[9] The conclusion that B will tend to gravitate *infinitesimally* close to A requires a slight modification in the particular case before us, but not in general. In note 8 it was seen that when A and B are sufficiently close together, the analytic expressions for the prices, and consequently the profits, are different. By a simple algebraic calculation which will not here be reproduced it is found that B's profits $\pi_2$ will increase as B moves from the centre towards A, only if the distance between them is more than four-fifths of the distance from A to the centre. If B approaches more closely his profit is given by $\pi_2 = bc(3l - a - 3b)$, and diminishes with increasing $b$. This optimum distance from A is, however, an adventitious feature of our problem resulting from a discontinuity which is necessary for simplicity. In general we should consider $q_1$ and $q_2$ as continuous functions of $p_1$ and $p_2$, instead of supposing, as here, that as $p_2 - p_1$ falls below a certain limit, a great mass of buyers shift suddenly from B to A.

$$c \int_0^a t dt$$

or $\frac{1}{2} c a^2$. Altogether the sum is

$$\frac{1}{2} c \left( a^2 + b^2 + x^2 + y^2 \right)$$

Now if the places of business are both fixed, the quantities $a$, $b$ and $x + y$ are all determined. The minimum total cost for transportation will be achieved if, for the given value of $x + y$, the expression $x^2 + y^2$ is a minimum. This will be the case if $x$ and $y$ are equal.

But $x$ and $y$ will not be equal unless the prices $p_1$ and $p_2$ are equal, and under competition this is not likely to be the case. If we bar the improbable case of A and B having taken up symmetrical positions on the line, the prices which will result from each seeking his own gain have been seen to be different. If the segment $a$ in which A has a clear advantage is greater than $b$, then A's price will be greater than B's. Consequently some buyers will ship their purchases from B's store, though they are closer to A's, and socially it would be more economical for them to buy from A. If the stores were conducted for public service rather than for profit their prices would be identical in spite of the asymmetry of demand.

If the stores be thought of as movable, the wastefulness of private profit-seeking management becomes even more striking. There are now four variables, $a$, $b$, $x$ and $y$, instead of two. Their sum is the fixed length $l$, and to minimise the social cost of transportation found above we must make the sum of their squares as small as possible. As before, the variables must be equal. This requires A and B to occupy symmetrical positions at the quartiles of the market. But instead of doing so they crowd together as closely as possible. Even if A, the first in the field, should settle at one of these points, we have seen that B upon his arrival will not go to the other, but will fix upon a location between A and the centre and as near A as possible.[10] Thus some customers will have to transport their goods a distance of more than $\frac{1}{2} l$, whereas with two stores run in the public interest no shipment should be for a greater distance than $\frac{1}{4} l$.

If a third seller C appears, his desire for as large a market as possible will prompt him likewise to take up a position close to A or B, but not between them. By an argument similar to that just used, it may be shown that regard only for the public interest would require A, B and C each to occupy one of the points at distances one-sixth, one-half and five-sixths of the way from one end of the line to the other. As more and more sellers of the same commodity arise, the tendency is not to become distributed in the socially optimum manner but to cluster unduly.

The importance and variety of such agglomerative tendencies become apparent when it is remembered that distance, as we have used it for illustration, is only a figurative term for a great congeries of qualities. Instead of sellers of an identical commodity separated geographically we might have considered two competing cider merchants side by side, one selling a sweeter liquid than the other. If the consumers of cider be thought of as varying

---

[10] With the unimportant qualification mentioned in note 8.

by infinitesimal degrees in the sourness they desire, we have much the same situation as before. The measure of sourness now replaces distance, while instead of transportation costs there are the degrees of disutility resulting from a consumer getting cider more or less different from what he wants. The foregoing considerations apply, particularly the conclusion that competing sellers tend to become too much alike.

The mathematical analysis thus leads to an observation of wide generality. Buyers are confronted everywhere with an excessive sameness. When a new merchant or manufacturer sets up shop he must not produce something exactly like what is already on the market or he will risk a price war of the type discussed by Bertrand in connection with Cournot's mineral springs. But there is an incentive to make the new product very much like the old, applying some slight change which will seem an improvement to as many buyers as possible without ever going far in this direction. The tremendous standardisation of our furniture, our houses, our clothing, our automobiles and our education are due in part to the economies of large-scale production, in part to fashion and imitation. But over and above these forces is the effect we have been discussing, the tendency to make only slight deviations in order to have for the new commodity as many buyers of the old as possible, to get, so to speak, *between* one's competitors and a mass of customers.

So general is this tendency that it appears in the most diverse fields of competitive activity, even quite apart from what is called economic life. In politics it is strikingly exemplified. The competition for votes between the Republican and Democratic parties does not lead to a clear drawing of issues, an adoption of two strongly contrasted positions between which the voter may choose. Instead, each party strives to make its platform as much like the other's as possible. Any radical departure would lose many votes, even though it might lead to stronger commendation of the party by some who would vote for it anyhow. Each candidate "pussyfoots," replies ambiguously to questions, refuses to take a definite stand in any controversy for fear of losing votes. Real differences, if they ever exist, fade gradually with time though the issues may be as important as ever. The Democratic party, once opposed to protective tariffs, moves gradually to a position almost, but not quite, identical with that of the Republicans. It need have no fear of fanatical free-traders, since they will still prefer it to the Republican party, and its advocacy of a continued high tariff will bring it the money and votes of some intermediate groups.

The reasoning, of course, requires modification when applied to the varied conditions of actual life. Our example might have been more complicated. Instead of a uniform distribution of customers along a line we might have assumed a varying density, but with no essential change in conclusions. Instead of a linear market we might suppose the buyers spread out on a plane. Then the customers from one region will patronise A, those from another B. The boundary between the two regions is the locus of points for which the difference of transportation costs from the two shops equals the difference of prices, *i.e.* for which the delivered price is the same whether the goods are bought from A or from B. If transportation is in straight lines (perhaps by aeroplane) at a cost proportional to the distance, the boundary will be a hyperbola, since a hyperbola is the locus of points such that the difference of distances from the foci is constant. If there are three or more sellers, their regions will be separated from each other by arcs of hyperbolas. If the transportation is not in straight lines, or if its cost is given by such a complicated function as a railroad freight schedule, the boundaries will be of another kind; but we might generalise the term hyperbola (as is done in the differential geometry of curved surfaces) to include these curves also.

The number of dimensions of our picture is increased to three or more when we represent geometrically such characters as sweetness of cider, and instead of transportation costs consider more generally the decrement of utility resulting from the actual commodity being in a different place and condition than the buyer would prefer. Each homogeneous commodity or service or entrepreneur in a competing system can be thought of as a point serving a region separated from other such regions by portions of generalised hyperboloids. The density of demand in this space is in general not uniform, and is restricted to a finite region. It is not necessary that each point representing a service or commodity shall be under the control of a different entrepreneur from every other. On the other hand, everyone who sells an article in different places or who sells different articles in the same place may be said to control the prices at several points of the symbolic space. The mutual gravitation will now take the form of a tendency of the outermost entrepreneurs to approach the cluster.

Two further modifications are important. One arises when it is possible to discriminate among customers, or to sell goods at a delivered price instead of a fixed price at store or factory plus transportation. In such cases, even without an agreement between sellers, a monopoly profit can be collected from some consumers while fierce competition is favouring others. This seems to have been the condition in the cement industry about which a controversy raged a few years ago, and was certainly involved in the railroad rebate scandals.

The other important modification has to do with the elasticity of demand. The problem of the two merchants on a linear market might be varied by supposing that each consumer buys an amount of the commodity in question which depends on the delivered price. If one tries a particular demand function the mathematical complications will now be considerable, but for the most general problems elasticity must be assumed. The difficulty as to whether prices or quantities should be used as independent variables can now be cleared up. This question has troubled many readers of Cournot. The answer is that either set of variables may be used; that the $q$s may be expressed in terms of the $p$s, and the $p$s in terms of the $q$s. This was not possible in Cournot's example of duopoly, nor heretofore in ours. The sum of our $q$s was constrained to have the fixed value $l$, so that they could not be independent, but when the demand is made elastic the constraint vanishes.

With elastic demand the observations we have made on the solution will still for the most part be qualitatively true; but the tendency for B to establish his business excessively close to A will be less marked. The increment in B's sales to his more remote customers when he moves nearer them may be more than compensation to him for abandoning some of his nearer business to A. In this case B will definitely and apart from extraneous circumstances choose a location at some distance from A. But he will not go as far from A as the public welfare would require. The tempting intermediate market will still have an influence.

In the more general problem in which the commodities purveyed differ in many dimensions the situation is the same. The elasticity of demand of particular groups does mitigate the tendency to excessive similarity of competing commodities, but not enough. It leads some factories to make cheap shoes for the poor and others to make expensive shoes for the rich, but all the shoes are too much alike. Our cities become uneconomically large and the business districts within them are too concentrated. Methodist and Presbyterian churches are too much alike; cider is too homogeneous.

SIXTY-TWO

# The Mathematical Economics of Professor Amoroso*

FRANCIS EDGEWORTH

Source: *Economic Journal* 30 (September), 1922, pp. 400–7.

THE high reputation earned by the Italian school of mathematical economics will be enhanced by this publication. Professor Amoroso appears to especial advantage when dealing with that part of economics which is most amenable to mathematical treatment, the theory of value. He restates felicitiously the relations of value to utility. He smooths and straightens the path struck out by the pioneers, Gossen, and Jevons, and Walras. He presents in juxtaposition the two views of the subject which we might distinguish as hedonic and economic. According to the first view there is a function which represents and *measures* the satisfaction derived from a certain quantity of commodity considered as the variable. According to the second view the function is only an *index* increasing with the increase and decreasing with the decrease of satisfaction, but not measuring that subjective quantity. According to both views there exist very generally functions such that the differential coefficient of the function with respect to a variable, say $x$, representing the amount of a commodity, divided by the corresponding differential coefficient for another commodity $y$, represents the value of $x$ in exchange for $y$; the price of $x$, we may say, if $y$ is the monetary substance – that is, supposing that there is fulfilled a certain condition purporting that purchasers of $x$ will have obtained as much as they demand at the price. As a simple form suited to act as a representative of "ophelimity," or at least as an "index-function," Professor Amoroso uses $cx^a$, where $c$ is a positive constant and $a$ is a positive proper fraction. There is then fulfilled the primary condition that the function should increase with the increase of the variable. There is also fulfilled the supplementary condition above referred to, since $ca(a-1)x^{a-2}$ (the second differential coefficient) is negative. The function may involve more than one variable. Professor Amoroso instances $Ax^\alpha + By^\beta + Cx^\alpha y^\beta$. Here the first differential coefficients with respect to $x$ and $y$ correspond to the respective prices; and two supplementary conditions are furnished by the second differential coefficients. Here we interject a query: Is there not required a *third* supplementary condition to make sure of economic equilibrium? Say $x$ and $y$ denote respectively quantities of bread and beef. The two supplementary conditions stated by our

---

* Book Review on *Lezioni di Economia Mathematica*. Luigi Amoroso. (Bologna: Zanichelli. 1921. P. 478.)

author (page 86) secure that, the consumption of beef being supposed fixed, the purchasers of bread will obtain just what they demand at the price; and likewise, if the supply of bread were fixed, that the purchasers of beef would be satisfied. But is it made sure that the purchase of *sandwiches* of the form $\lambda x + \mu y$ (where $\lambda$ and $\mu$ are any positive constants) – the concurrent consumption of the two commodities – will come to a stop when $x$ and $y$ have the values above determined? Professor Amoroso, a distinguished mathematician, does not need to be reminded that in order to secure a true maximum for a function of two variables, there are in general *three* conditions which must be satisfied by the second differential coefficients.

After fully and clearly describing the "equilibrium of the consumer," Professor Amoroso goes on to the "equilibrium of the producer." He makes good use of a construction which he names the "curve of unitary costs"; unitary cost being the total cost of production divided by the amount produced. The construction is much the same as Professor Pigou's "curve of marginal production." It is much required when we are dealing with the case of decreasing costs (increasing returns). In this connection we note that Professor Amoroso defines decreasing costs by the condition that the *unitary* cost is decreasing. Some might prefer to take as the essential attribute of increasing returns the decrease of *marginal* cost. But all must agree that Professor Amoroso's statement contrasts favourably with that of literary economists who often leave it uncertain whether they mean unitary or marginal cost (Cp. *Economic Journal*, XXI, p. 293 *et seq.*). The charm of lucidity, indeed, pervades our author's work. Very clearly he distinguishes the *régime* of monopoly, in which the producer is free to vary the price, and the regime of competition, in which the producer can only vary the quantity which he will supply at the given price. What price the monopolist will fix is investigated on the lines of Cournot. There are some interesting deductions concerning the displacement of the "Cournot point" to the detriment or benefit of the consumers by means of a tax or bounty.

Beyond this stage we are unable to follow the author's investigation of monopoly, when he extends to the case of two monopolists the reasoning which he had applied with success to the case of one. This extension appears to us illegitimate, for reasons which have been stated in the articles on Monopoly in the *Giornale degli Economisti* for 1897. We shall here direct our objections to the example given by Professor Amoroso (p. 258). He supposes the law of demand for a certain commodity to be such that the quantity $x$ is demanded at the price

$$450/(2 + x) \tag{a}$$

(the sloping line signifying division). The commodity is supplied by two competing monopolists, Primus and Secundus, who produce it under similar conditions. The cost to Primus of producing $y$ is

$$30y - y^2 + \frac{1}{4}(y - 5)^2(y - 8)^2 \tag{b}$$

And likewise the cost to Secundus of producing $z$ is

$$30z - z^2 + \frac{1}{4}(z - 5)^2(z - 8)^2 \tag{c}$$

The quantity at any time supplied being the sum of the amounts supplied by each producer, we may put $y + z$ for $x$ in the expression (a) for the price. We have thus for the net profits of Primus and Secundus, respectively,

$$y450/(2 + y + z) - (30y - y^2 + \frac{1}{4}(y - 5)^2(y - 8)^2)  \tag{d}$$

$$z450/(2 + y + z) - (30z - z^2 + \frac{1}{4}(z - 5)^2(z - 8)^2)  \tag{e}$$

Accordingly, argues Professor Amoroso, Primus will vary $y$ so as to make (d) a maximum; and likewise Secundus will vary $z$ so as to make (e) a maximum. Whence we obtain two simultaneous equations:

$$450(2 + z)/(2 + y + z)^2 - 30 + 2y - \frac{1}{2}(y - 5)(y - 8)(2y - 13)  \tag{f}$$

$$450(2 + y)/(2 + y + z)^2 - 30 + 2z - \frac{1}{2}(z - 5)(z - 8)(2z - 13)  \tag{g}$$

The solution of this system determines the position of equilibrium, which is accordingly attained when Primus supplies 5, and Secundus 8.

This procedure appears to us inappropriate to pure monopoly. It might be appropriate to a kind of *kartel* in which each producer is free from time to time to alter the amount of commodity which he puts on the market, the price being allowed in the interval between such changes to accommodate itself to the total supply. But this convention appears unduly to limit the characteristic freedom of the monopolist to vary price. If Primus were an alert business man, he would not acquiesce in an arrangement according to which his rival made a profit 64 while he himself, producing under equally favourable conditions, netted only 25 (as follows from substituting 5 and 8 for $y$ and $z$, respectively, in both (d) and (e)). Primus would "cut" the price, charging instead of 30 (the price when $x = y + z = 5 + 8 = 13$) $30 - \kappa$; where $\kappa$ is very small, just large enough for Primus to draw off from his rival as much custom as he likes. How much will he like? The amount which it will be most advantageous for him to supply is that value of $y$ which maximises $(30 - \kappa)y - (b)$; i.e.

$$y^2 - \frac{1}{4}(y - 5)^2(y - 8)^2 - \kappa y  \tag{h}$$

Proceeding as usual we find that this expression is (or would be if $\kappa$ were zero) approximately a maximum when $y = 9.444$. The net profit of Primus will therefore be

$$9.444(30 - \kappa) - 9.444 \cdot 30 + 9.444^2 - \frac{1}{4}(4.444^2 \cdot 1.444^2)$$

that is, all but 79 – an improvement upon 25! Meanwhile, Secundus will have lost a great part of his custom, which will be reduced in the ratio of 8: (13 – 9.444). If to this residue he supplies, at the price 30, what it demands at that price, viz. 3.556, he will make a profit of about 2.35! Faced thus with the loss of custom and profits he will no doubt cut the price anew. Primus will retort; and thus the price will be continually lowered. Conceivably it might descend to a figure at which each monopolist, or rather the one who has made the last cut of the price, say Primus, will earn next to nothing. This limit is found to be in the neighbourhood of 21.5717. For in general corresponding to any assigned reduction, $\kappa$, from the original price 30, the value of $y$ which is most advantageous to Primus, is that which maximises $(h)$. Accordingly, when $\kappa = 8.4283$, the best that Primus can do for himself is to put about 8.97 on the market. But that best is very bad; for, with the said values of $\kappa$ and $y$, $(h)$ reduces to 1.15! At this stage it may be thought that equilibrium will have been reached. But this would only occur in the particular case where at the limiting price one of the monopolists can supply the whole demand of the market. But this is very far from being the case in the example before us. At the price 21.5717 the demand of the market, found by equating $(a)$ to that figure, is nearly 18.89. Thus Primus supplies a little less than half the total demand. One might suppose that when Primus announced the price 21.5717, his establishment would be besieged by a long queue, of which only about half could be satisfied. The remainder would turn to Secundus, who can satisfy the greater part of them on the same terms. But it will occur to Secundus that, as he is indispensable to the unsatisfied "tail" of Primus' queue, there is no necessity for him to adopt Primus' terms. Why not fix a price more advantageous to himself? The price that is most advantageous under the circumstance may be found thus. According to $(a)$ $x$, the amount of commodity that would be absorbed by the full market consisting of all possible customers at any price $p$, is $(450 - 2p)/p$. The amount, then, that will be absorbed by the portion of the (homogeneous) body of customers with which Secundus has now to deal is to $x$:: as $(18.89 - 8.97)$: 18.8607; say, 1: 1.9. Whence $p = 450/(2 + 1.9z)$. Therefore the net profit to Secundus from the output $z$

$$= z450/(2 + 1.9z) + z^2 - 30z - \frac{1}{4}(z - 5)^2(z - 8)^2 \qquad (i)$$

The value of $z$ which renders this expression a maximum is found to be approximately 3.9. Substituting this value in $(i)$ we find the net profit of Secundus to be about 80. His price will be about 47.8. Primus will certainly not be content to make only 1.15 while his rival is making 80. Primus will fix a price a little below 47.8, and so draw off custom from Secundus. Secundus will retort with a fresh cut; and so the price will again descend, again to mount.

It is to be understood that the details in this illustration have been filled in to "fix the ideas," as the mathematicians say. Thus we need not assume that Primus after the cut which brought the price down to 21.5717 satisfied completely a minority of the market, while the majority – the "tail" of the queue which the lowered price attracted – went away empty. It comes to the same if Primus partially satisfied a majority. Nor is it to be supposed that the price will really be beaten down to the limit at which profits vanish. Long before that limit is reached one or other of the monopolists will ask himself whether it would not be more profitable, instead of cutting his rival's price, to raise the price on the customers left to him. Suppose, for instance, that the price has been beaten down (from 30) to 25.208, the last cut having been made by Primus; at that price the amount which

Primus will find it most advantageous to put on the market (as determined from $(h)$, $\kappa$ being now 4.792) will be 9.2. Accordingly, the net profit of Primus will be 34.2. Secundus may count on a profit only slightly less than this if he cuts the price. The advantage of the alternative course is thus reckoned. Whereas (by $(a)$) the amount demanded by the whole market at the price 25.208 would be 15.85, the "tail" of custom left to Secundus when Primus has supplied 9.2 is to the whole market as 6.65 is to 15.85, say as 1: 2.38. It is proper therefore to substitute 2.38 for 1.9 in $(i)$. Proceeding as usual we shall find that the value of $z$ which maximises the expression thus presented is approximately 3.7, corresponding to price 41.6, and net profit nearly 49. It will be more profitable, therefore, for Secundus to withdraw from the direct competition and deal separately with the customers left to him by his rival's last cut. But it is not certain that Secundus will raise his price to the theoretic height of 41.6. Practical considerations may induce him to make a less violent jump. For Primus it will then be a matter for deliberation whether he should cut the price fixed by Secundus, or, jumping to a still higher price, deal separately with the custom left to him by Secundus. We cannot foresee what the jumps will be; theory predicts only that the jumping will go on for ever, as long as the monopolists are uncombined.

We should give judgment in this matter against Professor Amoroso with more confidence if he had not appealed to Professor Pareto. We have not seen the note by Professor Pareto to which our author makes reference (p. 260). But from the writings of Professor Pareto with which we are acquainted we do not gather that he differs seriously from the conclusions reached in the article on Monopoly to which we have referred. He indeed raises the nice question whether from a mathematical point of view it is proper to describe as "indeterminate" a position which is too much determined, there being more equations than unknowns. But that is not to dispute the statement that there is not a "determinate and definitive" position of equilibrium (Giornale, *loc. cit.*, p. 22), not the same sort of stability in duopoly as in monopoly and in perfect competition. We believe that Professor Amoroso is alone among high authorities in siding with Cournot in this matter. The view that in monopolistic competition "the output is indeterminate" . . . "is now commonly accepted," says Professor Pigou; and, he adds, "appears to me to be the correct one" (*Wealth and Welfare*, p. 193).

Altogether our author's teaching about duopoly cannot be regarded as part of accepted science. We should recommend the omission of this topic, if it were proposed to translate the work into English with the view of supplying the much-felt need of an introduction to mathematical economics. If excision were permitted, we should also advise pruning the redundancy of digressions. It is disconcerting to a beginner to encounter at the ninth page a digression of ten pages on the determination of the present value of national capital. Herodotus was not more fond of digressions. But the father of History is not so good a model in this respect as the father of Political Economy, whose classical Digressions are few and far between. We speak in the interest of tiros. For the mature student our author's digressions are good reading. The same may be said, indeed, of the disputable passages which we think unsuited to beginners. It is good to consider views different from our own presented with ability and perspicuity.

As a second example of the last-named advantage, we shall refer to our author's treatment of the cases in which two or more monopolists produce each a *different* article. Professor Amoroso applies to this case the same reasoning as he had applied to the case of the *same* article produced by two monopolists. The reasoning is more plausible when the different articles are *complementary*. This case is not well illustrated by Professor Amoroso's example. For there is a *singularity* in the data instanced by him which render them unsuitable for a simple representation of the *general* theory. In general it may be presumed that the curves corresponding to (*f*) and (*g*) [in the figure] *intersect* at the point which they have in common. Consider, for instance, in the annexed figure, the curves FF' and GG'. Here FF' is the locus of points such that if Secundus supply any assigned quantity O$z$ of his commodity, the quantity O$y$ which it will then be most advantageous for Primus to supply is determined by the intersection of a horizontal through $z$, with the curve FF'. The curve GG' likewise determines the ordinate $z$ corresponding to any assigned $y$. If then P is the intersection of the two curves, it would seem that neither party has an interest in moving from that position. It is not now, as before, the interest of Primus to lower his price. By so doing he would only diminish his own profits while increasing the profits of the other monopolist. Nevertheless, it is not against his interest to move a *little* way from P on the horizontal through P: although – or rather, just because – P is a position of maximum. Suppose, then, Primus moves to $f_1$. It will then be the interest of Secundus to lower his supply to $g_1$. It will not now be the immediate interest of Primus to move again to the left. But if he does so, it is likely to prove advantageous to him, since Secundus will then descend to $g_2$; and it is in general advantageous to Primus to descend *some way* on the curve GG' (cp. Giornale, *loc. cit.*, p. 26, where the argument is not affected by the difference in the slope of the curve corresponding to GG', nor by the circumstance that the curves there relate to prices and here to quantities). No doubt this excursion must come to a stop. But then Secundus may initiate a similar deviation.

And there will go on vibration inconsistent with that determinate equilibrium which is characteristic of pure competition. So far supposing that the different articles are *complementary*. A fortiori if the articles are *rival* or, in Professor Amoroso's phrase, "supplementary." For then there are superadded to the dance just now described the leaps and bounds before exhibited. If Primus is the purveyor of beef and Secundus of mutton they will go on making moves against each other very much as if they were producers of the same article. Accordingly, we cannot, with Professor Amoroso (p. 418), regard the regime

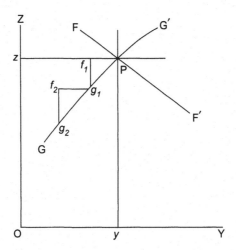

in which every industry is monopolised as comparable in respect of equilibrium with a regime of pure competition. The determinateness which theoretically exists in the latter case is theoretically absent in the former.

Again, we are unable to accept Professor Amoroso's views about Protection. He seems to think that there is on balance of pros and cons no general presumption in favour of Free Trade. "On the contrary, it is particular historical circumstance varying from time to time and from place to place that require the adoption sometimes of one solution, sometimes of the other, most frequently of a solution between the two" (p. 322). In the scales of our judgment the two policies are not so evenly balanced. Nor are we convinced by the "equations which represent that profits are zero" (p. 408; cp. p. 178). No number of equations or authorities will persuade us that this doctrine is other than paradoxical.

But while differing from our author on some cardinal points, we recognise that he has evinced great ability in defence of positions which we regard as indefensible. If they were defensible,

"Si ... dextrâ

Defendi possent, etiam hâc defensa fuissent."

# SIXTY-THREE

# Existence and Computation of Mixed Strategy Nash Equilibrium for 3-Firms Location Problem

AVNER SHAKED

Source: *Journal of Industrial Economics* 31 (September–December), 1982, pp. 93–6. Reprinted by permission of Blackwell Publishers.

Location problems of firms on a closed interval were introduced by Hotelling [3] and later investigated by Eaton & Lipsey [2]. Firms sell a homogeneous product at a fixed price, customers distributed along the interval buy one unit each from the firm nearest to them and firms aim to maximize the number of their customers. It is well known that where the customers are evenly distributed along the interval and the number of firms is other than 3 the location problem has a pure strategy Nash equilibrium (see [2]).

The case of 3 firms is peculiar in that no pure strategy Nash equilibrium exists, for in any situation one of the extreme firms (not located between the other two) can increase its revenue by either moving towards or away from the other two firms. The existence of mixed strategies is not obvious because the payoff functions are discontinuous whenever two or more firms are located at the same point.

In a recent paper Dasgupta and Maskin [1] investigate a class of games, all derived from economic problems and all with some discontinuities in their payoff functions. They demonstrate that the discontinuities in the payoff functions do not prevent the existence of mixed strategies Nash equilibria in the games investigated. In particular, location problems of the type described earlier have such "weak" discontinuities and hence possess a mixed strategy Nash equilibrium. Although their proof is constructive, offering a method of approaching these equilibria as a limit of equilibria of finite games, the equations involved very quickly become unmanageable. In this note we compute a mixed strategy Nash equilibrium for the 3 firms location problem.

Let the customers be evenly distributed along [0, 1] then a mixed strategy is a probability measure over [0, 1]. The symmetry of the problem suggests that the solution will be doubly symmetric in that all firms choose the same mixed strategy and that this strategy is symmetric around $\frac{1}{2}$ (symmetric locations are given the same probabilities). Dasgupta and Maskin confine their analysis to doubly symmetric solutions and prove that the strategies in any doubly symmetric equilibrium are atomless.

Given the symmetric nature of the game and following the analysis of Dasgupta and Maskin we shall confine ourselves here to such doubly symmetric equilibria. We demonstrate here that *the 3 firms location problem has a unique doubly symmetric mixed strategy equilibrium*, given by:

$$g(x) = \begin{cases} 2 & \frac{1}{4} \le x \le \frac{3}{4} \\ 0 & \text{otherwise} \end{cases} \tag{$*$}$$

This implies that firms in equilibrium avoid the extreme quartiles and choose locations in the remaining half with equal probability.

Let two firms choose their location according to a symmetric (atomless) density probability function $f(x)$; we compute the payoff function for the third firm. For an equilibrium $f(x)$ the payoff function of the third firm assumes a single value over the support of $f$ and a lower value outside the support. We assume without loss of generality that the support of $f$ is a subset of $[\alpha, 1 - \alpha]$ for $0 \le \alpha < \frac{1}{2}$.

Define:

$$Q(x) = \int_\alpha^x f(t)dt$$

$$R(x) = \int_x^{1-\alpha} f(t)dt = 1 - Q(x)$$

Then:

$$Q'(x) = f(x) = -R'(x)$$

Let the third firm locate itself at $z$, its payoff there is given by:

$$A(z) = 2 \int_\alpha^z f(x)Q(x)\left(1 - \frac{z+x}{2}\right)dx \; + 2 \int_\alpha^z \int_z^{1-\alpha} f(x)f(y)\frac{y-x}{2}dydx$$
$$+ 2 \int_z^{1-\alpha} f(x)R(x)\frac{x+z}{2}dx. \tag{1}$$

The first integral represents payoff when the two firms are located to the left of $z$, and the last integral when both firms are to the right of $z$, the second integral corresponds to the case of one firm on each side of $z$.

Differentiating w.r.t. $z$:

$$A'(z) = 2f(z)Q(z)(1-z) - \int_\alpha^z f(x)Q(x)dx + f(z)\int_z^{1-\alpha} f(y)(y-z)dy$$
$$- f(z)\int_\alpha^z f(x)(z-x)dx - 2f(z)R(z)z + \int_z^{1-\alpha} f(x)R(x)dx. \tag{2}$$

Since:

$$R + Q \equiv 1, \quad \int f(x)Q(x)dx = \frac{1}{2}Q^2(x), \quad \int_{\alpha}^{1-\alpha} xf(x)dx = \frac{1}{2},$$

equation (2) becomes:

$$A'(z) = \left(\frac{1}{2} - Q(z)\right) + f(z)\left[3\left(\frac{1}{2} - z\right) - 2\left(\frac{1}{2} - Q(z)\right)\right]. \tag{3}$$

We are looking for a function $Q(z)$ (with $Q'(z) = f(z)$) such that $A'(z) = 0$ whenever $f(z) \neq 0$. Under the transformation

$$h(z) = \frac{\frac{1}{2} - Q(z)}{\frac{1}{2} - z}$$

the differential equation $A'(z) = 0$ becomes:

$$h'(2h - z)\left(\frac{1}{2} - z\right) = 2h(h - 2) \tag{4}$$

This is a simple separable equation whose solution is implicitly given by:

$$h^3(h - 2) = K\left(\frac{1}{2} - z\right)^{-4}, \tag{5}$$

where $K$ is a constant.

Let $K = 0$, this defines one acceptable solution for $h : h \equiv 2$ (the other solution, $h \equiv 0$ implies $Q \equiv \frac{1}{2}$ and is therefore ruled out).

Hence

$$Q(z) = 2\left(z - \frac{1}{2}\right) + \frac{1}{2} = 2\left(z - \frac{1}{4}\right)$$

which is the $Q(z)$ derived from the distribution $g(x)$ defined in (*). To show that this is an equilibrium we need to demonstrate that the payoff outside the support is lower than in it. For $z \leq \frac{1}{4}, f(z) \equiv 0$ and the payoff at $z$ is:

$$A(z) = 2\int_{1/4}^{3/4} f(x)R(x)\left(\frac{x + z}{2}\right)dx$$

This is an increasing function of $z$ and since $A(z)$ is continuous and symmetric in $z$, the payoff is highest in the support.

We now demonstrate that no other solution of the differential equation is suitable as an equilibrium. Let $Q(z)$ and $h(z)$ be the solutions of (4) for $K \neq 0$. Let $z$ be the first point for which $Q(z) = \frac{1}{2}$, then $z$ is the limit of points in the support. If $z < \frac{1}{2}$ (or $z > \frac{1}{2}$) then by the definition of $h$: $h(z) = 0$ but since (5) holds at that point, $h(z)$ cannot be zero, hence $z = \frac{1}{2}$. Rearranging the terms in (5):

$$\left[ h(z)\left(\frac{1}{2} - z\right) \right]^3 (h(z) - 2)\left(\frac{1}{2} - z\right) = K.$$

By the definition of $h(z)$ this becomes:

$$\left(\frac{1}{2} - Q(z)\right)^3 \left(2z - Q(z) - \frac{1}{2}\right) = K.$$

Taking the limit as $z \to \frac{1}{2}$, the left hand side converges to 0, i.e. $K = 0$. Hence (5) represents a solution to (4) only for $K = 0$.

### References

DASGUPTA, P. and MASKIN, E., "The Existence of Equilibrium in Discontinuous Economic Games", ICERD, LSE, London.

EATON, B. C. and LIPSEY, R. G. (1975), "The Principle of Minimum Differentiation Reconsidered: Some New Developments in the Theory of Spatial Competition", *Review of Economic Studies*, 42(1), No. 129, January, 27–49.

HOTELLING, H. (1929), "Stability in Competition", *Economic Journal*, 39, March, 41–57.

# SIXTY-FOUR

# Busting a Trust: Electrical Contractors Reel Under Charges That They Rigged Bids

ANDY PASZTOR

*Source*: *Wall Street Journal*, November 29, 1985.

Washington – One spring morning three years ago, William Baxter, then the head of the Justice Department's antitrust division, received a startling letter alleging rampant bid-rigging among many of the nation's largest and most respected electrical contractors. The letter accused the contractors of secretly inflating bids and routinely conspiring to divvy up billions of dollars of contracts nationwide since the early 1970s. The tipster identified more than a dozen specific projects where he claimed executives engaged in or condoned blatantly anti-competitive behavior. The anonymous letter contained details that could have been written only by somebody with intimate knowledge of the industry's operations.

"A letter like that surely had to trigger an investigation," Mr. Baxter recalls, "unless we had some clear indication that the writer was an outright liar or a lunatic." As it turned out, says a senior Justice Department antitrust official, the unsolicited warning was "a prosecutor's dream come true." Investigators eventually traced the letter to William Schwartzkopf, a disgruntled former general counsel for Commonwealth Electric Co. of Lincoln, Neb., the fifth-largest electrical contractor in the U.S. Mr. Schwartzkopf now says that the importance of his role "has been blown somewhat out of proportion," and he declines to discuss what caused him to alert the government. But his tip has prompted an unprecedented flurry of federal and state prosecutions of the $5 billion-a-year industry, costing it at least an estimated $20 million so far in total fines, legal fees and private damage payments. (Commonwealth Electric was charged but acquitted.) Pending antitrust claims by alleged victims such as utilities, power plants and factory owners could cost the companies many times more.

So far, 18 federal grand juries have investigated bid-rigging by contractors, resulting in guilty pleas by or convictions of 33 companies and 34 individuals in at least 15 states. At least 14 executives have received jail sentences and eight more await trials in federal courts. Total federal and state prosecutions rival the bid-rigging actions against highway contractors in recent years. The Justice Department still has 13 grand juries investigating the industry, raising howls from electrical contractors that the government is being over-zealous. But Douglas Ginsburg, the newly confirmed assistant attorney general in charge of antitrust enforcement, maintains that despite the government's crackdown, bid-rigging among contractors "still is occurring on a wider basis than I would have believed possible." Mr. Ginsburg argues that company officials who file false bids in any industry are guilty of "theft at the wholesale level," and says, "I'd like to see them in the pen."

Depositions, filings and court testimony in numerous cases show that rigged bids for electrical contracting cost consumers and taxpayers incalculable millions of dollars. Prosecutors claim violations range from work on multibillion-dollar nuclear power plants in the Pacific Northwest to Pennsylvania steel mills and Indiana auto plants. Attorneys for one defendant company, for instance, told a federal judge that prices for certain work on oil refineries in Pennsylvania were inflated by as much as 21%. Evidence gathered by prosecutors shows that contractors commonly used padded invoices, kickbacks, secret code words and clandestine meetings in clubs or hotels to allocate lucrative contracts. Prosecutors contend the low bidder typically was chosen a few days or weeks in advance, while other conspirators kept their bids artificially high. Prosecutors in North Carolina say executives in that state exchanged information in such an unconcerned, business-as-usual manner that some contractors signed blank bid forms for certain jobs and simply gave them to the designated low bidder to fill out and turn in on their behalf. Nine small companies have pleaded guilty in state courts to rigging bids on a medical complex for Eastern Carolina University. And Bryant-Durham Electric Co. of Durham, N. C., paid an $80,000 fine in 1983 in federal court in Raleigh for participating in another conspiracy to rig bids on several hospital projects in the state.

Federal court records in Pennsylvania show that starting as early as 1967, major contractors set up a complicated rotation system for allocating contracts in that state. The system was based on the size of the bids, whose turn it was to be the "designated hitter" to win a contract and which of the participants most needed the work. Precise records were kept and, according to court documents, the conspiracy was suspended temporarily in those rare instances when the group felt one of the authorized bidders couldn't be trusted. In a recent opinion, Federal Judge Joseph McGlynn in Philadelphia said the conspiracy was so strong in Pennsylvania that "there was no fear or hesitation" recruiting new participants. During one secret meeting at a hotel near the Pittsburgh airport, the judge said, the president of Sargent Electric Co. of Philadelphia "apologized" to his counterparts "for the mistake" of underbidding a competitor previously designated to receive a contract from U.S. Steel Corp. Sargent even agreed to "lose a turn" obtaining contracts from U.S. Steel Corp., the judge said. (Nevertheless, he dismissed charges against Sargent and other contractors. He indicated that he did so because they already had been convicted or pleaded guilty to similar charges in the state.) In many states, "this really was the way of life in the industry until a few years ago," asserts Charles F. Rule, a deputy assistant attorney general. Rigging of bids was so prevalent, Mr. Rule contends, that "it would be difficult for me to say" that the top executives of major companies "wouldn't have known something about the practices."

The list of convictions and guilty pleas already reads like a Who's Who of the industry. It includes Dallas-based Fischbach  Moore Inc., the nation's largest electrical contractor, two of its subsidiaries and several company executives; Howard P. Foley Co. of Washington, D.C., and its former president, Bancroft T. Foley, who served five months in jail;

New York-based Lord Electric Co. and Paul Arbogast, one of its vice presidents; and Sargent Electric. The list also includes about two dozen smaller companies. Additional prosecutions are likely to be started in the next few months before the five-year statute of limitations runs out. In federal court in Covington, Ky., Lord Electric, its president and chief executive, Peter F. Matthews, and another senior company manager are under indictment on charges of rigging bids on a $9 million coal-fired generating station built for a group of rural electric cooperatives in the northeastern corner of the state. In this case, the government contends that Lord provided an illegal $50,000 payoff to Wente Construction Co. of Hamilton, Ohio, in order to ensure that the smaller contractor would cooperate in the conspiracy. Last year, Wente pleaded guilty to fraud charges for its part in the alleged scheme to get Lord the contract. The other defendants pleaded innocent and are contesting the charges.

Apart from going after bid-riggers, the government also has indicted a former Foley branch manager in California and a number of other defendants from other companies for obstructing justice by allegedly destroying or failing to turn over internal company documents demanded by investigators. In a separate case, Lord and Mr. Arbogast, a vice president in Portland, Ore., pleaded guilty to charges filed in federal court in Tucson, Ariz., of improperly concealing that they provided thousands of dollars of free trips to a contracts administrator for the Washington Public Power Supply System between 1979 and 1982. Lord was a major contractor for WPPSS during those years.

Industry officials charge that the Justice Department is going too far. "I think they simply lost their judgement in this area," asserts attorney Gordon Spivack, a former government trustbuster who represents Fischbach Moore in several criminal cases. "The department is charging everything anyone can possibly think of," Mr. Spivack argues. "It's straining to find cases." Industry officials complain that most of the violations ended years ago. They also emphasize that many of the guilty individuals either quit or were dismissed from their jobs, while most large contractors have instituted tough new internal guidelines to prevent a recurrence of improper information-swapping with competitors.

Some critics who aren't involved in the bid-rigging cases also worry that the Justice Department is squandering scarce resources to prosecute relatively minor criminal defendants, while maintaining a hands-off approach to most civil antitrust matters. Democratic Sen. Joseph Biden of Delaware says that "the folks currently running Justice only think in terms of criminal prosecutions" for antitrust violations instead of challenging mergers and acquisitions that also hurt consumers by reducing competition. "Unfortunately, a lot of illegal behavior by companies and executives may not lend itself to this approach," he argues. But even some critics of the department's antitrust policies praise the tenacity with which individual criminal cases are pursued. "Those parts of the law which they are enforcing, they are enforcing very vigorously," says Robert Pitofsky, a former member of the Federal Trade Commission who now is the dean of Georgetown University's law school.

The government's biggest defeat has resulted from such zealous prosecution, but the loss has taken an ironic turn. In February 1984, a jury in Helena, Mont., acquitted Fischbach Moore, three other large contractors and six of their top executives of conspiring to rig bids on a trio of nuclear power plants in Indiana and Washington state. Jurors said the Justice Department failed to prove that all the rigged contracts were part of a single conspiracy. Now, some defense attorneys want to argue exactly the opposite. To try to fend off further prosecution, the industry has seized upon an ingenious legal argument informally dubbed the "super conspiracy" theory. Instead of asserting that their clients were never involved in any bid-rigging, these defense attorneys concede that evidence gathered by the government shows efforts to inhibit competition were part of the rituals necessary to survive in the industry during those years. They say the government's evidence shows bids may have been fixed on more than 80 jobs as part of the overall scheme.

In light of the interconnected nature of the violations uncovered by prosecutors, these attorneys argue, it is unfair and unconstitutional for the government to continue singling out individual conspirators for independent prosecution. Court papers filed in Philadelphia on behalf of Sargent Electric contend that certain companies "could be counted on to go along with the conspiracy, regardless of the location of a particular project." As a result, the company told the court, "for them it had become a way of doing business."

Whether the alleged conspiracy took place in Utah, Washington or Kentucky, Lawrence Bader, an industry defense lawyer, suggested during a federal hearing in Ashland, Ky., in another case in October 1984 that the five largest contractors "were the core of an ongoing conspiracy.... Nobody was shocked, or surprised, or amazed" to receive a telephone call or other signal revealing the size of a competitor's bid or which company was in line to win a particular job. "Those were terms that didn't have to be explained to them," Mr. Bader maintained. But Justice Department officials deny defense assertions that continuing prosecutions will subject defendants to double jeopardy for the same crime. The irony behind the defense arguments hasn't escaped Joseph Hood, who presided over the Ashland hearing and rejected arguments to dismiss charges against several defendants. "For the first time in my memory," the magistrate says in an interview, "you have some major companies and their executives bent on convincing the courts that they participated in a truly nationwide conspiracy to fix prices and that, in fact, they got away with it for many years."

# SIXTY-FIVE

# "Isn't it Great that We Don't Get Any More Pesky Calls during Dinner Asking Us to Switch Long-Distance Companies?"

ROB ROGERS

*Source*: © 1999 United Feature Syndicate, Inc., courtesy of Knight Features, London.

# PART FIFTEEN
# Entry

# Introduction

Models of entry by new competitors vary even more than models of pricing, and in ways that necessity forces on us. If different things happen in different situations in reality, then so must they in our models. It is a pleasant surprise, therefore, when an article helps us to sort out existing models rather than creating new ones we must understand. Fudenberg and Tirole's "Fat Cat" paper is one of those. It appeared in the *American Economic Association Papers and Proceedings*, which has contained quite a number of influential short pieces like this over the years. These papers do not go through the usual submission procedure, but must, on the other hand, be short, and so they are a good occasion for top economists to try something unconventional. The cartoon, "Henry and the Candy Shop," illustrates one of their points: entrants and incumbents alike may be better off not to be too greedy.

I commented in the last part that the basic tasks of antitrust is to stop price fixing and monopolistic mergers, rather than solve tougher problems like the Microsoft case. The article, "Drugs: Novel Heart-Drug Deal...," is about one of those tougher problems. Innovation is one way to enter a market, but patents and the licensing arrangements that result from them can block entry.

I have included just one of my own papers in this volume, my "Aphorisms on Writing, Speaking, and Listening". These are notes I have accumulated over my years teaching doctoral students and writing referee reports. I value the opportunity to include them here, not just for students, but so that mid-career economists will read them, reform their writing style, and write better papers for me to read. Please do!

# SIXTY-SIX

# The Fat-Cat Effect, the Puppy-Dog Ploy, and the Lean and Hungry Look

DREW FUDENBERG AND JEAN TIROLE

Source: *American Economic Review, Papers and Proceedings* 74 (May), 1984, pp. 361–6.

> Let me have about me men that are fat....
> *Julius Caesar*, Act 1, Sc. 2

The idea that strategic considerations may provide firms with an incentive to "overinvest" in "capital" to deter the entry or expansion of rivals is by now well understood. However, in some circumstances, increased investment may be a strategic handicap, because it may reduce the incentive to respond aggressively to competitors. In such cases, firms may instead choose to maintain a "lean and hungry look," thus avoiding the "fat-cat effect." We illustrate these effects with models of investment in advertising and in *R & D*. We also provide a taxonomy of the factors which tend to favor over- and underinvestment, both to deter entry and to accommodate it. Such a classification, of course, requires a notion of what it means to overinvest; that is, we must provide a benchmark for comparison. If entry is deterred, we use a monopolist's investment as the basis for comparison. For the case of entry accommodation, we compare the incumbent's investment to that in a "precommitment" or "open-loop" equilibrium, in which the incumbent takes the entrant's actions as given and does not try to influence them through its choice of preentry investment. We flesh out the taxonomy with several additional examples.

Our advertising model was inspired by Richard Schmalensee's (1982) paper, whose results foreshadow ours. We provide an example in which an established firm will underinvest in advertising if it chooses to deter entry, because by lowering its stock of "goodwill" it establishes a credible threat to cut prices in the event of entry. Conversely, if the established firm chooses to allow entry, it will advertise heavily and become a fat cat in order to soften the entrant's pricing behavior. Thus the strategic incentives for investment depend on whether the incumbent chooses to deter entry. This contrasts with the previous work on strategic investment in cost-reducing machinery (Michael Spence, 1977, 1979; Avinash Dixit, 1979, our 1983a article) and in "learning by doing" (Spence, 1981; our 1983c article) in which the strategic incentives always encourage the incumbent to overaccumulate. Our *R & D* model builds on Jennifer Reinganum's (1983) observation that the "Arrow effect" (Kenneth Arrow, 1962) of an incumbent monopolist's reduced incentive to do $R \& D$ is robust to the threat of entry so long as the $R \& D$ technology is stochastic.

Our examples show that the key factors in strategic investment are whether investment makes the incumbent more or less "tough" in the post-entry game, and how the entrant reacts to tougher play by the incumbent. These two factors are the basis of our taxonomy. Jeremy Bulow et al. (1983) have independently noted the importance of the entrant's reaction. Their paper overlaps a good deal with ours.

## 1.  Advertising and Goodwill

In our goodwill model, a customer can buy from a firm only if he is aware of its existence. To inform consumers, firms place ads in newspapers. An ad that is read informs the customer of the existence of the firm and also gives the firm's price. In the first period, only the incumbent is in the market; in the second period the entrant may enter. The crucial assumption is that some of the customers who received an ad in the first period do not bother to read the ads in the second period, and therefore buy only from the incumbent. This captive market for the incumbent represents the incumbent's accumulation of goodwill. One could derive such captivity from a model in which rational consumers possess imperfect information about product quality, as in Schmalensee (1982), or from a model in which customers must sink firm-specific costs in learning how to consume the product.

There are two firms, an incumbent and an entrant, and a unit population of *ex ante* identical consumers. If a consumer is aware of both firms, and the incumbent charges $x_1$, and the entrant charges $x_2$, the consumer's demands for the two goods are $D^1(x_1, x_2)$ and $D^2(x_1, x_2)$, respectively. If a consumer is only aware of the incumbent (entrant), his demand is $D^1(x_1, \infty)$ and $(D^2(\infty, x_2))$. The (net of variable costs) revenue an informed consumer brings the incumbent is $R^1(x_1, x_2)$ or $R^1(x_1, \infty)$ depending on whether the consumer also knows about the entrant or not, and similarly for the entrant. We'll assume that the revenues are differentiable, quasi concave in own-prices, and they, as well as the marginal revenue, increase with the competitor's price (these are standard assumptions for price competition with differentiated goods).

To inform consumers, the firms put ads in the newspapers. An ad that is read makes the customer aware of the product and gives the price. The cost of reaching a fraction $K$ of the population in the first period is $A(K)$, where $A(K)$ is convex for strictly positive levels of advertising, and $A(1) = \infty$.[1] There are two periods, $t = 1, 2$. In the first period, only the incumbent is in the market. It advertises $K_1$, charges the monopoly price, and makes profits $K^1 R^m$. In the second period the entrant may enter.

To further simplify, we assume that all active firms will choose to cover the remaining market in the second period at cost $A_2$. Then assuming entry, the profits of the two firms, $\Pi^1$ and $\Pi^2$, can be written

---

[1]  See Gerard Butters (1977), and Gene Grossman and Carl Shapiro (1984) for examples of advertising technologies.

$$\Pi^1 = [-A(K_1) + K_1 R^m] + \delta[K_1 R^1(x_1, \infty) + (1 - K_1)R^1(x_1, x_2) - A_2]$$
$$\Pi^2 = \delta[(1 - K_1)R^2(x_1, x_2) - A_2] \tag{1}$$

where $\delta$ is the common discount factor.

In the second period, the firms simultaneously choose prices. Assuming that a Nash equilibrium for this second-stage game exists and is characterized by the first-order conditions, we have

$$K_1 R_1^1(x_1^*, \infty) + (1 - K_1)R_1^1(x_1^*, x_2^*) = 0 \tag{2}$$

$$R_2^2(x_1^*, x_2^*) = 0 \tag{3}$$

where $R_j^i \equiv \partial R^i(x_1, x_2)/\partial x_j$, and $x_i^*$ is the equilibrium value of $x_i$ as a function of $K_1$.

From equation (2), and the assumption that $R_{ij}^i > 0$, we see that

$$R_1^1(x_1^*, \infty) > 0 > R_1^1(x_1^*, x_2^*)$$

The incumbent would like to increase its price for its captive customers, and reduce it where there is competition; but price discrimination has been assumed impossible.

Differentiating the first-order conditions, and using $R_{ij}^i > 0$, we have

$$\begin{aligned} \partial x_1^*/\partial K_1 &> 0 & \partial x_1^*/\partial x_2^* &> 0 \\ \partial x_2^*/\partial K_1 &= 0 & \partial x_2^*/\partial x_1^* &> 0 \end{aligned} \tag{4}$$

The heart of the fat-cat effect is that $\partial x_1^*/\partial K_1 > 0$. As the incumbent's goodwill increases, it becomes more reluctant to match the entrant's price. The large captive market makes the incumbent a pacifistic "fat cat." This suggests that if entry is going to occur, the incumbent has an incentive to increase $K_1$ to "soften" the second-period equilibrium.

To formalize this intuition we first must sign the *total* derivative $dx_1^*/dK_1$. While one would expect increasing $K_1$ to increase the incumbent's equilibrium price, this is only true if firm 1's second-period reaction curve is steeper than firm 2's. This will be true if $R_{11}^1 R_{22}^2 > R_{12}^1 R_{21}^2$. If $dx_1^*/dK_1$ were negative the model would not exhibit the fat-cat effect.

Now we compare the incumbent's choice of $K_1$ in the open-loop and perfect equilibria. In the former, the incumbent takes $x_2^*$ as given, and thus ignores the possibility of strategic investment. Setting $\partial \pi^1/\partial K_1 = 0$ in (1), we have

$$R^m + \delta(R^1(x_1^*, \infty) - R^1(x_1^*, x_2^*)) = A'(K_1) \tag{5}$$

In a perfect equilibrium, the incumbent realizes that $x_2^*$ depends on $K_1$, giving first-order conditions

$$R^m + \delta(R^1(x_1^*, \infty) - R^1(x_1^*, x_2^*) + (1 - K_1)R_2^1(dx_2^*/dK_1)) = A'(K_1) \tag{6}$$

As $R_2^1$ and $dx_2^*/dK_1$ are positive, for a fixed $K_1$ the left-hand side of (6) exceeds that of (5), so if the second-order condition corresponding to (6) is satisfied, its solution exceeds that of (5).

The fat-cat effect suggests a corollary, that the incumbent should underinvest and maintain a "lean and hungry look" to deter entry. However, while the "price effect" of increasing $K_1$ encourages entry, the "direct effect" of reducing the entrant's market goes the other way. To see this, note that

$$\Pi_k^2 = \delta[(1 - K_1)R_1^2 \ (dx_1^*/dK_1) - R^2] \tag{7}$$

The first term in the right-hand side of (7) is the strategic effect of $K_1$ on the second-period price, the second is the direct effect. One can find plausible examples of demand and advertising functions such that the indirect effect dominates. This is the case, for example, for goods which are differentiated by their location on the unit interval with linear "transportation" costs, if first-period advertising is sufficiently expensive that the incumbent's equilibrium share of the informed consumers is positive. In this case, entry deterrence requires underinvestment.

## 2. Technological Competition

We now develop a simple model of investment in $R \ \& \ D$ to illustrate the lean and hungry look, building on the work of Arrow and Reinganum. In the first period, the incumbent, firm 1, spends $K_1$ on capital, and then has constant average cost $\bar{c}(K_1)$. The incumbent receives the monopoly profit $V^m(\bar{c}(K_1))$ in period 1. In the second period, both the incumbent and firm 2 may do $R \ \& \ D$ on a new technology which allows constant average cost $c$. If one firm develops the innovation, it receives the monopoly value $V^m(c)$. Thus the innovation is "large" or "drastic" in Arrow's sense. If both firms develop the innovation, their profit is zero. If neither firm succeeds, then the incumbent again receives $V^m(\bar{c})$. The second-period $R \ \& \ D$ technology is stochastic. If firm $i$ spends $x_i$ on $R \ \& \ D$, it obtains the new technology with probability $\mu_i(x_i)$. We assume $\mu_i'(0) = \infty, \mu_i' > 0,$ $\mu_i'' < 0$. The total payoffs from period 2 on are

$$\begin{aligned}
\Pi^1 &= \mu_1(1 - \mu_2)V^m(c) + (1 - \mu_1) \ (1 - \mu_2)V^m(\bar{c}) - x_1 \\
\Pi^2 &= \mu_2(1 - \mu_1)V^m(c) - x_2
\end{aligned} \tag{9}$$

The first-order conditions for a Nash equilibrium are

$$\begin{aligned}
\mu_i'[V^m(c) - V^m(\bar{c})] \ (1 - \mu_2) &= 1 \\
\mu_2'V^m(c) \ (1 - \mu_1) &= 1
\end{aligned} \tag{10}$$

We see that since the incumbent's gain is only the difference in the monopoly profits, it has less incentive to innovate than the entrant. This is the Arrow effect.[2] We have

---

[2] For large innovations, the monopoly price with the new technology is less than the average cost of the old one. Richard Gilbert and David Newbery (1982) showed that for "small" innovations, because the sum of the

derived it here in a model with each firm's chance of succeeding independent of the other's, so that we have had to allow a nonzero probability of a tie. Reinganum's model avoids ties, because the possibilities of "success" (obtaining the patent) are not independent.

Because $\mu_i' > 0$ and $\mu_i'' < 0$, the reaction curves in (10) slope downward – the more one firm spends, the less the other wishes to. Since increasing $K_1$ decreases the incumbent's gain from the innovator's we expect that the strategic incentive is to reduce $K_1$ to play more aggressively in period 2. As in our last example, this is only true if the reaction curves are "stable," which in this case requires $\mu_1'' \mu_2'' (1 - \mu_1) (1 - \mu_2) > (\mu_1' \mu_2')$.[2] This is true for example for $\mu_i(x) = \max(1, bx^{1/2})$, with $b$ small. We conclude that to accommodate entry the incumbent has a strategic incentive to underinvest. Because $K_1$ has no direct effect on $\Pi^2$, we can also say that to deter entry the incumbent has an incentive to underinvest.[3]

## 3.  Taxonomy and Conclusion

In the goodwill model the incumbent could underinvest to deter entry, while in the R & D model the strategic incentives always favored underinvestment. To relate these results to previous work, we next present an informal taxonomy of pre-entry strategic investment by an incumbent. In many cases, one might expect both "investment" and "production" decisions to be made post-entry. We have restricted attention to a single post-entry variable for simplicity. We should point out that this involves some loss of generality. Strategic underinvestment requires that the incumbent not be able to invest after entry, or more generally that pre- and post-entry investments are imperfectly substitutable. This was the case in both of our examples. However, if investment is in productive machinery and capital costs are linear and constant over time, then underinvestment would be ineffective, as the incumbent's post-entry investment would make up any previous restraint.

Before presenting the taxonomy, it should be acknowledged that since Schmalensee's (1983) article, several authors have independently noticed the possibility of underinvestment. J. Baldani (1983) studies the conditions leading to underinvestment in advertising. Bulow et al. (1983) present a careful treatment of two-stage games in which either production or investment takes place in the first period, with production in the second, and costs need not be separable across periods. They focus on cost minimization as the benchmark for over- and underinvestment. The starting point for the Bulow et al. (1983) paper was the observation that a firm might choose not to enter an apparently profitable market due to strategic spillovers on other product lines. This point is developed in more detail in K. Judd (1983).

---

duopoly profits is (typically) less than $\Pi^m(c)$, the incumbent loses more than the entrant gains if the entrant obtains the patent. With a deterministic R & D technology, the incumbent's incentive to innovate thus exceeds the entrant's, because the incumbent's current patent is certain to be superseded and thus the current profits are not "sacrificed" by the incumbent's R & D. Reinganum showed that with stochastic R & D and a small innovation, either effect can dominate. In her R & D model the reaction curves slope up.

[3] For small innovations the direct effect goes the other way.

Our taxonomy classifies market according to the signs of the incentives for strategic investments. Because only the incumbent has a strategic incentive, given concavity, we can unambiguously say whether the incumbent will over- or underinvest to accommodate entry (compared to the open-loop equilibrium).[4] We continue to denote the incumbent's first-period choice $K_1$, the post-entry decisions $x_1$ and $x_2$, and the payoffs $\Pi^1$ and $\Pi^2$. For entry deterrence there are two effects, as we noted before: the "direct effect" $\partial \Pi^2 / \partial K_1$, and the "strategic effect" $\partial \Pi^2 / \partial x_1^* \dot{\partial} x_1^* / \partial K_1$. We saw in the goodwill case that these two effects had opposite signs, and so the overall incentives were ambiguous. In all the rest of our examples, these two effects have the same sign.

In Table 1, first the entry-accommodating strategy and then the entry-deterring one is given. The fat-cat strategy is overinvestment that accommodates entry by committing the incumbent to play less aggressively post-entry. The lean and hungry strategy is underinvestment to be tougher. The top dog strategy is overinvestment to be tough; this is the familiar result of Spence and Dixit.

Last, the puppy-dog strategy is *underinvestment* that accommodates entry by turning the incumbent into a small, friendly, nonaggressive puppy dog. This strategy is desirable if investment makes the incumbent tougher, and the second-period reaction curves slope up.

One final caveat: the classification in Table 1 depends as previously on the second-period Nash equilibria being "stable," so that changing $K_1$ has the intuitive effect on $x_2^*$.

Our goodwill model is an example of Case I: goodwill makes the incumbent soft, and the second-period reaction curves slope up. The $R \, \& \, D$ model illustrates Case II. Case III is the "classic" case for investing in productive machinery and "learning by doing" (Spence, 1981; our paper, 1983c) with quantity competition. Case IV results from either of these models with price competition (Bulow et al. (1983), our paper, 1983b; Judith Gelman and Steven Salop, 1983). A more novel example of the puppy-dog ploy arises in the P. Milgrom and J. Roberts (1982) model of limit pricing under incomplete

**Table 1**

| Slope of Reaction Curves | Investment Makes Incumbent: | |
|---|---|---|
| | *Tough* | *Soft* |
| Upward | *Case IV* | *Case I* |
| | $A$: Puppy Dog | $A$: Fat Cat |
| | $D$: Top Dog | $D$: Lean and Hungry |
| Downward | *Case III* | *Case II* |
| | $A$: Top Dog | $A$: Lean and Hungry |
| | $D$: Top Dog | $D$: Lean and Hungry |

$A$ = Accommodate entry; $D$ = Deter entry.

---

[4] This does not generalize to the case in which both firms make strategic decisions. In our paper on learning by doing (1983c), we give an example in which one firm's first-period output declined in moving from the precommitment to the perfect equilibrium. The problem is that if, as expected, firm 1's output increases when it plays strategically, firm 2's strategic incentive to increase output can be outweighted by its response to firm 1's change.

information, if we remove their assumption that the established firm's cost is revealed once the entrant decides to enter, and replace quantity with price as the strategic variable. To accommodate entry, the incumbent then prefers the entrant to believe that the incumbent's costs are relatively high.

We conclude with two warnings. First, one key ingredient of our taxonomy is the slope of the second-period reaction curves. In many of our examples, downward slopes correspond to quantity competition and upward slopes to competition in prices.[5] These examples are potentially misleading. We do not intend to revive the Cournot vs. Bertrand argument. As David Kreps and José Scheinkman (1983) have shown, "Quantity Precommitment and Bertrand Competition Yield Cournot Outcomes." Thus, "price competition" and "quantity competition" should not be interpreted as referring to the variable chosen by firms in the second stage, but rather as two different reduced forms for the determination of both prices and outputs. Second, our restriction to a single post-entry stage eliminates many important strategic interactions. As our 1983a paper shows, such interactions may reverse the over- or under-investment results of two-stage models.

*References*

ARROW, K. (1962): "Economic Welfare and the Allocation of Resources to Innovation," in R. Nelson (ed.), *The Rate and Direction of Economic Activity*, New York: National Bureau of Economic Research.

BALDANI, J. (1983): "Strategic Advertising and Credible Entry Deterrence Policies," mimeo, Colgate University.

BULOW, J., GEANAKOPLOS, J. and KLEMPERER, P. (1983): "Multimarket Oligopoly," Stanford Business School, R. P. 696.

BUTTERS, G. (1977): "Equilibrium Distributions of Sales and Advertising Prices," *Review of Economic Studies*, October, 44, 465–96.

DIXIT, A. (1979): "A Model of Duopoly Suggesting a Theory of Entry Barriers," *Bell Journal of Economics*, Spring, 10, 20–32.

FUDENBERG, D. and TIROLE, J. (1983a): "Capital as a Commitment: Strategic Investment to Deter Mobility," *Journal of Economic Theory*, December, 31, 227–50.

——— and ———, (1983b): "Dynamic Models of Oligopoly," IMSSS T. R. 428, Stanford University.

——— and ———, (1983c): "Learning by Doing and Market Performance," *Bell Journal of Economics*, Autumn, 14, 522–30.

GELMAN, J. and SALOP, S. (1983): "Judo Economics," mimeo, George Washington University.

GILBERT, R. and NEWBERY, D. (1982): "Preemptive Patenting and the Persistence of Monopoly," *American Economic Review*, June, 72, 514–26.

GROSSMAN, G. and SHAPIRO, C. (1984): "Informative Advertising with Differentiated Goods," *Review of Economic Studies*, January, 51, 63–82.

JUDD, K. (1983): "Credible Spatial Preemption," MEDS D. P. 577, Northwestern University.

KREPS, D. and SCHEINKMAN, J. (1983): "Quantity Precommitment and Bertrand Competition Yield Cournot Outcomes," mimeo, University of Chicago.

MILGROM, P. and ROBERTS, J. (1982): "Limit Pricing and Entry under Incomplete Information," *Econometrica*, 50, 443–60.

---

[5] Bulow et al. (1983) point out that while these are the "normal" cases, it is possible, for example, for reaction curves to slope up in quantity competition.

REINGANUM, J. (1983): "Uncertain Innovation and the Persistence of Monopoly," *American Economic Review*, September, 73, 741–8.

SCHMALENSEE, R. (1982): "Product Differentiation Advantages of Pioneering Brands," *American Economic Review*, June, 72, 349–65.

——(1983): "Advertising and Entry Deterrence: An Exploratory Model," *Journal of Political Economy*, August, 90, 636–53.

SPENCE, A. M. (1977): "Entry, Capacity, Investment, and Oligopolistic Pricing," *Bell Journal of Economics*, Autumn, 8, 534–44.

——(1979): "Investment Strategy and Growth in a New Market," *Bell Journal of Economics*, Spring, 10, 1–19.

——(1981): "The Learning Curve and Competition," *Bell Journal of Economics*, Spring, 12, 49–70.

# SIXTY-SEVEN

# Drugs: Novel Heart-Drug Deal Protects Sales, Spurs Suit

RALPH T. KING JR.

*Source: Wall Street Journal*, August 21, 1998.

When does a drug company's payment to a generic rival to stay out of a market become price-fixing? A group of consumers is going to court to find out. They have sued drug makers Hoechst AG and Andrx Corp., alleging that an unusual deal they struck is protecting one of the nation's most popular heart drugs from cheaper, generic competition. A lawsuit filed yesterday in San Francisco Superior Court charges that Germany's Hoechst conspired with Andrx to fix prices by agreeing to pay the small Fort Lauderdale, Fla., company $40 million a year to keep its generic version of Hoechst's Cardizem CD off the market. The suit, alleging antitrust violations, says the deal lets Hoechst in effect overcharge consumers of Cardizem CD, which treats high blood pressure and chest pain. Hoechst has put other potential rivals in regulatory limbo, the suit says. The reason: Continuing litigation between Hoechst and Andrx is holding up Food and Drug Administration action to approve other generic versions of Cardizem CD, thus shutting them out of the market too.

The case spotlights the heated marketplace battle between generic drug makers and brand-name pharmaceuticals firms. If the suit is successful, it could speed access to cut-rate substitute drugs for millions of consumers. If it fails, other drug makers may try to copy Hoechst's approach. In a separate antitrust suit filed earlier this year by one of its commercial rivals, Hoechst already faces similar charges. The consumer suit, which is seeking class-action status, increases the pressure on Hoechst.

Cardizem CD, a so-called calcium channel blocker, ranks among the top 20 best-selling drugs in the U.S., where it generated about $700 million in revenue for Hoechst last year, according to market researchers IMS Health. About 50 million Americans, many of them elderly, suffer from hypertension or chronic chest pain.

Hoechst's deal with Andrx, which both parties disclosed when they struck it last September, came after Andrx announced plans to launch its product in late 1995. Usually a generic drug can't be introduced until a brand's patent, or patents, expire. In the case of Cardizem CD, some patents extend for at least another decade. But a generic manufacturer can jump the gun if certain conditions are met, such as proving that its product doesn't infringe the patent of the brand-name drug. In this case, Andrx's product has the same active ingredient, but Andrx claims it uses a different release mechanism in the body.

Hoechst sued Andrx for patient infringement in 1996, triggering a regulatory provision that blocked the generic drug's launch for 30 months. The 30-month period ended last month, giving Andrx the go-ahead even though the patent suit is pending. But, both companies announced, Andrx decided not to proceed to market in exchange for Hoechst's payment of $10 million a quarter. Those payments will continue until the patent suit is resolved or until the Cardizem CD patent at issue expires. The payments began accruing in July, when Andrx won final Food and Drug Administration approval to market its Cardizem CD generic.

The California complaint calls the arrangement an "outright bribe," and an "unconscionable and per se illegal restraint of trade that assures that [Hoechst] will continue to set maintain artificially high prices" for Cardizem CD. A Hoechst spokesman, Charles Rouse, says the Andrx deal doesn't harm consumers because a variety of less expensive calcium blockers, albeit in other formulations, are available. "I don't see where consumers are left in the lurch from a cost or a brand perspective," Mr. Rouse says. The deal, he adds, "enables us to manage the downside risk for both companies" pending resolution of the patent suit. Mr. Rouse said the company hadn't reviewed yesterday's lawsuit and declined to comment on it. But he did say the Andrx deal is an "acceptable, legal agreement. I can tell you it's not violating antitrust laws." An Andrx official said the company also hadn't seen the suit and declined to comment on it.

The deal makes economic sense for Hoechst. The availability of a generic alternative once a drug's patent expires can quickly slash its premium price by at least 25% and erode its market share. Thus, Hoechst's $40 million annual payment is a relatively cheap way to protect its highly profitable $700 million product. Andrx, for its part, cashes in without the costly burden of marketing and distribution. The company also averts the possibility of having to pay Hoechst triple damages if it loses the patent suit. (Damages accrue only if an infringing product is sold.) "That could potentially bankrupt this company," said Elliot Hahn, Andrx's president. If Andrx wins, Hoechst agreed in the September 1997 deal to pay Andrx $100 million in lost profits per year, including the quarterly $10 million payments, which are nonrefundable.

Even as the deal keeps Andrx from putting its product on the market, the continuation of the patent litigation is letting Hoechst keep other competitors at bay. U.S. drug law gives the first company to go to market with a generic version of a drug six months of exclusivity before any other generic firm can enter the same market. Thus, until Andrx launches its product – or resolves its patent case – two other would-be entrants, Canada's Biovail Corp. International and Australia's F.H. Faulding Co. are shut out. The two companies both have applications before the FDA, but the agency won't approve them while Andrx's patent remains in dispute, an FDA official says.

In March, Biovail filed an antitrust suit against Hoechst in Newark, N.J., federal court, citing the Hoechst-Andrx deal and other conflicts arising from a 1995 Federal Trade Commission consent decree. The decree involved a dispute over a brand-name calcium blocker, Tiazac, that Hoechst and Bioval had once co-developed and which Biovail now sells. Hoechst declined to comment on Biovail's suit. Meanwhile, Biovail has also developed a generic form of Cardizem CD and is seeking FDA approval to sell it. A spokesman for Faulding, which Hoechst also sued for patent infringement, declined to comment on the situation.

The consumer suit could benefit Biovail's case, and there are some connections between them. Stephen Lowey, the plaintiff's lawyer on the consumer case, contacted Biovail in June and obtained information about its case, says Kenneth Cancellara, Biovail's general counsel. That relationship grew even closer when Mr. Cancellara subsequently retained Mr. Lowey to research Biovail's other legal options in the U.S. But Mr. Cancellara says Biovail didn't initiate yesterday's action and that Biovail won't share in any proceeds from the litigation. Biovail and Mr. Lowey also share a public-relations firm – Sitrick  Co. of Los Angeles. Mr. Lowey, whose firm Lowey Dannenberg Bemporad  Selinger is in White Plains, N.Y., was unavailable to comment on his ties to Biovail.

The overall market for calcium blockers exceeds $4 billion, led by Pfizer Inc.'s two drugs, Norvasc and Procardia XL, neither of which faces generic competition yet. Cardizem CD ranks as the third most popular in the category, but it is the most widely prescribed brand for treating chronic chest pain, Hoechst's spokesman said. Despite this success, there is a long-standing scientific controversy over whether calcium blockers are more effective at preventing heart attacks or strokes than cheaper medications, such as beta blockers and diuretics, which have been available in generic form for years.

SIXTY-EIGHT

# Aphorisms on Writing, Speaking, and Listening

Eric Rasmusen*

*Source*: Unpublished notes, February 2000.

This article collects aphorisms on the mechanics of doing research in economics, emphasizing writing, speaking, and seminar participation. They are intended for both students and for scholars and are useful beyond just economics.

## 1. Introduction

Some fifteen years ago I wrote down some thoughts on how to write papers for the students in my Ph.D. game theory classes. I have taught that course almost every year, and each year I have updated and improved the notes, which itself is an example of how writing can always be improved. Now, finally, I will publish these notes. They are aphorisms – ideas expressed in sentences or paragraphs rather than pages, often expressed in striking ways, and only loosely linked. Because they run from one idea to another and use plentiful helpings of rhetoric, aphorisms make for rather a rich diet, so you might want to read a few at a time, as a break from drier consumption. You will find my tone to be informal but dogmatic. The most important idea is that the author should make things clear to the reader and save him unnecessary work. Bluntness aids clarity.

I will assume throughout that you already know the following.

1　Benefits are to be weighed against costs. It is optimal for writing to be somewhat unclear if the alternative is costly, just as tissue paper is the optimal writing medium if you are smuggling a journal article out of a prison. More usually, we face tradeoffs between improving tenth drafts and writing first drafts.

2　I am still learning how to write. I have never looked over any of my papers without finding ways to improve it, even though I am accounted a good writer and do many drafts. So do not be surprised when you read my published papers and find violations of my own rules.

* Professor of Business Economics and Public Policy and Sanjay Subhedar Faculty Fellow, Indiana University, Kelley School of Business, BU 456, 1309 E 10th Street, Bloomington, Indiana, 47405–1701. Office: (812) 855-9219. Fax: 812-855-3354. Erasmuse@indiana.edu; Php.indiana.edu/~erasmuse. Copies of this paper can be found at Php. indiana.edu/~erasmuse/GI/write.pdf.

I would like to thank Thom Mitchell for helpful comments.

3   You may violate any rule, including rules of grammar and spelling, if you have a
    good reason. Just be sure you do it deliberately.[1] If you know you write poorly,
    do not even break the rules deliberately. Having drunk a fifth of whisky, an
    economist, being rational, refrains from driving home even though he may feel
    not only confident but exceptionally confident in his driving ability in such
    circumstances.

Care in writing is important, and writing up your results is not just a bit of fringe to
decorate your idea. Besides the obvious benefit of helping the reader, clear writing fosters
clear thinking. If you have to write an abstract, to decide which results to call propositions,
and to label all your tables and diagrams, you will be forced to think about what your
paper is all about.

## 2   Background

### 2.1   Motivation

In my experience, students generally do not take their papers seriously, which is defeatist,
though realistic. MBA and PhD students, if not undergraduates, eventually will be trying
to write important reports or articles, and they ought to start practicing.

In writing a paper, think about whether anyone else would want to read it. Other than
recreation, here are the reasons people read a paper:

1   They can cite it in arguing for a position because it pins down a certain fact or
    logical connection.
2   It is better written than other papers on the same subject, even though it contains
    nothing new. As Pascal said, "Let no one say that I have said nothing new ... the
    arrangement of the subject is new. When we play tennis, we both play with the
    same ball, but one of us places it better."[2]
3   It contains an important idea that readers want to understand.

Most people should not count on reason (3), since it requires that the reader already
believe the paper contains an important idea. People read George Stigler's papers because
they believe that, but most of us do not have that reputation (nor did the young Stigler).
Reason (1) is more important. Even a student can write something citable, and however
trivial the cite, it is a useful contribution to the world. A badly written summary of
someone else's work, on the other hand, or an original variant on an existing model, may
be completely useless.

Especially, do not scorn the small fact. The small fact is the foundation of science,
and since it is the kind of contribution anyone can make, experts are less likely to throw away
a paper by an unknown which modestly purports to establish a small fact. Of scholars,
someone said,

---

[1]   This is similar to the idea that a gentleman is never unintentionally rude.
[2]   Blaise Pascal, *Pensées*, translated by W. Trotter, www.orst.edu/instruct/ph1302/tests/pascal, I-22. (1660/
August 18, 1999).

It suffices, if many of them be plain, diligent and laborious observers: such, who though they bring not much knowledge, yet bring their hand, and their eyes incorrupted; such as have not their brains infected by false images, and can honestly assist in the examining and registering what the others represent to their view.[3]

## 2.2 Thinking

Most people are confused in their everyday conversation and thinking. If you had a transcript of your conversation and your thoughts you would be shocked by their incoherence. That is a big reason to write down your thoughts. Writing helps thinking. It is hard to hold an entire argument in your head at once and even harder to find which part has a flaw. This goes not only for the mathematics but for the explanations. Thus, start writing as soon as you think you have a worthwhile idea.

## 2.3 The reader

The reader, like the customer, is always right. That is not to be taken literally, but it is true in the sense that if the reader has trouble the writer should ask why, and not immediately blame the reader's lack of intellect or effort.

Copyeditors are a different matter. Especially at law reviews and scholarly journals, they are often pedantic young college graduates who rely on rules but ignore clarity. (In my experience, book copyeditors are much better.) Don't trust them unthinkingly. But please don't shoot the reader; he's doing his best.

At some point in a paper's history, you should write up your results for your reader, not yourself. The first draft is for you and only you but unless the paper ends up in the "cylindrical outbox" it will reach a point where you want other people to read it. So write for them.

This means doing a lot of work that will take up very few lines in the paper – finding a statistic or a cite, or running a test that is mentioned only to say it found nothing interesting. It also means putting figures and tables in the text, not at the end of the paper, using English for variable names rather than Computerese, and cutting out all the propositions that are true and hard but boring.

## 2.4 Checking for mistakes

In looking for mistakes, spread your effort across all parts of your analysis. Suppose it has five steps. If you have done the first draft efficiently, you have put most of your effort into the hardest steps in such a way as to equate the marginal product of effort across steps. As a result, the likelihood of error in the easiest step, on which you spent very little effort, may be just as great as that of error in the hardest step.

---

[3] Thomas Sprat probably wrote this around 1700, but I can't find the source. For some purposes, if you cannot verify a citation or a fact you should leave it out. In these aphorisms, however, I am usually quoting because someone has said something well rather than because he is an authority, so the point of the citation is to give credit, not credibility. In view of that, I have decided to keep quotations for which I do not have adequate sources. Please let me know if you find the source of any of them. I'll have a link on my web page for any new citations I find.

## 2.5  A football metaphor

Don't go charging off at full speed immediately, or you'll confuse the sidelines with the goal lines.[4] Looking where you're running saves time in the end, and prevents head injuries. At the same time, if you don't start, you don't finish.

# 3  Writing, Generally

## 3.1  Effort

Professors and parents may or may not care about how much work you did to write your paper. In the wider world, nobody cares in the slightest; all they care about are results. Thus, do not include material just to show how hard you worked. A paper with one useful regression will be more highly regarded than a paper with the same useful regression plus ten useless regressions.

Students often think that if they write something down, it has to stay in the paper. If they cut a paragraph from the introduction, maybe they can put it in the conclusion, or the literature review, or an appendix, or, in desperation, as part of the caption of Figure 2. Be prepared to consign that paragraph to the dustbin, to complete annihilation. Any word that cannot justify its existence must die. This is not murder, but justifiable homicide – or perhaps self defense.

## 3.2  Role models

When the mathematician Niels Abel was asked how he gained his expertise he said, "By studying the masters and not their pupils."[5] As a model for writing, take the best economists, not the average article you read, and certainly not the average article published: George Stigler, Richard Posner, Paul Milgrom, Jean Tirole, Franklin Fisher, Adam Smith. To learn how to write good English, read it. George Orwell, Joseph Epstein, C. S. Lewis, David Hume, Thomas Macaulay, Isaac Asimov, Winston Churchill, Jack Vance, and Walter Durant would all be good influences, and one of these surely must have written on a subject that interests you. This is particularly important for those of you who are not native English speakers.

## 3.3  Reading aloud

Reading your paper out loud is the best way to catch awkward phrasing and typos. Have someone else proofread the final version for you if you can.

## 3.4  Revision

Serious papers require many drafts, where "many" means from five to twenty-five. Coursework does not, but students should be aware of the difference from professional

---

[4] Note my use of a contraction here. That is out of place in the formal writing of a journal article, but I use contractions here and there in these aphorisms for euphony and emphasis.

[5] I do not know the source for this quotation.

academic standards. A major if seldom noted purpose of graduate training is to teach people how to work hard. People don't know how to work hard naturally, and although students think they know what hard work means, most of them are in for a surprise. One of the tribulations of being a professor is that "What is written without effort is read without pleasure."[6] Do not be misled by the free and easy style of good writing. It rarely comes from pure ability without revision.

> True ease in writing comes from art, not chance,
> As those move easiest who have learn'd to dance.
> 'Tis not enough no harshness gives offense;
> The sound must seem an echo to the sense.[7]

It is useful to set aside a paper for a week or a month before going back to revise it. Not only will you approach it more as a reader would, but also your subconscious will have been working away at it. An economics article, like a poem, is never finished – only abandoned.[8] At some point the author, or rather, some editor, decides it is ready to be set into print. You should, however, be circulating drafts for comment long before that point. If your paper is repeatedly rejected for publication, the bright side is that it will have fifty years of steady improvement before you die.

## 3.5  Clarity versus precision

Clarity and precision are not the same. Usually clarity is preferable. Consider the following opening for a monopoly model:

> Let output be $q$.

versus

> Assume that a firm can produce a nonstochastic, finite quantity of an infinitely divisible good that is uniform in quality. Denote quantity by $q$, where $q$ is a non-negative real number bounded above by some sufficiently large number $\bar{q}$ and measured in units we need not specify here.

The first version is clearer, though the second is more precise.

## 3.6  Redundancy

A common vice of theorists is this trick of phrasing: "The price is high (low) if the quantity is low (high)." How quickly can you understand that statement compared to, "The price is high if the quantity is low. The price is low, on the other hand, if the quantity is high." Writing for people is different from writing for computers. Redundancy helps real people to read faster. That is why I didn't write "Rdnncy hlps pple rd fstr", even though the condensed sentence is precise, unambiguous, and short.

---

[6] Quote from Samuel Johnson, but I don't know the source.
[7] Alexander Pope, "Essay on Criticism," Part II, line 162 (1711).
[8] Original version by Paul Valery, but I don't know the source.

This goes for algebra too. "Suppose that there is a probability $\beta$ that the plaintiff will go to trial. The defendant's expected cost from turning down the settlement offer is then $(1 - \beta) * (0) + \beta(\alpha D + C_d)$." This algebraic expression is different from and superior to "$\beta(\alpha D + C_d)$" because it explains to the reader that there are two possible outcomes, in one of which the defendant has zero cost and in the other of which he has a cost of $(\alpha D + C_d)$. Algebra is not easier when expressions are boiled down to their shortest versions.

Another example is $\frac{1}{1+\rho_{cb}}$ versus $\beta_{cb}$ for discount factors. We have enough to think about in the world without having to remember the difference between a discount rate and a discount factor. Interest rates are foremost in our minds, so write $\frac{1}{1+\rho_{cb}}$ and do your comparative statics in terms of the discount rate.

This is a metaphor for writing generally. In these notes, I am saying both "Don't be verbose!" and "Don't be afraid of redundancy if it makes things clearer!" These are not contradictions. You must ask of each word: "Does it help the reader?" Some hurt, some help.[9]

## 3.7  Verbosity

Keep your signal to noise ratio high. To modify Eleazar ben Azariah,

> "He whose words are more abundant than his data, to what is he like? To a tree whose branches are abundant but whose roots are few, and the wind comes and overturns it, as it is written, *For he shall be like the tamarisk in the desert, and shall not see when good cometh; but shall inhabit the parched places in the wilderness, in a salt land and not inhabited.* But he whose data is more abundant than his words, to what is he like? To a tree whose branches are few but whose roots are many, so that even if all the words in the world come and blow against it, it cannot be stirred from its place, as it is written, *He shall be as a tree planted by the waters, and that spreadeth out her roots by the river, and shall not see when heat cometh, but her leaf shall be green; and shall not be careful in the year of drought, neither shall cease from yielding fruit.*[10]

Do not say, "The price controls which were introduced by Nixon." Rather, say, "The price controls Nixon introduced" to avoid a passive and save 38 percent in words. In revising, cut out words that are not doing any work. They are barnacles sticking to the ship and slowing down its progress.[11]

---

[9] Here you have observed an example of a purposeful and correct violation of the rules of grammar. I thought carefully about inserting an "and" or a semicolon in that sentence.

[10] *Mishna Perke Aboth*, 3.22. Eleazar is speaking of the evil of wisdom exceeding deeds, but as a Calvinist economist I'd reverse him. The two quotations I have italicized are Jeremiah 17:6 and 17:8. Verse 9 is also pertinent: *The heart is deceitful above all things, and desperately wicked: who can know it?* We must all be careful of bias.

[11] Cutting out useless words is a theme running through most discussions of good writing. Consider what two mathematicians have said. (1) "You know that I write slowly. This is chiefly because I am never satisfied until I have said as much as possible in a few words, and writing briefly takes far more time than writing at length." Gauss, as quoted in G. Simmons, *Calculus Gems*, p. 177, New York: McGraw Hill (1992). (2) "My Reverend Fathers, my letters haven't usually followed so closely or been so long. The small amount of time I've had caused both. I wouldn't have been so long except that I didn't have the leisure to be shorter." ("Mes Reverends Pères, mes lettres n'avaient pas accoutumé de se suivre de si près, ni d'être si étendues. Le peu de temps que j'ai eu a été causé de l'un et de l'autre. Je n'ai fait celle-ci plus longue que parce que je n'ai pas eu le loisir de la faire plus courte.") Blaise Pascal, *Lettres Ecrites à un Provincial*, Letter 16, p. 233, Paris: Flammarion, 1981 (first published in 1656).

## 3.8 Novel formats

To good and brave writers, I offer the suggestion that they think about using unusual formats. Consider using dialogues,[12] parables,[13] aphorisms,[14] hyperlinked web files, allegories, book reviews,[15] letters, legal briefs, disputations,[16] or the Socratic method.[17] I wouldn't suggest blank verse or stream-of-consciousness, but there are lots of possibilities. For most papers, the straightforward pattern of Introduction–Model–Propositions–Evidence–Implications–Conclusion is best, but think about whether it is best for your particular paper.

# 4. Words and Notation

## 4.1 Word choice

- "And so forth" is better than "et cetera."
- "I present a theoretical model in which there are two players, each of whom..." is better than "I present a theoretical model where there are two players, each of whom..."
- Avoid "to assert" and "to state." In over 95 percent of the examples I've seen they are misused. The word "to say" is fine old Anglo-Saxon and closer to what is meant.

## 4.2 Groups of related connecting words

- And, furthermore, besides, next, moreover, in addition, again, also, similarly, too, finally, second, last.
- Therefore, thus, then, in conclusion, consequently, as a result, accordingly, finally, the bottom line is.
- But, or, nor, yet, still, however, nevertheless, to the contrary, on the contrary, on the other hand, conversely, although, though, nonetheless.[18]

## 4.3 Gender-neutered language

Political correctness has had an unfortunate impact on academic writing. In English, "he" and "his" have two uses. I use "he" when I want to refer to a male. I also use "he" when I

---

[12] Kenneth Dau-Schmidt, Michael Alexeev, Robert Heidt, Eric Rasmusen and Jeffrey Stake, "Review Discussion: Game Theory and the Law," *Law and Society Review*, 31: 613–29 (1997); pages 476 to 480 of Eric Rasmusen and Jeffrey Stake, "Lifting the Veil of Ignorance: Personalizing the Marriage Contract," *Indiana Law Journal*, 73: 454–502 (Spring 1998).

[13] See the story at the start of David Hirshleifer and Eric Rasmusen, "Cooperation in a Repeated Prisoner's Dilemma with Ostracism," 12 *Journal of Economic Behavior and Organization* 87–106 (August 1989).

[14] The article you are now reading.

[15] Thomas Macaulay, "Mill on Government," *Edinburgh Review*, (March 1829); Sam Peltzman, "The Handbook of Industrial Organization," *The Journal of Political Economy* (February 1991) 99: 201–17.

[16] Thomas Aquinas, *Summa Theologica*, www.Newadvent.org/Summa (August 17, 1999).

[17] Plato's *Meno* is a dialog in which Socrates takes a slave boy step by step through a mathematical proof. Classics.mit.edu/Plato/meno.html (August 17, 1999).

[18] This list is based on p. 62 of Mary Munter's 1992 book.

want to be bland and not specify gender. It has become common to throw in "she" and "her" for the second use. In reading along, we are thinking "no special sex" until we hit "her," when a flag goes up and we wonder if gender must matter. After that first flag, a second flag goes up, "Ah, perhaps this is just an expression of the writer's political correctness," the reader thinking this with satisfaction or with irritation depending on his or her political views. In either case, the reader is distracted from what is being written, which is bad unless the writer considers working to destroy patriarchy more important than whatever he (or she!) is writing about.

There are milder forms of political correctness. One is to use "he or she" (as above). This has the disadvantage that it is three times as long as "he" and rather distracting to the reader, who wonders why the author is being so verbose. Another, more insidious form is to resort to the third person, and use "they". This sounds more natural, because we often do that in daily conversation when we want to be purposely vague, not knowing who is doing some particular thing. That vagueness is less desirable in writing, where the singular is generally more desirable because of its extra precision and punch.

## 4.3   Notation

Think about your notation. "By relieving the brain of all unnecessary work, a good notation sets it free to concentrate on more advanced problems, and, in effect, increases the mental power of the race."[19] Bad notation, on the other hand, irritates readers and provokes them to blunt criticism, as in the review that said of one paper, "This paper gives wrong solutions to trivial problems. The basic error, however, is not new: if the reviewer has correctly understood the author's undefined notations and misprints, the stress–strain relations used are those once proposed by St.-Venant..."[20]

1   Use conventional notation, such as $r$ for the interest rates and $p$ for price.
2   To avoid trouble in seminars, avoid using the same letter in both upper and lower case (e.g. $Y$ for output and $y$ for the log of output).
3   Macroeconomists commonly use a symbol for the logarithm of a variable, but I find this irritating, since it weakens intuition considerably. I would rather see "$Y = M/P$, where $Y$ is output, $M$ is money, and $P$ is price" than "$Y = M - P$, where $Y$ is the logarithm of output, $M$ is the logarithm of the money supply, and $P$ is the logarithm of the price."
4   Be careful about using 1 and 2 as subscripts for anything but time. If you have a static model, though, 1 and 2 may do well for denoting countries or companies.
5   Just because you define your notation once does not mean the reader is going to remember what $\mu_{ji2}$ meant ten pages later. If possible, define all your notation on one page so the reader knows where to flip back to, even if you don't use a particular variable till later. Also, try to use both words and symbols. Don't say "This shows that as $\mu_{2i}$ gets bigger, crime falls." Rather, say "This shows

---

[19] Alfred Whitehead, as quoted in P. Davis and R. Hersh, *The Mathematical Experience*, Boston: Birkhauser (1981).
[20] Clifford Truesdell, *Mathematical Reviews* 12:561 (1951).

that crime falls as $\mu_{2i}$, the second-period return to a particular crime, gets bigger."

6  Don't define notation you're not going to use. Someone might, for example, pretend that their model is more general than it is by saying that agent $i$ has ability $a_i$ and agent $j$ has ability $a_j$ while later assuming that $a_i = a_j = a$. It would be better just to say that all agents have ability $a$ from the start.

## 4.4  Anecdotes

Data is the plural of anecdote. Anecdotes are highly useful if true. One data point is much better than none, an application of the principle of diminishing returns. More data may add less than you think. More often than we like to believe, our data points are not independent, in which case eighty observations may be no better than one. Finding that eighty managers all predict a fall in demand next year has a different meaning if they all based their opinion on the same article in a trade journal.

Try to find one concrete illustration to carry through the paper, using that illustration to explain the mathematical propositions. "The more abstract the truth is that you would teach, the more you have to seduce the senses to it."[21]

## 4.5  Jargon

Duangkamol Chartpraser found in experiments that college students rated an author higher in expertise if he wrote badly, and rated him higher the longer they had been in college, even though they also said they liked simpler writing better.[22] "Such labour'd nothings, in so strange a style, Amaze th' unlearn'd, and make the learned smile."[23] You must decide who you want to impress, the learned or the unlearned. On this rests whether you should use "impact" as a verb.

## 4.6  Acronyms

Do not say "The supra-national government authority (SNGA) will..." and then use SNGA throughout your paper. Say "The supra-national government authority ("the Authority") will..." The use of acronyms is a horrible vice akin to requiring the reader to learn a foreign language. The reader will not bother to learn foreign terms just to read a paper as insignificant as yours. If the term's length makes using it throughout your paper awkward, the problem is the term, not the number of letters used to represent it. Let the author be warned: when he finds his writing is awkward, that is often a sign his thinking is muddy. Political scientists, take note!

---

[21] Friedrich Nietzsche, *Beyond Good and Evil*, 4–128, from *Basic Writings of Nietzsche*, translated by Walter Kaufmann, New York: Modern Library, (1968) (*Jenseits von Gut und Bose*, 1886). Just across the page, he writes, "It was subtle of God to learn Greek when he wished to become an author – and not to learn it better" (4–121), a nice observation on the advantage of using a plain style in a popular language rather than, say, the Greek of Sophocles.)

[22] Duangkamol Chartpraser "How Bureaucratic Writing Style Affects Source Credibility," *Journalism Quarterly*, 70: 150–9 (Spring 1993). The article itself is rather poorly written.

[23] Alexander Pope, "Essay on Criticism," Part II, line 126 (1171).

## 5   A Paper From Start to End

### 5.1   Starting

To overcome writer's block, put together an outline in any order of the points you want to make. Then order them. Start writing without worrying about style, and later revise heavily or start over. Starting twice today is better than waiting three months and starting once. It is better, *a fortiori*, than waiting forever.[24]

Pascal said, "The last thing one knows when writing a book is what to put first."[25] Don't write your introduction first; write it last. Setting it into the context of the literature, motivating the idea, and so forth are for your reader, not for you. Do, however, at some early stage write up the part of your paper which intuitively explains your idea.

### 5.2   Numbering

Number each page of text so the reader can comment on particular pages. Number each equation in drafts on which you want comments. If you have appropriate software, label each line.

### 5.3   Title pages

The title page should always have the date, your address, your phone number, and your e-mail address. You might as well put your fax number and web address down too, if you have them. The date should be the exact date, so that if someone offers you comments, you know what he mean when he says, "On page 5, line 4, you should say...". Save copies of your old drafts for this same reason.

### 5.4   Abstracts

A paper over five pages long should include a half-page summary of its main point. Depending on your audience, call this an abstract or an executive summary. In general, write your paper so that someone can decide within three minutes whether he wants to read it. Usually, you do not get the benefit of the doubt.

The plaintiff in a lawsuit writes up pleadings which state his complaint and suggested remedy. "John Doe, though driving carefully, hit me with his car and caused $5,000 in damages, which I should collect from him according to Section 103.2 of the Indiana Code." The judge may respond with a "summary judgement": "The Court dismisses the suit because even if what you say about Doe is true, Section 103.2 does not allow damages when the driver was careful." But if the plaintiff does not submit clear pleadings, the judge rejects his suit anyway: "The Court dismisses the suit for lack of a clear legal basis." A paper's abstract and introduction are like the pleadings in a lawsuit. The abstract should present the claims

---

[24] Depending, of course, on the substance of your paper.

[25] Blaise Pascal, *Pensées*, translated by W. Trotter, www.orst.edu/instruct/ph1302/tests/pascal, I–19, (1660/ August 18, 1999).

you make to the reader, with the proof to come later. If the claims are too weak, or, worse, if it is unclear what they are, the reader will not bother to go to the second page of the paper.[26]

## 5.5  Sectioning

It is often useful to divide the paper into short sections using boldface headings, especially if you have trouble making the structure clear to the reader.

## 5.6  Assumptions and definitions

On page 163 of his article on writing, William Thomson has an excellent discussion of examples.

> *When introducing a novel definition, give illustrative examples.* If the definition is a property that an object may or may not have, exhibit:
>
> 1  Objects that satisfy the definition;
> 2  Objects that do not satisfy the definition;
> 3  Objects that satisfy the definition but almost do not;
> 4  Objects that do not satisfy the definition but almost do.

Figure 1 and Definition 1 are my versions of Thomson's example. Note the importance of Figure 1d in pointing out the part of Definition 1 most likely to be misunderstood.

**Definition 1.**  A function $f : [0, 1] \to [0, 1]$ is **increasing** if for all $x_1$ and $x_2$, if $x_1 < x_2$ then $f(x_1) < f(x_2)$.

Examples are useful to elucidate not only mathematical definitions but economic policies and laws. You might, for example, suggest a particular anti-merger policy and provide the reader with four examples of mergers that could come under scrutiny.

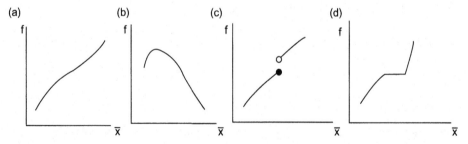

**Figure 1**  Examples to illustrate Definition 1. Functions (a) and (c) are increasing. Functions (b) and (d) are not.

---

[26] In federal courts, if a plaintiff has only ridiculously weak evidence or facetious claims, the judge will fine him under Rule 11 for pleading in bad faith. Something similar, but working through reputation, happens to people who write bad papers.

Thomson also says, "State your assumptions in order of decreasing plausibility or generality." Do it in this order for a payoff function: "A1: $u_i$ is continuous; A2: $u_i$ is bounded; A3: $u_i$ is strictly concave."[27] The last assumption, equivalent to risk aversion, is the one with bite, so put it at the end and flag it somewhere for your readers.

## 5.7  Propositions

Technical papers should present their results as *Propositions* (the interesting results, stated in words), *Corollaries* (subsidiary ideas or special cases which flow directly from the propositions), *Lemmas* (points which need to be proved to prove the propositions, but usually have no intrinsic interest), and *Proofs* (why something is true). Lemmas and proofs can be purely mathematical, but propositions and corollaries should be intelligible to someone who flips directly to them when he picks up the paper. That means they must be intelligible to someone who does not know the paper's notation. A reader must be able to decide whether the paper is worth reading just by reading the propositions.

Be content if your paper has one contribution to make – that is one more than usual in economics journals. If you include too many points, the reader won't be able to find the best one. Beware of listing numerous results as propositions. Three propositions to an article is plenty; someone who says that everything is interesting says that nothing is interesting.

## 5.8  The model

It is best to present the model quickly before pausing to explain the assumptions. That way, the experienced reader can grasp what the model is all about, and all readers can flip back and find the notation in one place. It is reasonable, and even desirable, however, to separate the model from the analysis of equilibrium. Such separation is particularly important for beginners in game theory, who have a wondrously difficult time separating out the rules of the game from the description of the equilibrium – "What could happen" from "What does happen."

## 5.9  Proof by example

Often a model's qualitative predictions depend on its parameters, preventing clean propositions. In such a case, consider dropping the general model and using two examples. A general proposition like

"Free trade increases conflict if $\alpha > \frac{3\beta^2}{log(\gamma)}$ and reduces it otherwise,"

really just means

"Free trade can either increase or reduce conflict, depending on the parameters."

Such a proposition can be proven by laying out two numerical examples, one where free trade increases conflict and one where it reduces conflict. Such a proof is more enlightening than one with pseudo-generality in $\alpha$, $\beta$, and $\gamma$.

---

[27] Thomson (1999, p. 169).

## 5.10 Headings

Headings should have what Munter calls "stand-alone sense."[28] Make all headings skimmable. The reader should glean some information from each of them. Instead of "Extensions", try "Extensions: Incomplete Information, Three Players, and Risk Aversion."

White space on the page is part of the writing too. This is obvious in tables and figures. Do you feel any temptation to fill up your figures with text just to save space, as in Figure 2? If you don't, don't feel any compulsion to do so in the tables or text either.

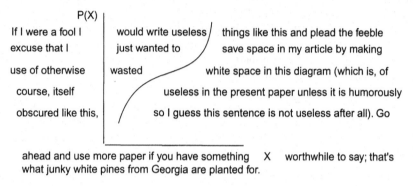

**Figure 2** Misusing your budget constraint, paperwise

## 5.11 The conclusion

Do not introduce new facts or ideas in your concluding section. Instead, summarize your findings or suggest future research.

## 5.12 Appendices

Appendices should be self-contained. If you put the proof of a proposition in an appendix, put a copy of the proposition too, and perhaps even a recap of the notation.

## 5.13 The reference list

Even a working paper should have a list of references, and these should be at the very end, after the appendices and diagrams, so the reader can flip to them easily. Law reviews do not publish lists of references, but you should have one anyway for the working paper version, including separately a list of cases and statutes cited. Include a few words of explanation after every case if you want to be especially helpful. Example: *United States v. O'Brien*, 391 U.S. 367 (1968) (upholding the conviction of a draft card burner).

[28] Munter (1992, p. 52).

## 6  Footnotes and Quotations

### 6.1  Footnotes

Scholarly references to ideas can be in parenthetic form, like (Rasmusen [1988]), instead of in footnotes.[29] Footnotes are suitable for tangential comments, citation of specific facts (e.g., the ratio of inventories to final sales is 2.6), or explanations of technical terms (e.g., Dutch auction).[30] These should be footnotes, not endnotes.[31] Every statistic, fact, and quotation that is not common knowledge should be referenced somehow. In deciding whether something is common knowledge, ask, "Would any reader be skeptical of this, and would he know immediately where to look to check it?" Economists can be sloppy in this respect, so do not take existing practice as a model.

Try not to have footnote numbers[32] in the middle of a sentence. If a sentence requires two footnotes, as when you say that the populations of Slobovia and Ruritania are 2 million and 24 million, just use one footnote for the two facts. You may even wait until the end of the paragraph if you think the reader will still know which facts are being footnoted.[33]

Footnotes have a quite different purpose in drafts, where they can be used for comments to oneself or to co-authors. I put comments to myself as footnotes starting with xxx, like this.[34] The practice is eccentric, but this helps me not to forget to add things later at the appropriate places.

### 6.2  Cites to books

References to books should usually be specific about which part of the book is relevant. Give the chapter or page number.[35] Note that I give 1776 as the year of Smith's work, rather than 1952, as the back of the title page of my copy says. The year could tell the reader one of two things: 1. the year the idea was published, or 2. what edition you looked at when you wrote the paper. Usually (1) is much more interesting, but you should also have (2) in the references at the end of the paper so the page numbers are meaningful.

---

[29] Like this: Rasmusen, Eric (1988) "Stock Banks and Mutual Banks." *Journal of Law and Economics*. October 1988, 31: 395–422.

[30] Like this tangential comment. Inventory ratio: 2.62 for 1992-III, *Economic Report of the President, 1993*, Washington: USGPO, 1993. In a Dutch auction, the price begins at a high level and descends gradually until some buyer agrees to buy.

[31] If this were an endnote, I am sure you would not read it.

[32] Like this one. A distraction, wasn't it? Go back up the page again and continue reading.

[33] The Slobovia population figure is from the 1999 *Statistical Abstract of Slobovia*, Boston: Smith Publishing. The Ruritania figure is for 1994, and is from the 1998 *Fun Facts From Fiction*, Bloomington, Indiana: Jones and Sons. In this case, I probably ought to have put the footnote at the end of the sentence containing the populations rather than waiting till the end of the paragraph. I should not, however, have two footnotes interrupting that sentence.

[34] xxx This is just a foonote to myself. Thus, I don't bother to get the typos out.

[35] Example: "Adam Smith suggests that sales taxes were preferred to income taxes for administrative convenience (Smith [1776], p. 383)." Or, "(Smith [1776], 5–2–4)." If you really wish to cite the entire book, then that is okay too: "Smith (1776) combined many ideas from earlier economists in his classic book."

## 6.3 Citation format

How to cite old books is a problem. I like the format of: Smith, Adam (1776/1976) *An Inquiry into The Nature and Causes of the Wealth of Nations*. Chicago: University of Chicago Press, 1976. This does not seem quite right for Aristotle, but for moderns like Smith it combines the two functions of saying when the idea originated and how the reader can obtain a copy with the cited page numbering.

There seems to be consensus in the journals that the reference list should cite Author, Year, Volume, Pages, Journal (or City and Publisher, for a book), and Title. Some journals like to have the month of publication, a good idea because it helps readers find the issue on their bookshelf. Legal style is to list only the first page, not the first and last pages, a bad idea because readers like to know how long the article is.[36]

If you have the author's first name, put it in the citation rather than just using his initial. If, however, he customarily uses a different name, use the name by which he is known. Thus, you should not write "J. Ramseyer," or "M. Ramseyer," or "John Ramseyer," but "J. Mark Ramseyer," for the Japan scholar who goes by the name "Mark."

## 6.4 Quotations

Long quotations should be indented and single-spaced. Any quotation should have a reference attached as a footnote, and this reference should include the page number, whether it is to an article or a book.

When should you use quotations? The main uses are (a) to show that someone said something, as an authority or an illustration; and (b) because someone used especially nice phrasing. Do not use quotations unless the exact words are important. If they are and you do quote, cite, if you have it, the exact page or section.

## 7 Tables, Figures, and Numbers

### 7.1 Highlighting numbers in tables

Circle, box, boldface, or italicize the important entries in tables. Often you will wish to present the reader with a table of 100 numbers and then focus on two of them. Help the reader find those two. Tables 1 and 2 show ways to do this.

The title of Table 2 illustrates an exception to three rules of good writing:

1 Use short words instead of long words.
2 Use Anglo-Saxon roots instead of Greek or Latin.
3 Use unambiguous words rather than words with more than one meaning.

I had to decide whether to use "illegitimacy," a long Latinate word with many meanings, or "bastardy" a shorter Anglo-Saxon word with only one meaning. I avoided

---

[36] One good style is: Davis, John (1940) "The Argument of an Appeal," *American Bar Association Journal* (December 1940) 26: 895–9.

**Table 1**   Arrests rates per 100,000 population

| | Under 18 | 18–20 | 21–24 | 25–29 | 30–34 | 35–39 | 40–44 | 45–49 | 50+ | All ages |
|---|---|---|---|---|---|---|---|---|---|---|
| 1961 | 1,586 | 8,183 | **8,167** | 6,859 | 6,473 | **6,321** | 5,921 | 5,384 | 2,594 | 3,877 |
| 1966 | 2,485 | 8,614 | 7,425 | 6,057 | 5,689 | 5,413 | 5,161 | 4,850 | 2,298 | 3,908 |
| 1971 | 3,609 | 11,979 | **9,664** | 6,980 | 6,016 | 5,759 | 5,271 | 4,546 | 2,011 | 4,717 |
| 1976 | 3,930 | 13,057 | 10,446 | 7,180 | 5,656 | 5,205 | 4,621 | 3,824 | 1,515 | 4,804 |
| 1981 | 3,631 | 15,069 | 11,949 | 8,663 | 6,163 | 5,006 | 4,176 | 3,380 | 1,253 | 5,033 |
| 1985 | 3,335 | 15,049 | 13,054 | 9,847 | 7,181 | **5,313** | 4,103 | 3,155 | 1,088 | 5,113 |

Over 50% of arrests are for "public order" offenses (e.g. drunk driving, prostitution), especially for older people. The [boldfaced] entries are mentioned in the text.

*Source*: BJS (1988c), pp. 26–27.

"bastardy" because it is somewhat archaic and the word "bastard" is most commonly used in slang, so that the reader would be distracted from my subject if I followed the three rules above. But I thought carefully before breaking the rules.

## 7.2   Summary statistics

If you do not have hundreds of observations, you should consider showing your reader all of your data, as I did in Table 2. Note that I gave the reader the regression residuals by observation, which reveals outliers that might be driving my results. It is not enough just to show which observations are outliers in the variables – D.C. is an outlier in both the dependent and explanatory variables, but it isn't one in the residual. Regardless of the number of observations, give the reader the summary statistics, as in Table 3.

I did not put the standard deviations in Table 3, even though we usually think of them as the most important feature of a variable after the mean. If a variable has a normal distribution, listing the mean and the variance (or, equivalently, the mean and the standard deviation) makes sense, because they are sufficient statistics for the distribution – knowing them, you know the exact shape of it. If the variable does not have a normal distribution, though, it may not be very useful to know the standard deviation, and such is the case in the data above. If the data might be highly skewed, the median may be useful to know, and if the data is bounded, the minimum and maximum are useful. If the data points are well known, such as states, countries, or years, it may be useful to give the reader that information too. I could have put the states in parentheses in the table above, like this:

Illegitimacy (%) | 11.1 (Utah) 23.4 24.5 22 59.7 (D.C.) |

## 7.3   Correlation matrices

Correlation matrices should be used more often than they are. You will want to look at them yourself while doing your multiple regressions to see how the variables are interacting. Table 4 shows an example.

Table 2  The illegitimacy data and the regression residuals

| State | Illegit-imacy (%) | AFDC ($/month) | Income ($/year) | Urbani-zation (%) | Black (%) | Dukakis vote (%) | Residual Illegitimacy (%) |
|---|---|---|---|---|---|---|---|
| Maine | 19.8 | 125 | 12,955 | 36.1 | 0.3 | 44.7 | 2.8 |
| New Hampshire | 14.7 | 140 | 17,049 | 56.3 | 0.6 | 37.6 | 2.3 |
| Vermont | 18.0 | 159 | 12,941 | 23.2 | 0.4 | 48.9 | −4.9 |
| Massachusetts | 20.9 | 187 | 17,456 | 90.6 | 4.8 | 53.2 | −6.2 |
| Rhode Island | 21.8 | 156 | 14,636 | 92.6 | 3.8 | 55.6 | −5.2 |
| Connecticut | 23.5 | 166 | 19,096* | 92.6 | 8.2 | 48.0 | 2.3 |
| **Delaware** | 27.7 | 99 | 14,654 | 65.9 | 18.9 | 44.1 | 2.1 |
| **Maryland** | 31.5 | 115 | 16,397 | 92.9 | 26.1 | 48.9 | −0.4 |
| DC | 59.7* | 124 | 17,464 | 100.0* | 68.6* | 82.6* | 0.5 |
| **Virginia** | 22.8 | 97 | 15,050 | 72.2 | 19.0 | 40.3 | −2.1 |
| **West Virginia** | 21.1 | 80 | 10,306 | 36.5 | 2.9 | 52.2 | 2.1 |
| **North Carolina** | 24.9 | 92 | 12,259 | 55.4 | 22.1 | 42.0 | −6.0 |
| **South Carolina** | 29.0 | 66 | 11,102 | 60.5 | 30.1 | 38.5 | −5.0 |
| **Georgia** | 28.0 | 83 | 12,886 | 64.8 | 26.9 | 40.2 | −3.5 |
| **Florida** | 27.5 | 84 | 14,338 | 90.8 | 14.2 | 39.1 | 5.0 |
| **Kentucky** | 20.7 | 72 | 11,081 | 46.1 | 7.5 | 44.5 | 1.4 |
| **Tennessee** | 26.3 | 54 | 12,212 | 67.1 | 16.3 | 42.1 | 5.7 |
| **Alabama** | 26.8 | 39* | 11,040 | 67.5 | 25.6 | 40.8 | 0.5 |
| **Mississippi** | 35.1 | 39* | 9612* | 30.5 | 35.6 | 40.1 | 2.4 |
| **Arkansas** | 24.6 | 63 | 10,670 | 39.7 | 15.9 | 43.6 | 1.3 |
| **Louisiana** | 31.9 | 55 | 10,890 | 69.2 | 30.6 | 45.7 | −1.4 |
| Oklahoma | 20.7 | 96 | 10,875 | 58.8 | 6.8 | 42.1 | −4.8 |
| **Texas** | 19.0 | 56 | 12,777 | 81.3 | 11.9 | 44.0 | 0.9 |
| Montana | 19.4 | 120 | 11,264 | 24.2 | 0.2* | 47.9 | 0.5 |
| Idaho | 13.0 | 95 | 11,190 | 20.0* | 0.4 | 37.9 | −0.6 |
| Wyoming | 15.8 | 117 | 11,667 | 29.2 | 0.8 | 39.5 | −2.3 |
| Colorado | 18.9 | 109 | 14,110 | 81.7 | 3.9 | 46.9 | 1.3 |
| New Mexico | 29.6 | 82 | 10,752 | 48.9 | 1.7 | 48.1 | 14.0* |
| Arizona | 27.2 | 92 | 13,017 | 76.4 | 2.7 | 40.0 | 12.0* |
| Utah | 11.1* | 116 | 10,564 | 77.4 | 0.7 | 33.8* | −14.0* |
| Nevada | 16.4 | 86 | 14,799 | 82.6 | 6.9 | 41.1 | 3.2 |
| Washington | 20.8 | 157 | 14,508 | 81.6 | 2.4 | 50.0 | −4.8 |
| Oregon | 22.4 | 123 | 12,776 | 67.7 | 1.6 | 51.3 | 1.5 |
| California | 27.2 | 191 | 16,035 | 95.7 | 8.2 | 48.9 | −6.8 |
| Alaska | 22.0 | 226* | 16,357 | 41.7 | 3.4 | 40.4 | −10.0* |
| Hawaii | 21.3 | 134 | 14,374 | 76.3 | 1.8 | 54.3 | 1.1 |
| United States | 24.5 | 124 | 14,107 | 77.1 | 12.4 | 46.6 | 0.0 |

Extreme values are italicized and starred. States defined as Southern are boldfaced. Residuals are from equation (34). Sources and definitions are in notes 23 and 25.

**Table 3**  A summary table of the data on illegitimacy by state

| Variable | Minimum | Mean Across States | Mean (U.S.) | Median | Maximum |
|---|---|---|---|---|---|
| Illegitimacy (%) | 11.1 | 23.4 | 24.5 | 22 | 59.7 |
| AFDC ($/month) | 39 | 112 | 124 | 109 | 226 |
| Income ($/year) | 9,612 | 13,440 | 14,107 | 13,017 | 19,096 |
| Urbanization (%) | 20.0 | 64.5 | 77.1 | 67.1 | 100 |
| Black (%) | 0.2 | 10.8 | 12.4 | 6.9 | 68.6 |
| Dukakis vote (%) | 33.8 | 46.0 | 46.6 | 44.7 | 82.6 |

N = 51. The District of Columbia is included. The U.S. mean is the value for the U.S. as a whole, as opposed to the equal-weighted mean of the 51 observations. Sources and definitions are in footnotes 23 and 25.

**Table 4**  A correlation matrix for the illegitimacy data

| | Illegitimacy | AFDC | Income | Urbanization | Black | South | Dukakis vote |
|---|---|---|---|---|---|---|---|
| Illegitimacy | 1.00 | | | | | | |
| AFDC | −.25 | 1.00 | | | | | |
| Income | .18 | −.36 | 1.00 | | | | |
| Urbanization | .24 | −.09 | −.09 | 1.00 | | | |
| Black | .76 | −.17 | .00 | .14 | 1.00 | | |
| South | .48 | −.17 | −.28 | −.05 | −.66 | −1.00 | |
| Dukakis vote | .18 | −.06 | .06 | .17 | .03 | .07 | 1.00 |

N = 51. The District of Columbia is included. Sources and definitions are given in notes 23 and 25.

## 7.4  Normalizing data

In empirical work, normalize your variables so the coefficients are easy to read. A set of ratios (.89, .72, .12) can be converted to percentages: (89, 72, 12). Incomes can be converted from (12,000, 14,000, 78,100) to (12, 14, 78.1), making the units "thousands of dollars per year" instead of "dollars per year" and making the coefficient on that variable .54 instead of .0054. Z-scores, the variables minus their means divided by their standard deviations, may be appropriate for numbers without meaningful natural units, such as IQ scores or job satisfaction.

If you do decide to write a full number such as "12,345," it helps to put the comma in to separate out thousands. Leave out meaningless decimal places. 15,260 is better than 15260.0. In fact, if you are talking about incomes, there is a case to be made for using 15 instead, and measuring in thousands of dollars. That discards information, to be sure, but the number is simpler to work with, and if the data measurement error has, say, a standard deviation of 3,000, the loss in information is small.

Note that I said "data measurement error," not "the size of the disturbances." We often forget that there is measurement error in the data even before we start doing regressions with it and adding disturbances to represent specification error, omitted variables, and so forth. Remember the story of the man who was asked how old a certain river was and said "That river is 3,000,021 years old." When asked how he knew that precise number, he said, "Well, I read in a book that it was 3 million years old, and the book is 21 years old."[37]

## 7.5 Variable names

There is no need to use peculiar code names for variables. "Density" is a much better name than the unpronounceable and mysterious "POPSQMI."

Use words as well as numbers, or instead of them. Say "Because of the differentiability assumption (A2)...," not "Because of (A2)..." As William Thomson says on p. 161 of his article, "The argument that numbers and abbreviations save space is not very convincing given that they will not shorten a 20-page paper by more than five lines, and they certainly will not save time for your reader."

## 7.6 Table location

Always refer to tables in the text. Otherwise, the table is like a paragraph that has no link to the paragraphs before and after it. Put tables and figures in the text, not at the end of the paper. Journals often ask authors to put tables and figures at the end for ease in processing manuscripts, but don't do it till the paper is accepted. The common practice of putting them at the end in working papers is a good example of the author being lazy at the expense of his readers.

## 7.7 Table titles

Give useful titles to every table and every diagram. Do not label a table as "Table 3." Say, "Table 3: Growth in Output Relative to Government Expenditure." (When you refer to the table in the text, though, you can just refer to "Table 3," since it will be apparent from the context what the table is about.) Also don't title a table "Regression Results" or "Summary Statistics." Those are useless names – anybody can look at a table and tell it is regression results or summary statistics. "Executive Pay Regressions" and "Executive Pay Summary Statistics" are better names.

## 7.8 Diagram axes

In diagrams, use words to label the axes, not just symbols. Say: "$X$, the education level," not just "$X$."

## 7.9 Econometrics

It is good to present several specifications for a regression, but pick your favorite specification and use it as your base. Discuss it in detail, and only say what happens in

---

[37] The story is from Chapter 3, "Specious Accuracy," pp. 62–69 of Oskar Morgenstern, *On the Accuracy of Economic Observations*, 2nd edn, Princeton, Princeton University Press (1963) (1st edn, 1950.) Note the precedent of a theorist criticizing econometrics – and considering it important.

other specifications for comparison with the base regression, because your reader will find one regression hard enough to understand. You might use $y = \beta x + \gamma z$ as your base, for example, because it represents your theory best, but then present (1) $y = \beta \log(x) + \gamma \log(z)$; (2) $y = \beta x + \gamma z$, but excluding 10 outlier observations; and (3) $y = \beta x$. That way you have done three robustness checks, which together span three dimensions of specification space.

If you report the F-statistic, the Aikake Information Criterion, or anything else, do it for a reason. Don't report it just because your fancy regression program spewed it out. A common example of a useless statistic is the F-statistic for the test that all the coefficients in a regression equal zero. The reader can deduce for himself that if you bothered to report the estimated coefficients in your paper, it must be the results were not complete garbage.

Here is a sample of how you might report a regression result:

A simple regression of illegitimacy on AFDC and a constant yields the following relationship:

$$Illegitimacy = 26.91 - \mathbf{0.034} * \mathbf{AFDC},$$
$$(3.05) \quad (\mathbf{0.026})$$

(1)

(standard errors in parentheses) with $R^2 = .03$. Equation (1) implies that high AFDC payments reduce the illegitimacy rate, but this is, of course, misleading because the simple regression leaves out important variables. Regression (2) more appropriately controls for a variety of things which might affect the illegitimacy rate:

$$Illegitimacy = 15.74 + \mathbf{0.016} * \mathbf{AFDC} - 0.00011 * Income\ 0.024 * Urbanization$$
$$(3.65) \quad (\mathbf{0.021}) \qquad (0.00042) \qquad (0.033)$$

$$- 1.60 * South + 0.56 * Black,$$
$$(1.71) \qquad (0.06)$$

(2)

with $R^2 = 0.79$. Equation (2) would leave us with the conclusion that AFDC payments have almost no effect on the illegitimacy rate. Nor, surprisingly, do any of the other variables except *Black* have large or significant coefficients. The coefficients are small enough, in fact, that one might doubt whether increasing the size of the dataset would change the conclusions: the variables are insignificant not because of large standard errors, but because of small coefficients.

## 8   Miscellaneous

### 8.1   Backups

Xerox your paper before you give it to anyone, or, better yet, retain two copies on disk, in separate locations for fear of fire.

## 8.2   Computers

For each paper, have a separate directory with a short name – for example, STIGMA. Then have the following subdirectories: _Literature, _Comments, _Letters, _Old, _Figures, _Old.Drafts. Also create a file called AaChronology.stigma that has the dates different things happen – when you begin, you circulate a draft, you send to a journal, and so forth. Each time you present the paper or submit it, create a new subdirectory, e.g., _JPE, _ALEA.97. The subdirectories should all start with "_" so that they are together, not mixed in with the various uncategorized or active files in the main directory.

## 8.3   The Net

Email and the Net are increasingly important. Plain-text ASCII – the letters you type in from the regular typewriter keys – is the only universally readable type of file. Don't expect people to tussle with Wordperfect, Postscript, or other specialized formats. Just because everybody at Podunk University uses Wordperfect doesn't mean everyone in the world does. Most people should rather have something readable, even if it loses all the equations, tables, and figures, than something which would be beautiful if they could read it, but they can't. (Admittedly, foolish people and business students are exceptions, who are happier with nothing than with something messy. Those people must be denied anything but hardcopy of final drafts.) Transmitting non-ASCII files by email can be done, with various coding programs, but do not expect it to always work. The same goes for posting on the Net. One approach is to post both an ASCII version and a Postscript or other special version, so that everybody can read something and some people can read everything in your paper. A packager such as Adobe Acrobat is also useful. Acrobat creates a pdf file which is easily transferred across the Net and can be read with a public-domain reader that people can download at the same time as they download the pdf file.

Instead of emailing papers as attachments, post them to the Web and email the websites. That way you do not clog up email inboxes.

Always include the web address and your email address on any web page you create, including pages for your papers.

## 8.4   Referees

In dealing with journals, remember that ordinarily the editor, and even the referee, is much smarter than you are. They often get things wrong, but that is because they are in a hurry or feel obligated to give objective reasons for rejecting a paper when the real reason is that it is trivial or boring. If a referee has given some thought to the paper, he is probably correct when he suggests changes. Suggesting changes is a sign he has given some thought to his report. Referees who have just skimmed the paper usually do not suggest any changes. Whether changes are suggested is also a way to distinguish the Big Problem from the Fatal Flaw.

## 8.5  Copyright

Many journals have unscholarly policies of requiring authors to give away the copyright and all their rights. Unless an exception is written in, this means that the author cannot legally xerox his own article![38] The journal then charges well above the monopoly price for use of the article in class packets. Scholars should resist this even though journals, while insisting on obtaining the authority to sue authors who disseminate their writings, seem unlikely to carry out their threats. All that a journal really needs is a non-exclusive license to publish the article.

It is hard to turn down an article acceptance, but I have pulled out from submitting articles to journals of this sort (e.g., *Management Science*, *JEMS*), and I am reluctant to referee for them without being paid. I encourage other people to refuse to referee for such journals. Most of us referee only from a sense of public duty, a duty we do not owe to journals that try to suppress dissemination of research.

# 9  Speaking

## 9.1  Empathy

Sympathize with your audience. Put yourself in their place.

## 9.2  Purpose

When I was a student at MIT, Peter Temin told us that presentations have three purposes:

1  To tell something to people
2  To receive comments
3  To impress the audience

Purpose 3 is perfectly appropriate to a job talk, but it tends to conflict with purposes 1 and 2.

In any case, strive to get your meaning across first. Only then should you defend your assumptions.

## 9.3  Starting

Write out the introduction word for word. This will help you to over came the nervousness of starting to talk.

---

[38] It probably also means the journal has the legal right to publish or republish the article under someone else's name, or to cut out half the article and publish the rest. The only limitations would be that the publication cannot ruin the author's reputation, and, perhaps, that his consideration for signing away his rights was that he hoped to have his name on the publication. Copyright ownership is not a small thing.

## 9.4   Notes

Munter (1992, p. 107) suggests the following if you use notes:

1   Use large print.
2   Leave a margin of one-third of the page on the right for last-minute notes.
3   Do not break a paragraph between two pages.
4   Do not staple the notes; it is better to slide pages to one side.
5   For a talk in which exact phrases are important enough that you will actually read your notes verbatim, or if you have to read them because your command of the seminar language is poor, leave the bottom third of the page blank so your head does not go down as you read.

An addition I will make to Munter's points is that you should circle quotations or numbers that you will need to read exactly, so they are not lost in the middle of words that you do not need to read.

## 9.5   The outline

Use the blackboard or a transparency to outline your talk before you start. Do not write this on the board before you start. Instead, write a short outline as you are concluding the introduction. For example, you might write

1   Intro
2   The bargaining problem.
3   Nash solution.
4   Many periods.
5   Incomplete info.

Then check off sections as you finish them.

## 9.6   Feedback

In the Preface to the *General Theory*, Keynes wrote, "It is astonishing what foolish things one can temporarily believe if one thinks too long alone, particularly in economics..."[39] Sometimes even the act of trying to explain an idea (your own or another's) can show you the folly of what you thought you knew. This can even be true when you are trying to explain the idea to yourself. At about the same time and place as Keynes, Ludwig Wittgenstein was writing, "Wovon man nicht sprechen kann, daruber muss man schweigen."[40]

---

[39] John Maynard Keynes, *The General Theory of Employment, Interest, and Money*, Preface, p. vii, New York: Harcourt, Brace & World, 1964 (1936).

[40] "Whereof one cannot speak, one must be silent", Ludwig Wittgenstein, *Tractatus Logico-Philosophicus*, Section 7.000, London: Routledge and Kegan Paul, (1974) (*Logisch-Philosophische Abhandlung* in *Annalen der Naturalphilosophie*, 1921). Usually, I would quote the English translation and put the German in footnotes (if I included it at all). Here, the quotation was short and famous, and ended a sentence in a choppy format so that the reader's progress would not be inappropriately disrupted. I therefore reversed the order for dramatic effect.

## 9.7 Questions

Answering questions is more important than reaching the end of your talk. If you rush the talk, few people will understand the last part anyway. Think of the talk as a gathering of people to discuss your work for 90 minutes, not as a gathering of people to hear you read 33 pages of an article.

Look out to the audience to see if anyone has a question, or, if you are too busy writing, pause and ask for questions occasionally. Mary Munter says that if you can remember what people looked like after your talk, you had good eye contact.[41]

Invite questions along the way. If the audience must wait until the end they will be reluctant to raise questions that were relevant earlier, and disagreements will take the form of long speeches instead of short questions. Asking for questions is also a good way to show you have reached the end of a section of your talk.

Don't be embarassed to defer a question, but make a note on the board (the questioner's name or the topic) to come back to it, and tell the questioner to remind you later if you forget.

A common problem is for a young economist to present a model in such a way that nobody understands even the slightest thing about it. If the audience does not grasp the notation, the theorems are irrelevant. If you do not convey the model to them, whether you can defend it is irrelevant.

Obfuscation does prevent embarassing criticism, of course, but it is no more effective than standing up and saying "goo-goo-goo" for ninety minutes. Joe Sixpack may think your babbling means you're saying something profound; scholars will just think you're feeble-minded. Someone who with clarity lays out an interesting idea that crumbles under repeated and varied attacks will leave a far more favorable impression. Partly this is for the same reason that lions like Christians in the arena, but partly it is because the audience has actually learned something. "It is more important that a proposition be interesting than that it be true. This statement is almost a tautology. For the energy of operation of a proposition in an occasion of experience is its interest and is its importance. But of course a true proposition is more apt to be interesting than a false one."[42]

## 9.8 Excuses

When someone asks you, "Why did you make Assumption X?" do not answer, "Because that's standard in the literature." The implication is that you blindly follow other people's mistakes and that you don't even know the standard lame excuses for Assumption X. It is, however, acceptable to say that X is standard after you give a substantive explanation, so that the questioner knows that you are not doing odd things just because of an artistic temperament.

---

[41] Munter, p. 147. Or, it might just be that you were seriously traumatized.

[42] Alfred Whitehead, as quoted in W. H. Auden and L. Kronenberger, *The Viking Book of Aphorisms*, New York: Viking Press (1966).

## 9.9 Handouts

Handouts are useful for tables, figures, equations, notation, technical definitions, abstracts, and statements of propositions. The length should be one to three pages, no more. Unless your audience has the entire paper, you should distribute at least a one-page handout. This is particularly important in a Chicago-style seminar, since you may not reach your main point, and it must be on the handout for the audience to learn it. Handouts are also useful as doodling paper. Don't pass out handouts identical to your overheads; think first, because handouts should have a higher idea to paper ratio. Put extra handouts near the door, so that latecomers can pick them up as they come in.

## 9.10 Notation

If your paper is technical, write up the notation on a handout or put it on the board and do not erase it. This is crucial, unless you have a handout with the notation.

## 9.11 Proofs

If your paper is technical, you should keep in mind that your propositions are probably more important than your proofs. Usually, the audience is completely uninterested in the proofs. This is not always true – sometimes the whole point of an article is the new way that you prove an old theorem – but spending two-thirds of a theory seminar going through your proofs is like spending two-thirds of an empirical seminar going through how you collected and cleaned the data. In both cases, the speaker will actually derive much benefit from being forced to think systematically about the least glamorous parts of his paper, but think twice before inflicting this on the audience unless you are paying them to listen. (This kind of exercise is better suited to a "solitary seminar" in which you prepare and give a talk to an empty seminar room late at night just to clarify your own thinking.)

## 9.12 Diagrams

Label all axes on diagrams you draw on the board.

## 9.13 Electrical equipment

If you are using electrical equipment such an overhead projector, test it before the talk starts. If you are talking as a guest of someone else, be sure to tell them well in advance if you need a room with a screen. Have a backup plan for if the equipment fails entirely. This goes double for computer equipment, unless you bring along your own.

## 9.14 Overhead slides

Use boldface on overheads, especially for numbers. Circle important numbers with a red marker. Use lots of color, for interest, putting boxes around propositions and underlining key terms. In preparing slides, it is fine either to use computer-printed slides (if the font is large enough) or to write them by hand. I most often print out the slides in black ink and then write on them in color with a water-soluble marker. I use a penny to scratch out typos in the printing, and I have an oil-base marker to correct the typos.

## 9.15   Equation numbers on overheads

Should equation numbers match between the paper and the overheads? Matching them might require some extra work, depending on the word processor. Here are some acceptable alternatives:

1   Let the numbers be inconsistent, but point this out to your audience.
2   Make all the numbers consistent.
3   Use a marker to cross out the typeset inconsistent numbers and put in the numbers in the paper.
4   Leave all the numbers off of the overheads. (But then the audience cannot ask about specific equations, unless you write some of them back in with a marker, or write in some marks like ∗, ∗∗, and ∗∗∗.)

## 9.16   Visibility

Test visibility if you have time. Can people at the back of the room read your overheads and the blackboard? Remember to keep overheads high up if the heads of people in front will block the lower part of the screen, as often happens at conferences.

## 9.17   Redundancy

Remember that people blank out frequently when listening. This means the speaker ought to occasionally summarize what he has done, and structure his talk so that if a listener misses any single thirty-second block he can catch up again later.

## 9.18   Calculations

Write down all calculations in your notes. At the board it is hard to remember even that $7(19) = 133$. If you perform a series of, say, ten arithmetic operations, a mistake is likely, and finding it will take as long as the first try on all ten operations combined.

## 9.19   The length of a seminar

As an economist, keep budget constraints in mind and don't grumble about not having enough time. Any paper can be presented in any length of time, just as any idea can be written up in any number of pages. This does not mean that you should use up all the available time, though, just as it is counterproductive for a slaveowner to work his slaves for 18 hours a day even though he may be legally entitled to do so. (A reminder: the slave in the analogy is not you, but the listener.)

Students generally are very bad at delivering papers. Even though seminars often run an hour and a half, students are well-advised to schedule them for an hour. More people will attend, and often the comments received in the first hour make the last third of the paper irrelevant anyway.

## 9.20   My audience for these notes

Much of my advice is directed to speakers with boring topics and poor delivery. That is because most seminars are given by speakers with boring topics and poor delivery. Don't take it personally.

## 9.21   Suspense

Don't rely on suspense, or delay announcing your main results until the end. After an hour, people usually stop listening anyway, and if your idea is worth spending time on, it is complex enough that people will need to hear the idea at the beginning to understand it by the end. Also, experienced economists often can figure out the middle of your argument by themselves better than a novice can explain it, once they have heard the assumptions and the conclusions. Without the conclusions, though, it's harder to make sense of why particular assumptions were chosen.

## 9.22   The option value of time

Why only look at your watch after an hour and then speed up to cram everything into your time slot? Look at your watch early, and you will be able to *choose* which parts to rush through. Do not think, "I have an hour left, so I have plenty of time." Many a seminar – especially many a student seminar – is severely behind after the first half hour.

## 9.23   Towards the end

Towards the end, say things like "My final result is..." to give hope to your fading audience and stimulate them to a final effort to stay awake. And do not disappoint them.

## 9.24   Closing remarks

If the host asks if you have any closing remarks, that usually means you should have finished five minutes ago. He does not really want closing remarks; he wants you to stop. Your reply should be either (1) "No, I do not have any closing remarks. Thank you," or (2) Three sentences summarizing the main results; or (3) a closing joke.

## 9.25   The punchline

The composer of a musical has failed unless the audience leaves humming a tune. The same goes for you. Make them leave with a conclusion that they can't get out of their heads for the rest of the day.

### 9.26   Finish on time

Martin Luther said, "There are three things, so to speak, which every good preacher should do: First, he takes his place; second, he opens his mouth and says something; third, he knows when to stop."[43] The first rule of speaking is to finish on time. Perhaps I should rephrase that:

FINISH ON TIME!!!

In your notes, mark certain paragraphs or sections to be dropped if you run out of time. Do not run late unless you sense that your talk is extraordinarily interesting to the people who matter.

Put more pungently: "When you strike ile, stop boring; many a man has bored clean through and let the ile run out through the bottom."[44] Running late stimulates much more hostility than saying stupid things. Ending early is quite acceptable. People do not really say, "The food here is inedible, and, besides, the portions are so small."

## 10   Listening

### 10.1   Notation

Write down the notation.

### 10.2   The first question

Do not be afraid to ask the first question. In fact, try to ask it, to break the ice. Ask even if it isn't such a good question. Hold back only if you are a guest at an unfamiliar workshop, where boring, questionless, presentations may be the social custom.

### 10.3   Discussion

Discussion is usually the point of a seminar. Without questions, reading the paper almost always dominates listening to an oral presentation. If questions are not asked along the way, then (a) the audience becomes confused, (b) the speaker can slip through with incorrect or controversial assertions, (c) it is hard to make small comments of the kind useful to the speaker, and (d) when questions are asked, at the end, they tend to be irrelevant, and turn into general, solipsistic, speeches. In the humanities, this is what usually happens.

---

[43] Martin Luther, *Luther's Works, Volume 21, The Sermon on the Mount*, p. 7, translated by Jaroslav Pelikan, St. Louis: Concordia Publishing House (1956).
[44] Josh Billings, As quoted on p. 80 of Francis Wellman, *The Art of Cross Examination*, 4th edition, New York: The Macmillan Company (1936, 1st edition 1903).

## 10.4  Notes

Write notes on the seminar paper (literally) if you have a copy, so you will not lose them later, and to make filing easier.

## 10.5  Comments

During the seminar, write down comments to give the speaker afterwards. This is especially useful if (a) your question would be too distracting because it is off the current topic, (b) too many other questions are being asked for you to have a chance to ask your question, or (c) the custom is not to ask questions, and you are bursting with frustration. Speakers are very appreciative about written comments, and you may have nothing better to do.

## 10.6  Doodling

In my opinion, doodling is perfectly appropriate, and a good use of your time, though Hahnlike drawings are acceptable only if Hahn does them.[45] Knitting, whittling, etc. will be seen as peculiar, but can be socially useful.

## 10.7  Leaving early

It is often customary to let the speaker know beforehand if you must leave early. This can be presumptuous. I've sometimes thought to myself, "Why should I care if this person leaves early? He's not important enough for me to feel insulted even if I knew his motive was boredom." If you think the speaker has special concern for your opinions, though, you should certainly let him know if you must leave early.

## 10.8  Board typos

Ignore spelling errors the speaker makes at the blackboard, but instantly point out mathematical typos. You need not raise your hand for this kind of comment.

## 10.9  Helpful questions

If you realize that other people are confused and do not understand something, ask their question for them.

## 10.10  Long questions

Keep your questions as short as you can. Sometimes people feel obligated to state their question three times, to show what an important question it is. ("Could inflation be the cause? It seems like inflation might be the cause. So do you think inflation might be the cause? Inflation does seem important.") Resist this.

---

[45] One person drawing naked women during seminars is eccentric. Thirty of them is a bore.

## 10.11  Questions about assumptions

Don't object to a model's assumption simply as being unrealistic or too simple. Those are not valid objections. What is a valid objection is that the assumption leads to a false conclusion about the way the world works. For example, suppose that someone is presenting a general equilibrium model with two goods to show that if a change in tastes increases production of one good, it must decrease production of other goods in the economy. It is a valid objection to question whether that conclusion would also be true in a three-good economy. It would be best to ask the question with some hint of why you think it might make a difference, saying, for example, "It seems to me that if you had three goods, then when demand for good 1 increased, production of good 2 would also increase, if it were a complement. Isn't your model oversimplified, since complements are impossible in a 2-good economy?" If, on the other hand, the speaker uses a 3-good economy to show that if demand for one good rises, output of the two other goods might or might not fall, then objecting to the model limiting itself to 3 goods is not valid. To be sure, three is an unrealistically small number, but that is unimportant. A model with 4 or $N$ goods would be unnecessarily complicated for the point being made.

## 10.12  Answers

It is quite proper to point out that the speaker did not answer your question. In academic discussions, this is usually because the speaker did not understand your question. If he is being purposely evasive, fry him. This does not usually happen in academic seminars.

## 10.13  References

It is often helpful if someone brings a *Statistical Abstract* or an *Economic Report of the President* to a seminar, to look up the odd fact.

## 10.14  Laser pointers

If you have a laser pointer, bring it along. You can use it to ask questions, pointing to the overhead or blackboard tables and equations.

## 10.15  Pacing

Pace yourself. If you are too tired, you will gain nothing from sitting through a seminar. Don't bother to go unless politeness demands it. At conferences, the problem is usually not sleepiness, but burnout. Plan to skip some good sessions, and force yourself to rest.

## Further Reading

Any scholar who uses econometrics has more than one econometrics text in his office, even though all econometrics texts cover essentially the same material. Should the same be true for scholars who use writing?[46] Here are some suggestions for further reading.

BASIL BLACKWELL, *Guide for Authors*. Oxford: Basil Blackwell (1985). A fine style guide by the publishers of the present article.

BOWER, RICHARD et al., "Protocol, Etiquette, and Responsibilities of Reviewers in Finance," *Financial Practice and Education* (Fall/Winter 1994) 4: 18–24. How to write referee reports.

DAVIS, JOHN, "The Argument of an Appeal," *American Bar Association Journal* 26: 895–9 (December 1940). Appellate argument in the 1920s turns out to be very similar to economics seminars in the 1990s.

EPSTEIN, RICHARD, "The Struggle Between Author and Editor over Control of the Text: Faculty-Edited Law Journals," *IIT Chicago-Kent Law Review*, 70: 87–94 (1994). Law reviews are a special kind of research outlet that more economists should learn about.

FOWLER, HENRY, *A Dictionary of Modern English Usage*, 2nd edn. New York: Oxford University Press, 1965. This is a classic, though I find its format not as useful as other style guides. A book similar in outlook but more systematic is Ernest Gowers, *The Complete Plain Words*, London: Her Majesty's Stationery Office, 1954.

GRAVES, ROBERT and ALAN HODGE, *The Reader Over Your Shoulder*, New York: The Macmillan Company, 1944. A book chock-full of real examples with discussion of how they should have been written. Of particular interest is the over 100 pages of word-by-word criticism of eminent writers (which Liddell Hart suggested be subtitled "A Short Cut to Unpopularity") in which the authors go after such excellent writers as T.S. Eliot, Ernest Hemingway, John Maynard Keynes, Bertrand Russell, and George Bernard Shaw, an excellent reminder to us that no writer is so good that he can't improve.

HALMOS, PAUL, "How to Write Mathematics," *L'Enseignement Mathematique*, 16: 123–52 (May/June 1970). Halmos was a prominent mathematician who cared deeply about writing.

HARMAN, ELEANOR, "Hints on Poofreading," *Scholarly Publishing*, 6: 151–7 (January 1975). Not only this article but the trade journal in which it appeared is good reading.

LEAMER, EDWARD, "Let's Take the Con out of Econometrics" *American Economic Review*, 73: 31–43 (March 1983). This is about econometrics, not writing, but Leamer's concern is ultimately the same: communicating ideas.

McCLOSKEY, DONALD, "Economical Writing," *Economic Inquiry*, 24: 187–222 (April 1985). Every economist should read this useful and entertaining article, later expanded into book form,

MUNTER, MARY, *Guide to Managerial Communication*, 3rd edn, Englewood Cliffs, N.J.: Prentice-Hall (1992). This book is oriented towards business writing and presentation.

POSNER, RICHARD, "Goodbye to the Bluebook," *University of Chicago Law Review* 53: 1343–52 (Fall 1986). The Bluebook is the standard law review guide to citation style, published by the students at the top law reviews. The University of Chicago has tried to reform legal citation in the direction of clarity and simplicity.

RASMUSEN, ERIC, *Games and Information*, 2nd edn. Oxford: Blackwell Publishers (1994). 3rd edn, 2001. See the preface and introduction especially.

SONNENSCHEIN, HUGO and DOROTHY HODGES, "Manual for *Econometrica* Authors," *Econometrica*, 48: 1073–81 (July 1980). This is more about mechanics than anything else, but we all need to worry about mechanics too.

---

[46] Maybe not. Just memorize my article and forget about my competitors!

STIGLER, GEORGE, "The Conference Handbook," *Journal of Political Economy*, 85: 441–443 (April 1977). This is humor, possibly with deep meaning (there really *are* questions that apply to every paper).

STRUNK, WILLIAM and E. WHITE, *The Elements of Style*. New York: Macmillan (1959). The classic; good writing hasn't changed. Attitudes have though, so recommend you read the third edition, not the 1999 fourth edition. In general, I avoid writing guides written after 1985; in recent years, English departments have decided that the politics of feminism, race, and class warfare are more important than clarity and beauty, with predictable results for how they teach writing.

THOMSON, WILLIAM, "The Young Person's Guide to Writing Economic Theory," *Journal of Economic Literature*, 37: 157–87 (March 1999). Good for tips on how to write up mathematics, in a style very similar to my article here.

TUFTE, EDWARD, *The Visual Display of Quantitative Information*. Cheshire, Conn.: Graphics Press (1983). A delightful book about graphs and charts, which is as good a coffee-table book as a guide to one's own writing.

TULLOCK, GORDON, "Does Mathematics Aid in the Progress of Economics?" pp. 201–14, *On the Trail of Homo Economicus: Essays by Gordon Tullock*, eds. Gordon Brady and Robert Tollison, Fairfax: George Mason University Press (1994). Useful hostility for those of us who use algebraic notation.

WEINER, E., *The Oxford Guide to the English Language*. Oxford: Oxford University Press (1984). Older style guides such as this are more likely to be correct, given the current popularity of political correctness and gender-neutered language among literature professors.

# SIXTY-NINE

# Henry and the Candy Shop

CARL ANDERSON

*Source*: © Allsorts Media Limited.

# Index